Michèle Brown read Modern History at Oxford and began her career as a presenter and reporter for both BBC and ITV television programmes.

She is the author of many books, most recently *Ritual of Royalty* about the ceremony and pageantry of Britain's royalty and (with Ann O'Connor) two volumes of quotations by and about women entitled *Woman Talk*.

Her husband is called Gyles, her children are called Benet, Saethryd and Aphra, her cats are called Oscar and Neville (the latter being a girl!) and her editor is called Emer. Some of these are in the book – some are not.

Michèle Brown

The New Book
of First Names

CORGI BOOKS

THE NEW BOOK OF FIRST NAMES
A CORGI BOOK 0 552 12257 2

First publication in Great Britain

PRINTING HISTORY
Corgi edition published 1985
Corgi edition reprinted 1986

Copyright © Michèle Brown 1985

This book is set in 10/11 pt. Souvenir

Corgi Books are published by Transworld Publishers
Ltd., 61–63 Uxbridge Road, Ealing, London W5 5SA, in
Australia by Transworld Publishers (Aust.) Pty. Ltd.,
15–23 Helles Avenue, Moorebank, NSW 2170, and in New
Zealand by Transworld Publishers (N.Z.) Ltd., Cnr. Moselle
and Waipareira Avenues, Henderson, Auckland.

Printed and bound in Great Britain by
Cox & Wyman Ltd., Reading, Berks.

For my three children
Benet, Saethryd and Aphra

Introduction

In the year 1500 the population of the world was probably around 420 million. In 1982 it increased by more than the total population of the British Isles and stands at around 5,000 million. When Magellan first circumnavigated the globe he set out in 1519 and returned almost exactly three years later. The present world record for the same feat is 45 hours and 19 minutes. So it is hardly surprising that in recent years parents have often chosen unusual personal names for their children, in an attempt to assert the individuality of the child against so much competition. Nor is it surprising that names are chosen from a wider range of countries and languages than ever before. Yet at the same time some parents have chosen to back away from the curious and unfamiliar names and opt for the security of good old-fashioned names like Tom, Harry, William, Abigail and Lucy, all of which have a reassuring no-nonsense air to them. After the excesses of the sixties and seventies the reaction was probably inevitable and few people are surprised to find that rock singer David Bowie now calls his son Zowie by the more pedestrian Joe. However some of the post-war names have become part of the basic stock used in English-speaking countries, and names like Darren, Glen, Wayne, Marilyn and Samantha are now quite conventional.

Even before the Norman Conquest of 1066 Britain's names had been imposed from outside. The first to import their names were the Romans who arrived in 54 B.C. and did not leave until 436 A.D. When the Romans left, their names survived mainly on the Celtic fringes of Britain while the majority of the country came under the influence of the tribes which invaded from Northern Europe.

Several Welsh names still familiar today are thought to be corruptions of Latin originals. Emlyn for instance is probably a corruption of the Roman name Aemilianus. In England itself the names of the Roman Empire were quickly superseded by names of Germanic origin. The Anglo-Saxon language (Old English)

7

which developed was very similar to the language (Old German) of the Teutonic invaders so the names used in Britain became similar to those used in what is now Germany, and also in Scandinavia. As a result when Northern Britain was invaded from Scandinavia in the 8th and 9th centuries the influence on names was not particularly noticeable, although one or two new ones were introduced. By and large the custom in all the countries of Northern Europe was for one name per person. Family connections were occasionally denoted by using names which sounded similar, perhaps because they began with the same letter or ended with the same syllable. Although St Augustine arrived in England in 597 and began the conversion of mainland Britain to Christianity these old pagan names survived, probably because even 1300 years ago people had by and large begun to give names without regard to their original meanings. Saints' names were sometimes used by priests or monks but seemed to have no influence on the rest of the community.

When the Normans arrived in 1066 they were naturally determined to impose their own culture, including their names, on the inhabitants of Britain. One way in which those who wished to co-operate with the Normans could show their readiness to adapt to the new order was by adopting the new names. Those peasants who could not expect to gain anything from co-operation were probably much slower to forget the old Anglo-Saxon names. However the Norman names were not a total innovation. The Normans themselves were of Viking stock and the names they tended to favour were often adaptations of Old German names which already had remarkably similar Old English equivalents. The Norman variations of these stock Northern European names were usually characterized by a softer overall sound (e.g. Roland for Hrodland). Later on they strayed further from the originals by their 'Latinization'. When the name was recorded in Latin, which was almost invariably the language used for written documents, it would be given a Latin form which eventually became accepted as the true spoken form as well. In addition to the new forms of the Teutonic names the Normans also brought to Britain names like Alan and Ivo, for the area of France they came from was basically Celtic and many of the original names had survived.

The next major influence on English names was that of Christianity. In the early Middle Ages the names of Saints became fashionable and naturally this was encouraged by the church. Some of the Saints' names came from the Bible but most were those of early converts, many of them martyrs. Since most lived under the rule of Rome their popularity introduced Roman names like Laurence, Sebastian, Eugenia, Lucia, Ursula and Sabina.

Certain saints became cult figures and many children were named in their honour. Catherine is one of the prime examples. It was popular throughout medieval Europe because of the virgin martyr St Catharine of Alexandria who was reputedly tortured on the Catherine wheel and the name has retained its popularity into the twentieth century. Another cult figure in England was St Etheldreda, a Queen of Northumbria before the Norman Conquest. Because of her cult the name survived despite the Norman invasion, although it was later corrupted to Audrey. A masculine example is Thomas, a name which owed much of its popularity to the veneration of St Thomas à Becket, martyred at the instigation of Henry II, whose shrine at Canterbury drew pilgrims from all over Europe.

In the early Middle Ages therefore there was a vast number of names from many different sources to choose from. Despite this initial variety, however, by the 13th century clear favourites had emerged which accounted for about half the names in the country. They are equally familiar today, names like John, Henry, William, Richard, Robert for boys, and Joan, Elizabeth, and Mary for girls. This narrow range combined with a rising population led to the development of surnames to distinguish one from another. The baptismal or Christian name became separate from the family name, and some names such as Jarman, Thurstan, Aldred, Osborne, Fabian and Bennett, became common as surnames but virtually ceased to be used as personal names. Totally new surnames also developed as the practice became more common. These were usually based either on parentage (eg Sanderson), occupation (eg Fowler), place of origin (eg London), or physical characteristics (eg Redhead). Diminutives and nicknames also helped to give a little more individuality to the recipients of common names and many of these such as Jack (John), Harry (Henry), Bess (Elizabeth), Polly (Mary), Austin (Augustin), and Barney (Barnabas) became independent names.

During the 16th century the classical influences of Renaissance

9

culture gave rise to a new source of first names, either directly from classical Greece or Rome or indirectly through Italian literature. Some, like Horatio, were authentic but many were coined literary names with classical allusions such as Araminta, Phyllida, Aspasia, Chloë and Silvia. The Protestant Reformation, which followed close on the heels of the Renaissance produced another set of names. In the 17th century many Protestants, particularly Puritans, rejected the names of non-Biblical Saints which had been popular for so long, because they smacked of 'popery'. They turned instead to the Bible, which was by then available in English for laymen to read, and chose from it names untainted by Catholicism. Some came from the New Testament but many also were from the Old Testament. Two of the most successful names from the Old Testament source are Sarah and Ruth while Jason, Timothy, Nathaniel and Deborah were among those brought into use from the New Testament. Puritans were inclined to use any name, however obscure, which occurred in the Bible, and many, especially those from the long genealogical lists in the Old Testament, did not last the course, even in New England where Puritan influence was strong. Names like Ezekiel, Zedekiah, Zephaniah, Uriah and Japheth had slipped back into obscurity by the beginning of the 19th century. Even more rapidly forgotten were the excessive names chosen by some Puritans to imprint their beliefs on the newly baptised child, including the oft quoted If-Jesus-Christ-Had-Not-Died-For-Thee-Thou-Hadst-Been-Damned-Barebones who wisely changed his name in later life to Nicholas Barbon. The more restrained Puritan 'virtue' names, Prudence, Patience, Faith, Hope, etc. have, however, become part of the basic stock of English names.

The 18th century saw the introduction of classical names in their Latin form for both men and women. It is from this period that we get names like Georgina, Augusta, Amelia, Sophia, Adolphus and Augustus. Although a lot of the feminine names are still used today the masculine names are rarely used for they sound alarmingly pompous. This is precisely because they were intended to sound pompous. They were introduced into Britain by the German House of Hanover, which succeeded to the throne on the death of Queen Anne in 1714. The fashion for classical names which had affected Europe in the 16th century had found most favour in the small German states whose rulers

10

had adopted Imperial titles like Augustus to bolster their prestige and self-esteem. The Hanoverians were no exception. The new royal family set a fashion for these names which was followed not only at home but in the colonies, although the American War of Independence did rather dampen the North American enthusiasm for Hanoverian names.

In the 19th century it was the US which followed most enthusiastically yet another new trend, that of using surnames as given names. In many instances it was simply a case of names which had once been used as given names, and which later developed as surnames, being used as personal names once again, eg Barrett, Garret and Warren. However other types of surname also became common, particularly where a mother's family name was used as her child's first name. The practice has become well-established in North America and Australia and increasingly in Britain, where surnames like Hilton, Lincoln, Grant, Scott, Glen and Thatcher are now used as first names. In the 19th century a variation on this theme was the very popular fashion for using aristocratic surnames as given names, even when there was no family connection whatsoever. A great number of these names have since become accepted as bona fide first names. They were particularly popular among the newly rich members of the middle class who wished to give their wealth a little more style and to underline their improved position in the world. Obvious examples are Howard, Sidney, Ashley, Courteney, Percy, Russell, Pelham and Greville. They were mainly used for boys but two 19th century fashions which applied only to girls' names were the jewel and flower names used at the end of that century. These are now regarded as rather old-fashioned but undoubtedly they will come back into favour again, indeed names like Lily, Daisy and Rose are already creeping back. Jewel names like Pearl and Ruby are currently rather neglected.

A 19th century fashion shared by both masculine and feminine names was for medieval and even pre-Conquest names. This was sparked off by the Romantic movement at the beginning of the 19th century and the general interest in the 19th century in medieval culture and religion. Examples of these names which had been neglected since the 16th century include Emma, Maud, Edith, Ella and Ethel for girls and Harold, Edwin, Edgar and Guy for boys.

In the 20th century one of the main influences over the choice of first names has been the cinema, particularly during the golden years of the Hollywood 'stars'. Names like Rita (Hayworth), Marilyn (Monroe), Gary (Cooper) and Dean (Martin) were as popular as the actors and actresses who bore them. Even manufactured names like Marlene (Dietrich) and Merle (Oberon) came into general use. Another feature of the 20th century has been the introduction into the stock of first names used in English-speaking countries of a wide range of European names, particularly Spanish, Italian and German. This is to a great extent a result of the large scale immigration of people from those countries into North America and Australia in the 19th and 20th centuries. In Britain the range has also increased because of Commonwealth immigration, particularly from India and Pakistan. A recent development has been the use by many young West Indians of African names rather than the English names used by their parents. Since the Second World War there has also been a more relaxed attitude to made-up names with no real history or meaning such as Cary, Maribel, Malva, Nedra, and Nolana. There really is no limit to the number of names available once you start inventing your own or creating your own variation of a more familiar name. Those who say that to give a child an invented name is to put it at a disadvantage forget that such firm favourites as Wendy, Vanessa and Lorna were concocted out of nowhere.

So nowadays there is a greater range of names to choose from than ever before, even if you do not wish to make up a totally new name. This book reflects that trend, for it contains not just traditional English names but a wide selection of European and North American names as well as a good sample of African, Indian and Moslem names. It also contains the most familiar of the surnames which have become accepted as first names, although to include every surname would have doubled the size of the book. If you want to increase your options beyond the 10,000 or so names and variations to be found here, books which will widen your range include the Bible, the Roman Martyrology, dictionaries of biography, dictionaries of Saints and the plays of Shakespeare. You may well find in them something to distinguish your child from the other 5,000 million inhabitants of the globe without being reduced to bizarre combinations such as Opelia Bumps, Oofty Goofty Bowman, Marmalade P. Vestibule, Constant Agony, Cherri Pancake and Noble Puffer (all quoted in John Train's *Even More Remarkable Names*). And with luck your child will not feel like saying, in the words of Groucho Marx, 'No it's not my real name; I'm just breaking it in for a friend'.

PART ONE

Names for Girls

A

AAKASH (pron. Akass)
Origin/meaning: Hindu 'sky'.

Found throughout India but considered rather unusual.

AARTI
Origin/meaning: Hindu.
The name of a prayer made with a candle either at home or in the temple.

This name comes from West India.

ABBEY, ABBY
Origin/meaning: Hebrew 'father of joy'.

Popular North American contraction of Abigail *q.v.* used as a name in its own right.

Example: Abby Brewster – one of the two old ladies in Joseph Kesselring's play *Arsenic and Old Lace*.

ABEBI
Origin/meaning: Yoruba 'asked for child'.

A Nigerian name. Abeje and Abeke have similar meanings.

ABIGAIL
Origin/meaning: Hebrew 'father's joy' or 'father (source) of joy'.

One of the wives of King David (1 Sam.xxv). Popular from the end of the 16th century in England, especially in the 17th century. In the 17th century play *The Scornful Lady* by Beaumont and Fletcher, Abigail was the handmaid and confidante of the heroine. As a result Abigail became synonymous with maid servant and its popularity waned. Now enjoying a revival.

Variations and abbreviations: Abigael, Abagail, Abaigael (Irish), Abbe, Abbi, Abbie, Abby, Abbye, Abigael, Gael, Gail, Gale, Gayel, Gayle.

14

Examples: Abigail Masham, 1680–1734, Queen Anne's influential confidante.
Abigail Adams, wife of US President John Adams, 1744–1818.

ABRA
Origin/meaning: Hebrew 'earth mother' or 'mother of many'. Feminine version of Abraham *q.v.*

Abra was one of the wives of King Solomon.

ACACIA
Origin/meaning: Greek 'guileless, innocent', 'acacia tree'.

The acacia tree is said to symbolize the resurrection and therefore immortality.

Variations and abbreviations: Cacia, Cacie, Casey.

ACANTHA
Origin/meaning: Greek, 'thorny', 'acanthus tree'.

In Greek mythology Acantha was the mother of Apollo, God of the Sun.

ADA
Origin/meaning: Old German Eda, Etta and Old English Eadda, 'happy'.

Also used as a short form of names like Adah, Adelaide, Adela, Adeline, etc *q.v.*

Popular in Britain in the 18th and 19th centuries. Byron's first daughter, the mathematician, b.1816, was christened Ada.

Variations and abbreviations: Ad, Adda, Addie, Addy, Adie, Aida (Ital) Eada, Eda.

Examples: Ada Leverson, 1862–1933, English novelist.
Ada Reeve, 1874–1966, British comedy actress.

ADAH
Origin/meaning: Hebrew 'ornament'.

The second female name in the Bible (Genesis ch.iv). Adah was one of Lamech's two wives, the other being Zillah *q.v.* This was one of the Puritan Biblical names popular in Britain and New England during the 17th century. Now found more frequently in the US.

Variations and abbreviations: Ada, Adaiha.

Examples: Adah Isaacs Menken, 1835–1868, US actress and poet.

ADALBERTA
Origin/meaning: Old German 'nobly bright' from 'adal' – noble.

A fem. version of Adalbert and Albert q.v. The shortened version Alberta, is now more usual.

Variations and abbreviations: Ada, Adelberta, Adell, Adella, Alberta, Albertina (Ital), Albertine (Fr).

ADAMINA
Origin/meaning: Hebrew 'of the red earth'.

A fem. version of Adam q.v. It is increasingly rare. Most popular in Scotland and in areas of Canada and Australia where many Scots settled.

ADELA
Origin/meaning: 'noble' from the Old German 'adal'.

Connected to other names from the same root word (Old German 'adal', adila. Old English 'aethel') eg Ethel, Adelaide, Alice, Adeline, etc q.v. Adela was brought over to England at the time of the Norman Conquest. It enjoyed a period of popularity in the 19th century because of the Victorian interest in medieval history and literature and the success of the fashionable French version Adèle.

Variations and abbreviations: Ad, Adel, Adèle (Fr), Adella, Adelle, Addie. See also Adelaide, Adelina, Alice.

Examples: Adela, daughter of William the Conqueror and mother of King Stephen.
Adela Rogers St John, US journalist.

ADELAIDE
Origin/meaning: Old German 'nobility'.

Like Adela and Adeline this name comes from the Old German root adal meaning noble, which, combined with the suffix – haidu, formed the original Old German version Adalheid. Old French corrupted Adalheid to Adeliz from which we get Alice q.v. Several versions were introduced into Britain with the Norman Conquest, but were never widespread until the 19th century when Adelaide, the French version, became popular in England very quickly after the accession to the throne in 1830 of William IV and his wife Queen Adelaide. The capital of the state of South Australia was named Adelaide after the Queen in 1836.

Variations and abbreviations: Ada, Adalheid, Addi, Addie, Adel, Adelaida (Ital), Adelheid (Ger), Della, Heidi (Ger). See also Adela, Adeline, Alice.

Example: Queen Adelaide, 1794–1849, wife of William IV.

ADÈLE
Origin/meaning: Old German 'noble'.

Popular French version of Adela q.v.

Example: Adèle Astaire, 1898–1981, US musical comedy star, sister of Fred Astaire.

ADELHEID
Origin/meaning: Old German 'nobility'.

This is the German original of Adelaide q.v. from 'adal' – noble.

Variations and abbreviation: Adalheid, Heidi. See also Adela, Alice, Adelaide.

ADELINE
Origin/meaning: Old German 'nobility', 'noble maiden'.

This has the same root, Adal – 'noble', as Adela and Adelaide. They were all brought to Britain with the Norman Conquest, but Adeline became much more popular than either. It was revived in the 19th century as part of a general medieval revival.

Variations and abbreviations: Addi, Addy, Adel, Adelena, Adelene, Adelina (Ital), Aline q.v., Edelina, Edolina.

Examples: Adelina Patti, 1843–1919, Italian opera singer. Adeline Whitney, 1824–1906, US writer.

ADEOLA
Origin/meaning: Yoruba 'crown has honour'.

A Nigerian name. One of several similar names such as Adedagbo – 'happiness is a crown', and Adeleke – 'crown achieves happiness'.

ADERYN
Origin/meaning: Old Welsh 'bird'.

Rare outside Wales. See Birdie.

ADINA
Origin/meaning: Hebrew 'voluptuous'.

Variations and abbreviations: Adena, Adine, Dina.

ADITI
Origin/meaning: Hindi. Meaning obscure.

In mythology Aditi was one of the wives of the Hindu Saint Kasnyapa. She gave birth to all the Gods. Another of his wives, Diti, gave birth to all the Demons.

ADOLPHA
Origin/meaning: Old German 'noble wolf'.

Feminine version of Adolphus *q.v.*

Variations and abbreviations: Adolfa (Ger), Adolfina (Ital), Adolfine.

ADRIANA
Origin/meaning: Latin 'from Adria'.

Feminine version of Adrian, *q.v.*

Variations and abbreviations: Adria, Adriane (Ger), Adrianna, Adrianne, Adrienne (Fr), Hadria.

ADRIENNE
Origin/meaning: Latin 'from Adria'.

A French feminine form of Adrian, now more popular in England than Adriana.

Example: Adrienne Corri, British actress.

ADUKE (pron. Adóokay)
Origin/meaning: Yoruba 'much loved child'.

A name from Nigeria. Like many popular African names it is now coming into use in the US and Britain.

AFIYA
Origin/meaning: Swahili 'health'.

An East African name.

AFRA
Origin/meaning: obscure. May be Latin 'African', an abbreviation of Greek, Aphrodite, or Hebrew 'house of dust'.

The last origin is probably correct for England since this was a common name in the 17th century when Biblical names were popular. However there is a 4th century saint called Afra, whose feast day is August 5th, and whose name probably comes from one of the other meanings.

Variations and abbreviations: Aphra, Ayfara, Aphry.

Example: Aphra Behn, 1640–1689, first English woman novelist.

AGATHA
Origin/meaning: Ancient Greek 'good'.

The name of a 3rd century Sicilian Saint, Agatha was a popular medieval name. William the Conqueror gave it to one of his daughters.

Variations and abbreviations: Agace (Old Fr), Agata (Ital), Agathe (Fr), Agathie, Aggie, Aggy, Agueda (Sp).

Example: Agatha Christie, 1891–1976, writer of detective fiction.

AGNES
Origin/meaning: Greek 'pure', chaste.

This was an extremely popular name during the Middle Ages and was found in a variety of forms. One of these, Annis, shows us how it used to be pronounced. It was again popular in the 19th century although it is currently unfashionable in English-speaking countries.

Variations and abbreviations: Aggi, Aggie, Agna, Agnella, Agnese (Ital), Agneta (Scand), Agnete (Ital), Annis (Med Eng), Annys, Ines (Sp), Inez, Nezza, Nessie, Nesta (Welsh), Ynes, Ynez. See also Senga.

Examples: Agnes Grey, the heroine of Anne Brontë's novel. Agnes Sorel, 1422–1450, mistress of Charles VII of France.

19

AGNETA
Origin/meaning: Greek 'pure', 'chaste'.

Scandinavian and German form of Agnes.

Variation: Agnetha.

Example: Agnetha Faltskog, singer with Swedish group ABBA.

AIDA (pron. Ayéeda)
Origin/meaning: Old German 'happy'.

Italian form of Ada, also found in English-speaking countries.

Example: Heroine of Verdi's opera *Aida*, 1871.

AIDA (pron. Ayéeda)
Origin/meaning: Arabic 'benefit'.

This name is quite separate from the European name.

AILEEN
Origin/meaning: Greek 'light' or 'bright'.

The Irish version of the immensely popular name Helen.

Variations and abbreviations: Ailene, Aleen, Ailene, Eileen, Ilene, Ileana.

AILSA
Origin/meaning: uncertain. Possibly Hebrew 'God is my satisfaction' or Old German 'noble'.

This is almost exclusively Scottish. There is no agreement on its meaning but like another Scottish name, Elsie, it may be a short form of Elizabeth. Alternatively, like Alice *q.v.* it may be a complicated development of the Old German Adalheid. Either way this would make it a direct equivalent of the German name Elsa, *q.v.* However it may simply be a native Scottish name with no certain meaning.

AIMÉE
Origin/meaning: French/Latin 'beloved'.

French version of Amy, *q.v.*

Example: Aimée Semple MacPherson, 1890–1944. American religious leader.

AITHNE (pron. Ethnee or Awnye)
Origin/meaning: Old Irish 'little fire', 'little fiery one'.

The feminine version of Aidan q.v. In Irish mythology Aine (pron. Awnye) was Queen of the Fairies. A consistently popular name in Ireland, it is increasingly found in Scotland where there is a revived interest in the old Celtic language and culture.

Variations and abbreviations: Aine (Old Celtic), Eithne, Ena, Ethne, Ina.

AIYETORO (pron. Aryétoro)
Origin/meaning: Yoruba 'peace on earth'.

This name comes from East Africa.

ALANNA
Origin/meaning: Celtic 'beautiful'.

The feminine form of Alan q.v. this name is rarely used although, like the male form, it has many variations.

Variations and abbreviations: Alaine, Alana, Alanda, Alane, Alayne, Alina, Allene, Allin, Allina, Allyn, Lana, Lanna.

Examples: Alana Ladd, US actress.

ALBA
Origin/meaning: Latin 'white', 'blonde'.

Relatively recent version of Albinia q.v.

Variation: Alva.

ALBERTA
Origin/meaning: Old German 'nobly bright'.

Feminine version of Albert q.v. and a shortened version of the original, Adalberta

Variations and abbreviations: Adalberta (Old Ger), Albertina (Ital), Albertine (Fr), Ally, Elberta, Elbertina, Elbertine, Berta, Bartie.

ALBINIA
Origin/meaning: Latin 'white' or 'blonde'.

The feminine equivalent of Alban it was introduced into England from Italy in the 17th century.

Variations and abbreviations: Alba, Albina (Ital), Alvina, Aubune (Fr).

See also Blanche.

ALCINA
Origin/meaning: Greek 'sea-maiden'.

Variations and abbreviations: Alcine, Alcinia.

ALDA
Origin/meaning: Old German 'old'.

A rare feminine form of Aldous q.v. More usual as a surname.

Variation: Aude (Fr).

ALETHEA
Origin/meaning: Greek 'truth'.

Like other virtues, Faith, Hope, Prudence etc, Alethea was a popular name in the Puritan England of 17th century and among Puritan settlers in America.

Variations and abbreviations: Alatheia, Aleta, Aletea (Sp), Alethia, Aletia, Aletta, Alithia.

Example: Alethea Charlton, British actress.

ALEXANDRA
Origin/meaning: Greek 'defender of men'.

The feminine form of Alexander q.v. Popular in Greece and Russia. Isolated examples of the name are found in England from the 13th century. The name achieved popularity in English-speaking countries in the 19th century with the marriage of the Prince of Wales, later Edward VII, to Princess Alexandra of Denmark in 1863.

Variations and abbreviations: Alejandra (Sp), Alessandra (Ital), Alex, Alexa, Alexandria, Alexandrina, Alexina, Alexine, Alexis, Ali, Alix, Alla, Alli, Lexi, Lexine, Sandi, Sandie, Sandra, Sandy, Sondra, Zandra, Zandria.

Examples: HRH Princess Alexandra of Kent.
Alexis Smith, US actress.

ALEXANDRINA
Origin/meaning: Ancient Greek, 'defender of men'.

An uncommon diminutive of Alexandra, the feminine form of Alexander *q.v.*

Variation: Alejandrina (Sp).

Example: Princess Alexandrina Victoria of Kent, later Queen Victoria, 1819–1901.

ALEXIA
Origin/meaning: Ancient Greek 'helper' or 'defender'.

The feminine version of Alexis *q.v.*
Alexis as a girl's name is generally a shortened form of Alexandra.

ALFREDA
Origin/meaning: Old English 'elf counsellor', 'good counsellor'.

A feminine form of Alfred *q.v.*

Variations and abbreviations: Alfie, Elfreda, Elfrieda, Elfrida.

ALGUNI
Origin/meaning: Hindu: The name of the 5th month of the year.

In this month there is a big religious festival in West and North India, which celebrates the arrival of Spring. A popular name among young Indians.

See also May.

ALICE
Origin/meaning: Old German 'nobility' or Greek 'truth'.

Although it is sometimes described as a form of Alethea (truth) *q.v.* Alice is more commonly a development of the Old German name Adalheid, from which we also get Adelaide *q.v.* It comes from the Norman French version of Adelaide – Adelize. When this name was translated into Latin in documents it became Alesia from which Alice eventually developed. Very popular in the Middle Ages, usually as Alys, it was revived in the 19th century as part of a general interest in mediaval culture. Its popularity was greatly increased by the success of Lewis Carroll's book *Alice's Adventures in Wonderland*, published in 1865.

Variations and abbreviations: Adelice, Adelize, Ali, Alicea, Alis, Alisa, Alison, Allison, Allyce, Allys, Alyss, Alyssa.

Examples: Alice Keppel, mistress of Edward VII.
Alice Delysia, French born actress.

ALICIA
Origin/meaning: Old German 'nobility'.

A Medieval Latinized variation of Alice *q.v.* now an independent name.

Variations and abbreviations: Alicea, Alysia.

Example: Alicia Markova, English ballerina.

ALINE
Origin/meaning: Old German 'nobility' from adal 'noble'.

Short form of Adeline *q.v.* Often used as an independent name. Sometimes confused with Aileen, the Irish form of Helen.

Variations: Alena, Alene, Alina, Alyna, Arleen, Arline.

Example: Aline Bernstein, 1882–1955, US theatrical designer.

ALISON
Origin/meaning: Old German 'nobility'.

A diminutive form of Alice *q.v.* which is itself a derivation of Adelaide *q.v.* It is now an independent first name.

Variations and abbreviations: Alicen, Allison, Alyson, Elsie.

Example: Alison Uttley, 1804–1976 English children's writer.

ALIX
Origin/meaning: Ancient Greek 'defender of men'.

Short form, popular in Scandinavia and Germany of Alexandra *q.v.*

Example: Queen Alexandra 1844–1925, wife of Edward VII, was known to her family as Alix.

ALLEGRA
Origin/meaning: Italian 'cheerful'.

An Italian name. Given to Lord Byron's daughter by his mistress Claire Clairmont.

ALMA
Origin/meaning: Latin 'kind' or Italian 'soul'.

24

This name enjoyed a vogue after the Battle of Alma, 1854, which was an incident in the Crimean War. Now rather unusual.

Examples: Alma Gluck, 1884–1938, US opera singer. Alma Mahler, wife of composer Gustav Mahler.

ALMERIA
Origin/meaning: Arabic 'princess'.

ALMIRA
Origin/meaning: Arabic 'truth'.

Variation: Elmira.

Example: Almira Phelps, 1793–1884, US writer and educator.

ALOYISIA (pron. Aloéesha)
Origin/meaning: Old German 'glorious battle'.

Rare feminine form of Aloysius *q.v.* and an old-fashioned form of Louise.

ALPHONSINE
Origin/meaning: Old German 'noble and ready'.

A French feminine form of Alphonse *q.v.* comparatively recent in origin.

Variations: Alfonsina (Ital), Alfonsine, Alonsa, Alonza.

ALTHEA
Origin/meaning: Greek 'wholesome'.

An uncommon name first found in the 17th century when names with classical meanings were popular. The poet Lovelace used it in his poem *To Althea from Prison*. Sometimes found as a form of Alethea *q.v.*

Variations and abbreviations: Althee, Altheta, Thea.

Example: Althea Gibson, US tennis player.

ALUNA (pron. Alóona)
Origin/meaning: 'come here'.

A name used in Kenya.

ALVA
Origin/meaning: Latin 'white', 'blonde'.

A Spanish name, one of many with this meaning, eg Albinia, Bianca, Blanche.

Variation: Alba.

Example: Alva Vanderbilt Belmont, 1853–1933, US socialite, architect, social reformer.

ALVINA
Origin/meaning: Old German 'noble friend'.

Feminine form of Alvin and Aylwin *q.v.*

Variations and abbreviations: Alwina, Alwine (Ger).

ALYSSA
Origin/meaning: Greek 'sane', 'wise'; also the name of a yellow rock plant, alyssum.

This may be an independent name or it can be regarded as a form of Alice *q.v.*

AMABEL
Origin/meaning: Latin/Fr. 'lovable'.

A Medieval name which became temporarily popular during the 19th century Medieval revival. The short form Mabel is more usual.

Variations and abbreviations: Amabelle, Amabella, Amable, Amabil, Belle, Mabel.

Example: Amabel Williams-Ellis, d.1984, writer wife of architect Clough Williams-Ellis, creator of Portmeirion.

AMADEA
Origin/meaning: Latin 'beloved of God'.

A rare feminine form of Amadeus *q.v.*

AMALIA
Origin/meaning: Latin, from the Roman clan name Aemelius. Sometimes confused with Amelia and given as Old German 'industrious'.

This is a common European form of Emily *q.v.*

Examples: Amalia, Duchess of Saxe-Coburg, 1739–1807, Regent of Weimar and patron of Schiller and Goethe.
Amalia James, US novelist.

AMANDA
Origin/meaning: Latin 'lovable'.

Another of the many names eg Amabel, Amy, Amyas, etc which originate from the Latin verb amare – to love. Amanda seems to have begun as a contrived name in the 17th century when names were made up to underline the personalities of characters in the plays of the time. Amanda and the shortened form Mandy, are currently very popular.

Variations and abbreviations: Manda, Mandie, Mandy.

Example: Amanda Lear, British singer.

AMARANTHA
Origin/meaning: Greek 'unfading'.

One of the 'classical' names popularized for a short while by 17th century English poetry, when characters were given names which described their personal attributes.

AMARIAH
Origin/meaning: Hebrew 'God has spoken'.

An Old Testament name, used mainly in England and New England during the 17th century when Biblical names were popular among Puritans. Not to be confused with Annamaria q.v.

AMARYLIS (pron. Amm/ah/ryllis)
Origin/meaning: Ancient Greek 'fresh stream'.

Used by the Greek and Roman poets as a name for a fresh country girl. In the 17th century English poets such as Milton, taking up the current fashion for giving characters names which expressed their virtues, used it in their own poetry.

AMATA
Origin/meaning: 'beloved'.

Italian form of Amy q.v.

AMBER
Origin/meaning: Arabic/French. The name given to a translucent yellow resin used as a semi-precious stone.

Although naming girls after jewels is not unusual, this name was only rarely used before the book *Forever Amber* by Kathleen Winsor, which was a best-seller in the 1950s.

See also Scarlett.

AMBROSINE
Origin/meaning: Greek 'divine', 'immortal'.

A French feminine form of Ambrose *q.v.*

Example: Ambrosine Phillpotts, English character actress.

AMELIA
Origin/meaning: Old German 'hard work', 'industrious'.

The original Old German name Amalburga became Amelie in France. Amelia is the Latinized version which the Hanoverians brought to England in the 18th century. George III named his youngest daughter Amelia. The name Emily *q.v.* was often used as an equivalent although it may have a different origin.

Variations and abbreviations: Amalea, Amalia (Ital), Ameliarane, Amalie (Ger), Amelie (Fr), Amilia (Scot), Amiline, Emilia, Emelina, Emiline, Emily, Emmeline.

Examples: Amelia Earhart, 1897–1937, US aviatrix.
Amelia Jenks Bloomer, 1818–1894, US pioneer of women's clothes reform.

AMELINDA
Origin/meaning: Latin 'beloved and pretty'.

A name without any real history. The better known name Linda has a different derivation.

Variations and abbreviations: Linda, Melinda.

AMETHYST
Origin/meaning: Greek 'amethyst'.

The name of a semi-precious violet stone, occasionally used as a girl's name.

AMICE (pron. Éhmeess)
Origin/meaning: Latin 'beloved'.

One of the names derived from the Latin verb amare, to love. It is similar to the masculine Amyas and closely connected to the

28

more familiar Amy.

Variations and abbreviations: Ameis, Amicia.

AMINA
Origin/meaning: Arabic 'honest', 'faithful'.

A very popular Muslim and North African name.

Variation: Aminah. See Honor, Sati.

AMINTA
Origin/meaning: Latin 'loving'.

A 17th century name. A variation of Araminta *q.v.*

Variation: Amynta.

AMITY
Origin/meaning: Latin/French 'friendship'.

AMY
Origin/meaning: Latin/French 'beloved'.

Amy became popular because of the 13th century St Amata, and was found in England in several forms. Sometimes a short form of Amice or Amabel *q.v.* Like many medieval names it enjoyed a 19th century revival especially after Sir Walter Scott's book *Kenilworth* about the Earl of Leicester's ill-fated wife Amy Robsart.

Variations and abbreviations: Aimée (Fr), Aimie, Amata (Ir/Sp), Ame, Ami, Amia, Amya, Amye, Anwyl (Wel), Esmé.

Examples: Amy Robsart, (1532–1560), wife of Robert Leicester, favourite of Queen Elizabeth.
Amy Johnson, 1903–1941, English pioneer aviatrix.
Amy Carter, daughter of former US President Carter.

ANASTASIA
Origin/meaning: Greek 'resurrection'.

The name of a 4th century Saint who was martyred in Yugoslavia. There are many legends connected with her life. Anastasia has always been more popular in Greece and Russia than in the West. The Grand Duchess Anastasia, daughter of Czar Nicholas II of Russia, is claimed to have escaped from the Bolsheviks who executed the rest of her family in 1918.

Controversy over the truth of this claim still lingers so that the name has enjoyed a small revival in English-speaking countries. Stacy is a popular short form and Anstice *q.v.* an old English variation.

Variations and abbreviations: Amstice, Ana, Anastasie (Fr), Anstice, Nastasia (It), Nastasya (Russ), Stace, Stacey, Stacie, Stacy.

Example: Anastasia Robinson, d.1755, wife of English soldier and politician, Charles, 3rd Earl of Peterborough.

ANCILLA
Origin/meaning: Latin 'handmaiden'.

Found as a first name since the 17th century but rare in the 20th century.

Variation: Annzella.

ANCRET
Origin/meaning: Old Welsh 'much loved'.

English form of the ancient Welsh name Angharad *q.v.* It was almost never found outside the area of the Welsh marches between England and Wales.

Variations and abbreviations: Anchóret, Anchoretta, Ancrett, Ingaret, Ingaretta.

ANDREA
Origin/meaning: Greek 'manly', 'brave'.

A Latinized feminine form of Andrew although the single version Andrew was originally used for girls as well as boys. In Italy Andrea is the masculine form. Comparatively recent in popularity but isolated examples are found from the Middle Ages onwards.

Variations and abbreviations: Andrée (Fr), Andreana, Andria (It), Andriana.

Example: Andrea Newman, English writer.

ANEIRA (pron. Ann-eye-ra)
Origin/meaning: Latin 'honourable'.

Feminine equivalent of the Welsh Aneurin *q.v.*

ANGELA
Origin/meaning: Greek 'messenger'.

Angel was the word used to translate the Hebrew word for messenger of God and it was occasionally used as a masculine name. The feminine form was first found as a proper name in the 16th and 17th centuries. It became popular at the end of the 19th century and has remained so ever since.

Variations and abbreviations: Angèle (Fr), Angelia, Angelica.

Examples: Angela Lansbury, British-born actress.
Angela Brazil, 1868–1947, English writer of schoolgirl stories.

ANGELICA
Origin/meaning: Greek 'messenger', 'Angelic woman'.

A 19th century variation of Angela q.v. which was introduced from Italy.

Variations and abbreviations: Angelika (Ger), Angélique (Fr).

Examples: Angelica Kauffman, 1741–1807, Swiss painter.
Angélique Arnauld, 1624–1684, French nun, religious heroine.
Angelica Garnett, painter daughter of Vanessa Bell.

ANGELINA
Origin/meaning: Greek 'messenger'.

A 19th century variation of Angela q.v.

Variation: Angeline.

ANGHARAD
Origin/meaning: Old Welsh 'much loved'.

A Welsh name which dates back before the Norman Conquest. It is still used in Wales today. Rare English forms are Ancret and Anchoret which were generally found in the border lands between England and Wales.

Example: Angharad Rhys, Welsh actress.

ANITA
Origin/meaning: Hebrew 'graceful', 'little graceful one'.

A Spanish and Italian diminutive form of Ann q.v. which was rather popular in the 1940s and 50s.

Variation: Nita.

Examples: Anita Loos, American writer.
Anita Harris, English singer.

ANJA (pron. Annyah)
Origin/meaning: Hebrew 'graceful'.

A Russian form of Ann *q.v.*

Variation: Anya.

Example: Anya Seton, US novelist.

ANN, ANNE
Origin/meaning: Hebrew 'graceful'.

Ann and its variations are all based on the Hebrew name Hannah *q.v.* St Anne was popularly supposed to be the mother of the Virgin Mary. The name came to the West from the Byzantine Empire via Russia at about the time of the Norman Conquest. Although slow to catch on, by the 17th century it was one of the most common English names. The accession of Queen Anne to the English throne in 1701 confirmed its popularity, although many Puritans, particularly in the American colonies, preferred to go back to the Biblical original Hannah. Both in English-speaking countries and in Europe, it is frequently combined with Mary to make names like Anna Marie, Mary Ann, Marian etc. Its brevity and the ease with which it can be varied have ensured its continuing popularity.

Variations and abbreviations: Ana, Anette, Anja (Russ), Anita (Sp/It), Anna (Ger/It/Dutch/Scand), Annetta, Annette (Fr), Anni, Annie, Anny, Anouska (Russ), Anya (Russ), Nan, Nana, Nancy, Nannie, Nita.

Examples: Anne Boleyn, wife of Henry VIII, 1507-1536.
HRH Princess Anne.

ANNA
Origin/meaning: Hebrew 'graceful'.

A Latin form of Ann which became popular in England in the 18th century when many names eg Adolphus, Louisa, were used in a Latin form. It is still used frequently and is the usual form of Ann in countries like Germany, Italy and Sweden.

Examples: Anna Pavlova, 1885-1931, Russian ballerina.
Anna Rosenberg, 1902-1983, US politician.

ANNABEL
Origin/meaning: Latin/French 'lovable'.

This name is Scottish and dates from the 12th century. There is no convincing evidence for the frequent assumption that it is a combination of Anna and Bella, meaning 'beautiful Ann', as it appears in Scotland well before the name Anne. It was probably an equivalent of the English Amabel which also dates from the 12th century. The 18th century Latinized form is Annabella.

Variations and abbreviations: Annabella (It), Annabelle, Annabla (Ir), Bella, Belle. See also Arabella.

Example: Annabel Leventon, English actress.

ANNAMARIA
Origin/meaning: Hebrew 'graceful/bitter'.

One of many combinations of Mary and Ann *q.v.* This version is Italian or Spanish.

Variations and abbreviations: Anna Maria, Anna Marie, Anne Marie, Annamarie, Annemarie.

ANNORA
Origin/meaning: Latin 'honour' or 'beauty'.

A medieval English spelling of the name Honora *q.v.*

ANNUNCIATA
Origin/meaning: Latin 'bearer of news'.

This is a name which refers to the occasion when the Virgin Mary was told by an angel that she was to be the Mother of Jesus. The day this event is celebrated in the Catholic Church is March 25th. The name is therefore given almost exclusively to girls born in March. Rare in English-speaking countries.

Variations and abbreviations: Annunziata (It), Annunciacion (Sp), Maria Annunciata (It).

ANONA
Origin/meaning: Latin 'yearly crops' or 'ninth born'.

Example: Anona Winn, English broadcaster.

ANSELMA
Origin/meaning: Old German 'helmet of God'.

A feminine form of the old masculine name Anselm. Rare in English-speaking countries but still found in Germany and Italy.

Variations and abbreviations: Anselmina, Aselma, Selma.

ANSTICE
Origin/meaning: Greek 'resurrection'.

A 17th century English form of Anastasia *q.v.*.

Variation: Anstis.

ANTHEA
Origin/meaning: Greek 'flowery'.

One of the 17th century literary names created to give characters names appropriate to their appearance or personality.

See also Flora, Fleur.

Examples: Anthea Askey, actress daughter of Arthur Askey. Anthea Redfern, English model and actress.

ANTOINETTE
Origin/meaning: from the Latin name Antonius, one of the Patrician families of Ancient Rome.

A French form of Antonia *q.v.* which has become familiar in English-speaking countries.

Examples: Antoinette Sibley, English ballet dancer. Marie-Antoinette, 1755–1793, wife of Louis XVI of France.

ANTONIA
Origin/meaning: from the Latin name Antonius, one of the Patrician families of Ancient Rome. Sometimes considered to mean 'inestimable' or 'priceless'.

A feminine form of Antony *q.v.*

Variations and abbreviations: Anthoine (Fr), Antoinette (Fr), Antonetta (Scand), Antonie (Ger), Antonietta (It), Antonina (It), Netta, Nettie, Netty, Toni, Tonia, Tonie, Tony.

Examples: Lady Antonia Fraser, English writer. Antonia White, 1899–1980, English novelist.

APOLLONIA (pron. Apollóhnia)
Origin/meaning: Greek mythology, from Apollo, God of the sun therefore 'sunny'.

An Italian feminine version of the masculine name Apollo or Apollonius. Rarely found in English-speaking countries but not uncommon in Europe.

Variation: Apolline. See also Bridget.

APRIL
Origin/meaning: Latin 'opening', 'beginning of Spring'. The name of the 4th month of the year.

A comparatively recent 20th century name, it is usually given to girls born in April. Sometimes confused with Averil *q.v.*

Variations and abbreviations: Avril (Fr).

Example: Avril Angers, English actress.

ARABELLA
Origin/meaning: Latin 'lovable'.

This name was originally found only in Scotland and dates from the 12th century. Like Annabel it is probably a form of Amabel *q.v.*. Arabella is the Latinized 18th century version of the medieval original Arabel. Since Ara Bella means beautiful altar in Latin it is sometimes given this meaning.

Variations and abbreviations: Arabel, Arabela, Arabele, Arabelle, Arbel, Arbella, Bel, Bella, Belle, Ella.

Examples: Lady Arabella Stuart, 1575–1615, niece of Mary Queen of Scots.
Arabella Mansfield, 1846–1911, first woman admitted to the US Bar.

ARAMINTA
Origin/meaning: Latin 'loving'.

A rare name in the 20th century, this name was one of many made-up names found in 17th century literature, which were taken up and used by real people. It is probably a version of Arabella *q.v.* which itself may come from Amabel *q.v.*

Variation: Aminta.

ARDATH
Origin/meaning: Hebrew 'flowering field'.

Used as a first name occasionally since the 19th century when Marie Corelli gave the name to a character in one of her novels.

Variations and abbreviations: Ardith, Ardyth, Aridatha.

ARDELLE
Origin/meaning: Latin 'warm, enthusiastic'.

Variations and abbreviations: Arad, Ardelia, Ardella, Ardene, Ardine.

ARETA
Origin/meaning: Greek 'virtue'.

The feminine version of the obsolete masculine name Aretas.

Variations and abbreviations: Aretha, Aretta, Retha.

Example: Aretha Franklin, US singer.

ARIADNE
Origin/meaning: Greek 'very holy one'.

Originally the name of the mythological heroine, the daughter of King Minos of Crete. She helped the Greek Theseus escape from the labyrinth where the Minotaur was waiting to kill him, by giving him a ball of silk to mark his route. An early saint also bore the name.

Variations and abbreviations: Ariane (Fr/Ger), Ariana, Arianna (It).

Example: Ariadne Nicolaeff, Russian playwright.

ARIANA
Origin/meaning: Greek 'very holy one'.

Latin version of Ariadne q.v. Ariane is the name given to the first European space rocket.

Variations: Ariane, Arianna.

Example: Arianna Stassinopoulos, Greek writer.

ARIANWEN
Origin/meaning: Old Welsh 'silver white'.

See also Albinia, Alva, Blanche.

ARLENE
Origin/meaning: Gaelic 'a pledge'.

This name is sometimes also used as a version of Aline q.v.

Variations and abbreviations: Arleen, Arlena, Arline, Lena, Lina.

Examples: Arlene Phillips, British choreographer.
Arlene Dahl, US actress.

ARMINE
Origin/meaning: Old German 'army person', 'a soldier'.

Rare feminine version of Armin, the English form of Armand and

Herman *q.v.* The variation, Arminel, is found in the Devon area of England.

Variations: Armina, Arminda, Arminel, Arminie, Armande (Fr).

Example: Jane Arminda Delano, 1862–1919, US nurse and Red Cross administrator.

ARNOLDINE
Origin/meaning: Old German 'eagle-power'.

Feminine version of Arnold, *q.v.*

Variation: Arnalda.

ARTEMISIA
Origin/meaning: Greek 'belonging to Artemis'.

Artemis was the Greek Goddess of hunting and the moon, the equivalent of the Roman Goddess Diana. A 4th century BC queen of Caria was called Artemisia. It is unusual in English-speaking countries and tends to run in certain families.

Example: Artemisia Gentileschi, 1590–1642, Italian painter.

ASCELINA
Origin/meaning: Old German 'noble'.

Feminine form of Acelin *q.v.*

ASELMA
Origin/meaning: Old German 'helmet of God'.

A version of Anselma, the feminine form of Anselm *q.v.*

ASMITA (pron. Asméeta)
Origin/meaning: Hindu 'self-respect'.

Found throughout India.

ASPASIA (pron. Asspáyzia)
Origin/meaning: Greek 'welcome'.

One of the 'new' names of 17th century England which were inspired by literature. Beaumont and Fletcher used the name in their play *The Maid's Tragedy*, 1619. It was originally the name of the mistress of the Athenian statesman Pericles. Rare now in England, it is still found in Italy and Germany.

Abbreviation: Spash.

ASTA

Origin/meaning: Greek 'star' or a short form of Augusta, Astrid or Anastasia q.v.

Popular in Germany and Scandinavia, where it is probably a contraction of one of the three above names which are all commonly found in those countries. Rare in English-speaking countries.

Variation and abbreviation: Astra.

ASTRID

Origin/meaning: Old Norse 'God's strength'.

A perennially popular name in Scandinavia and German-speaking areas. Used by Scandinavian Royal families since the 11th century when it was the name of the wife of the Norwegian King and Saint, Olaf.

Variations and abbreviations: Asta, Assa, Assi, Atti, Estrid.

Example: Princess Astrid of Sweden, 1905-1935, popular first wife of Leopold III of Belgium.

ATALANTA

Origin/meaning: Greek 'swift runner'.

In Greek mythology Atalanta was an athlete who would only marry someone who ran faster than she could. Suitors who lost the race were killed. Hippomenes was given three golden apples by the goddess Aphrodite which he placed in Atalanta's path. He then won the race because she stopped en route to pick up the golden apples.

Variations: Atalante, Allante, Atlanta, Tala.

ATALYA

Origin/meaning: Spanish 'guardian'.

ATHALIA

Origin/meaning: Hebrew 'God is exalted'.

Athalia is a Biblical name. She was the mother of Ahaziah, one of the Kings of Judah (II Kings ch.1, 8).

Variations and abbreviations: Atalia, Atalie, Athalea, Athalie.

Example: Athalie, heroine of French writer Racine's play of the same name, 1691.

ATHENA

Origin/meaning: Greek 'wisdom'.

Athena was the Greek goddess of wisdom. Her symbol was an owl. Athens was named in her honour and was under her protection. Rare in English-speaking countries.

Variation: Athene (Fr). See also Minerva.

Example: Athene Sayler, b.1889, British actress.

AUDREY

Origin/meaning: Old English 'noble strength'.

One of the many name derived from the Old German 'adal' and Old English 'Aethel' meaning noble. Audrey is a contraction of Etheldreda. After 1000 years Audrey became common as an independent name in the 16th century. The word tawdry comes from the name because of the lace and other cheap ornaments sold at St Etheldreda's fair on the Isle of Ely where the 7th century Saint of that name had founded an abbey. It was particularly popular in the 1930s.

Variations and abbreviations: Audi, Audie, Audrie, Audry, Audrye, Dee. (See also Adelaide, Alice.)

Examples: Audrey Hepburn, English film actress.
Audrey the Shepherdess in *As You Like It* by William Shakespeare.

AUGUSTA

Origin/meaning: Latin 'venerable', 'majestic'. Title given to female relations of the Roman emperors.

Feminine version of Augustus *q.v.* which was used by German princes of the Renaissance in imitation of classical heroes. The Hanoverians brought both the masculine and feminine versions to England in the 18th century and Augusta became popular in the 19th century. Now uncommon in English-speaking countries although still popular in Europe. Sometimes used for girls born in the month of August which is itself named after the Roman Emperor, Augustus.

Variations and abbreviations: Auguste (Dutch/Fr/Ger/Scand), Augustina, Augustine, Austina, Austine, Gus, Gussie, Gussy, Tina.

Examples: Augusta of Brunswick, elder sister of George III.
Augusta Maywood, 1825–1876, US Prima ballerina assoluta.

AUGUSTINA
Origin/meaning: Latin 'venerable', 'majestic'.

A diminutive feminine form of Augustus and Augustine *q.v.* A variation of Augusta.

AUREA
Origin/meaning: Hebrew 'daughter of Jehovah' or Old Celtic 'life'.

A Latin adjective occasionally used as a descriptive first name. Similar to Aurelia. Also found in Italy.

AURELIA (pron. Or-ráy-leah)
Origin/meaning: Latin 'golden', 'beautiful'.

Aurelius was the name of one of the great Patrician families of Rome. Aurelia has been used as a girl's name from time to time since the Renaissance revived interest in classical names.

Variations and abbreviations: Aureliana (It), Aura, Aurel, Auralea, Aurélie (Fr), Auriol, Ora, Oralia, Oralie, Orelia, Oriel.

Example: Aurelia, heroine of *The Twin Rivals* by George Farquhar, 1702.

AURIOL
Origin/meaning: Latin 'golden', 'beautiful'.

A modern form of Aurelia *q.v.*

Variations and abbreviations: Auriel, Oriel, Oriole.

AURORA
Origin/meaning: Latin 'dawn'.

In Roman mythology Aurora was the goddess of the dawn. It is one of many classical names revived during the Renaissance and popularized by 17th century literature. Oriana *q.v.* may be a version of the same name.

Variation: Aurore (Fr). See also Dawn, Roxane, Zarah.

Examples: Amandine Aurore Dupin, 1804–1876, French novelist, who used the pseudonym George Sand.
Aurora Leigh, heroine of a blank verse romance of the same name by Elizabeth Barrett Browning, 1856.

AVA
Origin/meaning: Latin 'birdlike' or possibly Old German 'refuge in battle'.

Ava may well be a 'manufactured' name with no real meaning at all though it may have some connection with the well-established Avis *q.v.* or come from the Latin word 'avis' – a bird. Another possibility is that it is a mis-spelling of the German name Eva which is pronounced Ava and is a Latinized spelling of the name Eve.

Example: Ava Gardner, Italian/US film actress, once voted the world's most beautiful woman.

AVELINA
Origin/meaning: Old French 'hazel tree' or Old Celtic 'pleasant'.

Possibly Old German name Avi. An early version of Eveline *q.v.*

Variation: Aveline.

AVERIL
Origin/meaning: Old English 'boar-battle'.

This name is now almost always feminine, despite its meaning, although it can be used for boys or girls. It is sometimes confused with Avril, the French form of April.

The original Anglo-Saxon form was Everild, which survives in the gypsy name Everilda. A 7th century Everild founded a nunnery in Yorkshire.

Variations and abbreviations: Averell, Averilla, Averyl, Everild, Everilda.

AVICE (pron. Aviss)
Origin/meaning: Old German 'battle struggle'.

The original Old German Haduwig name arrived in England at the time of the Conquest in the French form Havoise from which Avice derives. It went out of fashion during the 16th and 17th centuries but is again regularly used in the 20th century.

Variations and abbreviations: Avicia, Avis. See also Hedvig.

Example: Avice Landone, British actress.

AVIS/A
Origin/meaning: Latin 'bird'.

Sometimes confused with the much longer established name, Avice *q.v.* King John's first wife was Avisa, daughter of the Earl of Gloucester.

AYESHA (pron. Ay'sha)
Origin/meaning: Arabic 'life' or 'alive'.

This popular Moslem name commemorates Ayesha, 610–677, the favourite of Mohammed's nine wives. He died on the 8th June, 632, with his head resting on her lap.

Variations and abbreviations: Aisha, Ashaas (Swahili), Ay'sha, Ayeshah.

AYO
Origin/meaning: Yoruba 'joy'.

A Nigerian name. The word occurs in many other names such as Ayobami 'I am blessed with joy', Ayodele 'joy comes home', Ayoluwa 'joy of our people', Baye 'joy is found', Dayo 'joy arrives', Nayo 'we have joy' and Olubayo 'highest joy'.

AZALEA
Origin/meaning: Greek 'parched' from the flowering bush of the same name.

One of the more unusual of the flower names popular at the end of the 19th century. It is the beauty of the flower which the name intends to convey, not the Greek meaning which indicated its favourite growing conditions.

Variations and abbreviations: Azaleah, Azalia, Azelea, Zalea, Zelie.

Example: Emma Azalia Hackley, 1867–1922, US singer.

AZARIA
Origin/meaning: Hebrew 'whom God aids'.

A masculine name *q.v.* sometimes listed as feminine because of its 'feminine' ending.

AZIZA
Origin/meaning: Arabic 'precious'.

This is a common Muslim name.

AZURA
Origin/meaning: Persian/Arabic 'bright sky-blue', the colour of lapis lazuli.

Presumably a name to indicate eyes of a remarkable colour.

Variation: Azzurra (Ger/It/Swiss).

B

BABETTE
Origin/meaning: Hebrew 'God is my satisfaction'.
A short form of Elizabeth *q.v.* and occasionally of Barbara *q.v.*
Example: Alice Babette Toklas, 1877–1967, US writer.

BABS
Origin/meaning: Greek 'stranger', 'foreigner'.
A short form of Barbara *q.v.*

BAI
Origin/meaning: Hindi 'woman'.
Used in North India as a suffix to other names to indicate politeness or respect. Never used as a name on its own. For example its addition to the masculine name Shashi *q.v.* turns it into a feminine name, Shashi-bai.

BAPTISTA
Origin/meaning: Greek/Latin 'one who baptizes'.
This is the feminine form of the Latin word.
In English-speaking countries only the feminine version of this name seems to be used. Elsewhere in Europe the masculine, Baptiste, is also found. It is a name which honours John the Baptist.
Variations and abbreviations: Baptiste (Fr), Batista (It), Battistina (It), Bautista (Sp).

BARBARA
Origin/meaning: Greek 'stranger', 'foreigner'.
This was a popular medieval name in Europe given to girls in honour of a legendary St Barbara who was martyred by her own father. After the Protestant Reformation a reaction against Catholic non-Biblical saints' names put it out of favour in England and New England. It was revived in the 19th century

43

along with many other medieval names, eg Alice, and has remained consistently popular ever since. In the US the fact that it is found in many languages has contributed to its popularity.

Variations and abbreviations: Bab, Babbie (Scot), Babetta (It), Babette (Fr), Babita, Babs, Bar, Barbarina (It), Barb, Barbe (Fr), Barbie, Barbra (Dan), Barbro (Swed), Barby, St Barbe, Varina, Varinka, Varvara (Slav).

Examples: Barbra Streisand, US actress and singer.
Barbara Castle, British politician.
Barbara Bel Geddes, US actress.

BARRIE
Origin/meaning: Old Irish 'spear'.

An occasional feminine form of Barry.

BASILIA
Origin/meaning: Greek 'kingly'.

Rare feminine form of Basil q.v.

Variation: Basilie (Fr).

BATHSHEBA
Origin/meaning: Hebrew 'daughter of the oath' or 'voluptuous'.

Two meanings are generally listed for this Biblical name. In Book II of Samuel is the story of how King David sent Bathsheba's husband Uriah into the most dangerous area of battle so that he was killed. David was then able to marry her himself. Bathsheba became the mother of King Solomon. Despite Bathsheba's story the name was fairly common among 17th century Puritans. In I Chronicles 3:5 the name is given as Bathshua.

Variations and abbreviations: Bathshua, Batsheva, Sheba.
Example: Bathsheba Everdene was the heroine of Thomas Hardy's *Far From the Madding Crowd*, 1874.

BEA
Origin/meaning: Latin 'bringer of happiness'.

A short form of Beatrice q.v.

Variation: Bee.

Example: Bea Lilly, Canadian-born musical comedy star, b.1894.

BEATA (pron. Bay-árta)
Origin/meaning: 'happy'.

The name of one of the early unauthenticated saints. It was only occasionally found in England, although it is still popular in Italy. Sometimes confused with the similar Beatrice *q.v.*

BEATRICE (Pron. Béeatriss)
Origin/meaning: Latin 'bringer of happiness'.

This is the Italian form of the name. In Italy it is pronounced Bee-a-trée-chay, and the short form Bice is pronounced Beechee. The original Latin form Beatrix is also found in Britain as well as Germany and the Netherlands. The name was found with various spellings and pronunciations throughout the Middle Ages when it was given to honour St Beatrice, an early Roman martyr. Like other non-Biblical saints' names it went out of fashion after the Protestant Reformation. It was revived in the 19th century as part of a general re-awareness of medieval culture, particularly because of Dante's great poem *The Divine Comedy*. In this he describes meeting his ideal love, Beatrice, in Paradise. He gave the name Beatrice to his only daughter. Queen Victoria, who shared the 19th century liking for medieval names, called her youngest daughter Beatrice.

Variations and abbreviations: Bea, Beat, Beate, Béatrice (Fr), Beatricia, Beatrisa, Beatrix (Lat/Old Eng/Ger/Dutch), Beatriz (Sp), Bee, Beitris (Scot), Bettrys (Welsh), Bice (It), Biche (Fr), Trix, Trixi, Trixie, Trixy.

Example: Beatrice Webb, 1858–1943, English social reformer and economist.

BEATRIX
Origin/meaning: Latin 'bringer of happiness'.

Old (Latin) form of Beatrice *q.v.*

Examples: Beatrix Potter, 1866–1943, English writer, creator of Peter Rabbit.
Queen Beatrix of the Netherlands.

BECKY
Origin/meaning: Hebrew 'knotted cord' therefore 'fathful wife', or possibly 'heifer'.

A short form of Rebecca *q.v.*

Example: Becky Sharp, heroine of Thackeray's *Vanity Fair*, 1847–1848.

BEGUM
This is a Muslim title. In her family a woman is addressed simply by her personal name, but formally by her personal name plus her title: eg Jameela *Begum*.

BELINDA
Origin/meaning: Old German 'snake-like', 'sinuous'.

The word *linda* means snake. The prefix *Be* has no certain meaning. Snakes were regarded as magical or godlike by many communities including the Saxon peoples. This is therefore a complimentary name. It is first found as the wife of Roland in the medieval Charlemagne romances but was never very common. It was used by several 18th century writers, notably Alexander Pope in his *Rape of the Lock*, 1712, and this gave it a certain currency. It is probably more popular today than it has ever been, perhaps because of the Spanish sound of the name and the assumption that it derives from the Spanish word meaning beautiful. It has been particularly successful in Australia.

Variations and abbreviations: Bel, Belle, Linda.

Example: Belinda J. Montgomery, American actress.

BELLE
Origin/meaning: French 'beautiful'.

Also a short form of names such as Anabel, Arabella, Belinda, Isabel etc.

Variations and abbreviations: Anwen (Welsh), Bell, Bella. See also Shobha.

Examples: Belle Starr, 1848–1889, US outlaw, 'The Female Jesse James'.
Bella Abzug, US member of Congress and feminist.

BEN
Origin/meaning: Hindi 'sister'.

Used as a suffix in West India to indicate politeness or respect. Never used as a name on its own.

BENEDICTA
Origin/meaning: 'blessed'.

The Latin feminine form of Benedict *q.v.* Found in various forms since the Middle Ages.

Variations and abbreviations: Benedetta (It), Bénédicke (Fr), Benedikta (Ger), Benita (Sp), Benni, Bennie, Benny, Benoite (Fr), Binnie.

Example: Binnie Barnes, British-born actress and Hollywood star in the 1930s and 40s.

BENITA
Origin/meaning: Latin 'blessed'.

A Spanish feminine form of the masculine name Benedict (Benito in Spanish). Outside Europe mainly found in US which has a large population of Spanish origin. See also Benedicta.

Example: Benita Hume, 1906–1967, British-born actress wife of Ronald Coleman.

BERENGARIA
Origin/meaning: Old German 'bear-spear'.

A Latin feminine form of Berenger *q.v.* The wife of King Richard the Lion Heart was called Berengière, the French version and in Latin documents this became Berengaria. A famous transatlantic liner of the 1930s was named after her.

BERENICE
Origin/meaning: Greek 'bringer of victory'.

This Greek name originally began with ph and was pronounced Pherenika. Because B in Greek makes a similar soft *v* sound it was used instead and so the name came to be mistakenly pronounced with a hard B in Western Europe. As a result of the confusion between the sounds Berenice was sometimes taken to be the same name as Veronica *q.v.* As a Biblical name, Berenice was the daughter of King Agrippa (Acts xxv-xxvi); it had some popularity after the Protestant Reformation. The name is common in the US as Bernice.

Variations and abbreviations: Berenike (Ger), Bérénice (Fr), Berenice (It), Bernice, Bernie, Berny, Bunny.

Example: Bernice Rubens, British novelist, winner of the Booker Prize, 1970.

BERINTHIA
Origin/meaning: an 18th century literary name, found most

notably in the heroine of Vanbrugh's play *The Relapse*, 1696.
Abbreviation: Berry.

BERNADETTE
Origin/meaning: Old German 'resolute as a bear'.

A French feminine diminutive form of Bernard *q.v.* Its great
popularity in the 20th century particularly in Ireland and among
Catholics, is almost entirely due to St Bernadette of Lourdes,
1844–1879, who was born Marie Bernarde Soubirous. The grotto
at Lourdes where she was reputed to have seen visions of the
Virgin Mary has become one of the greatest Christian shrines.
See also Bernardine.

BERNARDINE
Origin/meaning: 'resolute as a bear'.

Rare feminine equivalent of Bernard *q.v.* now overtaken by the
French Bernadette *q.v.* because of St Bernadette of Lourdes.

Variations and abbreviations: Berna, Bernadene, Bernadetta (It),
Bernadette (Fr), Bernadina, Bernadine, Bernarda, Bernarde
(Fr), Bernardina (It/Sp), Berneta, Bernie, Berny.

BERTHA
Origin/meaning: Old German 'bright'.

This name is at present out of favour, perhaps because 'Big
Bertha' was the name given to one of the heavy guns in the First
World War. Bertha and Berta have been current in Europe since
Saxon times. Bertha, sister of Charlemagne, was the mother of
one of his most famous knights – Roland. Charlemagne's mother
was also called Bertha with large feet! Bertha was originally the
name of a pre-Christian goddess associated with fertility.
Because of its meaning the name was associated with the Feast
of the Epiphany (Jan 6th) when the Magi followed the bright star
to Bethlehem. So it became customary to give the name to girls
born at that season. Eventually Frau Bertha, the personification
of the Epiphany, became part of German folk-lore. She was
pictured as dressed in white, with large feet (obviously a
reference back to Charlemagne's mother) and she was used as a
threat to naughty children. She was also supposed to rock
children and babies to sleep when their nursemaids neglected
them. The Italian version, Befana (a corruption of Epiphania)
was also supposed to put presents in the children's stockings on

Twelfth Night. In the 19th century Bertha was revived along with many other previously neglected early names, such as Alice, Emma and Matilda.

Variations and abbreviations: Bert, Berta (Ger/It/Swed/Sp), Berte, Bertel (Ger), Berthe (Fr), Bertie, Bertina, Betty. See also Blenda, Candida, Theophania.

Example: Berthe Morisot, 1841–1895, French impressionist painter.

BERYL
Origin/meaning: Greek/Latin. A beryl is a precious stone, similar to an emerald, usually pale green, blue or white.

This is one of the precious stone names, like Ruby, which came into use at the end of the 19th century at about the same time as flower names.

Variation: Berylla.

Examples: Beryl Grey, British ballerina.
Beryl Reid, British actress.

BESS
Origin/meaning: Hebrew 'God is my satisfaction'.

An English familiar form of Elizabeth q.v. often used for Elizabeth I who was popularly known as 'Good Queen Bess'.

Variations: Bessie, Bessy, Betsy.

BETH
Origin/meaning: Hebrew 'God is my satisfaction'.

English familiar form of Elizabeth q.v. sometimes used as an independent name.

Example: One of the four March sisters in Louisa M. Alcott's *Little Women* was named Beth, 1869.

BETHANY
Origin/meaning: Aramaic 'house of poverty'.

A Biblical name (it was a small village near Jerusalem) this has been found from time to time in England and New England since the Reformation.

BETHIA
Origin/meaning: Hebrew 'daughter of Jehovah' or Old Celtic 'life'.

The first meaning is most likely as the name came into use during the 17th century when Biblical names were popular among Puritans. Its popularity in Scotland may have been due to its similarity to an older Celtic name which it replaced.

Variations: Bethiah, Bithiah.

BETTINA
Origin/meaning: Hebrew 'God is my satisfaction'.

An Italian short form of Elizabeth widely popular in the 1960s, perhaps because of the famous model Bettina, wife of the Aly Khan.

BETTRYS
Origin/meaning: Latin 'bringer of happiness'.

Welsh form of Beatrice q.v.

Variation: Beitiris (Scots Gaelic).

BETTY
Origin/meaning: Hebrew 'God is my satisfaction'.

English familiar form of Elizabeth q.v. now often found as an independent name.

Variations: Beithidh (Gaelic), Betta (It), Bette, Betti (Ger), Bettie, Bettina (It), Betsey, Betsy and see Elizabeth.

Examples: Bette Davis, US film actress.
Betty Ford, wife of former US President, Gerald Ford.

BEULAH
Origin/meaning: Hebrew 'married', 'matronly'.

Variation: Beula.

Example: Said by Mae West in the famous line: 'Beulah, peel me a grape'.

BEVERLEY
Origin/meaning: Old English 'from the beaver stream'.

A surname derived from a place in Yorkshire, this has been used as a first name for boys and girls. In the USA it is almost exclusively a girl's name, with the spelling Beverly. The reason for its popularity was originally the novel by G. B. McCutchan,

Beverly of Graustark, 1904. The heroine was a Southern belle. It is a common practice in the southern United States to give girls as well as boys family names as forenames. Mrs Wallis Simpson, who married the Duke of Windsor, is a famous example of this tradition.

Variations and abbreviations: Bev, Beverle, Beverlee, Beverly.

Examples: Beverley Sassoon, English writer on health and beauty.
Beverly Sills, US Opera Singer.

BHAVANA (pron. Báunah).
Origin/meaning: Sanskrit 'conception', 'faith', 'love'.

BIANCA
Origin/meaning: Italian 'white', 'fair'.

The Italian form of the better known French name Blanche *q.v.* Intended to imply fair in the sense of 'beautiful' as well as fair colouring as in Shakespeare's play *The Taming of the Shrew*.

Variations: Biancamaria, Biancha (Med Eng), Bianka.

Examples: Bianca Jagger, Nicaraguan model and socialite.
Bianca Cappello, 1548–1587, wife of Francesco de' Medici, Duke of Florence.

BIBI
This is a Muslim title, like – bai or- ben in India. A Muslim woman would be addressed formally by her personal name and her title, eg Azara *bibi*.

BIBIANA
Origin/meaning: Latin 'full of life'.

This is a version of Vivien *q.v.* which comes from the Latin meaning to be alive. The change in letter is a result of confusion because the letter B being pronounced *v* in Greek. St Bibiana or Viviana is one of the early Roman martyrs about whom there is no authentic history.

BICE (pron. Bee-chay)
Origin/meaning: Latin 'bringer of happiness'.

Popular Italian short form of Beatrice *q.v.*

BIDDY

Origin/meaning: 'strong one', 'mighty one'.

The name comes from the Irish Celtic goddess of fire.

Irish familiar form of Bridget q.v.

BILLIE

Origin/meaning: Old German 'helmet of resolution'.

A short form of feminine versions of William, eg Wilhelmina, Williamina. Sometimes given as an independent name.

Variations: Bill, Billee, Billi, Billy. See also Minnar, Minnie.

Examples: The appropriately named Billie-Jean King, US tennis player.
Billie Holiday, 1915–1959, US singer.
Billie Whitelaw, English actress.

BIRDIE

Origin/meaning: English 'little bird'.

Usually a nickname, occasionally in US found as a given name.

See also Aderyn.

BIRGITTA

Origin/meaning: Old Norse 'mountain stronghold' or Old Irish 'strong one'.

This is the Scandinavian form of Bridget q.v. It has a different origin and meaning from the original Irish name Brigit or Brighid but the two names and their variations have become totally interchangeable. The 14th century Swedish St Birgitta 1303–1373 was as popular in her country as St Brigit in Ireland. She was the wife of a nobleman and mother of eight children, including one other saint. She used her position at court to try and improve the behaviour and morals of the royal family. As a widow she founded the Order of the Holy Saviour (Bridgettines).

Variations and abbreviations: Berget, Birga, Birgit, Brig, Brigga, Brigitta, Brita, Britt, Britta, Gita, Gitta.

BLANCA

Origin/meaning: Spanish 'white', 'fair'.

Blanca of Castile married Louis VIII of France, and became the mother of Louis IX, St Louis. The French translated her name directly into their own language as Blanche. Her grand-daughter, who was named after her, brought the name Blanche to England when she married the Earl of Lancaster, a member of the English royal family.

BLANCHE
Origin/meaning: French 'white' from Old German 'blaecan' to whiten.

A French name in its own right since the early Middle Ages, it was also used to translate foreign names with the same meaning such as Blanca or Guinevere. Blanche of Castile, 1189–1242, the Queen of Louis VIII was a Spanish princess whose name was originally Blanca. It was introduced from France into the English royal family as an independent name, rather than a translation of English or Celtic names, by Blanche of Artois in the 13th century. It has since been used with various spellings including Blanchia and Blaunch. It was one of the medieval names popularized in the 19th century and has been used consistently since, although it has never been common.

Variations and abbreviations: Bianca (It), Blanca (Dan/Sp), Blanch, Blanchette (Fr), Blanchia, Blanka (Ger/Swed), Blaunch (Med Eng), Blinnie, Blinny. See also Albina, Arianwen, Alva, Blenda, Blodwen, Candida, Guinevere.

Examples: Blanche du Bois in Tennessee Williams' play *A Streetcar Named Desire*.
Blanche Sweet, US star of silent films.

BLENDA
Origin/meaning: Old German 'dazzling', 'bright white'.

A Swedish name. See also Blanche, Bertha, Bianca, Candida.

BLISS
Origin/meaning: Old English 'cause of delight'.

Rare English girl's name.

BLODWEN
Origin/meaning: Old Welsh 'white flower'.

Rare outside Wales.

Variation: Blodwyn.

BLOSSOM
Origin/meaning: Old English 'flower', 'flower-like'.

53

Popular in West Indies. See also Fleur, Chloë.

Example: Blossom Dearie, US singer.

BLYTHE
Origin/meaning: Old English 'gentle', 'cheerful'.

An unusual name which may also be used as a boy's name.

Variations: Blithe, Blyth.

BOBBIE
Origin/meaning: Old German 'bright flame'.

A popular short form, especially in the United States, of Roberta. Occasionally used as an independent name.

Variations: Bobbi, Bobby, Bobbye.

Example: Bobbie Gentry, US country singer.

BONITA
Origin/meaning: Latin 'good', Spanish 'pretty'.

A Spanish name also used in the United States.

Variations and abbreviations: Bona (It), Bonnie, Nita.

Example: Bonita Granville, child film actress in Hollywood 1930s films.

BONNIE
Origin/meaning: Scots dialect 'pretty' perhaps derived from Latin bonus – good.

A word used as a familiar form of many names beginning with B, eg Barbara, Bonita and sometimes found as an independent name.

Variations and abbreviations: Bonnee, Bonni, Bonny.

Example: Bonnie Langford, English actress and dancer.

BRANWEN
Origin/meaning: Old Welsh 'beautiful raven', 'raven-haired'.

Rare outside Wales. In the collection of old Welsh tales *The Mabinogion*, intended as a repertoire for young bards, Branwen was the beautiful daughter of the British King Llyr. She married the King of Ireland and was buried in the Isle of Anglesey off the Welsh coast. Another legendary Branwen was the maid of Iseult

(Yssalt) who mistakenly gave her mistress the love potion intended for her on her wedding night, when she was with her escort, Tristan. Their resulting ill-fated romance has been an inspiration for many writers and was used by Wagner in his opera *Tristan und Isolde*. Variations of the name are also found as surnames.

Variations: Brangwain, Brengwain. See also Bronwen, Isolde.

BRENDA
Origin/meaning: Old Norse 'sword'.

This name comes from the Shetland Isles off Scotland, which were settled by Viking invaders. It is the feminine form of Brand *q.v.* which is occasionally found in England. Brenda became known outside the Shetlands in the 19th century when Sir Walter Scott, the Scottish novelist with a passionate love for his country's history and traditions, used the name for one of the characters in *The Pirate*, 1821, which was set in the Shetlands. It appealed to the Victorians' love of 'historical' names and its popularity increased gradually but steadily into the 20th century. Sometimes used as a feminine of the Irish name Brendan 'dweller by the beacon'.

Abbreviation: Bren.

Example: Brenda Lee, US singer.

BRENNA
Origin/meaning: Old Irish 'raven', 'raven-haired'.

May be a feminine form of Brendan *q.v.*

See also Branwen.

BRIANA
Origin/meaning: Old Irish 'strong'.

Modern feminine form of Brian *q.v.*

Variations and abbreviations: Brianne, Bryana.

BRIDGET
Origin/meaning: Old Irish 'strong one', 'mighty one' from the name of the Irish Celtic goddess of fire. This is the English form of the Old Irish name Brigid.

St Brigid of Kildare, 450–523, was the founder of the first

convents in Ireland and she was so revered that she was known as 'the Mary of the Gael (Celts)'. Since the 17th century the names Brigid and Mary have been the most popular female names in Ireland. Before the 17th century they were considered too sacred to be used. The original popularity of St Brigid may have been helped by the association of her name with the Celtic goddess of light and fire, Brighid, who was the daughter of the Sun God. In Sweden a 14th century St Brigitta or Birgitta was equally popular. Her name is also Anglicized as Bridget, and it was probably to honour her that it was first used as a Christian name in England when it was given in the form Brigitte, to a daughter of Edward IV in 1480. The usual form however for a long time after that was Bride – or Bryde – reflecting the Irish pronunciation Bri-ide. There are many reminders of this today in place names throughout Britain such as East Kilbride. The popularity of both Saints has resulted in the widespread use of the name throughout Europe and in many variations.

Variations and abbreviations: Bedelia, Beret, Berget, Biddie, Biddy, Birga, Birgit (Ger), Birgitta (Swed), Birte, Birtha, Brid (Ir), Bride, Bridie, Brietta, Brig, Brigga, Brighid (Ir), Brigid (Ir), Brigida (It/Sp), Brigide, Brigit (Ir), Brigitta (Swed/Ger), Brigitte (Fr/Ger), Brita, Britt (Swed), Britta (Swed), Bryde, Ffaod (Welsh), Gita, Gitta.

Examples: Brigitte Bardot, French film actress.
Brigid Brophy, English novelist.

BRITANNIA
Origin/meaning: Latin 'Britain'.

Rare British first name.

Variation: Brittany.

BRITT
Origin/meaning: Old Irish 'strong one', 'mighty one' or Old Norse 'mountain stronghold'.

A Swedish short form of Bridget *q.v.* from the form Brigitta. The Swedish form of the name has a different origin and meaning from the Irish one.

Variations and abbreviations: Birte, Birtha, Brita, Britta. See Birgitta.

Example: Britt Ekland, Swedish film actress.

BRODIE
Origin/meaning: Old Irish 'ditch'.

A surname used as a first name for both boys and girls.

Variation: Brody.

BRONWEN
Origin/meaning: Old Welsh 'white breast'.

Common in Wales but rare elsewhere. It is a name which features in the collection of Welsh mythological tales *The Mabinogion* (instruction for young bards).

Variations and abbreviations: Bron, Bronwyn.

BROOKE
Origin/meaning: Old English 'at the brook'.

A surname used as a first name, particularly in the US.

Variation: Brook.

Examples: Brooke Shields, US film actress.
Brooke Astor, US socialite and philanthropist.

BRUNETTA
Origin/meaning: Italian 'brown-haired'.

Italian name occasionally used in English-speaking countries.

Variation: Brunella.

BRUNHILDA
Origin/meaning: Old German 'breast plate of battle', 'battle maid'.

The name of one of the Valkyrie, the twelve nymphs of Valhalla in ancient German and Norse legend, who chose which warriors were to be slain. The name became known in English-speaking countries because of the popularity of Wagner's opera sequence *The Ring of the Niebelung*.

Variations and abbreviations: Brunhilel, Brunhilde, Brunilda, Brunilla, Brynhild, Hilda.

BRYONY
Origin/meaning: a climbing plant found in English hedgerows.

An unusual plant name.

BUNTY

Origin/meaning: a term of endearment similar to bunting in the nursery rhyme *Bye Baby Bunting*. Probably meaning plump or cuddly.

A nickname given to girls irrespective of their given names. See also Bonnie, Bunnie.

C

CADENCE
Origin/meaning: Latin 'rhythm'.
Variations: Cadena, Cadenza (Ital).

CAITLIN
Origin/meaning: uncertain. Possibly Greek 'pure'.
An old Irish form of Kathleen. Similar to the Medieval English Catlin and the Medieval French Cateline.
Variation: Catlin (Eng).
Example: Caitlin Thomas, wife of Welsh poet Dylan Thomas.

CALANDRA
Origin/meaning: Greek 'lark'.
Variations and abbreviations: Cal, Calandre (Fr), Calandria (Sp), Callie.

CALLA (pron. Callár).
Origin/meaning: Greek 'good', 'beautiful'.
Variations and abbreviations: Cal, Calli, Callie, Cally.

CALLISTA
Origin/meaning: Greek 'most beautiful'.
Variations and abbreviations: Calesta, Calista, Callie, Calysta, Kalista.

CALTHA
Origin/meaning: Latin 'marigold'.

CALYPSO
Origin/meaning: Greek 'concealer'.
In Greek myth Calypso was a nymph, Queen of the Isle of Ogygia (Gozo, near Malta) who kept Odysseus as her captive for seven years.

CAMILLA

Origin/meaning: Latin 'attendant at a sacrifice'.

Camilla was a female attendant, Camillus a male. A roman hero who saved Rome from the Gauls was called Camillus. The masculine name did not survive the collapse of the Roman Empire as well as the feminine version which was occasionally found in the Middle Ages, although there is an Italian St Camillus, 1550–1619. In the 18th century classical revival Camilla became quite popular, perhaps because of Camilla, Queen of the Volsci, who appears in Virgil's great poem *The Aeneid,* and is killed by one of the followers of Aeneas. Fanny Burney's novel *Camilla,* 1796, may have contributed to its popularity. It currently enjoys something of a vogue in England.

Variations and abbreviations: Cam, Camila (Sp), Camille (Fr), Cammie, Kamilla (Ger), Millie, Milly.

CAMILLE

Origin/meaning: Latin 'attendant at a sacrifice'.

The French version of the Latin/Italian name Camilla *q.v.* The name has always been much more popular in France than elsewhere.

Example: *Camille,* the Dumas *fils* novel made into a film with Garbo, 1936.

CANDACE (pron. Cánndiss).

Origin/meaning: Greek 'glittering', 'bright white'.

One of many names like Candida, Blanche, Bianca, which mean white. Candace was the name given to the Queens of Ethiopia. Found in the Bible it has occasionally been used since the 17th century and is more popular today than ever before.

Variations and abbreviations: Candi, Candice, Candie, Candy, Kandace, Kandy.

CANDICE (pron. Cánndiss).

Origin/meaning: Greek 'glittering', 'bright white'.

An alternative spelling of Candace *q.v.*

Example: Candice Bergen, US film actress.

CANDIDA

Origin/meaning: Latin 'white', 'fair', 'pure'.

One of the many names with a similar meaning. Candida, a 1st century saint was often translated from Latin to a name with the same meaning, becoming St Blanche *q.v.* in France and St Blanca *q.v.* in Spain. Never popular in England the name has been given some currency over the last 80 years by George Bernard Shaw's play *Candida*, 1898.

Variations and abbreviations: Candi, Candide (Fr), Candy, Kandida (Ger).

Example: Candida Lycett-Green, English writer, daughter of John Betjeman.

CANDY
Origin/meaning: a familiar form of Carol, Candace or Candida – sometimes used as a given name.

CARA (pron. Cárr-a).
Origin/meaning: either Latin 'beloved' or Old Irish 'friend'.

Only becoming popular in the 20th century, in English-speaking countries this name is most likely to have the first meaning. The Italians themselves use Carita, a diminutive form, and not the original Latin. In the variation Kara, it is gaining popularity in the US and in Australia.

Variations and abbreviations: Carina (It), Carita (It), Carrie, Carry, Kara (US).

CARINA (pron. Carr-éena).
Origin/meaning: Latin 'keel' or diminutive of Cara *q.v.* 'beloved'.

An established Italian name recently introduced into English-speaking countries, the second meaning seems more likely than the first.

Variation: Karina (Ger).

CARITA
Origin/meaning: Latin 'love', 'charity'.

An Italian name similar to Charity *q.v.* occasionally used in English-speaking countries.

Variations and abbreviations: Cara, Caritina, Carrie, Carry.

CARLA
Origin/meaning: Old German 'man', meaning by association 'womanly'.

An Italian feminine form of Charles q.v.

Example: Carla Lane, British playwright.

CARLOTTA
Origin/meaning: Old German 'man', meaning by association 'womanly'.

An Italian feminine form of Charles q.v.

Variations and abbreviations: Carlie, Carly, Charlotte (Fr), Karly.

CARLY
Origin/meaning: Old German 'man', meaning by association 'womanly'.

A pet form of the feminine versions of Charles, and of the Italian form Carlotta in particular. Recently very popular in Australia and the US because of singer Carly Simon. Since singer/actress Twiggy named her baby after her it has begun to gain popularity in the UK as well.

Variations and abbreviations: Carlie, Karlie, Karly.

Example: Carly Simon, US singer.

CARMEL
Origin/meaning: Hebrew 'garden'.

The name of the famous Mountain in Israel, Mount Carmel, where Elijah had his contest with the priests of Baal (I Kings 18). In the 12th century a monastic order was founded on the mountain. The influential Order of Carmelite nuns was based on this foundation. Carmel thus came into use as a name for Catholic girls, particularly in Spain and Ireland.

Variations and abbreviations: Carmela (It), Carmelina, Carmelita, Carmen (Sp), Carmencita, Carmina, Carmine, Carmita, Charmaine (Fr), Lita.

Example: Carmel Snow, 1890-1961, US fashion writer.

CARMEN
Origin/meaning: Hebrew 'garden' or occasionally Latin 'song', 'poem'.

The Spanish form of Carmel q.v. The title of Bizet's opera.

Variations and abbreviations: Carma, Carmencita, Charmaine (Fr), Carmina.

Example: Carmen Miranda, Portuguese singer and actress.

CAROL
Origin/meaning: Old German 'man', meaning by association 'womanly'. Sometimes given as Old French 'joyous song'.

Although a comparatively recent 20th century name, Carol is probably connected to other feminine versions of Charles q.v. such as Carola, Carla, Carlotta, through the Latin masculine version Carolus. It may have begun as a shortened form of the 18th century form Caroline.

Variations and abbreviations: Carola, Carole (Fr), Carroll, Carrie, Caryl, Carry, Karol, Karole, Karroll, Karoly.

Examples: Carol Channing, US musical actress.
Carole Lombard, 1908–1942, US film actress.

CAROLA
Origin/meaning: Old German 'man', meaning by association 'womanly'.

An unusual feminine form of Charles, being the feminine of its Latin form Carolus. Found in Italy and, since the 17th century, in England.

See also Carol, Caroline, Charlotte.

Example: Carola Oman, 1897–1978, English writer.

CAROLINE
Origin/meaning: Old German 'man', meaning by association 'womanly'.

Carolina is an Italian pet feminine form of Charles from Carola, the feminine form of the Latin version Carolus. It was introduced into England from Germany in the French form Caroline, when Caroline of Brandenburg-Anspach married the future George II. It rapidly became widespread along with Charlotte, the other 18th century version of the name popularized by the wife of her grandson, George III. It has maintained a steady popularity ever since. In Australia, Canada and the US, the form Carolyn is currently preferred.

Variations and abbreviations: Carlin, Carlina, Carlyn, Carlynn, Caro, Carolin, Carolina (It/Sp), Carolyn, Carolynn, Carolynne, Carrie, Karoline (Ger), Karolyn, Lyn.

Examples: Caroline Kennedy, daughter of President Kennedy. Lady Caroline Lamb (Caro), 1785–1828, mistress of Lord Byron. Princess Caroline of Monaco.

CARRIE
Origin/meaning: Old German 'man', meaning by association 'womanly'.

A short form of Caroline, particularly popular in the 19th century.

Example: Carrie Fisher, US film actress.

CARYL
Origin/meaning: Old German 'man', meaning by association 'womanly'. Sometimes given as Old Welsh 'love'.

An unusual feminine form of Charles q.v.

See also Carol, Caroline, Charlotte.

Examples: Caryl Brahms, c.1900–1982, English novelist and dramatist.
Caryl Churchill, English playwright.

CASS
Origin/meaning: a short form of Cassandra, or Catherine, sometimes used as an independent name.

Variations: Cassie, Cassy.

CASSANDRA
Origin/meaning: Greek, uncertain, possibly 'disbelieved by men'.

Cassandra was a Trojan prophetess and the sister of their hero Hector. She offended the god Apollo and was punished by being able to see the truth but never being believed. She was written about in the stories surrounding the wars between the Greeks and Trojans. These tales were immensely popular in the Middle Ages and Cassandra became a fairly common European name. It is still used in Italy and France and survives, though it is rare, in English-speaking countries.

Variations and abbreviations: Casandra (Sp), Cass, Cassandre (Fr), Cassandry, Cassie, Cassy, Sandie, Sandy.

Example: Cassandra Austen, d.1845, elder sister of English novelist Jane Austen, 1775–1817.

CATHARINE/CATHERINE
Origin/meaning: uncertain, possibly Greek 'pure'.

A variant spelling of Katherine *q.v.* The two spellings were often used interchangeably. For example three of Henry VIII's wives bore the name but either spelling may be used for them. In the 1960s and 70s Catherine was a vogue name in Britain. Catherine is the usual French form of the name.

Variations and abbreviations: Caitlin (Ir), Caitrin (It), Cass, Cassy, Catalina (Sp), Catarina (It), Cate, Caterina, Cath, Catharina, Catharine, Catherina, Cathie, Cathleen (Ir), Cathlene, Cathrine, Cathryn, Cathy, Catie, Catriona (Scots).

See also Katherine.

Example: Catherine Bramwell-Booth, b.1883, Salvation Army Commissioner.

CATHLEEN
Origin/meaning: uncertain, possibly Greek 'pure'.

An Irish diminutive form of Katharine *q.v.*

Variations and abbreviations: See Kathleen, Katharine.

CATRIONA
Origin/meaning: uncertain, possibly Greek 'pure'.

Scottish form of Katharine *q.v.* Used by Robert Louis Stevenson as the title of one of his novels, 1893, and consequently popularized outside Scotland.

Variations and abbreviations: See Kathleen, Katharine.

CECIL
Origin/meaning: Latin 'blind'. From the Roman family Caecilius.

Now assumed to be always the masculine form, Cecil was often found in the Middle Ages as a feminine name. The usual modern feminine forms are Cecily or Cecilia.

Example: Cecil Woodham-Smith, English historian and biographer, 1896–1977.

CECILIA
Origin/meaning: Latin 'blind'.

Latin form of Cecily q.v. popular in the Middle Ages and used in documents which were written in Latin. It is the form generally used for St Cecilia, a martyr whose cult began in the 6th century and who was adopted as patron saint of music in the 16th century. This form of the name was again popular in the 18th century when Latinized names were fashionable and Fanny Burney published her novel *Cecilia. Memoirs of an Heiress*, 1782.

Variations and abbreviations: Caecilia, Celia, Cis.

CECILY (pron. Sissillee or Sessillee)
Origin/meaning: Latin 'blind'. From the Roman family Caecilius.

This is one of the few names where the feminine versions came before the masculine, Cecil q.v. Indeed Cecil was originally one of the feminine forms of the name. It was introduced into Britain by William the Conqueror, who gave it to one of his daughters. There were several versions, the other most popular form being Cecilia q.v. St Cecily or Cecilia, Patron Saint of music, ensured the name's continuing popularity, and it gave rise to several surnames. The modern pronunciation is sometimes Sessilee. The Irish form Shelagh q.v. is now a totally independent name with its own variations.

Variations and abbreviations: Cacilia, Cacilie (Ger), Cecil, Cécile (Fr), Cecilia, Celia, Cicely, Cissie, Cissy, Sheila, Shelagh (Ir), Sisley, Sissie, Sissy, Zazilie, Zilla.

Examples: Dame Cicily Courtneidge, 1893–1980, Australian/British actress.

CELESTE
Origin/meaning: Latin 'heavenly'.

A French variation of Celia q.v.

Variations and abbreviations: Cele, Celesta, Celestia, Celestina (It), Celestine (Fr), Celestyn, Celestyna, Celina.

Example: Celeste Holm, US film actress.

CELIA

Origin/meaning: either 'heavenly' from the Ancient Roman family Caelius or 'blind' from the Ancient Roman family Caecilius.

The first meaning is probably correct although Celia is often assumed to be an abbreviated form of the quite distinct name Cecilia q.v. Celia was a popular 17th century name when writers liked to give their characters names suitable to their characteristics, other examples are Amanda, Anthea and Phyllis. Celia is also used in Italy.

Variations and abbreviations: Caelia, Celiana (It), Célie (Fr), Celeste (Fr), Celestine (Fr), Zilia.

Example: Celia Johnson, 1908–1982, English actress.

CELINA

Origin/meaning: Latin 'heavenly'.

An alternative spelling of Selina q.v. which is probably nearer the original Latin.

See also Celeste and Celia.

CHANDRA (pron. Chandráh)

Origin/meaning: Sanskrit 'moon'.

The moon was once worshipped as a deity, and this is now a very popular name found throughout India, and not confined to Hindus. The male version q.v. is used as a polite form of address and the last 'a' is then not pronounced. It is therefore very important to voice the last syllable if this is used as a girl's name.

See also Diana, Kamaria, Selina, Sudha and the masculine name Shashi.

CHANTAL

Origin/meaning: a French place-name, Chantal or Cantal.

This French girl's name was particularly popular after the Second World War and is occasionally used in English-speaking countries. It honours St Jeanne Françoise de Chantal, 1572–1641. She was a friend of St Francis of Sales and founder of a religious order. Her grand-daughter was the Marquise de Sévigné whose letters give a first hand account of the Court of Louis XIV.

CHARIS (pron. Káriss)
Origin/meaning: Greek 'grace', 'love'.

A 17th century literary name used to emphasize the heroine's natural virtues. This word also is the origin of the word Charisma which means an ability to inspire devotion. Sometimes confused with Charity *q.v.* which ultimately derives from it.

Variations and abbreviations: Carissa, Carrie, Charissa. See also Grace.

CHARITY
Origin/meaning: Greek 'grace', Latin 'affection', English 'charity', 'Christian love'.

One of the three virtues, spoken of by St Paul in his first Epistle to the Corinthians: 'And now abideth faith, hope, charity, these three; but the greatest of these is charity'. In the 17th century this was one of the most popular of the Biblical names used by the Puritans in England and New England. There were three martyrs SS Faith, Hope and Charity venerated by the early church.

Variations and abbreviations: Carita (It), Caritina (It), Chattie, Cherry. See also Charis.

CHARLENE
Origin/meaning: Old German 'man', meaning by implication 'womanly'.

A feminine form of Charles, probably derived from Charlotte, more popular in the US than elsewhere.

Variations and abbreviations: Carleen, Carlene, Carline, Charleen, Karleen, Karlene, Sharleen, Sharline.

Example: Charlene Tilton, US actress (*Dallas*).

CHARLOTTE (pron. Shárlott)
Origin/meaning: Old German 'man', meaning by implication 'womanly'.

One of many feminine forms of Charles from the French pronunciation of Charles – Sharll. Introduced into England in the 17th century at about the same time as the masculine version. In the 18th century it was used by the royal family in particular Charlotte of Mecklenburg-Strelitz, wife of George III and Charlotte, Princess of Wales, daughter of George IV. Both these women were more popular than the male members of the House of Hanover and the name became fashionable. It is currently enjoying a revival in England and was in *The Times* list of most popular first names for girls, in 1983.

Variations and abbreviations: Carlota, Carlotta (It), Charleen, Charlene, Charie, Charlotta, Chatty, Karlotta, Karlotte, Lola, Lolita, Lotta, Lotte, Lotti, Lottie, Tot, Tottie. See also Carla, Carol, Caroline and Cheryl.

Example: Charlotte Rampling, British film actress.

CHARMAINE
Origin/meaning: Hebrew 'garden'.

The French form of the Irish Carmel and Spanish Carmen *qqv.*

CHARMIAN (pron. Kármean, Shármean, Chármean)
Origin/meaning: Greek 'joy'.

Charmian is a character in Shakespeare's play *Antony and Cleopatra*. The name has been in regular use since but has never been common. Sometimes confused with Charmaine *q.v.* the French form of Carmel.

Example: Charmian Innes, British broadcaster.

CHAUSIKU (pron. Chaooséekoo)
Origin/meaning: Swahili 'born at night'.

This name is found in East Africa.

CHERE (pron. Shehr)
Origin/meaning: French 'dear', 'darling'.

A French adjective used mainly in North America as a given name. There are many variations, including a misuse of the masculine adjective Cher. It is sometimes pronounced with a hard *ch* sound and from this the variations Cherry and Cheryl have developed.

Variations and abbreviations: Cher, Chérie (Fr), Chery, Cherry, Sher, Sherry.

Example: Cher Bono, US singer.

CHERRY
Origin/meaning: Latin 'charity'.

A short form of Charity or pet name for a little girl, sometimes given as an independent name.

Variation: Cherri.

CHERYL
Origin/meaning: Old German 'man', usually given as 'womanly'.

Short form of Charlotte *q.v.* A feminine form of Charles. In the last 30–40 years it has become a popular name in its own right. Almost unheard before. Sometimes considered a derivation of Chère.

Variations and abbreviations: Charil, Charyl, Cherlyn, Cherry, Sharyl, Sheryl.

Example: Cheryl Kennedy, British actress.

CHIPO
Origin/meaning: Shona 'gift'.

A Zimbabwe name corresponding approximately to Theodora or Dorothy.

CHIQUITA
Origin/meaning: Spanish 'little one'.

An endearment sometimes used as an independent name.

CHITRA
Origin/meaning: Hindu 'picture'.

CHLOË (pron. Klo-ee)
Origin/meaning: Greek 'a tender green shoot'.

Chloë was the name given to Demeter, the Greek goddess of the earth, in the summer when she made the earth green and fruitful. It corresponds to the English name Blossom. Chloë was used in classical Greece and Rome and a pastoral poem *Daphnis and Chloë* ensured its popularity in the Middle Ages. In the 17th and 18th centuries its meaning and classical allusions made it a popular literary name. Although originally a pagan name, it was also, paradoxically, used by the 17th century Puritans because of the Chloë mentioned in St Paul's first Epistle to the Corinthians. Almost obsolete in the 19th century except as a slave name, it is currently enjoying a minor revival.

Variations and abbreviations: Clo, Cloe (It).

CHRIS

Origin/meaning: Greek 'Christian'.

Short form of Christine and its variations.

Variations and abbreviations: Chrissie, Chrissy.

Example: Chris Evert-Lloyd, US tennis champion.

CHRISTABEL

Origin/meaning: Greek/Latin 'beautiful Christian'.

A Medieval English first name used by the Lake Poet Samuel Taylor Coleridge as the title of one of his best-known poems, *Christabel*, 1816. It contains the lines:

The lovely lady, Christabel,
Whom her father loves so well.

The poem probably accounts for the sporadic use of the name ever since.

Variations and abbreviations: Chris, Christabell, Christabella, Christabelle, Christobel, Christobella, Christy.

Example: Christabel Pankhurst, 1880–1958, English suffragette.

CHRISTIANA

Origian/meaning: Latin 'Christian'.

This is the Latin feminine adjective which has been used as a Christian name since the early Middle Ages. It was sometimes used without an 'a' in what we now think of as the exclusively masculine form, Christian. It was found concurrently with Christina, *q.v.* with which it shares short forms. Christina is now the more popular of the two. It is also related to the Scandinavian name Kirsten from which comes the Scottish name Kirsty.

Variations and abbreviations: Cairistiona (Scots), Chris, Christian, Christiania, Christiane (Fr), Cristiana (It), Cristiona (Ir), Kristyan,

Example: Christiana Brand, British thriller writer.

CHRISTINE/CHRISTINA

Origin/meaning: Old English 'Christian'.

This name, from the Old English word Christen, developed in England concurrently with the Latin form Christiana. The English version was itself Latinized in documents by the addition of an 'a' to give Christina. These versions continue to flourish while Christiana is now virtually obsolete. Because of its meaning the name occurs in slightly different forms in all European languages. The fame of St Christine, an early Christian martyr, also contributed to its popularity. The Scottish short form of Kirsty, currently popular, shows the influence of Scandinavian languages on that country.

Variations and abbreviations: Chris, Chrissie, Chrissy, Christa, Christen, Christer, Christiana, Christie, Christin (Ger), Christy, Christyna, Cris, Crissie, Crissy, Cristie, Cristina (It/Sp), Cristine, Cristy, Kirsteen (Scots), Kirsten (Scand), Kirstyan, Kris, Krissie, Kristina, Krystyna, Tina.

Examples: Christina Onassis, Greek shipping tycoon.
Christina Rossetti, 1830–1894, English/Italian poet.
Christina Stead, 1902–1983, Australian novelist.

CHRYSËIS
Origin/meaning: Greek 'daughter of the golden one'.

A name similar to Chrysogon. Chryseis is one of the many characters in Homer's poem, the *Iliad*. She was the daughter of Chryses, the priest of Apollo.

See also Cressida.

CHRYSOGON (pron. Krízzagon)
Origin/meaning: Greek 'golden born'.

Rare English first name dating from the Renaissance period. St Chrysogonus, a 4th century martyr, was a man, and the name was initially given in England to both men and women.

CIARA
Origin/meaning: Old Irish 'dark haired'.

The feminine equivalent of the Irish masculine Kieran.

Variation: Ciaran.

CICILY
Origin/meaning: Latin 'blind', from the Roman Coecilius family.

See Cecilia and Cecily.

CINDY
Origin/meaning: a pet form, particularly popular in the US, of names like Lucinda and Cynthia *q.v.* Sometimes given as an independent name.

Variation: Sindy.

Example: Cindy Buxton, British documentary film-maker.

CLAIRE

Origin/meaning: Latin 'bright', 'distinguished'.

French form of Clare *q.v.*

Example: Claire Bloom, English actress.

CLARA

Origin/meaning: Latin 'bright', 'distinguished'.

The Latin adjective from which the English Clare and French Claire derive. Used as their equivalent in Latin documents during the Middle Ages it became accepted as an independent name. Revived in popularity at the end of the 18th century when Latin forms of names were fashionable it is still used today.

Example: Clara Bow, 1905–1965, US film actress, the IT girl of the 1920s.

CLARE

Origin/meaning: Latin 'bright', 'distinguished'.

Originally there was an equally valid masculine form of the name, Clarus, but the great popularity of St Clare of Assisi, 1193–1253, a friend of St Francis and founder of the highly ascetic Order of Nuns the Poor Clares, led to the name being regarded as exclusively feminine. Appropriately, since the name is one of the most popular contemporary names, she is patron saint of television! Clare was also used as a surname from which the masculine name Clarence *q.v.* is formed.

Variations and abbreviations: Chiara (It), Clair, Claire (Fr), Clara, Clarabelle, Claribel, Clarice, Clarie, Clarinda, Clarissa, Clarita (Sp), Clarrie, Klara (Ger), Klarissa.

Example: Clare Rayner, English writer and broadcaster.

CLARIBEL

Origin/meaning: Latin 'bright and beautiful'.

A name from Shakespeare's play *The Tempest*, 1611. It is probably a coined literary name typical of the age, similar to Dulcibel. It seems to have been popular in the US in the 19th century.

Variation: Clarabelle.

Example: Claribel, Queen of Tunis in Shakespeare's *The Tempest*.

CLARICE
Origin/meaning: Latin 'bright', 'distinguished'.

French variation of Claire, introduced into England in the early Middle Ages and used in the medieval romance poems. The Latin form Clarissa became popular in the 19th century.

Variations and abbreviations: Claris, Clarissa, Clarry.

CLARINDA
Origin/meaning: Latin 'bright', 'distinguished'.

A form of Clare *q.v.* used in the 17th and 18th centuries when fanciful names which implied the person's virtues were a popular literary device. Robert Burns, 1759–1796, addressed his friend and correspondent Mrs McLehose as Clarinda.

Example: Clarinda in Spenser's poetic tribute to Elizabeth I, *The Faerie Queene*, 1590.

CLARISSA
Origin/meaning: Latin 'bright', 'distinguished'.

Latin version of the French name Clarice, a pet form of Claire. A popular medieval name revived by the publication of Richardson's novel, *Clarissa*, 1748.

Variations and abbreviations: Clarice (Fr), Claricia, Clarisse, Clarry.

CLAUDETTE
Origin/meaning: Latin 'lame'.

A French pet form of Claudia *q.v.*

Example: Claudette Colbert, French-born US film actress.

CLAUDIA
Origin/meaning: Latin 'lame'. Claudius was the name of two well-known Roman families.

Used in England since the end of the 16th century when Puritans chose Biblical names as a reaction against Catholic saints' names. Claudia is mentioned at the end of the second Epistle of St Paul to Timothy.

Variations and abbreviations: Claude (Fr), Claudette, Claudie, Claudina, Claudine, Gladys, Gwladys (Welsh), Klaudia (Ger).

Example: Claudia Cardinale, Italian film actress.

CLEA
Origin/meaning: a name used by Lawrence Durrell in his novel sequence *The Alexandria Quartet*. It may be a form of Clio *q.v.*

CLEMENCY
Origin/meaning: Latin 'gentleness', 'mercy'.

The feminine version of the name Clement. In the Middle Ages Clemence was the usual form. During the 17th century when it was customary for people to name children after virtues the noun Clemency became the accepted version.

Variations and abbreviations: Clem, Clemence, Clementia, Clementina, Clemmie, Clemmy.

Example: Clemence Dane (Winifred Ashton), 1885–1965, English playwright and novelist who took her pen-name from St Clement Dane's Church in the Strand.

CLEMENTINE
Origin/meaning: Latin 'gentle', 'merciful'.

Like Clemency *q.v.* a feminine form of Clement *q.v.* Particularly popular in the 19th century its currency was debased by the song *Oh My Darling Clementine*.

Variations and abbreviations: Clementia, Clementina, Klementina.

Example: Lady Clementine Spencer Churchill, 1885–1977, wife of Sir Winston Churchill.

CLEO
Origin/meaning: Greek 'fame', 'renown'.

Sometimes a short form of the rarely given Cleopatra which means 'renown of the father'.

Example: Cleo Laine, British singer.

CLIO
Origin/meaning: Greek 'I celebrate', 'I proclaim'.

In Greek and Roman mythology Clio was the goddess of epic poetry and history.

CLODAGH (pron. Clóh-dar)
Origin/meaning: Irish. It is the name of a river in Tipperary.

A 20th century innovation, the name was given by the late Marquess of Waterford to one of his daughters. It rapidly became popular in Ireland. It is beginning to spread to areas with Irish communities.

Example: Clodagh Rodgers, Irish singer.

CLORINDA
Origin/meaning: a literary name created by the Italian poet Tasso, 1544–1595, for his poem *Jerusalem Delivered*. It has been used occasionally since and may have been confused with Clarinda, a fanciful version of Clare.

CLOTILDA
Origin/meaning: Old German 'battle maid'.

Clotilda, d.545, was the wife of the Frankish King Clovis I. Her grandson was the St Cloud after whom the area outside Paris is named. Clotilda is revered as a saint in France where the name is not uncommon. It is also given occasionally to Catholics in English-speaking countries.

Variations: Clothilde (Fr), Klothilde (Ger).

COLETTE
Origin/meaning: Greek/Old French 'victory of the people'.

A French feminine diminutive of Nicholas through Nicolette, this name is the equivalent of the masculine Colin. Like Colin it was accepted early on as an English name and therefore several surnames such as Colet derive from it. St Colette, 1381–1447, (Nicholette Boylet) has ensured its popularity among Catholics. The French author, Colette, who wrote *Gigi*, has given an added boost to its popularity in the 20th century although it was her surname not her first name – which was Sidonie.

Variations and abbreviations: Colecta, Coletta, Collette.

COLLEEN
Origin/meaning: Old Irish 'girl'.

Rare in Britain and Ireland but popular in Australia and US where there are many people of Irish origin.

Example: Colleen McCullough, Australian writer (*The Thorn Birds*).

COMFORT
Origin/meaning: Latin, Old French 'strengthen', 'encourage'.

One of the 17th century Biblical names popular in Puritan England and New England and still found occasionally.

CONNIE
Origin/meaning: Latin 'constancy'.

A short form of Constance sometimes used as an independent name.

Example: Connie Francis, US singer.

CONSTANCE
Origin/meaning: Latin 'constancy'.

The name of one of William I's daughters it was introduced into England at the Conquest. Although the name of a saint it survived the Reformation by being adapted to Constancy, one of the virtues which were popular as names among Puritans in England and New England. At the end of the 18th century and in the 19th century the Latin original, Constantia, became fashionable, but is currently out of favour.

Variations and abbreviations: Con, Conni, Connie, Conny, Constancia, Constancy, Constantia, Constanze, Costanza (It), Konstanze (Ger).

Examples: Constance Cummings, English actress.
Konstanze Mozart, d.1842, wife of the composer.

CONSTANTIA
Origin/meaning: Latin 'constancy'.

A form of Constance *q.v.*

CONSUELO (pron. Konsooélla)
Origin/meaning: Spanish 'consolation'.

This is really a short version of Our Lady of Consolation, a popular epithet of the Virgin Mary in Spain where it is Nuestra Señora del Consúelo. Because, like Dolores, it is taken from a long phrase Consuelo is in fact a masculine word. It is now often changed to the feminine ending Consuela. A predominantly Catholic name.

Variations and abbreviations: Connie, Consolata, Consuela. See also Dolores, Mercedes, Pilar.

Example: Consuela Vanderbilt Churchill Balsan, US socialite married off by her mother to the English Duke of Marlborough in 1895.

CONTENT
Origin/meaning: 'satisfaction', 'pleasure'.

A word used frequently in the St James version of the Bible and adopted as a first name by Puritans in England and New England. Now rare.

CORA
Origin/meaning: Greek 'maiden'.

This is the direct use of a Greek word and has only been current since the last century. It is a popular name in the US, where it has developed many variations, and in France. In England the name Corinna, q.v. which comes from the same stem, is more authentic.

Variations and abbreviations: Corabel, Corabella, Corabelle, Corella, Coretta, Corette, Corie, Corry, Kora.

Example: Cora Pearl, 19th century courtesan.

CORAL
Origin/meaning: Greek 'red-pink coral'.

A comparatively modern name introduced at the end of the 19th century along with names like Beryl, Ruby.

Variations: Coralie (Fr), Coraline.

Example: Coral Browne, Australian-born actress.

CORDELIA
Origin/meaning: uncertain. Possibly Old Welsh 'jewel of the sea' or Latin 'warm-hearted'.

Cordula is a name found in Celtic areas of Britain, like Cornwall and Wales, which retained the Latin names in altered forms. This may be the origin of the name Cordeilla which Shakespeare

78

adapted from Holinshed's *Chronicles* for the heroine of his play *King Lear*. The use of Cordelia in England and its occasional appearance elsewhere is now probably entirely due to the play. However in Germany Kordula seems to be a survival of the more ancient Cordula.

Variations and abbreviations: Cordélie (Fr), Cordey, Cordie, Cordula, Cordy, Delia, Della, Kordela (Ger), Kordelia, Kordula.

CORINNA
Origin/meaning: Greek, from the word 'maiden'.

An ancient Greek name sometimes used for the goddess of Spring, Persephone. A 5th century poetess bore the name and in the 17th and 18th centuries it was used by several writers for their heroines.

Variations and abbreviations: Corena, Corene, Corina, Corinne (Fr). See also Cora.

Examples: Corinna King, US/human rights campaigner, widow of Martin Luther King.
Corinne Calvet, French-born US film actress.

CORNELIA
Origin/meaning: Latin, from the influential Roman family Cornelius. The name may be from 'horn' which implies kingship.

The feminine form of Cornelius *q.v.* It was the name of Julius Caesar's first wife.

Variations and abbreviations: Cornela, Cornelie (Fr), Cornie, Corry, Kornelia (Ger), Nelia, Nell, Nelly.

Example: Cornelia Fasset, 1831–1898, US portrait painter. She painted portraits of several Presidents.

COSIMA
Origin/meaning: Greek 'order', 'harmony', 'the universe'.

Italian feminine form of Cosmo *q.v.*

Variation: Kosima (Ger).

Example: Cosima Wagner, wife of composer Richard Wagner, 1813–1883.

CRESSIDA
Origin/meaning: Greek 'daughter of the golden one'.

The name Crysëis *q.v.* was wrongly used by Boccacio for the faithless daughter of Calchas, when he 'borrowed' the story of Troilus and Cressida from another author who had called her Briséida. Boccacio adapted the name slightly to Chryseida and Chaucer who copied the plot in his turn altered it slightly to Criseyde. When Shakespeare based his play *Troilus and Cressida* on the same story he altered the name once more. It is Shakespeare's version which is used occasionally today. However, the name has never gained great popularity since Cressida was regarded as the epitome of an unfaithful woman.

Abbreviation: Cressy.

CRYSTAL
Origin/meaning: Greek 'clear-ice', 'crystal'.

A modern girl's name dating from the end of the 19th century like Beryl, Pearl. Its use is almost totally confined to the US. Chrystal is also an increasingly rare Scottish form of Christopher *q.v.*

Variations: Chrystal, Krystle.

Examples: Crystal Gayle, US country singer.
Chrystal Herne, 1882–1950, US actress.

CYNTHIA
Origin/meaning: Greek 'from Mount Cynthas'. A title used for Artemis, the Greek goddess of chastity and hunting, who was born on Mount Cynthos.

Sometimes mistakenly used in England for Sanchia. Because of its classical origins it was used by 17th and 18th century writers. In the 19th century its popularity was revived by Mrs Gaskell's use of it in her successful novel, *Wives and Daughters*, 1866.

Variations and abbreviations: Cimmie, Cindee, Cindie, Cindy, Cynthie. See also Phoebe.

CYRILLA
Origin/meaning: Greek 'lordly'.
The feminine form of Cyril *q.v.*

D

DAGMAR

Origin/meaning: Old German 'glory of the Danes'.

A Danish name introduced into Australia and North America by immigrants. In Britain the name became familiar, although never popular, because of the Empress Dagmar of Russia, who was a sister of Queen Alexandra.

DAHLIA

Origin/meaning: Old Norse 'from the valley'.

A Mexican flower, the Dahlia was named after its discoverer, the Swedish botanist A. Dahl, d.1789. The flower name is occasionally given to girls.

DAISY

Origin/meaning: Old English 'day's eye'. The name of a flower, which opens in the sunlight and closes at night.

A late 19th century name, when it was fashionable to call girls after flowers or jewels. Sometimes it was used as a pet name for Margaret, since its French equivalent, Marguerite, is the modern French word for a daisy and Margaret is also an English word (now obsolete) for a daisy.

Example: Daisy Ashford, pen name of English writer Margaret Devlin 1881–1972.

DALE

Origin/meaning: Old English 'from the valley'.

A surname sometimes used as a first name, particularly in the US.

Variations and abbreviations: Dael, Dayle.

Example: Dale Rogers, US singer and entertainer.

DALILA

Origin/meaning: Swahili 'gentle'.

An East African name.

DAMARIS
Origin/meaning: uncertain, possibly Greek 'calf' sometimes given as 'gentle'.

One of the Biblical names popular after the Protestant Reformation. Damaris was an Athenian woman converted by St Paul (Acts 17:34).

Variations and abbreviations: Damara, Mara.

DANA
Origin/meaning: uncertain, possibly Scandinavian 'Danish'.

A surname used as a first name perhaps because of its similarity to Donna. Also used as a boy's name.

Example: Dana, Irish singer.

DANIELLE
Origin/meaning: Hebrew 'God has judged'.

French feminine form of Daniel q.v.

Variations and abbreviations: Danella, Danelle, Danette, Daniela (It/Sp), Darnella, Dannie, Danny.

Examples: Danielle Darrieux, French actress.
Danielle Steel, US novelist.

DAPHNE
Origin/meaning: Greek 'laurel bush', 'bay tree'.

Daphne in Greek mythology was a nymph loved by Apollo. She called on the gods to help her elude his advances and they obliged by turning her into a laurel bush. The name came into use as a girl's name at the end of the 19th century when flower names were popular.

Variations and abbreviations: Dafne, Daffie, Daph.

Example: Daphne du Maurier, English novelist.

DARIA
Origin/meaning: uncertain, probably Persian, possible meaning 'preserver' or 'possessor of riches'.

Feminine version of Darius q.v. and rare in English speaking areas. St Daria is listed as one of the Roman martyrs and the name is fairly frequently used in Italian and German-speaking countries.

DARLENE

Origin/meaning: Old English 'darling'.

Modern feminine version of the much older established masculine name Daryl *q.v.* Found mainly in North America.

Variations and abbreviations: Darla, Darleen, Darelle, Daryl, Darylyne.

DAVINA

Origin/meaning: Hebrew 'darling', 'friend'.

A Scottish feminine form of David. Dating from the 17th century, it is currently enjoying a slight revival in Britain. Davida is the English version.

Variations and abbreviations: Davida (Eng), Davidina, Davinia, Davita, Veda, Vida, Vita.

Example: Lady Davina Windsor, daughter of the Duke and Duchess of Gloucester.

DAWN

Origin/meaning: English 'sunrise'.

Surprisingly a modern 20th century innovation since the name is simple and evocative. There are many names of differing origins with the same meaning including Aurora, Zara, Roxanne and Oriana.

Example: Dawn Addams, English actress.

DEANNA (pron. Dee-anna)
Origin/meaning: Latin 'divine'.

A modern spelling of Diana *q.v.* Sometimes used as a feminine of Dean and pronounced Deena, in which case it means 'from the valley'.

Example: Deanna Durbin, Canadian actress and singer.

DEBBIE

Origin/meaning: Hebrew: 'bee'.

Short form of Deborah, *q.v.* now used as an independent name.

Variation: Debby.

Example: Debbie Reynolds, US actress and singer.

DEBORAH

Origin/meaning: Hebrew 'bee'.

Deborah was a Jewish prophetess (Judges 5) and the name was in use among Puritans in the 17th century. Its greatest popularity has been in the 20th century perhaps because of the influence of film stars such as Debbie Reynolds and Deborah Kerr.

Variations and abbreviations: Deb, Debor, Debora, Debra, Debbie, Debby. See also Melissa.

DECIMA
Origin/meaning: Latin 'tenth'.

A name given to a tenth child, equivalent to the masculine Decimus.

DEE
Origin/meaning: short form of names like Deirdre or Diana now frequently given as an independent name.

Example: Dee Wells, British journalist.

DEIRDRE
Origin/meaning: Old Irish 'sorrowful' or 'raging'.

Deirdre was the tragic heroine of a long established Celtic legend, one of the 'three tragic stories of the Irish', in which she committed suicide following the death of her lover and his brothers. At the turn of the century there was a strong revival of interest in Celtic culture. W. B. Yeats wrote *Deirdre* in 1907 and J. M. Synge wrote *Deirdre of the Sorrows* in 1910, both based on the same legend. The modern use of the name is a direct result of this literary activity.

Variations and abbreviations: Dede, Dee, Deerdre, Didi.

DELIA
Origin/meaning: Greek 'from Delos'.

Delia (like Celia) is one of the names given to the Greek goddess Artemis, in this case because she came from the island of Delos. Because of its classical associations it was a popular literary name in the 17th and 18th centuries. It may sometimes be used as a short form of the equally unusual Cordelia *q.v.* or Odelia *q.v.*

Variations and abbreviations: Dee, Della, Didi.

Example: Delia Smith, English cookery writer and broadcaster.

DELIGHT
Origin/meaning: Old French 'pleasure', 'joy'.

An occasionally used name which speaks for itself.

DELILAH
Origin/meaning: Hebrew 'delight'.

A Biblical name. Delilah betrayed Samson to the Philistines by cutting off the hair from which he derived his great strength (Judges 13-16). The name is rarely used because of Delilah's treachery.

DELLA
Origin/meaning: Old German 'noble'.

Familiar form of names like Adèle, Delia, sometimes used as an independent name, particularly in North America.

DELMAR
Origin/meaning: Spanish 'of the sea'.

Found in the US and Australia.

Variation: Delma.

DELPHINE
Origin/meaning: either Greek 'from Delphi' (a famous shrine of the god Apollo) or Greek 'larkspur', 'Delphinium' (a plant with a nectary resembling a dolphin).

An unusual name in English-speaking countries this name is popular in Germany and France. Delphine is the French version.

Variations and abbreviations: Delfa, Delpha, Delfina (It/Sp), Delfine (Ger), Delphina.

Example: Delphine Seyrig, French film actress.

DEMETRIA
Origin/meaning: Greek 'follower of Demeter'.

Demeter was the Greek goddess of agriculture and the corn-bearing earth. The Roman equivalent was the goddess Ceres. This pagan name became an acceptable Christian name because of the Roman martyr St Demetria. Only occasionally found in English-speaking countries but popular in Italy and Spain. The masculine equivalent is popular in Russia as Dmitri.

Variations and abbreviations: Demeter, Demtra, Demetris.

DENA

Origin/meaning: Old English 'from the valley'.

A modern feminine form of Dean q.v. which is itself a surname. Found principally in the US.

Variations: Deana, Dina.

DENISE

Origin/meaning: Greek, from the name of the god of fertility Dionysus.

French feminine version of Dennis q.v. Popular in English-speaking countries in the last 30–40 years, since it was re-introduced from France. The same name was found in England in the Middle Ages as Denis, Denise or in a form closer to its origin. Dionysia.

Variations and abbreviations: Denice, Denis, Denny, Denyse, Dion, Dionne.

Example: Denise Coffey, English actress and director.
Denise Robins, English romantic novelist.

DEODATA

Origin/meaning: Latin 'given by God', 'given to God'.

Italian version of Donata q.v.

DESIDERATA

Origin/meaning: Latin 'desired', 'longed for'.

Medieval English form of Désirée q.v. taken directly from the Latin word.

DÉSIRÉE (pron. Dáyzeeray)

Origin/meaning: Latin/French 'desired' 'longed for'.

This name has been borrowed from France in the 20th century by English-speaking countries. In the Puritan period the name Desire was sometimes used because of the frequent appearance of the word in the King James Bible. In the Middle Ages there was a masculine name Desideratus, taken directly from the Latin adjective, and this was occasionally used in the feminine form Desiderata.

Variations and abbreviations: Desiderata, Desideria (Ger), Desire.

Example: Désirée, early amour of Napoleon, subject of the film starring Jean Simmons and Marlon Brando.

DIANA

Origin/meaning: Latin 'divine'. The Roman equivalent of Artemis, the Greek goddess of Chastity, Hunting and the Moon.

The classical name came into use in Europe in the 16th and 17th centuries because of the Renaissance interest in classical culture. Shakespeare used it in his play *All's Well That Ends Well*, written at the beginning of the 17th century. It has been used consistently ever since and will presumably increase in popularity now it is the name of the Princess of Wales. Many of the more novel spellings originate from North America.

Variations and abbreviations: Deana, Deanna, Dede, Dee, Di, Diane (Fr), Dianna, Dianora (It), Didi, Dyana, Dyanna.

Examples: HRH The Princess of Wales.
Diana Dors, d.1984, English actress.
Diana Rigg, English actress.

DIANE

Origin/meaning: Latin 'divine'.

This is the French version of Diana *q.v.* After the Second World War it became immensely popular in the United States and from there it spread to Britain and Australia. The variant spellings so popular in the US have not spread so readily.

Variations and abbreviations: Deane, Deanne, Dede, Di, Diahann, Dian, Dianne, Dyan, Dyane, Dyann, Dyanne.

Examples: Dyan Cannon, US film actress.
Diahann Carrol, US singer.

DIANORA

Origin/meaning: Latin 'divine'.

An Italian version of Diana *q.v.*

DIDO

Origin/meaning: obscure, possibly Greek 'teacher'.

Dido was the legendary founder and Queen of Carthage. In the poem by the Roman, Virgil, he describes how she falls in love with Aeneas and kills herself when the gods order him to leave her.

DIEUDONNÉE
Origin/meaning: Latin 'given by God', 'given to God'.
French form of Donata q.v.

DILYS
Origin/meaning: Welsh 'perfect' or 'pure'.

A recent Welsh name used in the last hundred years. It has spread rapidly to the rest of Britain, but not to North America or Australia.

Examples: Dilys Powell, British film critic.
Dilys Watling, British actress.

DINAH
Origin/meaning: Hebrew 'lawsuit' therefore 'avenged'.

In Genesis chapter 34, Dinah is the daughter of Leah and Jacob. When she is dishonoured by Shechem her brothers avenge her. Like so many Biblical names it came into use in the 17th century both in England and New England. Its recent popularity may be due to confusion with Diana.

Variations and abbreviations: Dena, Di, Dina.

Examples: Dinah Shore, US singer.
Dinah Washington, US singer.

DIONNE
Origin/meaning: Greek 'follower of Dionysus'.

A modern version of Denise q.v. found particularly in the US.

Variations and abbreviations: Dion, Dione, Dionis.

Example: Dionne Warwick, US singer.

DIVINA
Origin/meaning: Latin 'divine' or 'super-human'.

A Latin adjective occasionally used as a first name.

Example: Divina Galica, Anglo-Polish racing driver and speed skier.

DODIE
Origin/meaning: Greek 'gift'.

A pet form of Dora and Dorothy *q.v.*

Variations: Dodo, Dody.

Example: Dodie Smith, English playwright.

DOLLY
Origin/meaning: Greek 'gift of God'.

A short form of Dorothy *q.v.* which had been used as an independent name since the Middle Ages. It was so popular that in the 18th century it became the word which we still use today for toy babies although by then it was being overtaken by other short forms such as Dora. For a while it was used as a term for a loose woman.

Variations: Dol, Doll, Dollie.

Example: Dolly Parton, US country singer and actress.

DOLORES (pron. Do-láw-rez)
Origin/meaning: Spanish 'sorrows'.

This is a shortened form of the Spanish phrase for the Virgin Mary in her manifestation as the suffering mother, Maria de los Dolores. When used in Spain and by Catholics elsewhere it is understood that it encompasses the entire name. This custom came about because for a long time in Spain, as in Ireland, the name of the Blessed Virgin was considered too sacred to use. With the influence of Mexico on the United States it has gained a much wider currency. However, it has never numbered among the top fifty names in an English-speaking country.

Variations and abbreviations: Delores, Doloreita, Deloris, Dolorita, Lola, Lolita. See also Consuelo, Mercedes.

Example: Dolores Del Rio, 1905–1983, Mexican film actress.

DOMINA
Origin/meaning: Latin 'lady'.

Occasionally used as a first name. The modern Italian equivalent Donna, *q.v.* is far more popular.

DOMINICA
Origin/meaning: Latin 'of the Lord'.

Latin feminine adjective used in the Middle Ages. The equivalent of Dominic *q.v.* When spoken the girl's name may have been pronounced simply Dominic like the boy's. Nowadays the French Dominique is used.

Variations and abbreviations: Domenica (It), Dominga (Sp), Dominika (Ger), Dominique (Fr).

DOMINIQUE
Origin/meaning: Latin 'of the Lord'.

French feminine form of Dominic *q.v.* equivalent of the Medieval English Dominica. Nowadays in English-speaking countries if the name is used the French form is preferred in line with the fashion for French names like Danielle, Michelle and Denise. Sometimes used for a child born on Sunday, the Lord's day.

DONATA (pron. Donn-árt uh)
Origin/meaning: Latin 'given by God', 'given to God'.

Short form of the more cumbersome Latin Deodonata, which is also occasionally found as a first name. It has the same meaning as Theodora and Dorothy and their variants.

Variations: Deodata (It), Dieudonnée (Fr), Dieudonne.

DONNA
Origin/meaning: Italian 'lady'.

The use of the Italian word as a girl's name is confined to the 20th century. It quickly gained popularity in the US after the Second World War and has more recently become popular in Britain and Australia.

Variations and abbreviations: Doña (Sp), Donella, Donia, Donnie. See also Domina.

Examples: Donna Summer, US singer.
Donna Hartley, British athlete.

DORA
Origin/meaning: Greek 'gift'.

A short form of Dorothy or Theodora *q.v.* it became popular as a name in its own right at the end of the 19th century.

Variations and abbreviations: Dodie, Doralyn, Dorelle, Dorena, Doretta, Dorja (Russ), Dorrie, Doro, Dory.

Example: Dora Bryan, English actress.

DORCAS
Origin/meaning: Greek 'antelope', 'gazelle'.

This is the direct Greek translation of the Hebrew name Tabitha. In the Acts of the Apostles ch.9, Tabitha, translated as Dorcas, is spoken of for her good works. Dorcas thus became a popular Biblical name among Puritans in both England and New England. Now rare.

DOREEN
Origin/meaning: uncertain, either Old Irish 'sullen' or an Irish diminutive of Dorothy 'gift of God' as Maureen is a diminutive of Mary.

Introduced into England from Ireland around the turn of the century when there was a renewed interest in Celtic language and history. It reached the peak of its popularity in Britain and Australia between the wars.

Variations and abbreviations: Dora, Dorene, Dorine.

Example: Doreen Wells, British ballet dancer.

DORIA
Origin/meaning: Greek 'Dorian', 'from Doris'.

The feminine form of Dorian, an inhabitant of the Doris region of Ancient Greece. The existence of this name increases the likelihood that Doris *q.v.* is simply another version of Dorothy.

DORINDA
Origin/meaning: 'gift of God'.

An 18th century form of Dorothy *q.v.* very typical of the style of the period.

DORIS
Origin/meaning: Greek 'gift'.

The name of a nymph who married the sea god Nereus in Greek mythology. It is also the name of a small independent country in Ancient Greece. The name came into use in Britain, Europe and North America in the 19th century. It was popular in English-speaking countries between the wars and is currently popular in German-speaking countries. Despite its apparent classical origins it is more likely to be a variation of the once immensely popular Dorothy *q.v.*

Variations and abbreviations: Dorice, Dorise, Dorita, Dorris, Dory.

Examples: Doris Day, US film actress.
Doris Lessing, South African novelist.

DOROTHEA
Origin/meaning: Greek 'gift of God'.

The Latinized version of Dorothy q.v. which was popular in England in the 18th century. It is the form popular in Germany today.

Examples: Dorothea Brooke in George Eliot's novel *Middlemarch*, 1872.
Dorothea Jordan, 1762–1816, Irish actress, mistress of the Duke of Clarence, later William IV.

DOROTHY
Origin/meaning: Greek 'gift of God'.

A back-to-front version of Theodora q.v. which has the same meaning. Despite the 3rd century martyr, St Dorothy, who made the name popular in Europe the name was not found in England until the 16th century when most Catholic saints' names were going out of favour. Its great popularity lasted well into the 19th century when it was somewhat superseded by variations like Dora and Doris. The short form Dolly q.v. has become a bona fide English word for a baby-toy. The Scottish/Irish short form Dorrit, which Dickens used for his novel *Little Dorrit*, 1857, produced a Scots word for doll, a dorrity. At the end of the 18th century the Latinized Dorothea became fashionable and the even more fanciful Latinized Dorinda. It is currently most popular in German-speaking countries along with the variation Doris.

Variations and abbreviations: Darja (Russ), Dody, Doll, Dollie, Dolly, Dora, Doreen (Ir), Dorinda, Dorofeja (Russ), Doro, Dorotea (It/Sp), Dorothea (Ger), Dorothée (Fr), Dorrit (Ir), Dortea (Dan), Dorthea (Dan), Dorthy, Dory, Dot, Dottie, Dotty.

Examples: Dorothy Parker, 1893–1967, US satirist and humorist.
Dorothy L. Sayers, 1893–1957, English writer.

DORY
Origin/meaning: a familiar form of names like Dorothy, Dora, Doris, Doria.

Variations: Dorey, Dori.

Example: Dory Previn, US singer songwriter.

DOTTY
Origin/meaning: Greek 'gift of God'.

A diminutive of Dorothy q.v.

Variations: Dot, Dottie.

DOWSABEL
Origin/meaning: Latin 'beautiful and sweet'.

A medieval name (the surname Dowson comes from it) which seems to have been usurped by the modern name Dulcie. In the 18th century the Latin form Dulcibella was sometimes used.

Variations and abbreviations: Douce (Fr), Dowse, Dowzabel, Dulcibel, Dulcibella, Dulcie.

DULCIE
Origin/meaning: Latin 'sweet'.

Since the Middle Ages there have been names derived from dulcis, the Latin meaning sweet. They include Dowse (from the French word douce – sweet) Dulcia, a version with a Latin adjectival ending used in documents and Dulcibelle a typical 18th century variation along the lines of Annabelle, Rosabel and Claribel. Dulcie is the modern form found since the end of the 19th century. It may have been taken from the Spanish Dulcia or Dulcinea since it is found in the US at the same time as other Spanish names such as Consuelo and Mercedes.

Variations and abbreviations: Delcine, Dulce, Dulcea, Dulcia, Dulciana, Dulcibelle, Dulcine, Dulcinea, Dulcy.

Example: Dulcie Gray, English actress and novelist.

DYMPHNA
Origin/meaning: Old Irish either 'eligible' or 'white wave'.

The legend evolved that Dymphna was the daughter of an Irish Prince. When his Christian wife died he became besotted by his daughter, also a Christian. She and her confessor fled from him to Gheel near Antwerp where they were found and killed by her father. Their remains were discovered in the 13th century and she became confused with the Irish St Damhnait. Dymphna is regarded as patron saint of the mentally ill. A hospital for them

Doris, Doria.

founded in her honour at Gheel still flourishes.

Variation: Dympna.

Example: Ellen Dymphna Cusack, Australian writer.

E

EADITHA
Origin/meaning: Old English 'rich war'.
A medieval spelling of Edith *q.v.*

EASTER
Origin/meaning: this name was given to both boys and girls born around the time of the Festival of Easter.
In pre-Christian times Easter was a Saxon goddess who was worshipped in the Spring.
See also Pascale, Sidony, Theophania.
Variations and abbreviations: Eacy, Estrild (Old English 'Eastre's battle').

EBUN
Origin/meaning: Yoruba 'gift'.
A Nigerian name.

EDE
Origin/meaning: Old English 'rich'.
Nowadays a short form of Edith *q.v.* this was found as an independent name throughout the Middle Ages.
Variations: Eda, Eden.

EDEN
Origin/meaning: Hebrew 'delight' or Old English 'rich'.
The second meaning refers to Eden when used as a form of Ede and Edith *q.v.* during the Middle Ages.

EDINA
Origin/meaning: Old English 'rich friend'.
This is a Scottish variation of Edwina, the feminine form of Edwin *q.v.*

EDITH

Origin/meaning: Old English 'rich war'.

This is the modern form of the Anglo-Saxon name Eadgyth. It was one of many names given in the hope that they would turn a wish into reality. Like other names beginning Ead or Ed, it was a name closely associated with the Royal House of Wessex. Edward the Confessor's wife was called Edith and Eadgyth (later known as Matilda) wife of Henry I was a descendent of Alfred the Great. Their marriage in 1100 united the Norman and Saxon lines. Like the male names of the House of Wessex Eadgyth survived better than most Anglo-Saxon names which quickly became obsolete after the Conquest. Perhaps, like Edward, Edwin, Edgar and Edmund, it survived not just because of its royal connections but also because it was borne by several Saints. One, St Edith (Eadgyth) of Wilton, 961–989, was an illegitimate daughter of King Edgar. However the Normans adapted Eadgyth to suit the sounds of their own language so that it evolved as Eaditha, a name that was common in the Middle Ages. It declined in the 16th and 17th centuries when saints' names were unpopular, but was revived at the end of the 18th century because of the influence of the Romantic movement and in the 19th century when medieval names, like Alice, were fashionable. It has been rarely used since the Second World War.

Variations and abbreviations: Eaditha (Med Eng), Eda, Ede, Edie, Edita (It), Editha, Edithe, Edwa, Edyth, Eyde, Eydie.

Examples: Edith Cavell, 1865–1915, English nurse and heroine of the First World War.
Dame Edith Evans, 1888–1976, British actress.

EDIVA

Origin/meaning: Old English 'rich gift'.

This is the Medieval Latin written form of the Anglo-Saxon name Eadgifu. Its origin and sound are similar to Edith *q.v.* and the Normans frequently treated them as one and the same name.

See also Ede, Eden.

EDNA

Origin/meaning: uncertain, Hebrew 'rejuvenation'.

A Biblical name which occurs several times in the Apocrypha. In the Book of Tobia Edna is the mother of Sara and mother-in-law of Tobia. The name was not used before the 19th century when its similarity to the Anglo-Saxon names currently in vogue may have been a contributory factor. Charlotte Yonge used it in her novel *Hopes and Fears*, 1860, but does not list it in her *History of Christian Names*, 1863. The popular 19th century novelist Edna Lyell, 1857–1903, made the name familiar and introduced it into the US, although Edna was in fact a partial anagram of the author's real name, Ada Ellen Bayly. Edna was a vogue name in Britain in the 1920s.

Variations and abbreviations: Ed, Eddie, Ednah.

Examples: Edna O'Brien, Irish novelist.
Edna St Vincent Millay, 1892–1950, US poet.
Edna Ferber, 1887–1968, US dramatist.

EDWINA
Origin/meaning: Old English 'rich friend'.

A modern feminine form of Edwin *q.v.* it dates from the 19th century revival of the original Anglo-Saxon masculine name.

Variations and abbreviations: Edina (Scots), Edwine.

Example: Edwina Mountbatten, 1901–1960, Vice-reine of India, wife of Lord Mountbatten of Burma.

EFFIE
Origin/meaning: Greek 'fair speech', implying either 'silence' or 'honour'.

A short form of Euphemia. Used in the 19th century as an independent name, particularly in Scotland.

EGLENTYNE
Origin/meaning: Old French 'prickly', an old-fashioned name for sweet-briar.

This flower name was used occasionally in the Middle Ages. It was revived in the 19th century but without great success.

Variations: Eglantine, Eglentine.

EILEEN (pron. Eyeleen or Evleen)
Origin/meaning: Greek 'light' or 'bright' or Old Irish 'pleasant'.

Like Aileen, this name is often used in Ireland as the Irish equivalent of Helen *q.v.* However the alternative pronunciation seems to indicate that it is sometimes a version of Eveline, in which case it takes on the second meaning. Its wider popularity stems from the increased interest in native Irish names at the beginning of the 20th century.

Variations and abbreviations: Aileen, Eily, Eveline.

EITHNE
Origin/meaning: Old Irish 'little fire', 'little fiery one'.

The modern spelling of the Old Irish name Aithne *q.v.*

Variation: Ethne. See also Ena.

ELAINE
Origin/meaning: Greek 'light' or 'bright'.

This Medieval French form of the Greek name Helen *q.v.* indicates its original pronunciation – Ellayni. The name was used in medieval literature and in particular the legends surrounding King Arthur and his Knights of the Round Table. In Victorian times all forms of medieval culture were admired and copied. The Victorian poet Laureate, Tennyson, wrote his own blank verse version of the legends, *Idylls of the King*, 1859, and took much of his inspiration from Sir Thomas Malory's 15th century poem which included the tale of Princess Elaine's doomed love for Sir Lancelot. In one of the many conflicting tales based on King Arthur and his Knights, Elaine was the mother of Sir Galahad. The baby's father was Sir Lancelot, who was in love with Queen Guinevere and who anyway was sworn to celibacy. Seeing her love was clearly doomed from every point of view, Elaine pined to death. At her request her body, with a letter explaining the circumstances, was placed on a barge and taken to King Arthur. When he read of the manner of her death Arthur had Elaine buried with all the pageantry of a Queen and with her story engraved upon her tomb. The success of the poem made the name a favourite among the Victorians and it enjoyed a second period of popularity in the 1920s and 1930s.

Variations and abbreviations: Elain, Elana, Elane, Elayne.

Examples: Elaine Stritch, US actress.
Elaine Delmar, US singer.

ELEANOR (pron. Ellinah or Ellyanore)
Origin/meaning: Greek 'bright', 'light'.

Like Elaine this is a Medieval French form of the Greek name Helen (Ellayni). It was introduced into England on the marriage of Eleanor of Aquitaine (1122–1204) with Henry II at the end of the 12th century. This formidable woman spelled her name in the Provençale fashion – Alienore. Eventually the spelling Eleanor became usual and the name gained popularity because of Edward I's much loved queen, Eleanor of Castile. On her death in 1290 he erected the famous stone crosses which marked the resting places of her body on its journey to London for burial. The best known of these is Charing Cross, which is, in fact, a replica of the original. Like other medieval names such as Alice, Emma and Edith, it was popular during the 19th century.

Variations and abbreviations: Alienore, Eleanora, Eléanore (Fr), Elenore, Eleonore (It), Elianora, Elinor, Elinore, Ella, Ellie, Elly, Leonor (Sp), Lenore, Leonora, Leonore, Nell, Nellie, Nelly, Nora.

Examples: Eleanore Roosevelt, 1884–1962, US journalist, wife of President Roosevelt.
Eleanor Bron, English actress.
Eleanora Duse, 1859–1939, Italian actress.

ELEN
Origin/meaning: Greek 'light' or 'bright'.

This is the Welsh form of Ellen q.v. a form of Helen q.v. The name was popular in Wales long before it was introduced into England by the Normans.

Variations: Elin, Ellen, and see also Helen.

ELFLEDA
Origin/meaning: Old English 'elf-clean'.

An Anglo-Saxon name revived for a short period during the Romantic Movement at the beginning of the 19th century. In the Teutonic legends of Northern Europe elves were super-natural beings capable of great good or great harm. By incorporating them into a name the Anglo-Saxons hoped to ensure the elves' capricious power was used for the child and not against it.

ELFRIDA
Origin/meaning: Old English 'elf-strength'.

A pre-Conquest Anglo-Saxon name revived at the beginning of the 19th century. Elfrida was the second wife of King Edgar *q.v.* and the mother of Ethelred the Unready, 968–1016.

Variations and abbreviations: Elfreda, Elfrid, Freda. See also Elfleda.

ELGIVA

Origin/meaning: Old English 'elf-gift'.

A pre-Conquest name which survived into the early Middle Ages. It was revived in the 19th century along with names of similar origin, such as Edith, Edgar and Emma.

See also Elfleda.

ELIANA

Origin/meaning: Greek 'sun'.

This is an Italian name occasionally used in English-speaking countries. It is sometimes considered a feminine form of Elias/Elijah *q.v.*

Variation: Elaine (Fr/Ger).

Example: Eliana Gianini Belotti, Italian feminist.

ELINOR

Origin/meaning: Greek 'bright', 'light'.

The spelling of Eleanor *q.v.* (form of Helen *q.v.*) which was popular in the 17th and 18th centuries.

Variation: Elinore.

Example: Elinor Glyn, 1864–1943, English romantic novelist.

ELISABETH

Origin/meaning: Hebrew 'God is my satisfaction'.

The usual European spelling of Elizabeth *q.v.* which comes via the Greek form.

Example: Elisabeth Schwarzkopf, German soprano.

ELISE

Origin/meaning: Hebrew 'God is my satisfaction'.

A French short form of Elizabeth now used as an independent name.

Variations and abbreviations: Elyse. See also Elizabeth.

ELIZA
Origin/meaning: Hebrew 'God is my satisfaction'.

A short form of Elizabeth. Used as a pet name for Elizabeth I in the 16th century, it became popular as an independent name in the 19th century. Shaw chose it for the heroine of his play *Pygmalion* which was adapted as the musical *My Fair Lady*.

Variations and abbreviations: Lisa, Liza, Elisa, Elise (Fr). See also Elizabeth.

ELIZABELLA
Origin/meaning: Hebrew 'God is my satisfaction'.

A 16th century version of Elizabeth. The use of the Italian word for beautiful, bella, as the last syllable, was presumably intended as a compliment to Elizabeth I. It may also have been intended as an Anglicized form of the usual Scottish form of Elizabeth – Isabel, *q.v.*

Variations and abbreviations: See Elizabeth.

ELIZABETH
Origin/meaning: Hebrew 'God is my satisfaction'.

This is the usual English spelling of the name. It comes via the Latin spelling whereas the continental spelling, using 's' instead of 'z' comes directly from the Greek. It is Biblical, being the name of the mother of John the Baptist and the wife of Aaron (in the form Elisheba). In the Middle Ages, the form Isabel *q.v.* was more popular. However in the 16th century the long and successful reign of Elizabeth I, 1533–1603, the daughter of Henry VIII and Anne Boleyn, brought the name from comparative obscurity to the point where nearly one girl in four was baptized Elizabeth. Not only did the Queen give glamour to the name but her success in firmly re-establishing the Protestant reformation after the reign of her Catholic sister Mary, made it a popular choice among those who wished to affirm both their Protestantism and their patriotism. The name Mary suffered a corresponding decline in England while climbing to new heights of popularity in

Catholic Ireland.

Since the 16th century Elizabeth has maintained its position as one of the most frequently used girls' names. This is especially true if the multitude of variations and short forms are included. At different times different variations have found favour. For example, Bess in the 16th century, Betty in the 18th century and again in the mid-20th century, Eliza at the end of the 18th century and the 19th century. Lisa and Liza are fashionable at the moment. Several of these variations, eg Elsie and Bettina, have become firmly established as independent names. The accession of Elizabeth II in 1952 was undoubtedly a boost to the name although it has never recovered the popularity of the 19th century. The familiar form used for Queen Elizabeth II when she was a child was Lillibet.

Variations and abbreviations: Babette (Fr), Belita (Sp), Belle, Bess, Bessie, Bessy, Beth, Betsey, Betsy, Betta, Bette, Betti, Bettie, Bettina (It), Bettine (Fr), Betty, Ealasaid (Scots Gaelic), Eilis (Ir), Elisa (It), Elisabet (Scand), Elisabeth, Elisabetta (It), Elise (Fr), Elissa (It), Eliza, Elizabella, Elizabet, Elly, Elsa (Ger/Dutch/Scand), Elsbeth (Scot), Else (Ger/Dutch/Scand), Elsey, Elsie (Scot), Elspet (Scot), Elspeth (Scot), Elsy, Elyse, Helsa, Isabel, Isabella (Sp/It), Isabetta (It), Isobel (Scot), Lib, Libbie, Libby, Liesel (Ger), Lieschen (Ger), Lillibet, Lisa, Lisabeth, Lisavetta (Slav), Lisbeth, Lise (Ger), Liselotte (Ger), Lisette (Fr), Lissa, Liz, Liza, Lizabeth, Lizbeth, Lizzie, Lizzy, Ysabel (and see Isabel).

Examples: Elizabeth Taylor, English-born actress.
Elizabeth Jane Howard, English novelist.
Elizabeth Barrett Browning, 1806–1861, English poet.

ELLA

Origin/meaning: uncertain, probably Old German 'all'.

A popular medieval name brought to England by the Normans. Like many other medieval names such as Alice, Elaine and Emma, it was revived in the 19th century. In the US it was frequently used in compound names such as Ella-Jane and Ella-May. Its use has declined sharply since the 19th century. It may also be used as a short form of Ellen, Elizabeth and Eleanor and of names such as Isabella or Arabella.

Variations and abbreviations: Ellaline, Ellie, Elly.

Examples: Ella Fitzgerald, US singer.
Ella Wheeler Wilcox, 1855–1919, US writer.

ELLEN
Origin/meaning: Greek 'light' or 'bright'.

This is the form of Helen used in medieval England and pre-Conquest Scotland and Wales. It gradually fell out of favour after the 16th century and was replaced by Helen. However it remained popular in Scotland and Ireland so that it is sometimes mistakenly described as a Scottish or Irish name. It was revived in the 19th century along with many other medieval names including the other medieval forms of Helen – Eleanor and Elaine.

Variations and abbreviations: Ella, Ellie, Ellin, Ellyn.

Examples: Ellen Terry, 1848–1928, English actress.
Ellen Wilkinson, 1891–1947, British politician.

ELLIE
Origin/meaning: short form of many names including Elizabeth, Ellen, Eleanor, Elaine.

Variation: Elly.

ELMA
Origin/meaning: a 19th century combination of Elizabeth and Mary.

This is an unusual girl's name, perhaps because it sounds like the boy's name Elmer *q.v.*

ELOÏSE (pron. Elloweeze)
Origin/meaning: Old German 'flourishing and strong'.

This is an Anglicized spelling of the French Héloïse and German Heloise. The Normans adopted the name from the Old German Helewidis and brought it to England in the form Helewis. It died out as a first name in the Middle Ages but survived as the surname Elwys or Elwes. In the Romantic Movement of the 19th century when medieval themes were popular, the story of the doomed love of the monk Abelard (1079–1142) for his pupil Héloïse, 1101–1163, revived interest in the name. It is sometimes mistakenly confused, because of its pronunciation, with the quite separate name Louise.

Variations: Eloisa (It), Helewise (Med Eng), Héloïse (Fr).

ELSA

Origin/meaning: Old German 'noble' or Hebrew 'God is my satisfaction'.

This predominantly German name may be a development of the Old German name Adalheid along the same pattern as Alice *q.v.* Or, like Elsie, it may be a short form of Elizabeth *q.v.* It was introduced to English-speaking countries in the 19th century when Wagner used it for the heroine of his opera *Lohengrin*, 1848.

Variations: Else, Ilsa, Ilse and see Elizabeth.

Examples: Elsa Lanchester, British film actress.
Elsa Martinelli, Italian film actress.

ELSIE

Origin/meaning: Hebrew 'God is my satisfaction'.

A Scottish short form of Elizabeth from the Scottish variation Elspeth *q.v.* Used as an independent name since the end of the 19th century but currently unfashionable. It may also be a short form of Alison.

Variations and abbreviations: See Elizabeth.

ELSPETH

Origin/meaning: Hebrew 'God is my satisfaction'.

An almost exclusively Scottish variation of Elizabeth.

Variations and abbreviations: Eilasaid, Elsbeth, Elsie, Elspet, Elspie. See also Elizabeth/Isobel.

Example: Elspet Gray, British actress.

ELUNED (pron. Éllinedd)

Origin/meaning: uncertain. Possibly a reference to the Old Welsh word meaning 'idol'.

A popular Welsh name occasionally used in England. Its short form Lyn and the Medieval French form Lynnet have proved more popular in English-speaking countries than the original.

Variations and abbreviations: Eiluned, Elined, Linet, Luned, Lyn, Lynn, Lynnet, Lynette.

ELVINA
Origin/meaning: Old English 'elf-friend'.

One of the pre-Conquest Anglo-Saxon names revived in the Romantic Movement at the beginning of the 19th century.

Variation: Elvine. See also Elfleda.

ELVIRA
Origin/meaning: uncertain, possibly Old German 'elf-counsel' or 'elf-ruler'.

This is a Spanish name which is found several times in literature, most notably as the woman seduced by Don Juan and as the heroine of Verdi's opera *Ernani*. The name probably developed from the Teutonic German along the same pattern as English names like Elvina, Elfrida and Elfgiva.

Variation: Elvire (Fr). See also Elfleda.

EMBLEM
Origin/meaning: French. A precious stone, green in colour.

A medieval spelling of the name revived in the 19th century as Emmeline *q.v.*

EMERALD
Origin/meaning: French. A precious stone, green in colour.

This is one of the jewel names popular at the end of the 19th century. It was possibly helped by the popularity of Victor Hugo's *The Hunchback of Notre Dame* in which the young girl loved by Quasimodo is called Esmeralda, the Spanish for Emerald.

Variations and abbreviations: Em, Emmie, Emeraude (Fr), Esmeralda (Sp/It), Meraud.

Example: Emerald Cunard, d.1948, English society hostess between the two World Wars.

EMILY
Origin/meaning: Latin, from the Roman clan name Aemelius.

Sometimes confused with Amelia and given as Old German 'industrious'.

This is a Medieval Italian name popularized by the Italian Renaissance poet Boccaccio. He used it in *Il Teseide*, which was read throughout Europe. Chaucer in *The Knight's Tale* (1380) borrowed both the plot and the name from Boccaccio's story. Chaucer used various spellings, including the Italian Emilia and the form we are still familiar with, Emily. Shakespeare used Emilia for Iago's wife in his play *Othello*. In the 18th century the Hanoverians brought to England the Old German name, Amelia. Its similarity to Emilia resulted in the English 'translating' Amelia into the native Emily, although they are in fact two separate names. The apparent royal use of the name immediately made it popular in a way it had never been before. It is a quite separate name from the Saxon Emma *q.v.*

Variations and abbreviations: Amalia, Aimil (Scots), Em (Med Eng), Em, Emalia, Emelye, Emerlee, Emilia (It/Sp), Emilie (Ger), Émilie (Fr), Emmie, Emmy.

Examples: Emily Brontë, 1818–1848, English novelist.
Emily Dickinson, 1830–1886, US poet.

EMMA
Origin/meaning: Old German 'universal' or from the name of the Teutonic god-hero Irmin.

This name probably began, like the German names Irma and Erma, as a short form of names like Ermintrude and Ermengard. The name was popular in the Western part of the Frankish empire (the area roughly corresponding to France). It was adopted by the Normans and in 1002 Emma, daughter of Richard I, Duke of Normandy, brought it to England when she married Ethelred the Unready. In 1016 after being widowed she married his successor, King Canute. Queen Emma was a popular figure and the name has been used ever since. From the 12th century to the 18th century the usual form was Em and the pet form Emmot. Since the 18th century when the old forms of many names were revived, Emma has been considered the correct form and Em its diminutive. Emma is sometimes mistakenly assumed to be a pet form of names like Emily and Emmeline rather than a name in its own right. It can however be considered a short form of Ermintrude *q.v.*

Variations and abbreviations: Em, Emm, Emmie, Emmot, Erma (Ger), Imma, Irma (Ger).

Examples: Emma, Lady Hamilton, 1765–1815, Mistress of Admiral Nelson.
Emma, the heroine of Jane Austen's novel, published in 1816.

EMMANUELLE
Origin/meaning: Hebrew 'God with us'.

Feminine form of Emanuel q.v.

EMMELINE
Origin/meaning: Old German 'little industrious one'.

This is a diminutive of Amalburga, the original form of Amelia q.v. It was introduced by the Normans who had adopted and adapted many Saxon names. As with most medieval names the spelling varied considerably. However it was as Emmeline that it was revived as part of the Romantic Movement's interest in medieval culture at the beginning of the 19th century. It is sometimes wrongly assumed to be related to Emily and Emma q.v.

Variations and abbreviations: Amelia, Em, Emblem, Emblin, Emelia, Emlin, Emlyn, Emmaline, Emmy.

Example: Emmeline Pankhurst, 1857–1928, British suffragette leader.

ENA
Origin/meaning: Old Irish 'little fire' or 'little fiery one'.

This is an English form of the Celtic Aithne/Eithne through the original name Aine (pron. Awnye) who was Queen of the Fairies. Although generally considered Irish the name is increasingly found in Scotland. It is sometimes mistakenly described as a short form of Eugenia (well-born). This is because Queen Victoria's grand-daughter, the future Queen Victoria Eugénie of Spain, 1887–1969, was generally known as Ena. In fact this was her real name, not a short form of Eugénie. She had been christened Victoria Eugénie Julia Ena. Ena was intended as a compliment to the Scots for the baby had been born and christened at Queen Victoria's beloved Scottish residence,

Balmoral. One of her brothers had the Scottish Donald included among his many names for the same reason. Ena, especially if found in the form Ina, may also be a short form of names such as Georgina.

ENID (pron. Welsh Ehnid, Eng Eenid)
Origin/meaning: uncertain, possibly Welsh 'tree-bark'.

This is another of the names, probably Welsh in origin, which have become more widely familiar because of being found in the tales of King Arthur and his Knights of the Round Table. Enid was the wife of Sir Geraint *q.v.* and wrongly considered by him to be unfaithful. However her selfless nursing when he was wounded convinced him he was mistaken and they lived happily ever after. Enid's virtues have sometimes led to the meaning of the name being given as 'purity'. Like Elaine and Lynette *q.v.* the name was made fashionable in the 19th century when Tennyson chose the tale of Enid as one of the episodes in his poem *Idylls of the King*, 1859, based on the many tales of King Arthur and his Knights.

Example: Enid Blyton, d.1968, English children's author.

ERICA
Origin/meaning: Old Norse 'ever-ruling'.

This is the feminine form of Eric *q.v.* Although popular for over 1000 years in Scandinavia it was not used in England until the 19th century when the masculine Eric was also revived. Since the fashion for early names coincided with the 19th century fashion for flower names. Erica was sometimes assumed to be a flower name since it is the Latin name for heather.

Variations and abbreviations: Eri, Ericha, Erika (Ger/Scand)), Rickie, Rikkie.

Example: Erica Jong, US poet and novelist.

ERIN
Origin/meaning: Old Irish 'peace'.

This is an alternative Celtic name for Ireland. Its use as a personal name is modern.

Variations: Erina, Erinna.

Example: Erin Pizzey, British writer and campaigner for battered wives.

ERMA
Origin/meaning: Old German 'universal' or from the name of the Teutonic god-hero Irmin.

An alternative form of Irma q.v. Erma is the older form and matches the English form Emma.

Variations: Emma, Irma. See also Irmgard, Ermintrude.

Example: Erma Bombeck, US writer.

ERMENGARDE
Origin/meaning: Old English/Old German 'under Irmin's protection'.

The equivalent of the German name Irmgard q.v. this pre-Conquest English name survived into the early Middle Ages, despite the Norman Conquest. Like Irmgard in Germany, Ermengarde was revived in England during the Romantic Movement of the late 18th century and early 19th century, but without the same lasting success.

ERMINTRUDE
Origin/meaning: Old German 'universal strength' or 'strength of Irmin'. Irmin was one of the god-heroes like Ing.

A pre-Conquest name similar to the German names Irma and Irmgard. Like Ermengarde it was revived in the early 19th century during the period of interest in early history which inspired the Romantic Movement in art and literature. Rare today.

Variations: Ermentrude, Ermyntrude, Irmintrude, Trudie, Trudy.

ERNESTINE
Origin/meaning: Old German 'earnestness' or 'vigour'.

This is a feminine form of Ernest from the French diminutive version Ernestin. It was used in the 19th century when Ernest was a popular name, but it is unusual in English-speaking countries today.

Example: Ernestine Carter, English fashion journalist, d.1983.

ESMÉ
Origin/meaning: French/Latin 'loved'.

This is a variation of Amy q.v. It was introduced from France to Scotland in the 16th century when relations between the two countries were very close. It was originally a boy's name but by the time it spread to England it was also used for girls. It is now considered primarily as a girl's name. Esmé may also be a short form of the Spanish name Esmeralda. As a feminine name it may also be a form of the Scottish Ismay q.v.

Variations: See Amy.

ESMERALDA
Origin/meaning: Spanish 'emerald'.

An extremely popular Spanish name. Its use by the Romantic writer Victor Hugo in his novel *The Hunchback of Notre Dame*, 1831 and the opera *La Esmeralda*, 1837, made the name familiar in France and England.

Variations and abbreviations: Emerald, Esmé, Esmeraldah.

ESTELLE
Origin/meaning: Latin 'star'.

This is a French form of the name Stella. Occasionally used in English-speaking countries since Dickens gave Estella to a character in his novel *Great Expectations*, 1861.

Variations and abbreviations: See Stella.

Example: Estelle Kohler, English actress.

ESTHER (pron. Esster)
Origin/meaning: uncertain. Probably Persian 'myrtle' or 'star'.

In the book of the Old Testament which carries her name, Esther is a Jewess who is chosen by King Ahasueras for her great beauty. In ch.2 v.7, it is explained that Esther is the equivalent of the Hebrew Hadassah, meaning myrtle. The two meanings given for the name may not conflict since the myrtle has star-like flowers. The pronounciation of *th* with a hard *t* sound is a result of the Greek spelling. Among non-Jewish people the name came into use in the 17th century when Biblical names were popular. The play *Esther*, 1689, written by the

French playwright Racine for the pupils of Mme de Maintenon's school for poor girls, may have given the name extra publicity.

Variations and abbreviations: Essa, Essie, Essy, Esta, Ester (It), Ettie, Etty, Hadassah, Hester, Hesther, Hettie, Hetty.

Examples: Esther Williams, US film actress, specializing in swimming spectaculars.
Esther Rantzen, British television presenter/producer.

ESTRILD
Origin/meaning: Old English 'Easter battle'.

This name occurs in the *History of Britain* written by Geoffrey of Monmouth, 1100–1154. Estrildis was the mistress of Locrin (see Gwendolyn and Sabrina). The name became rare after the Norman Conquest.

Variations: Estrildis, Estrella (Sp).

ETHEL
Origin/meaning: Old English 'noble'.

This is a simplification of Aethel, the Old English equivalent of the Teutonic Adel, which appears directly or indirectly in many names, eg Adelaide, Alice, Albert, etc. The prefix Ethel was not used on its own in pre-Conquest times but always as part of compound names such as Ethelred or Ethelfleda. When there was renewed interest in these obsolete names early in the 19th century, Ethel developed as an obvious short form. It survived as an independent name after names such as Etheldreda had sunk back into obscurity because of their unfamiliarity and complexity. It was used in several popular 19th century novels, notably Thackeray's *The Newcomes*, 1855, which undoubtedly helped to establish it. The astounding popularity of the Romantic novelist Ethel M. Dell, 1881–1939, may have influenced many mothers to choose the name during the period between the two World Wars.

Variations and abbreviations: Eth, Ethyl.

Examples: Ethel Merman, US musical comedy actress.
Ethel Barrymore, 1879–1959, US film actress.

ETHELBURGA
Origin/meaning: Old English 'noble fortress'.

The name of a pre-Conquest saint, sister of St Etheldreda. The name was revived unsuccessfully during the period of the Romantic Movement.

ETHELDREDA
Origin/meaning: Old English 'noble strength'.

An early form of the original Aethelthryth, commonly known since the 16th century by its much corrupted form Audrey *q.v.* St Etheldreda's, 630–679, popularity ensured the survival of the name after the Norman Conquest. She was one of several daughters of King Anna of the East Angles, who all became saints. The others were SS Sexburga, Ethelburga, Withburga and Saethryda. Although Etheldreda was revived during the Romantic Movement it had no lasting success but the simpler version Audrey continues to flourish.

Variations and abbreviations: Audrey, Ethel, Etheldred, Ethelia, Ethelred, Theldred.

ETHELINDA
Origin/meaning: Old English/Old German 'noble serpent'.

The serpent was regarded as having supernatural powers in pre-Christian Northern Europe, perhaps because of its ability to 'renew' itself by shedding its old skin. The name is therefore a flattering one, like the similar, Belinda. It was revived during the Romantic Movement at the end of the 18th century and is still used occasionally today.

Variations and abbreviations: Athelinda, Ethel, Etheline, Ethelyne.

ETTA
Origin/meaning: Old German 'home-ruler'. Or an abbreviation of Henrietta *q.v.* used as an independent name.

Variation: Ettie, Etty.

Example: Etta Cone, 1870–1949, US art connoisseur and collector, major benefactor of the Baltimore Museum of Art.

EUDORA
Origin/meaning: Greek 'gifted' or 'generous'.

Variations and abbreviations: Dora, Eudore (Fr).

Example: Eudora Welty, US writer.

EUDOXIA
Origin/meaning: Greek 'of good repute'.

This ancient Greek name has a similar meaning to Euphemia *q.v.* It is rare in English-speaking countries.

Variations and abbreviations: Docie, Doxy, Eudocia, Eudosia, Eudossia (It).

Example: Princess Eudoxia, b.1898, daughter of Ferdinand of Bulgaria.

EUGENIA
Origin/meaning: Greek 'noble', 'well-born'.

The Italian feminine form of Eugene, Eugenia was the name of an early Christian martyr. It was used in the Middle Ages when saints' names were at the height of their popularity. The stylish wife of the French Emperor Napoleon III, the Empress Eugénie, 1826–1920, created a fashion for the French form of the name in the 19th century.

Variations and abbreviations: Eugénie (Fr), Gene, Genia, Ginny.

Example: Eugenia Sheppard, US journalist.

EULALIA
Origin/meaning: Greek 'fair spoken' or 'well spoken of'.

A pre-Christian Greek name borne by one of the early Spanish martyrs. On her death a white dove was said to have flown out of her mouth. She is the patron saint of Barcelona. Rare in English-speaking countries. It has a masculine counterpart – Eulogius – which is not often used except in Spain, the home of St Eulogius.

Variations: Eulalie (Fr), Lallie.

EUNICE (pron. Yéwniss or Yewníghsee)
Origin/meaning: Greek 'happy victory'.

This is a pre-Christian Greek name. It was adopted as a Christian name by 17th century Puritans because of Eunice, the name traditionally given to the mother of St Paul's disciple Timothy (Acts xvi, 1 and 2). Although the second pronunciation,

113

in three syllables, along the same lines as Aphrodite, is more correct, the first pronunciation was soon the most common. It is rare outside Britain and usually does not appear in American or European name-books.

Variations and abbreviations: Euny, Unice.

EUPHEMIA
Origin/meaning: Greek 'fair speech' implying either 'silence' or 'honour'.

An old Greek name used as a Christian name to honour the 4th century martyr St Euphemia. It was used in the Middle Ages in England when saints' names were popular. In Scotland the short form Effie was popular and is still found today.

Variations and abbreviations: Effie, Effy, Eufemia (It/Sp), Euphémie (Fr), Phemie.

Example: Euphemia (Effie) Gray, d.1897, wife of John Ruskin, 1819–1900, the critic, and later of the painter John Millais, 1829–1896.

EUSTACIA
Origin/meaning: Greek 'fruitful'.

This is the Latin feminine form of Eustace q.v. Like many other names with Latin endings it was in use in the 18th century. In the Middle Ages Eustace was probably used equally for men and women in speech with the form Eustacia used as the feminine version in Latin documents.

Variations and abbreviations: Eustace, Eustachia.

EVA
Origin/meaning: uncertain. Possibly Hebrew 'life-giving'.

The Latinized form of Eve q.v. which is used in Italy, Scandinavia, Germany and Spain. In English-speaking countries it was used increasingly after the publication of Harriet Beecher Stowe's book *Uncle Tom's Cabin*, 1852, which had the popular character 'little Eva'.

Examples: Eva Perón, 1919–1952, wife of Juan Perón, former President of Argentina.
Eva Gabor, Hungarian-born actress.

114

EVADNE (pron. Eváddnee)
Origin/meaning: uncertain. Possibly Greek 'fortune'.

Evadne is a name from Greek legend. She was the wife of Capaneus and she killed herself by leaping onto his funeral pyre and being burned with him. The name was given by the dramatists Beaumont and Fletcher to the heroine of *The Maid's Tragedy*, 1611. It recurs from time to time in literature but is rarely given as a name.

EVANGELINE
Origin/meaning: a name coined by the US poet Longfellow, 1807–1882, for his poem Evangeline, 1847. Evangel is an archaic word for gospel, -ine is a French feminine ending, as in Ernestine, Ambrosine, etc. The poem was popular and the name, with its religious overtones, was taken into use, especially in the US. Nowadays, it is a rare name.

See also Fiona, Lorna, Miranda, Ophelia, Pamela, Vanessa, Wendy.

EVE
Origin/meaning: uncertain. Possibly Hebrew 'life-giving'.

This is the name given to the first woman by Adam (Genesis 3 v.20). Because it was Eve who tempted Adam with the apple so that they were forced out of Paradise, the name was never greatly popular though it was used in the Middle Ages.

Variations and abbreviations: Eva, Evie, Evita (Sp).

EVELEEN
Origin/meaning: Old Celtic 'pleasant'.

One of the possible sources of the English name Eveline/Evelyn *q.v.*

EVELINA (pron. Eveléena)
Origin/meaning: Old French 'hazel tree' or Old Celtic 'pleasant'.

Latinized version of Eveline *q.v.* which was used in medieval manuscripts. In the 18th century Latinized versions of names eg Augusta, Sophia, were extremely popular and Fanny Burney chose this name for the heroine of her novel *Evelina*, published in 1788.

EVELINE (pron. Éevlyn, Évellin or Evellighn (Scots)
Origin/meaning: Old French 'hazel-tree' or Old Celtic 'pleasant'.

The variation Evelyn, which is now more popular than the original spelling, is probably copied from the masculine Evelyn, *q.v.* which comes from an old German name.

Variations and abbreviations: Avelina, Aveline, Avelyn, Eveleen, Evelina, Evelyn.

EVELYN (pron. Éevlin)
Origin/meaning: Old French 'hazel-tree', Old Celtic 'pleasant'. Possibly from the old German name Avi.

The usual modern spelling of Eveline *q.v.* It probably imitates the masculine Evelyn *q.v.* which is a family name used as a first name. The masculine Evelyn developed independently from Avi.

Variation and abbreviations: See Eveline.

Example: Evelyn Laye, English actress.

F

FABIA (pron. Fáybea)
Origin/meaning: Latin. Of the Roman Fabius family.

This name is the root form of the diminutives Fabiana and Fabiola.

Example: Fabia Drake, English actress.

FABIOLA
Origin/meaning: Latin. Of the Roman Fabius family. It is a diminutive form 'little Fabia'.

St Fabiola, d.399, was a member of the Fabius family. She was a friend of St Jerome and St Paula and founded a large hospice for the needy at Porto. The name has been given mainly in Spain and Italy in her honour. It is rare in England although the masculine form Fabian was used.

Variations and abbreviations: Fabia, Fabiana.

Example: Queen Fabiola of the Belgians.

FAITH
Origin/meaning: Latin 'trust', 'faith'.

This, with Hope and Charity, was one of the three virtues referred to by St Paul in his first Epistle to the Corinthians. It was a popular Puritan name and is still used today.

Abbreviation: Fay.

Examples: Faith Brown, English comedienne.
Faith Brook, English actress.

FANCHON (pron. Fanshon)
Origin/meaning: Medieval Latin 'from France', 'free'.

This is a French familiar form of Françoise (Frances) q.v.

FANCY
Origin/meaning: Medieval Latin 'from France' or 'free'.

A variation of Frances q.v. used only in the US.

117

FANNY

Origin/meaning: Late Latin 'free' or 'from France'.

A familiar form of Frances q.v. Used since the 18th century as an independent name.

Variation and abbreviation: See Frances.

Examples: Fanny Burney, 1752–1840, English novelist and diarist.
Fanny Cradock, English cookery writer.
Fanny Farmer, 1858–1915, US cookery writer.
Fanny Brice, 1891–1951, US comedienne.

FATIMA (pron. Fáhteema)

Origin/meaning: Arabic 'daughter of the prophet' or 'weaned'.

Fatima was the youngest daughter of the Prophet Mohammed. She married Ali q.v. the first convert to Mohammedanism. Their descendants, the Fatimites, ruled over Egypt and North Africa from 969–1171.

There is also a similar Swahili name Fatuma (weaned) used for Fatima in parts of Africa.

Example: Fatima Whitbread, British athlete.

FAY

Origin/meaning: either 'fairy' or an abbreviation of Faith q.v.

Like May, which may be the month or an abbreviation of Mary, Fay is a name which originated in the 19th century.

Variations and abbreviations: Fayanne, Faye, Fayette (Fr).

Examples: Fay Weldon, English novelist and dramatist.
Faye Dunaway, US film actress.

FELICIA

Origin/meaning: Latin 'fortunate'.

This is a feminine form of Felix. It was popular in the Middle Ages when it was probably given to honour St Felicia, one of the many early martyrs. After the 17th century when Protestants shunned Catholic saints' names and favoured abstract virtues the form Felicity was used. Because of the similar sounds it was sometimes confused with Phyllis.

Variations and abbreviations: Felice, Felicity, Felis, Félise (Fr), Phelisia.

Examples: Felicia Hemans, 1793–1835, English poet.
Felicia Skene, 1821–1899, English novelist, correspondent of Florence Nightingale.

FELICITY
Origin/meaning: Latin 'happiness'.

This virtue name was adopted by 17th century Puritans in preference to the saint's name Felicia. Both names have more or less the same meaning. It is now considered the feminine equivalent of Felix and has remained moderately popular into the 20th century.

Variations and abbreviations: Fee, Felicia, Félicité (Fr), Felicidad (Sp), Felicita (It), Felicissima (It), Felizia (Ger).

Example: Felicity Kendal, British actress.

FENELLA
Origin/meaning: Old Irish 'white shoulders'.

This is the Scottish form of an old Celtic name, and the one which is most familiar in England, because Sir Walter Scott used it in *Peveril of the Peak*, 1823. In Celtic legend Fionnghala was a princess who was changed into a white swan.

Variations and abbreviations: Finella, Finnuala, Finola (Ir), Fiona, Fionnula, Nula.

Example: Fenella Fielding, English actress.

FERN
Origin/meaning: Sanskrit 'feather'.

This is the name of a woodland plant renowned for its feathery fronds. Ferns were popular houseplants in Victorian times and it is not surprising that Fern should have come into use at the end of the 19th century when flower names were fashionable. Fern is sometimes found as a short form of the Italian name Fernanda *q.v.*

FERNANDA
Origin/meaning: Old German 'journey venture', ie, 'adventurer'.

An Italian feminine form of Ferdinand. It is rare in English-speaking countries but used regularly elsewhere in Europe.

Variations and abbreviations: Ferdinanda (It/Ger), Ferdinande, Ferdinandina, Ferdinandine, Fern, Fernande (Fr), Fernandina.

FFION
Origin/meaning: Welsh 'roses'.
This is the Welsh equivalent of Rose or Rosanna.

FILIPA
Origin/meaning: Greek 'lover of horses'.
This is an unusual English spelling of Philippa q.v.

FINOLA
Origin/meaning: Old Irish 'white shoulders'.
A modern Irish form of Fenella q.v.
Example: Finola Hughes, English dancer.

FIONA (pron. Feeówna)
Origin/meaning: Old Irish 'fair'.

This is a pen-name invented by the Scottish novelist William Sharp, 1855–1905. As Fiona Macleod, he wrote a series of novels inspired by the old Celtic myths and legends. Although the name Fiona was a fabrication, it is now usually assumed to be a genuine Scottish name. It was presumably based on the Old Irish word fionn-fair, beautiful (the equivalent of the Old Welsh gwen-). The name is now well-established and has become increasingly popular since the Second World War.

Variations: Ffiona (Wel), Fionna.

See also Evangeline, Miranda, Ophelia, Lorna, Pamela, Perdita, Vanessa, Wendy.

FLAVIA (pron. Fláyvia)
Origin/meaning: Latin. From the Flavius family.

This was a well known Roman name and is thought to be derived from the word flavus – yellow. It is therefore the equivalent of the Greek Xanthe. An early martyr, St Flavia, made it an acceptable Christian name.

Variations: Flaviana, Flavilla.

FLEUR
Origin/meaning: French 'flower'.

This is a modern equivalent of the classical name Flora q.v. It was used by John Galsworthy for a character in his novel sequence The Forsyte Saga, 1926–1930, and has been used from time to time since then.

Variations and abbreviations: Fflyr (Wel), Flora, Florence, Flore (Med Fr), Flower.

Example: Fleur Adcock, New Zealand poet.

FLORA

Origin/meaning: Latin. The name of the Roman goddess of flowers and spring, and lover of the West Wind, Zephyr. Her festival was called the Floralia.

This name was used from time to time in the Middle Ages because of St Flora, martyred at Cordova in 851. It was popularized as a first name in Europe during the Renaissance when classical names from Greece and Rome became fashionable. It was first used in France in the form Flore, and was taken from there to Scotland which had close connections with France. In Scotland it was sometimes used to 'translate' the native name Finghin. Flora did not become popular in England until long afterwards, perhaps because it was frequently used as a name for a pet spaniel, Flora being regarded as a typical Spanish name and therefore appropriate. There is a rare masculine form Florus.

Variations and abbreviations: Fflyr (Wel), Fleur (Fr), Fleurette (Fr), Floella, Flor, Flore (Fr/Scots), Florella, Floretta, Floria, Floriane, Floris, Florrie. See also Fleur, Flower, Kusum.

Examples: Flora Macdonald, 1722–1790, Scottish heroine who aided the escape of Bonnie Prince Charlie.
Dame Flora Robson, English actress, 1902–1984.

FLORENCE

Origin/meaning: Latin 'in bloom' or 'prosperous'.

This name, often in the Latin form of Florentia, was used in England in the Middle Ages. There was also a masculine form, Florentius. Because it was a familiar name it was sometimes given to boys or girls born in Florence, a town which gained its name because of its flourishing trade. Shelley gave his son the name because he was born there. From the end of the 19th century in England it became exclusively a feminine name. This is because of the great fame of the pioneer nurse and heroine of the Crimean War, Florence Nightingale, 1820–1910. She herself had been given the name because she was born in Florence. By 1875 from being a rare name it had become one of the ten favourite English names, giving way only to names like Sarah and

Anne. It was also popular in North America and Australia. Although it is no longer a common name, it has become a firmly established one.

Variations and abbreviations: Fiorenza (Ir), Flo, Flora, Florance, Flore, Florencia (Sp), Florentina, Florenza (It), Florentia (Ger), Florenzia (Ger), Florenzina, Floria, Florie, Florina, Florinda, Floris, Florrie, Florry, Flossie, Flossy.

Example: Florence Lawrence, 1886–1938, US star of silent films, known as the Biograph Girl.

FLORIANE
Origin/meaning: Latin 'flowering'.

A medieval feminine name usually considered a form of Flora.

Variation: Floriana (It).

FLOSSIE
Origin/meaning: Latin 'in bloom' or 'prosperous'.

A familiar form of Florence q.v. which was sometimes used at the end of the 19th century when Florence was a vogue name.

Variations and abbreviations: See Florence.

FLOWER
Origin/meaning: 'a flower'.

This word, like the French Fleur, has occasionally been used as a first name. However it is rare. The long-established Latin name Flora is usually preferred.

FOLUKE (pron. Folóokee)
Origin/meaning: Yoruba 'placed in God's care'.

This name comes from Nigeria.

FRAN
Origin/meaning: Old German 'a Frank', Medieval Latin 'from France'.

A short form of Frances q.v. sometimes used as an independent name.

Variations: See Frances.

FRANCES
Origin/meaning: Medieval Latin 'from France' of 'free', both

122

meanings from old German 'a Frank'.

This is the feminine form of the masculine name Francis q.v. Like Francis it was introduced to England in the Tudor period. A niece of Henry VIII's was given the name because her mother had previously been married to the King of France. The child, Lady Francis Brandon, was given what we now think of as the masculine version, though 400 years ago such distinctions were not so important. The contemporary short form Frank is now considered a masculine form only, although Frankie is still used by both boys and girls. By the mid-17th century Frances and Francis were considered two separate names. The earliest form of the name, Francesca, which originated in Medieval Italy as a nickname to indicate French associations or ancestry, is currently a vogue name in Britain.

Variations and abbreviations: Fan, Fanchette (Fr), Fanchon (Fr), Fancy (US), Fanni, Fannie, Fanny, Fran, Francelia, Francesca (It), Francesse, Francine, Francisca (Sp/Port), Francoise (Fr), Francyne, Frangag (Wel), Frank, Frankie, Frannie, Franny, Franziska (Ger), Frasquita (Sp), Zissi.

Examples: Frances de la Tour, English actress.
Frances Hodgson Burnett, 1849-1924, English/US novelist.
Frances Gumm (Judy Garland), 1922-1969, US entertainer.

FRANCESCA (pron. Franchéska)
Origin/meaning: Medieval Latin 'from France'.

This is the Italian form of Frances q.v. It is the earliest form of the name although a name of similar origin, Franka q.v. predates it. Francesca probably began simply as a nickname and like the masculine Francesco (Francis) it became an established name because of the fame of St Francis of Assisi, 1182-1226.

Variations and abbreviations: See Frances.

Examples: Francesca Annis, English actress.
Francesca da Rimini, d.1285. Earliest example of the name. Her unhappy story is incorporated by Dante into his poem *The Divine Comedy*.

FRANÇOISE (pron. Frónswahze)
Origin/meaning: Medieval Latin 'from France'.

This is the French form of Frances q.v. Like the Italian

123

Francesca it dates from the 13th century and probably became established as a Christian name because of the fame of St Francis of Assisi who lived then. Its popularity in France was increased by the fame of the renaissance king Francis (François) I, who flourished in the early 16th century. Françoise is occasionally used in English-speaking countries.

Variations and abbreviations: See Frances.

Example: Françoise Sagan, French novelist.

FRANKA
Origin/meaning: Old German 'a Frank' or 'free'.

This is the feminine equivalent of the name Frank which existed as an independent name long before the name Francis/Frances which is derived from it. The Franks gave their name to a Latin word meaning free.

Variations and abbreviations: Franca (It), Francine (Fr), France (Fr).

FREDA
Origin/meaning: Old German 'peaceful friend'.
A short form of Frederica q.v., Alfreda q.v. or Winifred q.v. An alternative spelling of Frieda.

FREDERICA
Origin/meaning: Old German 'peace-rule'.

The feminine form of Frederick q.v. It dates from the 18th century when many masculine names were feminized on the Latin pattern by adding 'a'. Other examples are Augusta and Georgina.

Variations and abbreviations: Federica (It), Fred, Fredi, Freddie, Freddy, Fredericka, Frédérique (Fr), Friederike (Ger), Fritza, Fritzi, Rica, Ricki, Rickie, Ricky, Rikky, Rixi.

Example: Queen Frederica of Greece, 1917–1981.

FREYA
Origin/meaning: Old Norse. The goddess of love and of the night.

Freya was the equivalent in Norse mythology of the Roman goddess Venus. She was the daughter of Niörd, the spirit of water and air and the sister of Frey, the god of fertility. Odin, the chief of the gods, married her but deserted her when he discovered she loved finery more than she loved him. Her chariot is pulled across the sky by two cats. Freya is a rare name in Britain but it is the name from which the word Friday comes.

Variations and abbreviations: Freia, Freija, Freja, Frigga.

Example: Freya Stark, English travel writer.

FRIDAY
Origin/meaning: Old Norse 'Freya's day' (Freya was the Norse goddess of love), or old English 'peace-strong' a corruption of Frideswide.

FRIDESWIDE (pron. Frids' wid)
Origin/meaning: Old English 'peace-strong'.

One of the few pre-Conquest names which survived the Norman Conquest. St Frideswide, d.735, was daughter of a Mercian king. She founded a religious house at Oxford and is the patron saint of the city and the university. The name, in several forms which reflected the pronunciation, survived until the general reaction against saints' names after the Protestant Reformation.

Variations and abbreviations: Frediswid, Frévisse (Fr), Friday, Frideswid, Frithswith (Old Eng), Fryswyde.

FRIEDA
Origin/meaning: Old German 'peace'.

An alternative spelling of Freda, *q.v.*

Example: Frieda Lawrence, German wife of D. H. Lawrence.

G

GABRIELLE
Origin/meaning: Hebrew 'strong man of God'.

As with names like Francis and Peter, in the Middle Ages the same form of this name, Gabriel, *q.v.* was used for men and women. The 'a' on the end of the feminine form was used only in the Latin documents of the time. The Italian Gabriella and French/German Gabrielle are fairly recent innovations in English-speaking countries in any form.

Variations and abbreviations: Gabey, Gabi, Gabie, Gabriela, Gabriel (Ger), Gabrielle (Fr), Gaby, Gavrila (Russ).

Examples: Gabrielle (Coco) Chanel, 1883–1971, French fashion designer.
Lady Gabrielle Windsor, daughter of Prince and Princess Michael of Kent.

GAENOR
Origin/meaning: Old Welsh 'fair and yielding' or 'white wave'.

This form of Gwenhwyvar, the Welsh original of Guinevere *q.v.* is still used in Wales. It resembles the English form Gaynor.

Variations: Ganor, Gaynor (Eng), Gaynore, Guanor (Scots).
See also Guinevere.

GAIL
Origin/meaning: Hebrew 'father of joy' or 'father's joy'.

A short form of Abigail, found as an independent name since the Second World War.

Variations and abbreviations: Gale, Gayle.

Example: Gayle Hunnicutt, US actress.

GALATEA (pron. Galatáya)
Origin/meaning: Greek 'milky'.

In Greek mythology Galatea was a sea-nymph in love with Acis.

126

The jealous giant Polypheme crushed Acis with a huge rock but Galatea escaped to the sea. Both Handel and Lully wrote operas entitled *Acis and Galatea*.

Variations and abbreviations: Galatée (Fr), Galateia. See also Nerine, Nerissa, Nerita, Nyse.

GALIENA (pron. Galleeáyna)
Origin/meaning: Old German 'tall'.

This was a common medieval name. It may be the original form of Aliena which Shakespeare used as a typical rural name in his play *As You Like It*, 1600.

GALINA
Origin/meaning: Greek 'peace' or 'tranquility'.

A Russian name, which was very fashionable there in the 1960s. Also used in German-speaking countries.

Variations and abbreviations: Gala, Galya.

GARNET
Origin/meaning: Latin 'pomegranate'.

This dark red jewel was named because of its colour which resembles the flesh of the pomegranate. It was occasionally used at the end of the 19the century when jewel names were popular. It is also a rare masculine name of much earlier origin.

See also Hyacinth.

GAY
Origin/meaning: French 'merry', 'cheerful'.

This name, taken directly from the adjective, has come into use over the last 100 years.

Variations and abbreviations: Gae, Gaye.

Example: Gaye Brown, English actress.

GAYNOR
Origin/meaning: Old Welsh 'fair and yielding' or 'white wave'.

This is yet another form of the Welsh name Guinevere *q.v.* famous for being the name of the wife of King Arthur. It was a form used in Medieval England but then virtually obsolete until the 1950s. In the last 30 years it has been consistently used in

England though not yet in other English-speaking countries. Jennifer, the old Cornish form of Guinevere, was similarly neglected until 50 years ago and is now common.

Variations and abbreviations: Gaenor (Wel), Ganor, Gaynore, Guanor (Scots). See also Guinevere.

GEETA
Origin/meaning: Hindustani 'Holy Book'.

This is the Hindu equivalent of the Bible, being a collection of the sayings of Krishna. The name is found in all regions of India.

Variation: Gita.

Example: Gita Bali, Indian actress.

GEMMA (pron. Jemma)
Origin/meaning: Latin 'jewel'.

This is the origin of gem, the synonym of jewel. Its use in English-speaking countries dates only from this century although it has been a popular Italian name since the Middle Ages. Dante, the Italian poet, 1265–1321, despite his life-long devotion to Beatrice, married Gemma Donati by whom he had seven children.

Example: Gemma Jones, English actress.

GENE
Origin/meaning: Greek 'noble', 'well born'.

A short form of Eugene/Eugenia used as an independent name for boys and girls.

Variations and abbreviations: See Eugenia.

Example: Gene Tierney, US actress.

GENEVA
Origin/meaning: Latin, Old French/Dutch 'juniper'.

This name, especially the French form, Genèvre, is similar in appearance to Guinevere. It is sometimes wrongly assumed that Geneva is a form of Guinevere and therefore an equivalent of the best known form of the name Jennifer.

Variations and abbreviations: Gena, Genevra, Genèvre (Fr), Janeva.

GENEVIEVE (pron. Jéneveev)
Origin/meaning: uncertain. It includes the Gaulish French word

for 'tribe' but the rest is unknown.

This is an old French name sometimes used in England. It is often considered a form or close relative of Guinevere *q.v.* although in fact their meanings are quite dissimilar. St Geneviève, 420–500, is the Patron Saint of Paris. Her prayers were considered the reason for Attila the Hun turning his invading hordes away from Paris towards Orleans. Later her intercession with Clovis, King of the Franks, persuaded him to be lenient with his Parisian prisoners. Currently enjoying a minor vogue in Australia.

Variations and abbreviations: Geneviève (Fr), Genovefa (Ger), Genoveffa (It), Genoveva, Ginette, Vevo.

GENISTA (pron. Jennista)
Origin/meaning: Latin 'broom' (a shrub with bright yellow flowers common in sandy areas).

This is one of the more unusual plant names introduced at the end of the 19th century. Household brooms were originally made from the twigs of this plant.

GEORGETTE
Origin/meaning: Greek 'farmer'.

A French feminine form of George *q.v.*

Example: Georgette Heyer, 1902–1974, English historical novelist.

GEORGIA
Origin/meaning: Greek 'farmer'.

A feminine form of George *q.v.* It is used mainly in the US where it is associated with the State of Georgia, which was named after the English king George II, 1683–1760.

Example: Georgia Brown, English-born actress.

GEORGIANA
Origin/meaning: Greek 'farmer'.

A feminine form of George *q.v.* It was popular in the 18th and 19th centuries when George was the name of four successive English kings. By the mid 19th century the slightly simpler form Georgina had superseded it.

Abbreviation: Georgie.

129

GEORGINA

Origin/meaning: Greek 'farmer'.

A feminine form of George *q.v.* It came into use in the 18th century when George became a popular masculine name and has been regularly used ever since.

Abbreviation: Georgie, Gina.

Example: Georgina Hale, British actress.

GERALDINE

Origin/meaning: Old German 'spear-rule'.

This name originated as an adjective meaning 'of the Fitzgerald family'. Fitzgerald was the family name of the Earls of Kildare, one of the most powerful families in Ireland. They were descended from the 12th century Welsh princess Nesta, and Gerald of Windsor. The Earl of Surrey, 1517–1547, fell in love with Lady Elizabeth Fitzgerald and wrote poems to her addressed to 'the Fair Geraldine'. Subsequently Geraldine was used occasionally but was not really established as a name until the 19th century when Samuel Taylor Coleridge used it in his poem Christabel, 1816. It has since become a standard name used as the feminine of Gerald, though the German Geralde is probably a more exact equivalent.

Variations and abbreviations: Geralda, Geralde (Ger), Geraldina, Geraldine (Fr), Gerolda, Gerrie, Gerry, Giralda (It), Jerrie, Jerry.

Examples: Geraldine McEwan, English actress.
Geraldine Chaplin, actress daughter of Charlie Chaplin.

GERDA

Origin/meaning: Norse mythology. Gerda was the wife of Frey and daughter of the frost giant Gymer.

According to legend Frey, the god of Spring, married Gerda, the frozen earth and their children represented the fruitfulness of the earth when Spring banishes Winter. Gerda was used by the Danish writer Hans Christian Andersen for his story *The Snow Queen*. The popularity of his stories in Britain led to the occasional use of the name. However, it is largely confined to Scandinavia and to Germany where it is also used as a short form of Gertrude.

GERMAINE

Origin/meaning: Latin 'a German'.

This is the feminine form of German(us) *q.v.* through the French form Germain.

Variation: Germana (It).

Examples: Germaine Greer, Australian writer and feminist.
Anne Louis *Germaine*, Mme de Staël, 1766–1817, French writer.

GERTRUDE

Origin/meaning: Old German 'spear-strength'.

This, like Hilda, was the name of one of the Valkyries, twelve maidens who in Norse mythology watched over the battlefields. They picked out the greatest warriors to be killed and took them straight to Valhalla to feast with Odin the chief of the gods. In the Middle Ages the name was popular not for its connections with Norse history but because of two saints. The first, Gertrude of Nivelles, 626–659, was a young abbess who encouraged Irish monks in their missionary work in what is now Holland and Belgium. The second was Gertrude of Helfta, 1256–1302, a German nun whose mystic experiences are recorded in *Revelations of Gertrude and Mechtilda*. Both Saints attracted a lot of devotion and many girls were named in their honour. Shakespeare gave the name to Hamlet's mother in his play *Hamlet*, 1600. In the 19th century, when Gertrude was fashionable, the spelling which had been variable was standardized as Gertrude.

Variations and abbreviations: Gartrude, Gattie, Gatty, Geldrude (It), Gerda, Gertie, Gertraud (Ger), Gertrud (Ger/Scand), Gertruda, Gertrudis (Ger), Gerty, Trudie, Trudy.

Examples: Gertrude (Gertie) Lawrence, 1898–1952, English-born musical comedy actress.
Gertrude Stein, 1874–1946, US writer.

GERVASIA (pron. Jerrvázia)

Origin/meaning: uncertain. Possibly Old German 'spear' or Celtic 'servant'.

A rare feminine form of the masculine name Gervase *q.v.* most often found in Italy.

GHISLAINE (pron. Zheezlen)

Origin/meaning: Old German 'pledge'.

131

This is a form of Gisela *q.v.* found mainly in North Germany, Belgium and the Netherlands.

Variation: Gislaine. See also Gisela.

GIACINTA (pron. Jiacinta)
Origin/meaning: Greek 'hyacinth'.

This is the Italian form of the name more familiar in English-speaking countries as Hyacinth or Jacintha. It was the name of one of the early Roman martyrs.

Variations and abbreviations: See Jacintha.

GILBERTA
Origin/meaning: Old German 'bright pledge'.

An Italian feminine form of Gilbert, occasionally used in England.

Variations and abbreviations: Gilberte (Fr), Giselberta (Ger), Gisberta (Ger).

GILDA
Origin/meaning: Old English 'golden'.

A medieval name which probably began as a nickname. The well known modern variations are often nicknames used for people with other names. The name may have been given some extra popularity by the film *Gilda*, 1946, starring Rita Hayworth.

Variations: Golda, Goldie, Goldy.

GILLIAN
Origin/meaning: from Julius, a Roman family name, possibly meaning 'dowry'.

This name developed in the Middle Ages as a feminine form of Julian. It's pronunciation shows clearly that initially the male version (Julian) was not distinguished from the female version in speech. Only when written down in documents was the feminine 'a' added to make Juliana. Gillian was one of the most popular medieval names, so that it became almost synonymous for the word girl, for example in the expression 'Every Jack must have his Jill'. Because of this jilt (Gillet) came eventually to mean a flirt in the 17th century; and a harlot in the 19th century. Not surprisingly the name rather went out of fashion but has been popular again in Britain in the mid-20th century.

Variations and abbreviations: Gill, Gillet, Gillie, Gilly, Giula (It),

Giuletta (It), Giuliana (It), Juli, Julia, Juliana, Juliann, Julie (Fr), Julienne, Juliane, Juliet, Julietta, Juliette (Fr), Julita, Julitta.

GINA (pron. Jéena)
Origin/meaning: Latin 'queen'.

This is a short form of Regina, a medieval name. In Italy it is also used as a short form of Luigina, the Italian form of Louise q.v. In the 20th century Gina has become accepted as an independent name.

Examples: Gina Lollobrigida, Italian film actress.
Gina Fratini, British dress designer.

GINETTE
Origin/meaning: uncertain. Gaulish French 'tribe'.

A French short form of Genevieve q.v. Ginette has become an extremely popular independent name in France. In English-speaking countries sometimes used as a form of Jeanette.

GINGER
Origin/meaning: a pet form of Virginia q.v. or a nickname for people with red hair.

Example: Ginger Rogers (Virginia McMath) US dancer and actress.

GINNY
Origin/meaning: either Latin from the patrician Roman family Verginius ('Spring') or Latin 'maidenly', 'virginal'.

A short form of Virginia q.v. now commonly used as an independent name.

GIRALDA
Origin/meaning: Old German 'spear-rule'.

An Italian feminine form of Gerald q.v.

Variations and abbreviations: See Geraldine.

GISELA
Origin/meaning: Old German 'pledge'.

A short form of the many German names beginning with this syllable eg Giselburga, Giselmunda. It has been an independent name for over a thousand years. Gisèle, daughter of Charles III

133

of France, 879–929, was married to Rollo Duke of Normandy as part of the peace treaty between the two men. It is still a popular name in France and is familiar in English-speaking countries because of the ballet *Giselle*, 1841, by the French composer Adolphe Adam.

Variations and abbreviations: Ghislaine, Gila, Gisa, Gisèle (Fr), Giselle, Gisella (It).

Example: Queen Gisela of Hungary, wife of St Stephen, 975–1038.

GLADYS
Origin/meaning: Latin 'lame' from Claudius, the name of two eminent Roman families.

This is one of many Welsh surviving forms of Roman names. After the fall of the Roman Empire and the invasions by Vikings and Saxons the Latin names practically disappeared for several centuries from Britain but survived in the Celtic areas furthest from the new invaders. In Cornwall, another Celtic area, Claudia survived as Gladuse. Gladys has spread outside Wales since the end of the 19th century possibly because it was used by the romantic novelist Ouida (Louise de la Ramée), 1839–1908, in her novel *Puck*, 1870.

Variations and abbreviations: Glad, Gladusa (Cornish), Gladuse (Cornish), Gwladus (Wel), Gwladys (Wel).

Example: Gladys Cooper, 1888–1971, English actress.

GLENNA
Origin/meaning: Celtic 'valley', 'glen'.

A recent form of Glynis *q.v.* based on the modern masculine form Glenn.

Variations and abbreviations: Glen, Glenda. See also Glynis.

Example: Glenda Jackson, English actress.

GLENNIS
Origin/meaning: Celtic 'valley', 'glen'.

A form of Glynis *q.v.*

Variations: See Glynis.

GLORIA
Origin/meaning: Latin 'glory'.

This Latin word was not used as a name until the late 19th century when it seems to have been introduced in the US. Early usage may have been due to the phenomenal popularity of the US film actress Gloria Swanson, 1898–1982. It is now a well established name.

Example: Gloria Steinem, US author and feminist.

GLYNIS
Origin/meaning: Welsh Celtic 'valley', 'glen'.

The feminine form of Glyn q.v. This Welsh name has become more widespread in the 20th century.

Variations and abbreviations: Glenda, Glenna, Glennis, Glenys, Glynnis, Glynwen.

Example: Glynis Johns, English actress.

GODIVA
Origin/meaning: Old English 'God's gift'.

This is the feminine name similar to the masculine Godfrey q.v. and Geoffrey q.v. Godiva (the Latin form of the original Godgifu) was the wife of Leofric, Earl of Chester, and a generous benefactress of religious institutions. When her husband imposed crippling taxes on the city of Coventry he joked that they would be remitted if she would ride naked through the market place at midday. Godiva took up the challenge and the people of Coventry respected her by remaining indoors while she did so.

GOLDIE
Origin/meaning: Old English 'gold'.

An unusual modern name similar to Gilda q.v. which probably began as a nickname.

Variations and abbreviations: Gilda, Golda, Goldy.

Examples: Golda (Goldie) Meir, 1898–1979, Israeli Prime Minister. Goldie Hawn, US actress.

GRACE
Origin/meaning: Latin 'grace'.

Although used in the Middle Ages this name really established itself in England in the 17th century. Puritans on both sides of the Atlantic used it in the sense of God's favour or bounty. It was also used in the same sense as the Greek word Charis – love, and so is connected with the names Charity and Charissa. In the 19th century, this name seems to have been used to mean physical rather than spiritual grace although Gracilia *q.v.* is a more accurate name in that respect. For a long time it was used to 'translate' the native Irish name Gráinne *q.v.* and therefore was often used where there were Irish connections. Princess Grace of Monaco (Grace Kelly), 1928–1982, is an example.

Variations and abbreviations: Engracia (Sp), Gracia (Med Eng), Gracie, Gratia, Gratiana, Grayce, Grazia (It).

Examples: Grace Darling, 1815–1842, English heroine who rescued survivors of the sinking ship the *Forfarshire*.
Grazia Deledda, 1875–1936, Italian writer.

GRACILIA
Origin/meaning: Latin 'slender'.

An uncommon name sometimes used instead of the more familiar Grace *q.v.*

GRÁINNE
Origin/meaning: 'love'.

One of the most popular of the native Irish names brought back into use by the Celtic revival at the beginning of the 20th century. For many years it was usual for the English to change it to Grace, which has a similar meaning. In Irish Celtic legend Gráinne, daughter of Cormac MacArt, one of the five kings of Ulster, was wooed by the Mighty Finn (Fionn), an enormous giant. However she ran off with his nephew Diarmuid.

Variations and abbreviations: Grace, Graidhne (Ir), Grainé, Grania. See Dermot.

GRANIA
Origin/meaning: Old Irish 'love'.
A form of Gráinne *q.v.*

GREER
Origin/meaning: Greek 'watchman'.

This is a Scottish surname derived from a short form of Gregory *q.v.* It has occasionally been used as a first name in imitation of Greer Garson the film actress.

GREGORIA
Origin/meaning: Greek 'watchman'.

A coined feminine version of Gregory q.v.

Variation: Greer.

GRETA
Origin/meaning: Persian?/Greek/Latin 'pearl' or French/English 'daisy'.

A German and Scandinavian short form of Margaret q.v. used as an independent name since the 19th century.

Variations: Greda, Greet (Dut), Grete, Gretchen (Ger), Gretel. See also Margaret.

Example: Greta Garbo, Swedish film actress.

GRISELDA
Origin/meaning: Old German 'grey battlemaid'.

This name was introduced into England by Chaucer, who used Boccaccio's story of Patient Griselda as the basis for the Clerk's Tale in his *Canterbury Tales*. The daughter of a poor charcoal burner, she was married by the local lord. Unable to believe in her great goodness, he gave her three trials. First he took away her daughter, saying he had killed her. Next he took her son, giving the same explanation. After twelve years of marriage, he told Griselda he was divorcing her to marry another, and stripping her of all her finery he returned her to her father's cottage. To compound her humiliation her husband sent her to prepare his new wife for the wedding ceremony. On seeing that even then Griselda endured and was patient, without any sign of jealousy, he revealed that the new 'wife' was their daughter whom she thought dead. The family was reunited and Griselda's exemplary patience was finally rewarded. The tale has been the inspiration of many plays, poems and stories, including Thomas Dekker's play *Patient Grissil*, 1603.

Variations and abbreviations: Grisel, Griseldis (Ger), Grisell, Grishilda, Grisilda, Grissel, Grizelda, Grizel (Scots), Grizzie, Selda, Zelda.

Example: Griselda Harvey, English actress.

GRIZEL
Origin/meaning: Old German 'grey battlemaid'.

137

The Scottish form of Griselda *q.v.* still much in use today.

Variations and abbreviations: See Griselda.

Example: Lady Grizel Baillie, 1665–1746, Scottish poet.

GUDRUN
Origin/meaning: Old English 'secret writing'.

Used by D. H. Lawrence in his novel *Women in Love*, 1920. It is a popular Scandinavian name but unusual elsewhere. In Scandinavian legend Gudrun was a model of patience, like Griselda. She was a princess captured by the King of Norway. When she refused to marry him he punished her by making her do servile work unsuited to her upbringing. Eventually she was rescued by her brother and her betrothed, Herwig, whom she married – having readily forgiven the king.

GUENDOLEN
Origin/meaning: Welsh 'white moon/circle/brow'.

An alternative spelling of Gwendolyn *q.v.*

GUINEVERE
Origin/meaning: Old Welsh 'fair and yielding' or 'white wave'.

This is the familiar form of the Old Welsh name Gwenhwyvar and contains the Welshword Gwyn, meaning fair, white or beautiful. It was the name given to the wife of the legendary King Arthur. His exploits and those of his Knights of the Round Table formed a large part of the store of Celtic folklore. As a result the name, in varying forms, is found in all the Celtic areas; Wales, Scotland, Ireland, Cornwall, Normandy and Brittany. Each area has its own versions of the stories, some of which are particular to that area alone. In the 12th and 13th centuries, the stories were popular in England, where romance poems were fashionable. Not surprisingly the form Guinevere which became the standard English form, is similar to the Norman French version Guinèvre. A native form shortened in typical English fashion, was Gaynor, currently gaining popularity today. In the last 50 years the Cornish form Jennifer has re-established itself as a main-stream name. Guinevere was the daughter of Leodograunce of Camelyard. Extremely beautiful (called 'the grey-eyed') she became the much loved wife of King Arthur but entered into an illicit liaison with Sir Lancelot and possibly also with Arthur's

138

nephew Mordred. Arthur was mortally wounded in battle against Mordred and Guinevere entered a nunnery. For a long time her name was considered a synonym for adultress. The tales of King Arthur were re-written by Alfred Lord Tennyson under the title *Idylls of the King*, 1859–1872. Closely based on the Medieval French and English versions they reflected the Victorian passion for early history. As a result many of the names revived by Tennyson for his poems were brought back into currency. They, like Guinevere, often had Welsh origins. Examples include Enid, Lynette, Gareth, Gawain, Lancelot, and Elaine.

Variations and abbreviations: Gaenor (Wel), Ganor, Gaynor (Med Eng), Gaynore, Genevieve, Ginevra (It), Guener, Guenever, Guenevere, Guenieve, Guenna, Gwenhwyvar (Old Wel), Gwenore (Med Eng), Jenifer (Cor), Jennifer, Vanora (Scots), Wander (Scots).

GUNILDA
Origin/meaning: Old Norse 'battle-strife'.

A name introduced into Britain by the Danish invaders of the 9th and 10th centuries. Both the mother and daughter of King Canute were called Gunhild. The name survived the Conquest because it was also used by the Normans. From Gunilda we get our word gun, as a result of the masculine tendency to give weapons feminine nicknames. In this case it was Lady Gunilda, a large catapult at Windsor Castle which was first given the name. It was then applied to cannon which were in effect catapults which used gunpowder. An example of a similar feminine nickname is Mons Meg, the famous 16th century cannon at Edinburgh Castle.

Variations and abbreviations: Gunhild (Ger), Gunhilda (Scand), Gunne, Gunnell, Gunnilla, Quennell.

GUSSIE
Origin/meaning: Latin 'venerable', 'majestic'.

A familiar form of Augusta, sometimes used as an independent name.

Variation: Gussy.

Example: Gussie (Gorgeous Gussie) Moran, US tennis player.

GWAWL
Origin/meaning: Welsh 'light'.

One of the native names coming back into use in Wales.

GWEN
Origin/meaning: Welsh 'white', 'fair'.

An independent name, the equivalent of the masculine Gwyn *q.v.* or a short form of names beginning with that syllable, particularly Gwendolyn *q.v.*

Variations: Gwenda, Gwenno.

Examples: Gwen Watford, English actress.
Gwen Ffrangcon-Davies, Welsh actress.

GWENDOLYN
Origin/meaning: Welsh 'white (fair) moon/circle/brow'.

There is some confusion over the meaning of the second part of this name. However there is no doubt that Gwen is the word 'white' which occurs in many Celtic names such as Guinevere and Gwenfron. Like several other Welsh names, especially Gladys and Gwyneth, Gwendolyn spread beyond Wales in the 19th century. Geoffrey of Monmouth, the Welsh chronicler, who reworked many of the old Welsh legends into a supposedly true history (c. 1147) on which many of the legends of the Court of King Arthur are based, relates the story of Guendoloena. She was the wife of Locrin, son of Brute the first king of Britain. When Locrin divorced her, Guendoloena raised an army and defeated him. She then revenged herself on Estrildis, Locrin's new wife, and Sabre their daughter by throwing them into the River Severn. Another legendary Gwendolyn was a fairy, seduced by King Arthur and mother of his child Gyneth. Realizing Arthur intended to desert her she offered him a cup of poisoned wine. Before he could taste it, a drop fell on his horse who bolted in pain, causing Arthur to drop the cup. The poison was so powerful that the fairy's castle and everything in it was destroyed, including Gwendolyn herself. Sir Walter Scott used the story in his poem *The Bridal of Triermain*, 1813, which probably helped introduce the name to a wider public. In some versions of the Tales of King Arthur, Gwendolyn is the name of Merlin's wife.

Variations and abbreviations: Guendolen, Guendoloena, Guenna, Gwen, Gwenda, Gwendolen (Wel), Gwendolin, Gwennie, Gwynne, Winnie, Wynne.

GWENFREWI
Origin/meaning: Welsh 'blessed reconciliation'.

140

The Welsh form of the name known in English as Winifred *q.v.* Sometimes confused with Guinevere.

GWENFRON
Origin/meaning: Old Welsh 'white breast'.

A name rarely found outside Wales. It has the same meaning as Bronwen, but is much less popular.

GWENHWYVAR
Origin/meaning: Old Welsh 'white wave' or 'fair and yielding'.

This is the original form of Guinevere, the name of the wife of King Arthur. The name spread in different forms throughout the Celtic areas where the legends were known. Today the Welsh usually use the shortened form Gaenor.

Variations and abbreviations: See Guinevere.

GWLADYS
Origin/meaning: Latin 'lame'.

The Welsh spelling of Gladys *q.v.*

GWYNETH
Origin/meaning: Welsh 'white/fair maiden'.

This may be the same name as Gyneth, the daughter of King Arthur and Gwendolyn *q.v.* Arthur had promised that if the child were a girl she should marry the bravest knight in his kingdom. One day a beautiful girl arrived at his court to exact the promise. During the tournament to determine her husband many brave knights were killed, including Merlin's son Vanoc. Merlin therefore placed a spell on her which left her in a trance for 500 years until she was awakened by the valiant Knight De Vaux. Another meaning sometimes given to this name is the area of North Wales known as Gwynedd.

Variations and abbreviations: Gwyn, Gwynaeth, Gwynedd, Gynedd.

Example: Gwyneth Dunwoody, British politician.

H

HADAOSAH
Origin/meaning: Hebrew 'myrtle'.

The original name of the Jewish heroine Esther *q.v.* It has been used occasionally since the 17th century when many unusual Biblical names came into use.

HAIDÉE (pron. Háyday)
Origin/meaning: Greek 'a caress' – sometimes given as 'modesty'.

A Greek name used by Byron in his poem *Don Juan*, 1819–1824, since when it has been given from time to time.

HANNAH
Origin/meaning: Hebrew 'grace', 'graceful'.

The name of the mother of the prophet Samuel (Sam. I ch.20), it became popular in Europe as Ann, Anna *q.v.* In the 17th century Hannah was revived as an independent name because its clear Biblical origins recommended it to the Puritans of England and New England.

Variations and abbreviations: Hana, Hanna, Hanni, Hannie, Hanny. See also Ann, Anna, Nancy.

Examples: Hannah Gordon, Scottish-born actress.
Hannah Arendt, 1906–1975, German-American political philosopher.

HARRIET
Origin/meaning: Old German 'home-ruler'.

An English feminine form of Henry from its Medieval English form Harry. Its main period of popularity was the 18th and 19th centuries. It has become fashionable in Britain in the 1980s.

Variations and abbreviations: Harri, Harrie, Harrietta, Harriette, Harrio, Harriot, Hat, Hattie, Hatty.

Examples: Harriet Beecher Stowe, 1811–1896, US novelist (*Uncle Tom's Cabin*).

Harriette Wilson, 1786–1855, English courtesan.

HASINA
Origin/meaning: Swahili 'good'.

An East African name.

Variation: Hasanati.

HAYLEY
Origin/meaning: Old English 'high clearing'.

A surname used as a first name. It became popular when English actress Hayley Mills was a child star in the late 1950s and early 60s.

HAZEL
Origin/meaning: Old German 'hazel-tree'.

One of the many names taken from flowers and trees at the end of the 19th century.

Example: Hazel O'Connor, English actress and singer.

HEATHER
Origin/meaning: Middle English 'heather'.

A name taken from the plant common on heathland. It was first used, with many other flower names, like Ivy, Lily and Primrose, at the end of the 19th century.

Examples: Heather Harper, English singer.
Heather Sears, English actress.

HEBE (pron. Héebee)
Origin/meaning: Greek 'youth'.

In Greek mythology Hebe was the daughter of Zeus and Hera. She was goddess of youth and Spring and cup-bearer to the gods on Mount Olympus. The name is an unusual one.

HEDDA
Origin/meaning: Old German 'struggle'.

A short form of Hedwig q.v. long used in Germany and Scandinavia as an independent name. Ibsen used it for the heroine of his play *Hedda Gabler*, 1890, perhaps because of its meaning. In pre-Conquest times this was also found as a man's name.

Variations and abbreviations: See Hedwig.

Example: Hedda Hopper, 1890–1966, US actress and gossip columnist.

HEDY
Origin/meaning: Old German 'struggle'.

A short form of Hedwig *q.v.* Like Hedda it is often found as an independent name.

Variations and abbreviations: See Hedwig.

Example: Hedy Lamarr (Hedwig Kiesler), Austrian/US film actress.

HEDWIG (pron. Hédveeg)
Origin/meaning: Old German 'battle struggle'.

This is the modern German form of a name which has existed for about 1500 years. In English-speaking countries it is best known through its short forms, Hedda and Hedy. An English form Avice *q.v.* developed in the Middle Ages from the French Havoise.

Variations and abbreviations: Avice (Eng), Avis, Edvige (Fr), Edwige (It), Haduwig, Hadwig, Heda, Hedda, Heddy, Hedy, Hedvig (Swed), Hetta, Hetti.

Examples: St Hedwig, 1174–1243, wife of Henry I (the Bearded) of Silesia. She and her husband founded many charitable institutions.
Edwige Feuillère, French actress.

HEIDI
Origin/meaning: Old German 'nobility'.

Popular German short form of Adalheid, the German form of Adelaide *q.v.* Now found in the US and Australia which have large populations of German origin. Its popularity may also be associated with the classic children's story, *Heidi*, by Johanna Spyri.

HELEN
Origin/meaning: Greek 'light' or 'bright'.

This was the name of an early saint, the Empress Helen(a), 255–330. She was the mother of the Emperor Constantine and is associated with the supposed discovery of the remains of the Holy Cross. She was popular in the Eastern church and the name is found in varying forms throughout Eastern Europe. It was brought to England by the Normans after the Conquest of 1066. However it had been used well before then in the Celtic areas of Scotland and Wales, because it was believed, without any historical foundation, that St Helen had been the daughter of one of the old British kings, the Prince of Colchester, also known as Old King Cole. In Medieval England and the Celtic areas the name was found as Ellen or Elena, which is closer to the original Greek, Ellayni. However, Helen and Helena were introduced into England during the 16th century when the influence of Renaissance classical learning was strong. The popularity of the new form may have been in part due to the story of Helen, the wife of the King of Sparta who sparked off the Trojan war by leaving her husband for the Trojan prince Paris. Helen is now probably the most common form of the name in English-speaking countries having been encouraged by the Romantic Movement at the beginning of the 19th century and having been fashionable after the Second World War. It has been used in some languages to form composite names such as Annelene.

Variations and abbreviations: Aileen (It), Eileen (Ir), Elaine (Old Fr), Elana, Elane, Elayne, Eleanor, Eleanora, Eleen, Elena (Sp/It), Eleni (Gr), Elenore, Eleonore, Elianora, Elinor, Elinore, Ella, Ellen, Ellene, Ellie, Elly, Ellyn, Elyn, Helena, Helene, Hélène (Fr), Ilene, Lana, Lena, Lenka (Russ), Lenore, Leonora, Nell, Nellie, Nelly.

Examples: Helen Reddy, Australian singer.
Helen Keller, 1880–1968, US lecturer and writer, born deaf and blind.

HELENA
Origin/meaning: Greek 'light' or 'bright'.

The Latinized form of the Greek name Helen *q.v.* first used in England in the 16th centry when the Renaissance, inspired by the learning of ancient Greece and Rome, made classical names popular. With Helen, it soon overtook the earlier form Ellen *q.v.*
Shakespeare used it in *A Midsummer Night's Dream* and in *All's Well That Ends Well*.

Variations and abbreviations: See Helen.

Example: Helena Rubenstein, 1871–1965, French cosmetician.

HELGA
Origin/meaning: Old Norse 'holy'.

This name was introduced into England by Scandinavian invaders in the 9th century. It is now rare in Britain but found in the US which has many people of Scandinavian origin. The Russian form Olga is currently popular.

Variation: Olga (Russ). See also Sanchia.

HELOISE (pron. Elloweeze)
Origin/meaning: Old German 'flourishing and strong'.

The Norman French version of an Old German name. The usual English form is Eloïse q.v.

Variations and abbreviations: See Eloïse.

Example: Heloise, d.1164, Lover of Abelard.

HEMA
Origin/meaning: Sanskrit 'gold'.

A name found throughout India. The masculine equivalent is Hemchandra q.v.

HENRIETTA
Origin/meaning: Old German 'home-ruler'.

This is the Latinized form of Henriette, the French feminine form of Henry (Henri). It was introduced into England by the French wife of Charles I. She was really Henriette Marie but became known by the Latin forms of her name Henrietta Maria, 1609–1669, because of the English dislike of all things French. The English adopted the name but usually in the Anglicized form Harriet q.v. Henrietta enjoyed some popularity in the late 18th century when Latinized names were fashionable, and is still used today.

Variations and abbreviations: Enrichetta (It), Enriqueta (Sp/Port), Etta, Ettie, Etty, Hat, Hattie, Hatty, Heinrike (Ger), Hendrika (Dut), Henka, Hendrickje, Henna, Henrie, Henrieta, Henriette (Fr), Henryetta, Hetti, Hettie, Hetty.

Examples: Hendrickje Stoffels, mistress of Rembrandt van Rijn, 1606–1669, Dutch painter.
Henrietta, Marchioness of Tavistock, daughter-in-law of the Duke of Bedford.

HEPHZIBAH
Origin/meaning: Hebrew: 'my delight is in her'.

146

This is a Biblical name. Hephzibah was the wife of Hezekiah, and was also a name used for the city of Jerusalem. It has been used since the 17th century fashion for Biblical names but only rarely.

Variations and abbreviations: Hephsibah, Hephsibar, Hepsibah, Hepsibar.

Example: Hephzibah Menuhin, US-born pianist, sister of Yehudi.

HERMIA
Origin/meaning: Greek mythology. Hermes was the messenger of the gods.

This is a feminine form of Hermes. Shakespeare, influenced by the 16th century fashion for classical names, used it for one of the characters in his play *A Midsummer Night's Dream*, 1594.

See Hermione.

HERMINE
Origin/meaning: Old German 'army man'.

The feminine form of Herman *q.v.* Sometimes confused with Hermione *q.v.*

Variations and abbreviations: Armande (Fr), Armine (Eng), Erminia (It), Herma, Herminia, Herminie.

HERMIONE (Pron. Hermýohnee)
Origin/meaning: Greek mythology. Hermes was the messenger of the gods.

This, like Hermia *q.v.* is a feminine form of Hermes. Shakespeare used it for the wife of Leontes in *The Winter's Tale*, 1611. Hermione was traditionally the name of Helen's daughter by Menalaos, the husband she deserted to join Paris in Troy. Sometimes confused with the German name Hermine *q.v.*

Examples: Hermione Baddeley, British actress.
Hermione Gingold, British actress.

HERO
Origin/meaning: Greek 'chosen one'.

In Greek mythology Hera was the sister/wife of Zeus, the supreme god. She was therefore worshipped as the Queen of the Heavens. The name occurs several times in Greek mythology. The best known example is Hero, a priestess of the goddess of love, Aphrodite, at Sestos on the European shore of the

Hellespont. Leander, her lover, swam across the Hellespont each night to visit her. One night he drowned. In despair Hero threw herself into the Hellespont and died as well. Shakespeare used it in *Much Ado About Nothing*, 1598, and it has been used occasionally since. The name has also been used for men, notably the Greek mathematicians Hero of Alexander, 1st century AD, and Hero the Younger, 10th century AD.

HESTER

Origin/meaning: uncertain. Probably Persian 'myrtle' or 'star'.

A form of Esther *q.v.* which was popular in the 17th century.

Variation: Hetty, Hestor.

Examples: Lady Hester Stanhope, 1776–1839, British eccentric and traveller.
Hester Bateman, 1709–1790, US silversmith.
Hester Thrale, 1741–1821, English writer.

HETTY

Origin/meaning: Persian 'myrtle' or Old German 'home-ruler'.

Either a familiar or old form of Hester, a form of Esther *q.v.* or a familiar form of Harriet *q.v.* and Henrietta *q.v.* the feminine forms of Henry.

Variations and abbreviations: Het, Hetti, Hettie.

Example: Hetty King, 1883–1972, music hall star (*All the Nice Girls Love a Sailor*).

HIERONYMA

Origin/meaning: Hebrew 'God is high'.

A rare feminine form of Jerome *q.v.* from the Greek/Latin form Hieronymus.

Variation: Jeromia.

HILARY

Origin/meaning: Medieval Latin 'cheerful'.

Like many medieval names the same form of Hilary was used for boys and girls (see Peter, Francis, Eustace). Unlike the others Hilary has never had a separate feminine form, perhaps because it went out of favour before there was time to develop one. Both as a masculine and feminine name it was revived in the 19th

148

century when medieval names were fashionable. It is as a girl's name that it has survived most successfully in the 20th century although it is still rare in North America and Australia.

Variations and abbreviations: Hilaria (Ger), Hillaria, Ilaria (It), Illaria, Yllaria.

HILDA
Origin/meaning: Old German/Old English 'battle'.

Hild was the chief of the twelve Valkyrie in Norse mythology who rode through battles choosing who was to be slain and taken in glory to Valhalla. Hilda is the Latin version of the original. The name achieved early popularity in England because of St Hilda, 614–680, who founded the famous monastery for both men and women at Whitby in North East England. The Venerable Bede in his *History of the English Church and People*, speaks highly of her. 19th century nostalgia made Hilda a popular name again at the end of the last century. It may also be used as a short form of names like Brunhilda and Hildegarde.

Variations: Hild, Hilde, Hildy, Hylda.

Example: Hylda Baker, English comedienne.

HILDEGARD
Origin/meaning: Old German 'knowledge of war'.

This has been a popular German name for over a thousand years. Although a Teutonic name it became an established Christian name because of St Hildegard, 1098–1179. She was abbess of a large convent at Rupertsberg and was famous for her mystical visions and the prophecies she interpreted from them. Her nickname was the 'Sibyl of the Rhine'. Many of her writings, which cover a wide range of topics such as medicine, interpretations of the gospels and lives of the saints still survive. Although never obsolete, the name's popularity was greatly boosted in the 19th century by the Romantic Movement and its rediscovery of old names. Hildegard was taken to the US by the 19th century German immigrants and has become well established there.

Variations and abbreviations: Hilda, Hilde, Hildegarde (Fr), Ildegarda (It).

Example: Hildegarde Neff, German film actress.

HIPPOLYTA

Origin/meaning: Greek 'unfettered horse'.

In Greek mythology Hippolyta was the Queen of the Amazons, a race of female warriors. She owed her fighting skills to her father Mars, the god of War. Mars gave his daughter a girdle which became famous, and one of the twelve labours of Hercules was to take it from her. Shakespeare in *A Midsummer Night's Dream*, 1594, makes Hippolyta the wife of Duke Theseus of Athens. The occasional use of the name in England probably results from Shakespeare's play. In Catholic countries it is used to honour the Roman martyr St Hippolytus.

Variation: Ippolita (It).

HOLLY

Origin/meaning: Old English 'holly tree'.

This is one of the flower names which came into fashion at the end of the 19th century. It is gradually creeping back into use especially in North America. This may be due in part to the success of the film, based on Truman Capote's novel, *Breakfast at Tiffany's*, in which Audrey Hepburn played a character called Holly Holightly.

HONEY

Origin/meaning: English 'honey'.

This is a 20th century name. It seems to have developed from the US habit of using the word as an endearment.

Abbreviation: Hon.

HONOR

Origin/meaning: Latin 'honour' or 'beauty'.

The preferred 17th century Puritan form of the medieval name Honora *q.v.*

Example: Honor Blackman, British actress.

HONORA

Origin/meaning: Latin 'honour' or 'beauty'.

A popular medievel name given to honour SS Honoria and Honorata. It was particularly popular in Ireland where the short form Nora developed into an independent name. In the 17th century when Puritans reacted against saints' names and favoured virtues as baptismal names, the straightforward word Honor was popular. In the 18th century when Latinized endings were fashionable, Honoria came back into favour.

Variations and abbreviations: Annora (Med Eng), Honor, Honorata, Honoria, Honour, Nora, Norah, Noreen, Onora.

HONORIA
Origin/meaning: Latin 'honour' or 'beauty'.

A variation of Honor *q.v.*

HOPE
Origin/meaning: Old English 'hope'.

This is one of the three virtues listed by St Paul in his first Epistle to the Corinthians. It was used by Puritans from the 16th century when they showed a strong preference for names of abstract virtues or words/names from the Bible. Some which they used, like Temperance or Chastity, have fallen out of use. However Hope remains popular today.

See also Nadine.

Example: Hope Lange, US actress.

HORATIA (pron. Horáyshea)
Origin/meaning: Latin, from Horatius, the name of a patrician Roman clan.

The feminine of Horace/Horatio. This name was given to the daughter (1801–1881) of Lady Hamilton and Admiral Horatio Nelson.

HORTENSIA
Origin/meaning: Latin from the name of the Roman family Hortensius. Probably meaning 'belonging to a garden'.

This classical name is one of those revived during the Renaissance period. It has been most successful in France.

Variations and abbreviations: Hortense (Fr), Ortensia (It).

HUBERTA
Origin/meaning: Old German/Old English 'bright thought'.

A rare feminine form of Hubert *q.v.*

151

HUGUETTE (pron. Oogétt)
Origin/meaning: Old German 'understanding' or 'thought'.

A French feminine form of Hugh q.v. Rare in English-speaking countries.

HULDA
Origin/meaning: Old Norse/Old German 'gracious' or 'well-disposed'.

This name was taken to the US by German and Scandinavian immigrants and is now well established there. It is almost unknown in Britain. It is also an alternative spelling of Huldah q.v.

HULDAH
Origin/meaning: Hebrew 'mole'.

This is a Biblical name. Huldah was a minor prophetess of the 7th Century BC. She is referred to in the Second Book of Kings (ch.22 v.14). Huldah had some use in the 17th century period of Biblical names.

Variation: Hulda (Ger).

HYACINTH
Origin/meaning: Greek 'hyacinth flower', 'hyacinth jewel' (red topaz, zircon or garnet).

Hyacinth is really a masculine name from a character in Greek mythology (see Hyacinth(m)). The usual English feminine form is Jacintha q.v. However Hyacinth has always been a rare masculine name in English-speaking countries and since the end of the 19th century when flower names became fashionable, it has occasionally been used as a girl's name.

Variations and abbreviations: See Jacintha.

HYPATIA (pron. Hipáyshea)
Origin/meaning: Greek. Uncertain.

In 1853, Charles Kingsley, author of *The Water Babies*, and *Hereward the Wake*, wrote a novel based on the life of Hypatia (375–415) of Alexandria. She was a philosopher and teacher who was respected throughout the known world. She was killed in a riot by Christians inflamed against all non-Christian philosophy by their Bishop, Cyril of Alexandria. As a result of Kingsley's novel, the name has been occasionally used in England.

I

IANTHE (pron. Eeánnthee)
Origin/meaning: Greek 'violet flower'.

A name from Greek mythology; Ianthe was one of the sea nymphs. The name has been used from time to time in literature. Byron dedicated his poem *Childe Harolde*, 1817, to Ianthe, a pseudonym for Lady Charlotte Harley. Shelley's daughter, b.1813, was also named Ianthe.

Variation: Iantha. See also Violet and Hyacinth.

IDA
Origin/meaning: Old German 'industrious'.

Possibly derived from an old German name Idaberga, the name was introduced into England by the Normans. It was used in the Middle Ages but then fell out of favour. In the 19th century it was revived as part of a general interest in medieval culture and its popularity was boosted first by Tennyson's poem *The Princess*, 1847, then by the Gilbert and Sullivan operetta *Princess Ida*, 1884, which was based on it. It has been rarely used since the Second World War.

Example: Ida Lupino, US film actress and director.

IDONEA (pron. Iddonéeah)
Origin/meaning: Old Norse 'Idhuna' the goddess of Spring, or possibly Latin 'suitable'.

A popular medieval name, rare today.

Variations and abbreviations: Edony, Idonia, Idony.

IFE (pron. Eefée)
Origin/meaning: Yoruba 'love'.

A popular Nigerian name.

See also Amy, Lerato.

153

IGNATIA (pron. Ignáyshea)

Origin/meaning: uncertain. Possibly Latin 'fiery'.

A feminine form of Ignatius *q.v.* Usually used by Catholics.

ILA

Origin/meaning: Sanskrit 'world'.

ILEANA

Origin/meaning: Greek 'from Troy'.

Variation: Eliana.

IMAGINA

Origin/meaning: uncertain. Possibly Old Irish 'girl', 'daughter'.

An alternative spelling of Imogen *q.v.* However it may also be a quite separate name since it is occasionally found in Germany in the Middle Ages before Imogen's first appearance in the 16th century.

Variation: Imagine. See also Imogen.

IMOGEN

Origin/meaning: uncertain. Sometimes given as Old Irish 'girl' or 'daughter' or Greek 'beloved child'.

The regular use of this name in England dates from the present century, although a similar name, Imagina, was used in Europe in the Middle Ages. The source of the modern name is Shakespeare's play *Cymbeline*. However it appears that Shakespeare had intended Innogen which was the name used by Holinshed from whom Shakespeare took his plot. Innogen was definitely an established, though uncommon, name. Imogen therefore appears to be the result of a printer's error, and its meaning is derived from Innogen.

Variations and abbreviations: Imagina, Imogene, Imogine, Immy, Innagon, Innogen.

Example: Imogen Holst, d.1984, English composer and folklorist.

INDIA

Origin/meaning: Sanskrit 'river' or 'river Indus'.

The name of the country has sometimes been used by people who were born there. It was used for a grand-daughter of Earl Mountbatten, who had been the last Viceroy of India.

INDIRA
Origin/meaning: Sanskrit 'moon'.

This is based on the same word as the name Indu q.v.

Example: Indira Gandhi, 1917–1984, Indian Prime Minister.

INDU (pron. Indhú)
Origin/meaning: Sanskrit 'moon'.

A common Indian name. Indu was a famous female scholar who lived many thousands of years ago.

See also Chandra, Indira, Selina.

INEZ
Origin/meaning: Greek 'pure', 'chaste'.

The Anglicized version of Ines, which is the Spanish equivalent of Agnes, q.v.

Variations and abbreviations: Ines, Inessa, Ynes, Ynez.

INGARET
Origin/meaning: Old Welsh 'much loved'.

An English form of the Welsh Angharad q.v.

Variations: Anchoret, Ancret, Ingaretta.

INGE
Origin/meaning: Old Norse/Old German Ingvi or Ing, the name of one of the heroes of the Teutonic tribes.

This name is extremely popular in Scandinavia and German-speaking countries. It can be an independent name but it is frequently used as a double name with others eg Inge-Maria, Inge-Rose. Alternatively it may be a short form of names like Ingrid or Ingeborg. There is a masculine equivalent Ingo.

Variations: Ing, Inga. See also the masculine names Ingram and Ingmar.

INGRID
Origin/meaning: Old Norse/Old German 'Ingvi's ride' or 'beloved of Ingvi'.

One of the many German and Scandinavian names containing the name of the hero-god Ingvi or Ing. This name has become familiar in English-speaking countries because of the Swedish film actress Ingrid Bergman, 1915–1982.

Abbreviations: Inga, Inge, Inger. See also the masculine names Ingram and Ingmar.

INNOCENTIA
Origin/meaning: Latin 'harmless' 'innocent'.

Italian feminine form of Innocent q.v. sometimes used in English-speaking countries.

Variation: Innozentia.

IOLA (pron. Yóhla)
Origin/meaning: either a Welsh form of Julia q.v. or Greek 'dawn cloud'.

Iola is the name of a princess in Greek mythology. She was loved by Hercules who took her prisoner. An unusual name.

Variation: Iole.

IOLANTHE
Origin/meaning: Latin 'violet flower'.

A German form of the French name Yolande q.v. Probably influenced by the Greek name Ianthe q.v. Gilbert and Sullivan's Opera *Iolanthe* was first performed in 1882.

Variations and abbreviations: Iola, Jola, Jolanthe. See also Violet.

IONA (pron. Eye-ówna)
Origin/meaning: either Greek 'violet coloured stone' or the Scottish Hebridean island.

Although the first meaning is sometimes given the use of the name in Scotland indicates that the island is its real source. This may have been due to its connections with Celtic Christianity, for it is the site of St Columba's most important monastery founded about 563.

IRENE (pron. Eiréenee or Éireen)
Origin/meaning: Greek 'peace'.

Eirene is the Greek goddess of peace. In Britain, where the name appeared at the end of the 19th century and flourished in the first two decades of the 20th century, the first pronunciation is more usual. In North America and Australia the two syllable version is more usual, perhaps because it was used by people who had seen it written down rather than by people who had heard it. Although its use in English-speaking countries is comparatively recent, the name is a very old one. St Irene was burned alive in 304 for refusing to eat food which had been sacrificed to the gods, and for keeping Christian books.

Variations and abbreviations: Eirena, Eirene, Irena, Irina (Slav), Ira, Rena, Rene, Rina.

Examples: Irene Worth, US actress.
Irene Handl, British comedienne.
Irene, Byzantine Empress who began life as an Athenian orphan, 752–803.

IRIS
Origin/meaning: Greek 'rainbow'.

In Greek mythology Iris was a goddess who acted as the messenger of the gods. She was personified as a rainbow bridging heaven and earth and the iris flower was given its name because of its rainbow coloured varieties. The use of the name, which began in the 19th century, when flower names were popular, is probably intended to evoke the iris flower rather than the goddess.

Examples: Irish Murdoch, British novelist.
Iris Williams, Welsh singer.

IRMA
Origin/meaning: Old German 'universal' or from the name of the Teutonic god-hero Irmin.

A short form of the many German names which begin with this syllable. Now used in German-speaking countries as an independent name and occasionally found in English-speaking countries. The English form is the currently fashionable Emma q.v.

Variations: Emma (Eng), Erma.

Example: Irma Kurtz, US-born Agony Aunty and writer.

IRMGARD (pron. I'mguard)
Origin/meaning: Old German 'under Irmin's protection'.

Irmin was one of the Teutonic god-heroes who pre-dated Christianity. This old name was revived in the 19th century in

157

Germany when early names were fashionable. It is related to the English names Emma and Ermintrude *q.v.* One of its short forms – Irma – is found as an independent name.

Variations and abbreviations: Irma, Irmchen, Irmela, Irmengard, Ermengard (Old Ger), Ermengarda (It).

IRMINTRUDE
Origin/meaning: Old German 'universal strength'.

An alternative spelling of Ermintrude *q.v.*

ISA
Origin/meaning: Either a short form of Isabel (the Scottish form of Elizabeth) 'God is my satisfaction' or Old German 'iron'.

A name found mainly in the US and Scotland.

ISABEL
Origin/meaning: Hebrew: 'God is my satisfaction'.

This is an early medieval development of Elizabeth *q.v.* which began in Spain and Provence. Elizabeth became Ilsabeth and then Islabeau. Because beau is the French masculine adjective for handsome it seemed logical to change it to the feminine equivalent – belle. The name thus soon became Isabelle in France and in neighbouring Spain. Different spellings – Isabel, Isobel, Isabella – were interchangeable. Indeed for many years Isabel and Elizabeth were also used interchangeably. The name came to England with Isabella of Angoulême who married King John in 1200. In 1308 Edward II married Isabella of France and in 1396 Richard II married yet another Isabella of France. The name became well established in Medieval England although Elizabeth was also used. The name was introduced separately into Scotland from France which maintained a specially close relationship with that country. In Scotland where it has always been more popular than Elizabeth, the usual spelling is Isobel. Isa, Ishbel and Isla are three specifically Scottish short forms. In the 18th century the Latinized Isabella with the short form Belle, was the usual form.

Variations and abbreviations: Bell, Bella, Belle, Ib, Ibbie, Ibby, Ilsa (Ger), Ilse (Ger), Isa (Scot), Isabeau (Fr), Isabella (It), Isabelle, Isabetta, Ishbel (Scot), Isobel (Scot), Issie, Issy, Izabel, Ysabel.

Example: Isabella of Castile, 1451–1504, who united Spain by her marriage to Ferdinand of Aragon and funded Christopher Columbus on his 1492 voyage of discovery.

ISABELLA
Origin/meaning: Hebrew 'God is my satisfaction'.

An Italian and Spanish form of Isabel q.v. used in 18th century England.

Variations and abbreviations: Bella, Belle, Ella. See also Isabel, Elizabeth.

ISADORA
Origin/meaning: uncertain. Possibly Greek 'gift of Isis' (an Egyptian goddess).

The feminine form of an ancient Greek masculine name, Isidore. Now found mainly in Spain.

Variation: Isidora.

Example: Isadora Duncan, 1878-1927, American dancer and choreographer.

ISEULT
Origin/meaning: either Old Welsh 'fair one' or Old German 'ice-rule'.

This is the Celtic form of Isolda q.v.

ISLA (pron. Eyella)
Origin/meaning: Hebrew: 'God is my satisfaction'.

This is a Scottish short form of Isobel, which is itself a predominantly Scottish form of Elizabeth q.v.

Example: Isla St Clair, Scottish folk-singer.

ISMENIA
Origin/meaning: Greek 'learned'.

A medieval name possibly connected with Ismene (pron. Isménnee) the daughter of Oedipus and Jocasta. There is a 12th century romantic poem entitled *Ismene and Ismenias* which was incorporated in the poem *Confessio Amantis* by the 14th century English poet John Gower. Shakespeare used Gower's version as the basis of his play *Pericles of Athens*, 1608.

Variations and abbreviations: Ismay, Ismena, Ismene, Ysmena.

ISOBEL

Origin/meaning: Hebrew 'God is my satisfaction'.

The usual Scottish spelling of Isabel *q.v.* a variation of Elizabeth, which is extremely popular in Scotland. The form Elizabeth never gained favour there, perhaps because it was the name of the charismatic Elizabeth I, Queen of England, who at the time was regarded as an enemy of Scotland.

Variations and abbreviations: See Isabel, Elizabeth.

Example: Isabel Baillie, d.1983, English opera singer.

ISOLDA

Origin/meaning: either Old Welsh 'fair one' or Old German 'ice-rule'.

It seems likely that the Old Welsh Essylt and the Old German Isold developed separately but became synonymous before the Conquest. Isolda is the Latinized form of the German name, while Iseult and its variations which came to England with the Normans, seems to derive from the Celtic/Welsh version which would have been used in the Celtic areas of Normandy and Brittany. The romantic legend of Tristan and Isolde made it a popular medieval name. Interest in medieval culture and the Arthurian legends among writers like Tennyson, revived the popularity of the name in the 19th century as did Wagner's opera *Tristan und Isolde*. In the legend Isolda is brought from Ireland by Tristan (Tristram) to marry Mark, King of Cornwall. She accidentally drinks the love potion intended for her wedding night while in the company of Tristan. The guilty passion which they feel for each other, and the jealousy of Sir Tristan's wife, Isolda of the white hand, bring about the tragic death of both the lovers.

Variations and abbreviations: Essylt, Isaut, Iseut, Iseult, Isold, Isolde (Ger), Isolt, Isota, Yseult, Ysold, Ysolda, Ysolde, Ysolt, Ysonde.

ITA

Origin/meaning: Old Irish 'thirsty'.

A native Irish name, sometimes 'translated' into the English Ida *q.v.*

Variations: Ida, Ide, Ytha.

Example: St Ita, d.570, Irish abbess and ascetic.

IVY

Origin/meaning: Old English 'ivy plant'.

One of the flower and plant names which were popular at the turn of the century but went out of favour before the Second World War.

Examples: Ivy Benson, English Band leader.
Ivy Compton Burnett, 1884-1969, British novelist.

J

JACINTHA (pron. Jassinta)
Origin/meaning: Greek 'hyacinth flower', 'hyacinth jewel' (red topaz, zircon or garnet).

This is the English feminine version of the masculine Hyacinth q.v. It was a Greek name from the mythological character loved by Apollo and killed by Zephyr, the West Wind. It came into early use as a Christian name because there were several early Roman martyrs, men and women, who bore the name. St Giacinta (the Italian form of the name) is listed in the Roman martyrology. In Britain it has usually been considered a Catholic name. However the 19thc century vogue for flower names resulted in the English word Hyacinth sometimes being used as a flower name for girls, rather than a masculine saint's name.

Variations and abbreviations: Cynthia, Cynthie, Giacinta (It), Hyacinth, Hyacintha, Hyacinthe, Hyacinthia, Hyacinthie (Ger), Jacinta (Sp), Jacinthe, Jacynth.

JACOBA
Origin/meaning: uncertain. Possibly Hebrew 'supplanter'.

A feminine form of James used mainly in Scotland by followers of the Jacobite (Stuart) cause.

Variation: Jacobina. See also Jamesina, Jacqueline, Jacquetta.

Example: Jacoba of Bavaria, 1401–1436, a beautiful princess four times married, the last two times while already married.

JACQUELINE
Origin/meaning: uncertain. Possibly Hebrew 'supplanter'.

This is a feminine form of James from the French Jacques. It was used in the Middle Ages but has been most popular in the 20th century.

Variations and abbreviations: Jacki, Jackie, Jacky, Jaclyn, Jacquelyn, Jacqui. See also: Jacoba, Jacquetta, Jamesina.

Examples: Jacqueline du Pré, British cellist.
Jacqueline Kennedy Onassis, US socialite, wife of the late President Kennedy.

JACQUETTA
Origin/meaning: uncertain. Possibly Hebrew 'supplanter'.

A French feminine form of James from the French masculine form Jacques. It was known in the Middle Ages and Shakespeare used it in *Love's Labour's Lost*, 1594. It has never been as successful in English-speaking countries as the alternative Jacqueline.

Variations: Jacquenetta, Jacquenette, Jacquette, Jaquetta.

Example: Jacquetta Hawkes, British writer and archaeologist.

JADE
Origin/meaning: Old French/Spanish 'jade'.

The name of this greenish or bluish semi-precious stone has been used as a name since the late 19th century when gem names (Pearl, Ruby etc) became fashionable. It has been most successful in Spanish speaking countries. In English jade is an old fashioned word for a worn-out horse or a hussy.

Variation: Ijada (Sp).

Example: Jade Jagger, daughter of rock singer Mick Jagger.

JAEL
Origin/meaning: uncertain. Usually given as 'female wild goat' but may mean 'Jehovah is God'.

Jael was a Kenite who murdered Sisera, a guest, by driving a tent nail through his temple (Judges 4 and 5). This was justified by the fact that he was an enemy of her people and she was called 'Blessed above women'. As a Biblical name it was used from time to time by Puritans in England and North America but the gruesome circumstances seem to have prevented the name achieving great popularity.

JAMEELA
Origin/meaning: Arabic 'beautiful'.

A popular Muslim name.

Variation: Jamila. See also Belle, Nabulungi, Nomble.

163

JAMESINA
Origin/meaning: uncertain. Possibly Hebrew 'supplanter'.

A feminine form of James *q.v.* used mainly in Scotland in the 17th and 18th centuries by adherents of the Jacobite cause.

See also Jacoba, Jacqueline, Jacquetta.

JAN
Origin/meaning: Hebrew 'Jehovah has favoured'.

A short form of Jane (a derivative of Joan). Also a short form of Janice which developed from Jane.

Variations and abbreviations: Jana, Janetta, Janette, Janine, Janna (Ger). See also Joan.

Example: Jan Morris, English writer.

JANE
Origin/meaning: Hebrew 'Jehovah has favoured'.

This feminine form of John came into fashion in England in the 16th century. It usurped Joan, the original native form, and was considered more refined because, like the Scottish form Janet, it developed from the French form Jehane. Although Joan has made a come-back since the 19th century, and there are many alternative forms of the name such as Janice, Jean and Janet, Jane remains one of the most consistently used feminine names in English-speaking countries. Jana, a 'Latinized' form of Jane, has recently made an appearance in the US, probably because of its similarity to the German familiar form Janna.

Variations and abbreviations: Jana, Janey, Janie, Jayne. See also Joan.

Examples: Jane Austen, 1775–1817, English novelist.
Jane Russell, US film actress.
Jayne Mansfield, 1932–1967, US film actress.

JANET
Origin/meaning: 'Little Jane' a diminutive of Jane. Hebrew 'Jehovah has favoured'.

This has long been an independent name rather than a mere pet form of Jane. It was originally associated with Scotland but is now found in all English-speaking countries.

Variations and abbreviations: Jennet (Med Eng), Jonet, Netta, Nettie. See also Joan.

Examples: Janet Suzmann, South African actress.
Janet Baker, English singer.

JANICE
Origin/meaning: Hebrew 'Jehovah has favoured'.

A US form of Joan, probably from Jan, the short form of another variation, Jane. It has now spread to other English-speaking countries.

Variation: Janis. See also Joan.

JASMINE
Origin/meaning: Arabic/Persian 'jasmine flower'.

This is the English version of the Arabic Yasmin. Like other flower names it came into use at the end of the 19th century.

Variations and abbreviations: Gelsomina (It), Jasmin (Ger), Jasmina, Jessamine (Fr), Jessamy, Jessamyn, Jess, Jessie, Jessy, Yasmin (Arab).

JAYASHREE (pron. Jáyshree)
Origin/meaning: Sanskrit 'victory'.

A popular Indian name.

See also Victor, Vijay (masculine) and Victoria.

JEAN
Origin/meaning: Hebrew 'Jehovah has favoured'.

This is a Scottish form of the English name Joan. It has long been popular outside Scotland. Jean comes via the Old French form Jehane which was used in Scotland because of the close cultural and political ties between Scotland and France.

Variations and abbreviations: Jeanie, Jeanne (Fr), Jeannette. See Joan. See also Siné.

Examples: Jean Rook, British journalist.
Jean Simmons, British actress.
Jean Muir, British fashion designer.

JEANNE (pron. Sjhann)
Origin/meaning: Hebrew 'Jehovah has favoured'.

The French form of Joan/Jane *q.v.* Jeanette, Little Jeanne, is the equivalent of Janet.

Variations: Jeanette, Jeanine, Jeannette, Jeannine.

Example: Jeanne Moreau, French actress.

JEMIMA
Origin/meaning: Hebrew 'dove'.

This is a 17th century Biblical name. Jemima was one of Job's three daughters. The other two were Keziah and Kerenhappuch. The short form Jem is also an old short form of James and Jemima may therefore have been used as a feminine form of James. It is currently being revived along with other names popular at the same time such as Jessica, Abigail and Sarah.

Variations and abbreviations: Jamima, Jem, Jemie, Jemmie, Jemmy, Mimie.

JENNET
Origin/meaning: 'Little Joan' from the Hebrew 'Jehovah has favoured'.

A medieval form of names such as Jane/Jean/Janet, derived from Joan *q.v.*

Variations and abbreviations: See Janet and Joan.

JENNIE/JENNY
Origin/meaning: since the 1920s this has been the most common as a short form of the newly fashionable name Jennifer.

Prior to that it was considered a familiar form of Jane or Jean. In the US in the 1870s it was very fashionable and was even used as an independent name. An example is Jennie (Jeannette) Jerome, the American heiress who married Lord Randolph Churchill, 1874, and was the mother of Sir Winston Churchill.

JENNIFER
Origin/meaning: Old Welsh 'fair and yielding' or 'white wave'.

This is the Cornish form of the Old Welsh name Gwenhywvar (Guinevere). Variations of Guinevere were found in all the Celtic areas, including Cornwall, for the Tales of King Arthur formed an integral part of their folklore. It appeared in the rest of England in the 1920s and reached a peak of popularity in the

1940s. It has now established itself as a standard name in all the English-speaking countries. Gaynor, the Medieval English form of the same name, is also beginning to establish itself. Jennifer is sometimes mistaken for a form of Geneva which means juniper.

Variations and abbreviations: Jen, Jenifer, Jenni, Jenny. See Guinevere.

Example: Jennifer Jones, US actress.

JENYTH
Origin/meaning: Hebrew: 'Jehovah has favoured'.

A medieval diminutive form of Joan, similar to Jennet and Janet.

Variation: Janith. See also Joan.

JERRY
Origin/meaning: Old German 'spear-rule'.

A short form of Geraldine q.v. popular in the US where it is often used as an independent name.

Variations and abbreviations: See Geraldine.

Example: Jerry Hall, US model.

JESSAMINE
Origin/meaning: Arabic/Persian 'jasmine flower'.

A French form of Jasmine q.v.

Variation: Jessamyn.

JESSICA
Origin/meaning: Hebrew 'God beholds'.

Used by Shakespeare as the name of Shylock's daughter in The Merchant of Venice. It is probably a version of Iscah (Gen.11 ch.29). Rare, even among Jewish people, until the mid-20th century. It is now very popular.

Variations and abbreviations: Gessica (It), Jesca, Jess, Jessalin, Jessie, Jessy.

Examples: Jessica Tandy, British actress.
Jessica Mitford, British writer.

JESSIE
Origin/meaning: Hebrew 'Jehovah has favoured'.

167

A Scottish short form of Janet, itself a feminine form of John. Now found as an independent name.

Sometimes used as a short form of Jessica or Jasmine *q.v.*

Variations and abbreviations: Jess, Jessy.

Example: Jessie Matthews, 1907–1981, British musical comedy star.

JILL
Origin/meaning: from Julius, a Roman family name, possibly meaning 'dowry'.

This short form of Gillian/Juliana has been used since the Middle Ages. It is currently popular as an independent name.

Variations and abbreviations: See Gillian.

Examples: Jill Clayburgh, US actress.
Jill Bennett, British actress.
Jilly Cooper, British writer.

JO
Origin/meaning: a short form of names like Josephine and Joanna *q.v.*

Example: Jo Durie, British tennis player.

JOAN
Origin/meaning: Hebrew 'Jehovah has favoured'.

The most usual Medieval English feminine form of John *q.v.* It was often spelt Johan, which shows its connection with other North European forms of the name. It was so popular in the Middle Ages it eventually came to be considered vulgar. From the 16th–19th centuries Jane, which developed from the French feminine Jehanne was considered more acceptable. Since the 19th century when medieval names came suddenly back into fashion, Joan has been firmly re-established alongside Jane. The medieval diminutive of Joan was Jonet whereas the diminutive of Jane was Janet.

Variations and abbreviations: Gianna (It), Giannina (It), Giovanna (It), Hanna (Ger), Jan, Jana (US), Janella, Janelle, Janet, Janetta, Janette, Janey, Jania, Janice, Janie, Janine, Janis, Janith, Janka, Janna (Ger), Jannelle, Jany, Janyte, Jayne, Jean (Scots), Jeanette (Fr), Jeanie, Jeanne (Fr), Jeannette (Fr), Jeannine (Fr), Jennet, Jenni, Jennie, Jenny, Jenyth, Jess, Jessie,

Jessy, Jinny, Jo-Ann, Joan, Joana, Joanna, Joanne (Fr), Johanna (Ger), Joni, Jonie, Juana (Sp/Port), Juanita (Sp/Port), Netta, Nettie, Shena (Scot), Sheena (Scot), Sian (Wel), Siné (Scot), Sinead (Ir).

Examples: Joan of Navarre, 1370–1437, wife of Henry IV of England.
Joan Sutherland, Australian opera singer.
Joan Collins, English actress.
Joni Mitchell, US singer/song writer.

JOANNA
Origin/meaning: Hebrew 'Jehovah has favoured'.

This is the Latinized version of the medieval feminine form of John, Joan. It was sometimes used in the Middle Ages although the name Jo(h)anna in Latin medieval documents was almost certainly Joan when spoken. In the 18th century Joanna was used as an independent name when Latinized endings for feminine names were fashionable. In the mid-20th century Joanne, the French version, has been more popular than Joanna.

Variations and abbreviations: Jo, Joana, Jo-Ann, Joanne (Fr), Johanna (Ger).

Example: Joanna Lumley, English actress.

JOCASTA
Origin/meaning: Greek 'shining moon'.

In Greek legend Jocasta is the mother of Oedipus who unwittingly kills his father and marries his mother. When he realizes what he has done Oedipus goes mad and Jocasta kills herself. This rather gloomy tale gave Freud the name Oedipus complex, for his theory that a child is attracted to the parent of the opposite sex and therefore jealous of the other parent.

Example: Jocasta Innes, English writer.

JOCELYN
Origin/meaning: Old German 'man of the Goths'.

This pre-Conquest name was introduced into England by the Normans and until the 20th century was used exclusively as a male name. Recently, probably because of its similarity to two other feminine names, Joyce and Lynn, it has been used for girls

169

rather than boys.

Variations and abbreviations: Joceline, Jocelyn, Josceline, Joscelyn, Joss, Josselyn, Joycelin.

Example: Josceline Dimbleby, British cookery writer.

JODIE
Origin/meaning: Hebrew 'Jewish woman', 'from Judah'.

A modern diminutive of Judith q.v. currently a vogue name in North America, where it originated.

Variations: Jodi, Jody. See also Judith.

Example: Jodie Foster, US actress.

JOELLE
Origin/meaning: Hebrew 'Jehovah is god'.

A US feminine form of Joel q.v. created by adding a typical French feminine ending although it is not a French name. Joelle is found in France as a surname unconnected with Joel.

Variations: Joella, Joellen.

JONQUIL
Origin/meaning: the name of a flower similar to the narcissus.

This is one of the more unusual flower names which became popular at the end of the 19th century.

JORDAN
Origin/meaning: Hebrew 'flowing down'.

Jordan has been used as a masculine and feminine name since the Crusaders brought back the name of this river from the Holy Land in the Middle Ages.

Variations and abbreviations: Jordane, Jordane (Fr), Gordana (It).

JOSEPHINE
Origin/meaning: Hebrew 'May Jehovah increase'.

This is a French feminine diminutive form of Joseph q.v. meaning 'little Josepha'. Josepha or the French Josèphe were the original feminine forms of Joseph but nowadays they are neglected in favour of Josephine. The name came into use at the beginning of the 19th century because of Napoleon Bonaparte's wife (1763-1814). She was born Marie Joséphine Rose Tascher de la Pagerie, but was known throughout Europe as the Empress Josephine.

Variations and abbreviations: Fifi, Fina, Giuseppa (It), Giuseppina (It), Jo, Jo-Jo, Jolene (US), Josée (Fr), Josefa (Ger), Josefina (Sp/Port), Josefine, Josepha, Joséphine (Fr), Josette, Josie, Josy, Pepita (Sp), Peppina (It).

Examples: Josephine Butler, 1828-1906, British socialist reformer. Josephine Baker, 1905-1975, US dancer and singer.

JOSIE
Origin/meaning: Hebrew 'May Jehovah increase'.

A short form of Josephine used mainly in the US.

Variations: Josy. See also Josephine.

JOSS(E)
Origin/meaning: French, Celtic 'champion'.

An early medieval form of the name Joyce q.v. It was used for men as well as women.

Variations: See Joyce.

JOY
Origin/meaning: Latin 'rejoicing', French 'joy'.

A medieval Christian name Joy was rediscovered in the 19th century. Unlike some of the more difficult medieval names it remains firmly established in the 20th century. It is also used as a short form of Joyce.

Variations: Joia, Joya. See also Laetitia.

Example: Joy Adamson, 1910-1980, Kenyan wild-life expert renowned for her work with lions.

JOYCE
Origin/meaning: French Celtic 'champion'.

The English form of Judoc(us), the name of a Breton Saint, through the interim form Josse. Like many medieval names the same form was used for men and women, the distinction only being made in the Latin documents of the time which had separate written forms for male and female names. In the 19th century Joyce was one of a large number of medieval and

171

pre-Conquest names which came back into use. However, during this second period of popularity it has become an almost exclusively feminine name. Because of this the similar sounding name Jocelyn, which was originally a masculine name, is now also assumed to be a girl's name.

Variations and abbreviations: Joice, Joisse (Med. Fr), Josse (Med Eng), Joycelin.

Example: Joyce Grenfell, 1919–1979, British comedienne.

JUDITH

Origin/meaning: Hebrew 'Jewish woman', 'from Judah'.

Judith was the heroine of the Apocryphal Book of Judith. She saved the town of Bethulia by seducing Nebuchadnezzar's general Holofernes and then cutting off his head while he slept. It was always a popular Jewish name. Although there are several medieval examples including a niece of William the Conqueror, it did not become popular in Britain until the 17th century when Puritans favoured Biblical names. Interestingly it was not popular among American Puritans. Now it is a vogue name in the US in the familiar form Jodie.

Variations and abbreviations: Giuditta (It), Jodi, Jodie, Jody, Judi, Judie, Judintha, Juditha (Ger), Judy, Judye, Jutta.

Example: Judith Krantz, US writer.

JUDY

Origin/meaning: Hebrew 'Jewish woman'.

Originally a familiar form of Judith *q.v.* Now considered an independent name.

Variations and abbreviations: Judi, Judie. *See* also Judith.

Examples: Judy Garland, 1922–1969, US entertainer.
Judi Dench, English actress.
Judy Geeson, English actress.

JULIA

Origin/meaning: from Julius, a Roman family name, possibly meaning 'dowry'.

This is the direct equivalent of the masculine Julius and almost identical to Juliana and Gillian. It came into use in Europe during the Renaissance period when classical names were popular. It may have been Shakespeare who introduced the name into England when he used it for the Italian Giulia in his play *Two Gentlemen of Verona*, 1598. The name is sometimes used for girls born in July, the month named after Julius Caesar.

Variations and abbreviations: Giulia (It), Jule, Jules, Julie (Fr).

Examples: Julia Ward Howe, 1819–1910, US writer. Author of *The Battle Hymn of the Republic*.
Julia Morley, 'Miss World' promoter.

JULIANA
Origin/meaning: from Julius, a Roman family name possibly meaning 'dowry'.

This Latin feminine version of Julian *q.v.* is now the accepted feminine form although in the Middle Ages Julian was used for both boys and girls. It is exactly the same name as Gillian *q.v.* The two eventually developed as totally distinct names, but shared many of their short forms such as Jill. Juliana was the name of several saints, including St Juliana Falconieri, 1270–1341, who founded the community of Servite Nuns. St Juliana, a Roman martyr, was greatly venerated in the low countries and the name is still popular in Holland. Like many saints' names it went out of fashion in England after the Reformation. In the 18th century, the form was revived as part of a fashion for names with Latinized endings (Augusta, Amelia, Arabella etc) but did not make a great impact. Despite its popularity in Medieval England it now has a more 'foreign' feel to it than Gillian.

Variations and abbreviations: Giuliana (It), Juliane, Julianne, Julienne. See also Gillian.

Example: Ex-Queen Juliana of the Netherlands.

JULIE
Origin/meaning: from the Roman family name Julius, possibly meaning 'dowry'.

This French form of Julia *q.v.* has become very popular in English-speaking countries in the 20th century.

Variations and abbreviations: See Julia.

Examples: Julie Walters, English actress.
Julie Andrews, English singer/actress.

JULIENNE
A form of Juliana *q.v.*

JULIET

Origin/meaning: 'little Julia'. From the Roman Family name Julius, possibly meaning 'dowry'.

Shakespeare based his play *Romeo and Juliet* on a poem by Arthur Brooke called *The Tragical History of Romeus and Juliet*, 1562. Brooke had presumably 'translated' the Italian name Giuletta. The name was not known in England before the 16th century although the similar Julian/Gillian had long been popular, with its short form Gillet. Another similar name occasionally found in Medieval England was Julitta.

Variations and abbreviations: Jule, Juliette (Fr). See also Gillian.

Example: Juliet Mills, English actress.

JULIETTE

Origin/meaning: a French form of Juliet *q.v.*

Example: Juliette Greco, French singer.

JULITTA

Origin/meaning: uncertain. Possibly connected with Julia *q.v.*

The name of an early Christian saint and martyr. She and her three-year-old son Cyricus were executed at Tarsus about 304 although the facts are not well verified. The child is also known as St Cyr. Julitta was used in Medieval England before the 16th century when the name Juliet *q.v.* was introduced from Italy.

Variation: Giulitta (It).

JUNE

Origin/meaning: the sixth month of the year.

This month may have taken its name from Juno, the Chief of the goddesses and the patron of all female concerns from birth to death. Juno's festival was held on the Kalends of June and it is probably because of its association with her that since Roman times June has been considered the luckiest month for marriages. The name June has come into use in the 20th century with one or two examples in the 19th century.

Examples: June Whitfield, English actress.
June Allyson, US dancer/actress.

JUMOKE (pron. J'móhkee)

Origin/meaning: Yoruba 'everyone loves the child'.

A Nigerian name used for boys as well as girls.

JUNO
Origin/meaning: Old Irish, uncertain, possibly 'lamb'.

A variation of Oonagh *q.v.* best known for Sean O'Casey's play *Juno and the Paycock*, 1924. Sometimes wrongly assumed to be simply the name of the Chief Roman goddess Juno.

JUSTINE
Origin/meaning: Latin 'just'.

The French feminine version of Justin *q.v.* which is used in English-speaking countries.

Variations and abbreviations: Giustina (It), Justina (Sp).

Example: Justine, 1957, heroine of the first of the novels in *The Alexandria Quartet* by Lawrence Durrell.

K

KAILAS (pron. Kyelars)
Origin/meaning: Sanskrit. The name of a holy mountain in the Himalayas.

Hindus believe that the God Shiva *q.v.* and Parvati *q.v.* his wife live on Mount Kailas.

KAMARIA (pron. Kamaréea)
Origin/meaning: Swahili 'moon-like'.

A popular name in East Africa.

See also Chandra, Diana, Selina, Sudha.

KANOOM
This is a Muslim Title not a personal name. A woman is addressed formally by her personal name plus her title, eg Fatima Kānoom.

KAREN
Origin/meaning: uncertain. Possibly Greek 'pure'.

A Scandinavian form of Katharine *q.v.* It was introduced into the US by Scandinavian immigrants and has subsequently spread to other English-speaking countries where it is currently very popular.

Variations and abbreviations: Caren, Carin, Karim. See also Katharine.

KASHMIRA
Origin/meaning: Kashmin 'from Kashmir'.

A name given because Kashmir is considered a holy area by Indians.

KATE
Origin/meaning: uncertain. Possibly Greek 'pure'.

This is a short form of Katharine *q.v.* It was popular in the 16th and 17th centuries, Shakespeare's Katherina Minola, the 'Shrew' of his play *The Taming of the Shrew*, 1594, is constantly referred to as Kate. The name was again popular in the 19th century when Susan Coolidge (1835–1905) the US children's writer, wrote her classic series of Katy books. Kate has been a vogue name in Britain, the US and Australia for the last fifteen years.

Variations: Katie, Katy. See also Katharine.

Examples: Kate Millet, US feminist.
Kate Reid, Canadian actress.
Kate Bush, English singer.

KATHERINE/KATHARINE
Origin/meaning: uncertain. Possibly Greek 'pure'.

Although several later saints, notably the mystic St Katherine of Vienna, 1347–1380, reinforced the popularity of the name Katherine throughout Europe, it was the cult of St Katherine of Alexandria which initially spread the name throughout the areas of both the Eastern and Western church. Katherine of Alexandria may never have existed at all and may be simply a fiction to exemplify the highest Christian virtues of courage and steadfastness. Tradition has it that she was one of the virgin martyrs who died in Alexandria early in the 4th century. Aristocratic and beautiful she was also extremely erudite. When she protested to the Emperor Maxentius about the worship of idols she was able to counter the arguments of his fifty best philosophers. Attempts were made to torture her into submission including a spell on the spiked 'Catherine wheel' which miraculously disintegrated beneath her. Eventually Katherine was beheaded. Her body was carried by angels to Mount Sinai, where a church built in her honour became the centre of an influential cult, with the 'Catherine-wheel' as her symbol. The name was introduced to Western Europe by Crusaders who visited her shrine on Mount Sinai. In 1148 Queen Matilda founded a church in her honour by the Tower of London in the area of London still known today as St Katherine's dock. The name was soon popular, as the variety of forms and pet versions show. It proved equally successful in other European countries. After the 16th century Reformation Katherine, with its strong Catholic connotations, became less popular in Britain, except in Catholic Ireland where the form Kathleen was most common. Since the 19th century the name has recovered lost ground in English-

177

speaking countries. During the 20th century different forms have had periods of popularity with the Scandinavian form Karen now beginning to tail off in favour of Kate and Katy. In areas of high Irish immigration, Cathleen/Kathleen and the pet forms Cathy/Kathy remain popular. Catherine, the French spelling, has been the most popular post-war form.

Variations and abbreviations: Caitlin (Ir), Caitrin, Caren, Carin, Caryn, Cass, Cassie, Cassy, Catalina (Sp), Catarina, Cate, Catelin (Med Eng), Caterina (It), Catharina, Catharine, Cathee, Catherina, Catherine (Fr), Cathie, Cathleen (Ir), Cathlene, Cathrine, Cathryn, Cathy, Catia (It), Catie, Catlin (Med Eng), Catriona (Scots), Caty, Ekaterina (Ger/Russ), Karen (Scand), Karin, Kass, Kassia, Kassie, Kata, Katalin, Kate, Katerina, Katerine, Katey, Katha, Katharina (Ger), Kathi, Kathie, Kathleen (Ir), Kathryn, Kathy, Katia (Ger), Katie, Katina, Katinka (Russ), Katja (Russ), Katrina (Gk), Katrinka, Katya, Kay, Kaye, Kit, Kittie, Kitty, Treena, Trina.

Examples: Katherine (b.Kathleen) Mansfield, 1888–1923, New Zealand/British short story writer.
Katharine of Aragon, 1485–1536, first wife of Henry VIII of England.
Katharine II (the Great) of Russia, 1729–1796, Empress of Russia.

KATHLEEN
Origin/meaning: uncertain. Possibly Greek 'pure'.

The Irish diminutive form of Katharine *q.v.* used in Ireland and areas of Australia and North America with large populations of Irish origin.

Variations and abbreviations: Cath, Cathee, Cathleen, Cathie, Catty, Kay, Kath, Kathie, Kathy. See also Katharine.

Example: Kathleen Ferrier, 1912–1953, English singer.

KATHRYN
Origin/meaning: uncertain. Possibly Greek 'pure'.

An old-fashioned spelling of Katherine *q.v.* which has proved popular in the 20th century.

Variations and abbreviations: See Katherine.

Example: Kathryn Grayson, US singer/film actress.

KATINA
Origin/meaning: uncertain. Possibly Greek 'pure'.

Katina is a modern US form of Katherine *q.v.*

KATOON
This is a Muslim title, not a personal name. It is used on more formal occasions in conjunction with a personal name, eg Yasmin *Katoon*.

KAUR
The female equivalent of Singh. This is a Sikh religious name which is added to the personal name as a form of politeness. It is not used on its own.

KAVITA
Origin/meaning: Sanskrit 'poetry'.

This originated in West India but is now found throughout the country. Very popular nowadays, perhaps because of ease of pronunciation.

KAY
Origin/meaning: uncertain. Possibly Greek 'pure'.

A short form of Katharine *q.v.* The rare masculine name Kay *q.v.* has a quite separate origin.

Variations and abbreviations: Kaye. See also Katherine.

Example: Kay Kendall, 1927–1959, British film actress.

KELLY
Origin/meaning: Gaelic 'descendant of War'.

Celtic surname most commonly found in Ireland, now popular as a girl's first name, especially in Australia and the US.

Variation: Kellie.

KENDAL
Origin/meaning: Old English 'at the head of the valley'.

An English surname derived from a lake district place-name. Used as a first name, usually where there are family connections.

KENTIGERNA
Origin/meaning: Old Welsh 'head chief'.

This is the feminine equivalent of Kentigern *q.v.* There was a St Kentigerna d.733, who lived by Loch Lomond.

Variations: Caentigern, Quentigerna.

KEREN
Origin/meaning: Hebrew: 'horn of stibium'. (Stibium is a type of cosmetic used on the eyes.)

A short form of Kerenhappuch *q.v.* Now used, mainly in the US, as an independent name with no reference to its virtually obsolete original form.

KERENHAPPUCH
Origin/meaning: Hebrew 'horn of stibium'.

Stibium was a kohl-like substance used by the ancients as a cosmetic. Kerenhappuch was one of Job's three daughters. Her sisters were Kezia and Jemima. In the last chapter of the Book of Job they are described 'in all the land were no women found so fair as the daughters of Job'. Keren, the short form has now become a totally independent name while the clumsy original is virtually obsolete. Examples of its use are found among the early North American Puritans.

Abbreviation: Keren.

KERRIE
Origin/meaning: 'from Kerry', an Irish place-name, meaning the place of dark-haired people.

This has been used in North America and Australia in the 20th century presumably by families of Irish origin. The *ie* ending is regarded as more 'feminine'.

Variations and abbreviations: Keriann, Kerianne, Kerry, Kerryn. See also Kieran.

KETURAH
Origin/meaning: Hebrew 'fragrance'.

The name of the Patriarch Abraham's second wife, Keturah, was used mainly during the 17th and 18th centuries, when Puritans favoured Biblical names.

KEZIA
Origin/meaning: Hebrew 'cassia' (a type of cinnamon).

Kezia, with Jemima q.v. and Kerenhappuch q.v. was one of the three beautiful daughters of Job. The name was used by the Puritans.

Variation: Keziah.

Example: Harriot Kezia Hunt, 1805-1875, US Social reformer and pioneer woman doctor.

KHADIJA
Origin/meaning: Arabic 'born prematurely'.

Khadiia was the wife of Mohammed and is therefore a very popular name among Muslims.

Variation: Kedeja.

KIBIBI
Origin/meaning: Swahili 'little lady'.

An East African name.

See also Donna, Martha.

KIM
Origin/meaning: Old English 'cyne' – 'royal'. From the surname Kimball 'royal hill' or Kimberley 'royal meadow'.

This name became popular for boys after the publication in 1901 of Rudyard Kipling's book Kim. It has now become equally popular for girls. It is one of many modern feminine names beginning with K- and taken from surnames eg Kerry, Kyle, Kelly.

Examples: Kim Novak, US film actress.
Kim Wilde, British singer.

KIMBERLEY
Origin/meaning: Old English 'from the royal meadow'.

This is an English surname which has suddenly become popular as a girl's name in the US and Australia.

Variations and abbreviations: Kim, Kimmie.

Example: Kimberley Stewart, daughter of Scottish singer Rod Stewart.

KINEBURGA
Origin/meaning: Old English 'Royal fortress'.

The name of three Anglo-Saxon princess saints this name has many forms, one or two of which are occasionally found today.

Variations and abbreviations: Cyneburga, Cyniburg, Kinbarra, Kinborough, Kinburga.

KIRSTEN
Origin/meaning: Latin 'Christian'.

The Scandinavian form of the English names Christine, Christina and Christiana. This Northern European form influenced the Scottish versions Kirsty and Kirsteen, whereas in England the Italian and French versions had more influence.

Variations and abbreviations: Kerstin, Kerstina, Kirsteen (Scots), Kirsty, Kris, Krissy, Kirstin, Kristin, Kristina, Kristine. See also Christiana, Christine.

Example: Kirsten Flagstadt, 1895–1962, Norwegian opera singer.

KIRSTY
Origin/meaning: Latin 'Christian'.

This is a Scottish pet form of Christine/Christiana. It comes from the Scandinavian form Kirsten and illustrates the close connections which existed for several centuries between the Scots and the people of Scandinavia. Until the 1960s this name was confined almost totally to people of Scottish origin but it has recently become a vogue name in the rest of Britain and in Australia.

Variations and abbreviations: Kirstie. See also Kirsten and Christine.

KITTY
Origin/meaning: uncertain. Possibly Greek 'pure'.

A pet form of Katharine q.v. This was used in the Middle Ages and then went out of fashion. Like many medieval names it was brought back into fashion in the 19th century when it was often given as an independent name. In the second half of the 20th century it has begun to lose favour again.

Variations and abbreviations: See Katharine.

Example: Kitty Muggeridge, biographer, wife of Malcolm Muggeridge.

KORA
Origin/meaning: Greek 'maiden'.
An alternative spelling of Cora *q.v.*

KUSUM (pron. Kuhsoom)
Origin/meaning: Sanskrit 'flower'.

Popular throughout India.

Variation: Kusum kumari. See also Flower, Fleur, Flora and the masculine Kusum chandra.

KYLE
Origin/meaning: Gaelic 'narrow strait or sound'.

This is a place-name from Ayrshire in Scotland which has become a British surname. In the latter half of the 20th century it has been used, like Kerry and Kelly, as a feminine first name, particularly in the US. The familiar form Kylie is a native word in Western Australia for a boomerang. Kyle/Kylie is a popular girl's name in Australia where it may sometimes be given with the alternative meaning in mind.

Variations and abbreviations: Kylie, Kyly.

L

LAETITIA (pron. Letisha)
Origin/meaning: Latin 'joy', 'delight'.

The usual English form of this name was Lettice q.v. Laetitia was found occasionally in the Middle Ages but did not really establish itself until the 18th century when Latin names were highly fashionable. It is now rare.

Variations and abbreviations: Lätitia (Ger), Lece (Fr), Lecia, Leda, Letice, Leticia, Letitia, Letizia (It), Lettice (Eng), Letty.

Examples: Letizia Ramolino, 1750–1836, mother of Napoleon Bonaparte.
Letitia Landon, 1802–1838, English poetess.

LAKSHMI (pron. L'kshmee)
Origin/meaning: Hindi. The name of the goddess of Wealth and prosperity, the wife of Vishnu.

An extremely popular name throughout India.

Example: Lakshmi Bai, 19th century heroine of the fight for independence against the British.

LALAGE
Origin/meaning: Greek 'babbler'.

A name used by the poet Horace and found occasionally today, usually in the US.

LALLIE
Origin/meaning: Greek 'fair spoken' or 'well spoken of'.

A short form of Eulalia q.v.

Variation: Lalla.

LANA
Origin/meaning: a short form of either Helen (Greek 'light' or 'bright') or Alanna (Celtic 'beautiful').

184

Example: Lana Turner, US film actress.

LARA
Origin/meaning: uncertain. Possibly Greek 'cheerful'.

A Russian short form of Larissa *q.v.* which has become established in Europe and English-speaking countries only recently. Byron used it for his poem *Lara*, 1814.

Variations and abbreviations: See Larissa.

LARISSA
Origin/meaning: uncertain. Possibly Greek 'cheerful' or Pre-Hellenic 'castle'.

Larissa, with the short form Lara, has been one of the most popular names in the Soviet Union since the 1960s. It is presumably this name which is now being found in the West. Certainly the name has not been used prior to the last 30 years. It may well have been popularized by Pasternak's best-selling book *Doctor Zhivago*, which was also a successful film, for Lara is the heroine of Pasternak's novel. The name has been easy to introduce because it resembles other names like Laura, Clarissa and Melissa.

Variations and abbreviations: Lara, Larisa.

LATA (pron. L'ta)
Origin/meaning: Sanskrit 'climbing plant', 'bower'.

Example: Lata Mangeshkar – Indian singer.

LAURA
Origin/meaning: Latin 'bay tree' or 'from Laurentium' (city of laurels).

A feminine form of Laurence *q.v.* which probably evolved as a short form of the cumbersome original Laurencia. It is found early in the Middle Ages when its popularity may have been helped by the fact that the Italian writer Petrarch, 1304–1374, inspired by an unrequited passion for Laura (Lora) de Sade, addressed most of his poems to her. Since bay leaves were used to crown victors laureola was the Latin word for triumph and this too has been used as a variation of the name. In the 19th century when flower names were popular, Laurel was also found as a name. Laura is currently popular in Britain and the US and so is its variation Lauren.

Variations and abbreviations: Laure (Fr), Laureen, Laurel, Lauren, Laurence (Fr), Laurencia, Laurenzia, Lauretta (It), Laurette, Laurie, Laurine, Lora (It), Loreen, Loren, Lorene, Lorenza (It), Loretta, Lorette (Fr), Lori, Lorrie.

Examples: Laura Ashley, English designer.
Dame Laura Knight, 1877-1970, English painter.

LAUREL
Origin/meaning: Latin 'laurel' or 'bay tree'.

Used in the 19th century when flower names were in vogue. Laura q.v. is a longer established name with the same meaning. In the language of flowers laurel symbolizes victory and peace. The laurel/bay was associated with poetry, and it was said that sleeping on bay leaves would provide poetic inspiration.

Variations and abbreviations: See Laura.

LAUREN
Origin/meaning: Latin 'bay tree' or 'from Laurentum' (city of laurels).

Like Laura this is a short form of Laurencia, the feminine form of Laurence q.v. It is currently something of a vogue name, probably because of the film actress Lauren Bacall. Lauren is also a Swedish surname, derived from Laurence and in some cases in the US Lauren may be used as a first name because it is a family name.

Variations and abbreviations: See Laura.

LAURETTA
Origin/meaning: Latin 'little bay tree' or 'from Laurentium' (city of laurels).

A diminutive of Laura q.v. and Laurencia used since the Middle Ages.

Variation: Loretta. See also Laura.

LAVERNE
Origin/meaning: Old French 'alder tree'.

A French surname used as a feminine first name in the US. It may be used in the belief that it is connected with the Latin word vernus, meaning 'associated with the spring'.

Variation: Lavergne.

186

LAVINIA

Origin/meaning: uncertain. Possibly 'from Lavinium' (a town near Rome). Sometimes given as 'purified'.

Lavinia is a name from Roman literature. In Virgil's poem the *Aeneid* Aeneas, a Trojan hero, escapes after the fall of Troy and after many years of wandering and adventures reaches Italy. In one of his adventures he allies with Latinus whose daughter Lavinia is offered to him in marriage. To win her, he defeats a rival in single combat. Their son, Romulus, eventually becomes the founder of Rome. Lavinia was fashionable in the 16th century when names from classical Greece and Rome were being used. Shakespeare gave the name to the daughter of Titus Andronicus in his play of the same name, 1589, and that is probably the source of modern usage. In the 18th century it enjoyed another spell of popularity along with many other Latinized names.

Variations and abbreviations: Leni. See also Helen and Madelaine. Vinny.

LEAH

Origin/meaning: Hebrew 'heifer'. Sometimes given as 'weary'.

Leah was the first wife of Jacob, one of the patriarchs of the Old Testament. He worked for her father for seven years in order to marry her younger sister Rachel but was tricked into marrying the elder daughter first (Genesis 29–30). A popular Jewish name it was introduced as a Christian name by Puritans. An unusual name today, it is sometimes associated with the modern feminine name Lee.

LEE

Origin/meaning: Old English 'meadow'.

An English surname adopted in the 19th century as a first name. Originally a masculine name it is now used equally for girls.

Variations and abbreviations: Lea, Leigh.

Examples: Princess Lee Radziwill, sister of Jacqueline Kennedy Onassis.
Lee Remick, US actress.

LEILA (pron. Layla)

Origin/meaning: Persian 'night' or 'dark-haired as night'.

A popular Moslem name. It is found in the Persian legend of Leila and Majnoun. Byron used the name for a beautiful young concubine of the Caliph Hassan who, in his poem *The Giaour*, runs away from the harem with her lover Giaour. It was the success of the poem which introduced Leila as a name to English-speaking countries.

Variations: Layla, Leilah, Lela, Lelah, Lila.

Example: Leila Berg, British writer of children's stories.

LENA
Origin/meaning: Greek 'light' or 'bright' or Hebrew 'Woman of Magdala'.

A short form of Helena, now an independent name. When pronounced Layna it is a short form of Magdalena.

Variations and abbreviations: Leni. See also Helen and Madelaine.

Examples: Lena Horne, US singer.
Leni (Helene) Riefenstahl, German actress and film-maker.

LENORE
Origin/meaning: Greek 'bright', 'light'.

A German form of Eleanor *q.v.* (a form of Helen *q.v.*). Similar to the Italian name Leonora *q.v.*

LEO
Origin/meaning: Latin 'lion'.

A short form of names beginning with Leo, most but not all of which are derived from the Latin word for lion.

Variations: Leonore, Leonie, Leonarda, etc.

LEOLINA
Origin/meaning: Welsh 'like a lion'.

A Medieval feminine form of the Welsh name Llywelyn, from the English version Leoline. The feminine version was probably pronounced like the masculine and the Latin -a ending used only for the written form.

Variation: Leolin. See also Leonarda and Leonie.

LEONARDA
Origin/meaning: Latin/Old German 'lion bold'.

An Italian feminine of Leonard, occasionally used in English-speaking countries.

Variations and abbreviations: Leo, Leonharda (Ger).

LÉONIE
Origin/meaning: Greek 'lion'.

A French feminine form of the popular French name Léon q.v. It has occasionally been used in English-speaking countries, and without the accent.

Variations and abbreviations: Leo, Leona, Leonia (It), Leonzia (It).

LEONORA
Origin/meaning: Greek 'bright', 'light'.

An Italian form of Eleanor/a q.v. itself a form of Helen q.v. Like the similar German name Lenore it was introduced into Britain in the 19th century when the Romantic Movement in literature popularized many medieval names.

Variations and abbreviations: Leonore (Ger), Leonor, Leonore, Lora.

LEONTINE
Origin/meaning: Greek 'lionlike'.

A French feminine diminutive form of Léon q.v.

Variations and abbreviations: Leon, Leontina (It), Leontine, Leontyne.

Example: Leontyne Price, US opera singer.

LEOPOLDA
Origin/meaning: Old German 'people-bold'.

The Italian feminine form of Leopold q.v.

Variations and abbreviations: Leo, Leopolde, Leopoldine.

LERATO
Origin/meaning: Tswana 'love'.

A name from Botswana in South Africa.

See also Amy, Ife.

LESLEY
Origin/meaning: Scots Gaelic 'garden by the pool'.

This spelling of the Scottish surname is generally the one used for girls. Leslie is the preferred form for boys. The first use of Lesley as a first name seems to be for Lesley Baillie, the 'Bonnie Lesley' of the poem by Robert Burns, 1759–1796.

Variations and abbreviations: Les, Lesli, Leslie, Lesly, Lezley, Lezlie.

Examples: Leslie Caron, French actress and dancer.
Lesley Ann Down, English actress.

LETTICE
Origin/meaning: Latin 'joy', 'delight'.

The English form of Laetitia q.v. It was extremely popular throughout the Middle Ages but eventually became unfashionable in the 17th century. In the 18th century the Latin form Laetitia was introduced into England and Lettice became virtually obsolete.

Variations and abbreviations: See Laetitia.

Examples: Lettice Knollys, Lady in Waiting to Elizabeth I.
Lettice Cooper, English novelist.

LIBBY
Origin/meaning: Hebrew: 'God is my satisfaction'.

A short form of Elizabeth sometimes given as an independent name.

Variations and abbreviations: Lib, Libbie, and see Elizabeth.

Example: Libby Morris, Canadian actress.

LILIAS
Origin/meaning: Hebrew: 'God is my satisfaction'.

The Scottish form of Lillian q.v. a pet form of Elizabeth.

Variations and abbreviations: See Lillian.

LILITH
Origin/meaning: Hebrew 'belonging to the night' or Assyrian 'goddess of storms'.

In non-Biblical Hebrew mythology, Lilith was a wife of Adam before he gave his rib to create Eve.

LILLIAN
Origin/meaning: Hebrew 'God is my satisfaction'.

This is one of dozens of variations of the name Elizabeth. Its use as an independent name may well have been influenced by the flower name Lily, introduced at the end of the 19th century.

Variations and abbreviations: Lili, Lilian, Liliane, Lilias (Scots), Lilla, Lilli (Ger), Lillias (Scots), Lillie, Lilyan.

Examples: Lillian Gish, b.1896, US star of silent films.
Lillian Hellman, 1906–1984, US playwright.
Lillian Carter, 1898–1983, mother of the US President, Jimmy Carter.

LILY
Origin/meaning: Greek 'lily' or pet form of Elizabeth (Hebrew 'God is my satisfaction').

Since the late 19th century fashion for flower names Lily has undoubtedly been given as the name of the flower. Prior to that it may well, like Lillian, have been used as a pet form of Elizabeth, similar to the German Lilli (eg Lilli Palmer, Australian film actress).

Variations and abbreviations: Lil, Lilli, Lillie, Lilly. See also Susannah and Elizabeth.

Examples: Lillie Langtry, 1853–1929, Jersey-born actress, mistress of Edward VII.
Lily Dache, US couturière.

LINA
Origin/meaning: a short form of names ending in -ina, -ine, or -eine, such as Madeleine or Caroline. Most common in French and German speaking countries.

Variation: Line.

LINDA
Origin/meaning: Old German 'serpent'.

Linda is a short form of the many pre-Conquest names which contained the word. The best known nowadays are Belinda and Rosalind. Serpent may seem a strange meaning but in fact it was very flattering. In German mythology the serpent was regarded as a magical creature. In the 19th century many Old German names were revived in Europe as a result of the Romantic Movement in literature. The short form Linda rapidly became an independent name and has been one of the most popular 20th century names in English as well as German-speaking countries. It may have been helped by the fact that *linda* is also the Spanish word for pretty. Since the Second World War, Linda has suffered a sharp decline probably because at one time it seemed too popular.

Variations and abbreviations: Lindi, Lindy, Lynda.

Examples: Linda Darnell, 1923–1965, US film actress.
Lynda Lee-Potter, British journalist.

LINDSAY
Origin/meaning: Old English. Uncertain, possibly 'Lincoln's island'.

This is a common Scottish surname. It does, however, have aristocratic connections both because of the Earls of Lindsay and because it is the family name of the Earls of Crawford. Like several other Scottish surnames such as Leslie, Gordon and Keith, it came into use in the 19th century a period when many surnames were adopted as personal names. Lindsay has been particularly successful for both men and women and has developed several variations.

Variations and abbreviations: Lin, Lindsey (Eng), Linsay, Linsey, Lyn, Lynsey.

Example: Lynsey de Paul, English singer/songwriter.

LINET
Origin/meaning: uncertain. Possibly connected with the Old Welsh word meaning 'idol'.

This is the Medieval French form of the Welsh name Eluned *q.v.* which spread beyond Wales because it is the name of one of the characters in the legends of King Arthur and his Knights of the Round Table. The 19th century version Lynnet *q.v.* is now better known.

Variation: Lynnet.

LISA
Origin/meaning: Hebrew 'God is my satisfaction'.

A short form of Elizabeth, currently popular as an independent name.

Variations and abbreviations: Elisa, Elise, Elizabeth, Lissa.
Example: Lisa Alther, US writer and feminist.

LIZA
Origin/meaning: Hebrew 'God is my satisfaction'.

A short form of Elizabeth currently used as an independent name.

Variations and abbreviations: Elisa, Eliza, Elise, Lizzie, Lizzy. See Elizabeth.

Example: Liza Minelli, US actress and singer.

LIZZIE
Origin/meaning: Hebrew 'God is my satisfaction'.

A common English familiar form of Elizabeth q.v.

LOIS (pron. Lóys or Lówis)
Origin/meaning: Greek. Meaning uncertain.

A Biblicial name taken by 17th century Puritans from the second Epistle of St Paul to Timothy. In the 20th century it has become popular, particularly in the US. Modern pronunciation usually gives the name two syllables, perhaps because it is sometimes mistakenly thought to be a form of Louise. Its recent popularity may well have been affected by the fact that Lois Lane is the girlfried of the comic-strip character Superman.

Variation: Loyce.

Examples: Lois Maxwell, English actress.
Lois Nettleton, US actress.

LOLA
Origin/meaning: a Spanish diminutive of Dolores (Spanish 'sorrows') or Carlota (the Spanish form of Charlotte 'man').

Variation: Lolita.

Example: Lola Montes, 1818–1861, (Eliza Gilbert) Irish dancer, mistress of Ludwig I of Bavaria.

LORA
Origin/meaning: Greek 'bright', 'light'.

A short form of Leonora q.v. which is itself a variation of Helen. Sometimes used as an alternative spelling of Laura.

LORETTA

Origin/meaning: Latin 'baytree' or 'from Laurentum' (the city of laurels).

An alternative spelling of Lauretta, a diminutive of Laura *q.v.* Occasionally found, mainly among Catholics, as 'from Loreto' a famous Italian shrine of the Virgin Mary.

Example: Loretta Young, US film actress.

LORNA

Origin/meaning: this name was invented by the novelist R. D. Blackmore for his classic novel *Lorna Doone*, 1869.

Although the novel was set in Devonshire at the time of the English civil war the name was apparently adapted from the title of the Scottish Marquess of Lorne. Its easy sound has quickly established it as a popular name in English-speaking countries, though it is not used in Europe.

See also Evangeline, Fiona, Miranda, Ophelia, Pamela, Perdita, Vanessa and Wendy.

LORRAINE

Origin/meaning: French 'from Lorraine' (an area of France).

This has only come into use since the middle of the 20th century. Even in France it is an unusual name.

Variations and abbreviations: Larain, Lorain, Loraine, Lorri, Lorrayne.

LOTTIE

Origin/meaning: Old German 'man' by association 'womanly'.

A common familiar form (like Tottie) of Charlotte, a feminine form of Charles.

Variations: Lotte, Lotty. See also Charlotte.

Example: Lotte Lenya, German singer.

LOUELLA

Origin/meaning: a combination of Louise and Ella.

A pet name sometimes used as an independent name. Mainly confined to the US.

Variations and abbreviations: Loella, Lou, Luella.

Example: Louella Parsons, 1881–1972. Hollywood columnist.

LOUISA
Origin/meaning: Old German 'glorious battle'.

This is the Latin feminine form of the French name Louis *q.v.* Until the 20th century it was the most popular feminine form in English-speaking countries but has now been overtaken by the French Louise.

Variations and abbreviations: Lodovica (It), Loise, Lou, Louie, Louise (Fr), Louisette, Lu, Ludowika (Ger), Luigia (It), Luisa (It/Sp), Luise (Ger), Lulu.

Example: Louisa M. Alcott, 1832–1888, US children's writer, author of *Little Women*.

LOUISE
Origin/meaning: Old German 'glorious battle'.

The French feminine form of Louis *q.v.* Although Louis is a common French name the feminine form that used to be most popular in England and the US was the Latinized Louisa. In the mid-20th century Louise became fashionable in the US and later spread to Britain and Australia where it is currently a vogue name.

Variations and abbreviations: See Louisa.

Example: Louise Brooks, US actress.

LOVEDAY
Origin/meaning: Medieval English 'born on loveday'.

A loveday was an annual day set aside for settling disputes. In the 17th century it also came to mean a day when the young people of a town or village could look for a mate. The name is now rare and used only for girls.

LUCASTA (pron. Lookásta)
Origin/meaning: Latin 'light'.

A poetic form of Lucia/Lucy *q.v.* used in the 17th century. Richard Lovelace the Cavalier poet wrote a poem entitled *Lucasta* in 1649.

See also Lucy and Althea.

LUCIA
Origin/meaning: Latin 'light'.

The original Latin feminine form of Lucius from which the English Lucy and French Lucille are derived.

Variations and abbreviations: See Lucy.

LUCILLE
Origin/meaning: Latin 'light'.

A French feminine diminutive of Lucius q.v. It has recently been used in English-speaking countries.

Variations and abbreviations: Lucilla (It/Ger). See also Lucy, Lucinda.

Example: Lucille Ball, US comedienne.

LUCINA (pron. Looséena)
Origin/meaning: Lucina was a Roman goddess who presided over childbirth.

The name is probably, like Lucy and Lucille, connected with the Latin word for light. Lucina brought children into the light of day. It is a rare name today, except in Italy.

LUCINDA
Origin/meaning: Latin 'light'.

This, like Lucasta, is a 17th century form of Lucy. It was used in poetry and because of its Latin sound was not uncommon in the second half of the 18th century. It is currently enjoying a minor vogue in Britain in the wake of Lucy.

Variations and abbreviations: Lucinde. See also Lucy.

Example: Lucinda Green, British show-jumper.

LUCRETIA
Origin/meaning: Latin, belonging to the roman family Lucretius.

This is a classical name revived in Italy during the renaissance period and used in England mainly from the 16th–18th centuries. The main source of the name is the legend of Lucretia, wife of Lucius Tarquinius Collatinus. She was raped by Sextus, son of Tarquinius Superbus and overcome by shame, committed suicide. As a result the Tarquins were expelled from Rome and a republic established. This story inspired many poems and plays including Shakespeare's poem *The Rape of Lucrece*, 1594.

Variations and abbreviations: Lucrèce (Fr), Lucrecia (Sp), Lucresse, Lucrezia (It).

Examples: Lucrezia Borgia, 1480–1519, Duchess of Ferrara, daughter of Pope Alexander VI.

LUCY
Origin/meaning: Latin 'light'.

Lucy is the English form of Lucia, a Roman name. It became an acceptable Christian name because of St Lucia, d.304. She was a virgin martyr who met her death at Syracuse in Sicily during one of the persecutions by the Emperor Diocletian. As so often happened, preposterous stories grew up about the circumstances of her death. Because of the meaning of her name and the legend that during torture her eyes were torn out but miraculously replaced, she is a saint invoked against eye disease. She is sometimes represented holding two eyes on a dish. The name, probably brought to England by the Normans, was much used in the Middle Ages. It went out of use after the Protestant Reformation for Puritans preferred names without Catholic connections and St Lucy's name is mentioned in the Mass. Instead poetic versions such as Lucinda were used. In the 1970s and 80s it has become a vogue name in Britain. Lucy, and similar old-fashioned names like Jessica, Katy and Abigail, are coming back into favour, perhaps as a reaction against the Hollywood-influenced names of the 1940s and 50s and the new names invented in the 60s.

Variations and abbreviations: Luc, Lucasta (17th century), Luce (It), Lucetta, Lucette, Luci, Lucia (Ger/It/Lat), Luciana (It), Lucienne (Fr), Lucilia, Lucilla (It), Lucille (Fr), Lucina (It), Lucinda (17th century), Lucinde, Lucine, Lucky (US), Luz, Luzi, Luzia (Ger).

Examples: Luciana Avedon, US writer.
Luci Johnson Nugent, daughter of US President Lyndon B. Johnson.

LUDMILLA
Origin/meaning: Slav 'loved by the people'.

A name used mainly in Russia and Germany. Ludmilla, wife of the founder of the Bohemian Premyslid dynasty, was the grandmother of the Saint and King Wenceslas. Ludmilla herself was a Christian who was murdered by a political faction. She is therefore regarded as a saint and martyr.

Example: Ludmilla Tourischeva, Russian gymnast.

197

LULU
Origin/meaning: Old German 'glorious battle'.

A pet form of Louisa/Louise *q.v.*

LULU
Origin/meaning: Arabic 'pearl'.

A Muslim name quite unconnected with the European name. It has the same meaning as Margaret *q.v.*

LYDIA
Origin/meaning: Greek 'from Lydia' (an ancient kingdom of Asia Minor renowed for its wealthy King, Croesus).

This pre-Christian name occurs in the Acts of the Apostles. Lydia was sometimes said to be a daughter of Joseph of Nazareth. The name was first used in the 17th century but was most fashionable in the 18th century when classical and Latin name forms were at the height of their popularity. Jane Austen used the name for one of Mr Bennet's daughters in *Pride and Prejudice*, 1813.

Example: Lydia Lopokova, 1891–1981, Russian ballerina, wife of Maynard Keynes.

LYN
Origin/meaning: Old English 'pool' or a short form of the Welsh Eluned *q.v.* Possibly 'idol'.

The first meaning usually applies if the name Lyn is given because it is a family surname. Otherwise it is probably the short form, now used independently, of Eluned or its French variation Lynette, which came into general use in the 19th century. The similarity of Lyn to the endings of names like Caroline and Madeline has led to the modern trend of regarding the two spellings as interchangeable so that, for example, Caroline is frequently given as Carolyn, or Jacqueline as Jaquelyn. Lyn has also been added to other names. An obvious example is Mary which becomes Marilyn. Lyn is then used as a short form. In this way the Welsh girl's name Lyn has spread throughout the English-speaking world. Lyn is also used as a boy's name but one which is almost entirely confined to Wales.

Variations and abbreviations: Lynn, Lynne, Lynette.

Examples: Lynn Fontanne, 1887–1983, US actress.

Lynn Seymour, Canadian ballerina.
Lynne Reid Banks, English writer.

LYNNET

Origin/meaning: uncertain. Possibly connected with the Old Welsh word meaning 'idol'.

This is a variation of the well-established Welsh name Eluned *q.v.* from the short form, which is Lyn. In the Medieval French version of the Tales of the Court of King Arthur the form Linet is used. This was taken up, like a similar French name Elaine, by the poet Tennyson, when he wrote his own version of the Arthurian romances, *Idylls of the King*. It was Tennyson who first used the spelling Lynnet.

Variations and abbreviations: Eiluned, Elined, Eluned, Linet, Linette, Linnet, Luned, Lyn, Lynelle, Lynette, Lynne, Lynnet, Lynnette.

LYSIA

Origin/meaning: uncertain.

This is the traditional name given to the twin of St Thomas the Apostle.

See Thomas.

M

MABEL
Origin/meaning: Latin 'lovable'.

A short from of Amabel *q.v.* long established as an independent name. It was revived like many other medieval names in the 19th century.

Variations and abbreviations: Amabel, Mab, Mabella, Mabelle, Mable, Maybelle.

Example: Mabel Lucie Attwell, 1879–1964, English writer and illustrator.

MADELEINE
Origin/meaning: Hebrew 'woman from Magdala'.

This name comes from a corruption of Magdalene, the adjective which differentiates St Mary Magdalene from the other Marys named in the New Testament. Mary Magdalene was traditionally represented as a prostitute who repented and reformed. St Luke's story (ch.7 v.37) of a sinner who cleaned Christ's feet with ointment and wiped them with her hair is generally thought to refer to her. She was often referred to simply as 'the Magdalene' and this came to be used as an independent name. The old pronunciation was 'maudlin' which, because Mary Magdalene was patron saint of penitents, came to mean tearful. Both spelling and pronunciation were fairly early on supplanted by the French form Madeleine which remains the most usual form today.

Variations and abbreviations: Mad, Maddelena (It), Maddie, Maddy, Madeline (Eng), Madelon (Fr), Madelyn (US), Madlen, Madlon, Mado, Magda, Magdalena (Ger/Lat/Scand), Magdalene (Eng), Magdelone (Dan), Malena, Malina, Lena, Lene.

Examples: Madeleine de Scudery, 1608–1701, French novelist.

Marie-Madeleine, Comtesse de la Fayette, 1634–1693, French novelist, author of *La Princess de Clèves*.

MADGE
Origin/meaning: Persian?/Greek/Latin 'pearl' or French/English 'daisy'.

An English pet name for Margaret, sometimes used as an independent name.

Variations and abbreviations: See Margaret.

MADHURI (pron. Madtoorée)
Origin/meaning: Sanskrit 'sweet'.

This name comes from madhu, the Sanskrit word for honey or spring.

See also Dulcie, Honey, Mandisa and the masculine name Madhukar.

Example: Madhur Jaffrey, Indian actress and cookery writer.

MAEVE
Origin/meaning: Old Irish, meaning uncertain.

Maedbh was Queen of Connaught in the 3rd century who fought a great battle over a brown bull. This was the subject of an epic poem. The Irish 'dbh' becomes ve.

Example: Maeve Binchy, Irish novelist and journalist, author of *Light a Penny Candle*.

MAGDA
Origin/meaning: Hebrew 'Woman of Magdala'.

A German short form of Magdalena (Madeleine) sometimes used in English-speaking countries.

Variations and abbreviations: See Madeleine.

Example: Magda Lupescu, 1904–1977, Mistress and wife of Carol II of Rumania.

MAGDALENA
Origin/meaning: Hebrew 'Woman of Magdala'.

A Latin form of Magdalene/Madeleine q.v. Once popular it is now confined mainly to Catholic families. It is the usual form of the name in German and Scandinavia.

Variations and abbreviations: Magda, Lena. See also Madeleine.

Example: Magdalena Vásáryová, Czech opera singer.

MAGDALENE
Origin/meaning: Hebrew 'Woman of Magdala'.

An English form of Madeleine *q.v.* used in the Middle Ages and again in the 17th century when Puritans took it from the Biblical Mary Magdalene. In the Middle Ages it was pronounced 'maudlin' in imitation of the French. Magdalen College at Oxford retains the old pronunciation, while Magdalene College, Cambridge, uses the modern.

Variations and abbreviations: Magdalena (It). See also Madeleine.

MAGGIE
Origin/meaning: Persian?/Greek/Latin 'pearl' or Medieval French/Medieval English 'daisy'.

A short form of Margaret *q.v.* often used as an independent name.

Example: Maggie Smith, English actress.

MAHALAH
Origin/meaning: Hebrew. Meaning uncertain. Sometimes given as 'tenderness'.

Found as a masculine name in the Bible, this is now used exclusively for girls. It is a Biblical name found by the Puritans in their determination to avoid Catholic names. It has been more successful in the US than other English-speaking countries.

Variations and abbreviations: Mahala, Mahalia, Mehalah.

Example: Mahalia Jackson, 1911–1972, US gospel singer.

MAIA (pron. Mýar)
Origin/meaning: Latin 'exalted'. The name of a Roman goddess, the mother of Mercury. She may be based on a more ancient Indian deity, associated with visions.

This Italian name is sometimes considered the equivalent of the English name May, as that month is thought by some to have been named after the goddess. It is a popular name in Germany. Like May in England it may be used as a familiar form of Mary.

Variations and abbreviations: Maija (Fin), Maja (Ger/Scand).

MAIDIE
Origin/meaning: Hebrew 'bitter'.

A pet form of Mary *q.v.*

MAISIE
Origin/meaning: Persian?/Greek/Latin 'pearl' or French/English 'daisy'.

A Scottish familiar form of Margaret *q.v.* sometimes used as an independent name.

Variations and abbreviations: Mysie. See also Margaret.

Examples: Maisie Mosco, English novelist.

MAJA (pron. Mýar)
Origin/meaning: Latin 'exalted'. The name of a Roman goddess.

The German form of Maia *q.v.*

MALVINA
Origin/meaning: Scots Gaelic 'smooth/polished', 'fair'.

Malvina was probably, like Fiona, an invented name composed of Gaelic words. James Macpherson, 1736–1796, the writer of the Ossianic poems which he claimed he translated from the original Gaelic, was the first to use the name. It is sometimes considered a feminine form of Melvin *q.v.*

Variations and abbreviations: Malvine, Malwina (Ger), Melwine, Mel, Melva, Melvine.

MAMIE
Origin/meaning: Persian?/Greek/Latin 'pearl' or French/English 'daisy' (Margaret) or Hebrew 'bitter' (Mary).

This is an almost exclusively North American familiar form of two very common names, Margaret and Mary. It is sometimes given as an independent name. The European equivalent is Mimi.

Variations and abbreviations: Mame, Mimi. See also Margaret and Mary.

Examples: Mamie Eisenhower, wife of Dwight D. Eisenhower, 1860–1969, 34th President of the United States.
Mamie Van Doren, US actress.

MANDISA (pron. Mandéeza)
Origin/meaning: Xhosa 'sweet'.

A name from the South of Africa.

See also Dulcie, Honey and Madhuri.

MANON
Origin/meaning: Hebrew 'bitter' or 'wished for child'.

A French pet form of Marianne, a diminutive of Mary. Manon Lescaut is the heroine of a novel by Abbé Prévost, 1697–1763.

MANUELA
Origin/meaning: Hebrew 'God with us'.

A Spanish feminine form of Emanuel from the Spanish Manuel.

MARAH
Origin/meaning: Hebrew 'bitter'.

A form of the Hebrew name usually translated as Mary or Miriam. It was used by Puritans in the period of Biblical names.

MARCELLA
Origin/meaning: Latin 'little Marcus' from the name of Mars the Roman god of War.

Marcellus was a well-known Roman masculine name. Marcella, the feminine form, has been used occasionally in English-speaking countries. It is sometimes thought to be a form of Marcia *q.v.* Marcelle is a fairly popular name in France.

Variations and abbreviations: Marcella (Sp), Marcelia, Marceline, Marcelle (Fr), Marcellina (It), Marcelline. See also Marcia and Martina.

Example: Marceline Cox, US writer.

MARCIA (pron. Márssia or Marsha)
Origin/meaning: 'of Mars' (the Roman god of War) ie 'warlike'.

This name comes from the Roman family name Marcius. It is used as a feminine form of Mark or Marcus which have the same meaning. Marcia is sometimes considered the English form of the French name Marcelle.

Variations and abbreviations: Marcelia, Marcie (Fr), Marcy, Marquita, Marsha (US).

Examples: Marsha Hunt, US actress.
Marcia, Lady Falkender, English political worker, secretary to Harold Wilson, former Labour Prime Minister.

MARGARET
Origin/meaning: Persian?/Greek/Latin 'pearl' or Medieval French/ Medieval English 'daisy'.

The first meaning is probably the correct meaning of this name, although Margaret is an old word for daisy in English and Marguerite, the French form, is also the French word for an ox-eye daisy. Margaret was one of the most popular names in Medieval Europe. Initially it was given in a number of countries to honour one of the early martyrs St Margaret of Antioch, (also known as St Marina) who was the patron saint of childbirth and so likely to be remembered when names were chosen. These countries then produced their own saints bearing the name. One of these, being of royal birth, was particularly widely known and venerated. She was St Margaret of Scotland, 1045–1093, a grand-daughter of the English king Edmund Ironside. Her mother was German, she was born in Hungary and married Malcolm III of Scotland. Her daughter Matilda married the English king Henry I. These widespread connections ensured that her name was honoured throughout Europe. By the end of the Middle Ages it was used by most of the royal families which undoubtedly served to popularize it still further, especially since many of the recipients were remarkable women. Among the royal Margarets were Margaret of Anjou, 1429–1482, wife of Henry VI of England; Margaret Tudor, 1489–1541, sister of Henry VIII and wife of James IV of Scotland; Margaret, Queen of Navarre, 1492–1549, Margaret of Austria, 1480–1530, who ruled the Netherlands as Regent; Margaret of Parma, 1522–1586, who also ruled the Netherlands as Regent, and Margaret, 1353–1412, Queen of Denmark, Norway and Sweden. Not surprisingly Margaret and variations like Maggie, Marjory and Maisie are still popular Scottish names. When Queen Elizabeth the Queen Mother gave birth to her second daughter at Glamis Castle in Scotland Margaret was an almost inevitable choice of name, for

205

she was the first child in direct succession to the throne to be born in Scotland for 300 years. The present Queen of Denmark is Margrethe II, who uses the old-fashioned 'th' spelling. Because of its associations with Catholicism Margaret temporarily fell out of favour at the time of the Protestant Reformation. However it soon reasserted itself even in Calvinist Scotland. In the 20th century it has remained one of the most consistently popular of all feminine names.

Variations and abbreviations: Daisy, Greta, Gretel, Gritty, Madge, Mag, Maggie, Maggs, Maggy, Maisie, Mamie, Margareta (Swed/Ger), Margarete (Ger/Dan), Margaretha (Dutch/Ger), Margarette, Margarita (Sp), Margaux, Marge, Marged (Wel), Margery, Marget, Marghanita, Margherita (It), Margie, Margit (Swed), Margita (Swed), Margo, Margot, Margred (Wel), Margrethe (Dan), Margriet, Marguerita, Marguerite (Fr), Margy, Marina, Marjie, Marjorie, Marjory, May, Meg, Megan (Wel), Meggie, Meggy, Meghan, Megs, Meta, Mog, Peg, Pegeen, Peggi, Peggie, Peggoty, Rita.

Examples: Margaret Thatcher, British Prime Minister.
Margaret Mead, 1901–1978, US anthropologist.

MARGERY
Origin/meaning: Persian?/Greek/Latin 'pearl' or French/English 'daisy'.

An alternative English spelling of Marjorie *q.v.* which is a form of Margaret *q.v.*

Variations and abbreviations: See Margaret.

Example: Margery Allingham, 1904–1966, English writer of detective fiction.

MARGHANITA
Origin/meaning: Persian?/Greek/Latin 'pearl' or French/English 'daisy'.

A variation of Margaret *q.v.*

Example: Marghanita Laski, English novelist and critic.

MARGO
Origin/meaning: Persian?/Greek/Latin 'pearl' or French/English 'daisy'.

A variation of Margaret *q.v.* Identical in sound to the French Margot.

Variations and abbreviations: See Margaret.

Example: Margo Macdonald, former Scottish Nationalist MP.

MARGOT (pron. Margo)
Origin/meaning: Persian?/Greek/Latin 'pearl' or French/English 'daisy'.

A French short form of Margaret (Marguerite) *q.v.* sometimes given as an independent name.

Variations and abbreviations: See Margaret.

Examples: Dame Margot Fonteyn, English ballerina (born Margaret Hookham).
Margot Asquith, 1865–1940, British political hostess.

MARGUERITE
Origin/meaning: Persian?/Greek/Latin 'pearl' or French/English 'daisy'.

This is the French form of Margaret *q.v.* Margaret is an obsolete English word for a daisy. In France Marguerite is still the word for the ox-eye daisy. For this reason Daisy is sometimes used as a diminutive of Margaret. An example is the writer Daisy Ashford whose real name was Margaret Devlin.

Variations and abbreviations: See Margaret.

Example: Marguerite Chabert, President of a French wine co-operative, known as 'Queen of Beaujolais'.

MARIA
Origin/meaning: uncertain. Possibly Hebrew 'bitter' or 'wished for child'.

The Latin form of Mary used to translate the original Hebrew Mrym. All other forms of the name stem from it. It is the main form of Mary in Italy, Spain and Portugal, but is often used in countries which also have their own native form. It was very popular in England in the 18th century when Latin endings were fashionable.

Variations and abbreviations: See Mary.

Examples: Maria Callas, 1923–1977, Greek opera singer.
Maria Montessori, 1870–1952, Italian educationalist.

MARIABELLA
Origin/meaning: Latin 'beautiful Mary'.

A fanciful 17th–18th century literary version of Mary *q.v.*

MARIAMNE
Origin/meaning: uncertain. Possibly Hebrew 'bitter' or 'longed for child'.

One of the forms of Mary/Miriam found in the Old Testament.

Variations and abbreviations: See Miriam.

MARIANA
Origin/meaning: uncertain. Possibly Hebrew 'bitter' or 'wished for child'.

This is the Spanish/Italian diminutive of Mary (Maria) and means 'little Mary'. It was the most popular in England in the 18th century when names with Latin endings (eg Augusta, Lydia, Lavinia) were fashionable. At the same time Mary-Anne was a popular English double name and Mariana like the French Marianne, may have been used, as a more flamboyant version. Rare in English-speaking countries today.

Variations and abbreviations: See Marion.

MARIANNE
Origin/meaning: uncertain. Possibly Hebrew 'bitter' or 'wished for child'.

This is the French equivalent of Marion – 'little Mary'. It was used in the 18th century in England as a more up-market version of the double name Mary-Ann.

Variations and abbreviations: See Marion.

Example: Marianne Faithfull, English singer.
Marianne Moore, 1887–1972, US poet and writer.

MARIE
Origin/meaning: uncertain. Possibly Hebrew 'bitter' or 'wished for child'.

The French form of Mary, used in Scotland and currently in fashion in the US. In France, it is often used as part of a double name to honour the Virgin Mary, a practice dating from the time when French law made saints' names compulsory. Typical combinations are Marie-Claire, Marie-France, Marie-Christine and Marie-Rose. Marie is used for the same reason in combination with masculine names. An exclusively French familiar form is Manon.

Variations and abbreviations: See Mary.

Examples: Marie Curie, 1867–1934, French physicist.
Marie Stopes, 1880–1950, English pioneer of birth control.

MARIETTA
Origin/meaning: Hebrew 'bitter' or 'longed for child' plus Antoinetta (from the Roman Antonius family).

A contraction of Marie-Antoinette.

MARIGOLD
Origin/meaning: uncertain. Probably Medieval English, a combination of (the Virgin) Mary and gold.

This is one of the flower names which came into use at the end of the 19th century.

MARILYN
Origin/meaning: Hebrew 'bitter' plus Old English 'pool'.

A typical US combination of two popular names, Maria and Lyn. Its great popularity in the 1950s is undoubtedly due to the great popularity of the film star Marilyn Monroe (Norma Jean Baker), 1926–1962.

Example: Marilyn French, US writer and feminist author of *The Women's Room*.

MARINA
Origin/meaning: uncertain. Usually given as Latin 'of the sea'. May also be a form of Mary *q.v.*

Occasionally used in England in the Middle Ages, possibly like Stella (Maris) as an epithet for the Virgin Mary. She was known as the Queen of the Sea because of the similarity of Maria to the

Latin word mare – sea. The name has been mildly fashionable in Britain since the wedding in 1934 of Princess Marina of Greece, 1906–1968, with the late Duke of Kent.

Variation: Marinetta.

MARION
Origin/meaning: uncertain. Possibly Hebrew 'bitter' or 'wished for child'.

Marion means 'little Mary' and is the equivalent of the Irish Maureen. It has been used as an independent name since the Middle Ages, when Robin Hood and his Maid Marian are said to have flourished. Both Marion and the French equivalent, Marianne, are sometimes used with the intention of combining the names Mary and Anne. An example is the novelist George Eliot who changed her name from Mary Ann to Marian. In France Marion with an o is a boy's name.

Variations and abbreviations: Marian, Mariana (It/Sp), Marianna (It), Marianne (Fr), Maureen (It), See also Mary.

Examples: Marion Davies, 1898–1961, US actress, mistress of William Randolph Hearst.
Marion Mould, British showjumper.

MARISA
Origin/meaning: uncertain. Possibly Hebrew 'bitter' or 'wished for child'.

It probably derives from the Latin 'maris' – of the sea. Because of the similarity between Mary and the Latin word for the sea this was often assumed to be the name's meaning. A common title for the Virgin was therefore Stella Maris – star of the sea, and Maris became an accepted form of the name with the familiar forms Marisa, Mariska, Maristella and Marisella.

Variations and abbreviations: See Mary.

MARISKA
Origin/meaning: uncertain. Possibly Hebrew 'bitter' or 'wished for child'.

A Scandinavian familiar form of Mary q.v. through Maris q.v.

MARJORIE
Origin/meaning: Persian?/Greek/Latin 'pearl' or French/English

210

'daisy'.

This is a Scottish pet form of Margaret, used as an independent name since the 12th century. Like Isabel, the name came to Scotland from France, for the two countries had very close ties. Marjorie is a development of Margerie, a Medieval French diminutive of Marguerite. The name eventually came to England from Scotland and was fairly popular between the World Wars. It has been a separate name for so long it is sometimes mistakenly associated with the herb marjoram.

Variations and abbreviations: Margery, Marjory. See Margaret.

Example: Marjorie Proops, British journalist.

MARLENE (pron. Marrlayna)
Origin/meaning: Hebrew 'bitter' plus 'of Magdala'.

A combination of Maria and Lene (a common German short form of Magdalena). It was created for Marlene Dietrich the German singer/actress whose full name is Maria Magdalena von Losch. As it has become popular it has frequently been mispronounced as two syllables – Marrleen.

MARSHA
Origin/meaning: Latin 'of Mars' (the Roman god of War), ie 'warlike'.

An American form of Marcia q.v. which reflects the American pronunciation.

Example: Marsha Hunt, US film actress.

MARTHA
Origin/meaning: Aramaic 'lady'.

Martha is the feminine form of Mar, the Aramaic word for man or lord. Martha was the sister of Mary Magdalen and Lazarus. She was upbraided by Christ for allowing her chores to distract her from sitting and listening to him. Martha is appropriately the patron saint of housewives who often find their own higher interests submerged in the job of caring for others. The name was used in Europe in the Middle Ages, especially in France where, tradition has it, Martha and Mary Magdalen travelled after the death of Christ. In England it was not much used

211

until the 17th century when the Puritans favoured it and introduced it to New England. Its next period of popularity in English-
speaking countries was in the 19th century. It remains a well-
known but not particularly common name.

Variations and abbreviations: Marja (Russ), Marta (It), Marte,
Marthe (Fr), Mari, Martie, Martita, Marty.

Examples: Martha Washington, 1732–1802, wife of George
Washington, first President of the US.
Martha Graham, US dancer and choreographer.

MARTINA (pron. Martéena)
Origin/meaning: Latin 'of Mars' (the Roman god of War) ie
'warlike'.

This is the name of one of the early Roman martyrs. However the
name is more likely to have been given to honour the much
loved soldier/saint Martin of Tours, d.397. In the Middle Ages it
was probably used in the same form for both boys and girls and
the -a ending used in Latin documents to denote a girl. Modern
usage pronounces the -a.

Variations and abbreviations: Marta, Martie, Martine (Fr),
Marty, Martyna, Tina.

Example: Martina Navratilova, US-Czech tennis champion.

MARTY
Origin/meaning: Aramaic 'lady'.

The usual pet form of Martha, q.v.

Variation: Marti.

Example: Marti Caine, English entertainer.

MARY
Origin/meaning: uncertain. Possibly Hebrew 'bitter' or 'wished
for child'.

There are many meanings given to this name, a large number of
them due not to the origins of the word but to the qualities
ascribed to the Mother of God. The name in Hebrew was spelt
only with consonants – MRYM. The vowels have been added by
guesswork in translation, so that the Old Testament Miriam,
sister of Moses, does in fact hold the same name as the Virgin
Mary, although they now count as totally distinct names. The

212

Latin form Maria, used in Italy and Spain and popular in England in the 18th century was the intermediate source of Mary. When the Bible was translated from Hebrew into Latin MRYM sounded as though it had an accusative ending of a Latin feminine word ending in -a. The name was therefore given a Latin nominative form – Maria, without any grammatical justification, since there was no reason to suppose Hebrew names followed Latin rules! However the melodious sound of the resulting name and its religious significance resulted in its coming into use with other saints' names in the Middle Ages.

The English form Mary developed from the French form Marie with its typical French ending. Scotland, which at the time was more closely allied with France than England, tended to retain the original French form. After the 16th century Protestant Reformation the name's popularity declined sharply in Protestant countries because it was associated with the Catholic cult of the Virgin Mary which was considered idolatrous by many Protestants. In England this was coupled with the dislike of two notable Catholic women: Queen Mary, 1516–1558, whose reign had seen persecution of Protestants, and Mary Queen of Scots, who provided a focus for discontented Catholics plotting against the Protestant Elizabeth.

In the 18th century the name began to come back into favour, often in the Latinized form Maria, so that by the 19th century it was again one of the commonest names in Britain. In Ireland Mary, like Bridget, had been considered too holy to use in the Middle Ages. The two names came into use there in the 17th century probably as a show of Catholic defiance against English Protestantism, and are now the commonest Irish girls' names. The Irish form Máire (similar to the Welsh Mair and Scottish Moira) has re-established itself since the beginning of the 20th century. In Ireland respect for the Virgin Mary has also resulted in a special form – Muire – used exclusively for her. In Europe, and to a lesser extent in English-speaking countries, the name is combined with other names, such as the French Marie-Claude, the English Mary-Ann, and the American Mary-Lou. These combinations have sometimes been run together to create established independent names such as Marianne or common familiar forms like Meriel.

Variations and abbreviations: Maia, Maidie (Wel), Mair, Maire (Ir), Mairi (Scots), Maja (Ger), Mame, Mamie (US), Manette (Fr), Manon (Fr), Mara, Maria (It/Sp), Mariam, Mariamne,

Marian, Mariana, Marianna, Marianne, Marice, Marie (Fr), Mariel, Marietta, Mariette (Fr), Marilyn, Marion, Mariquilla, Mariquita (Sp), Maris, Marisa, Mariska, Marita (Sp), Maritsa, Marja (Slav), Marla, Marya, Maryann, Maryanne, Marysa, Maryse, Mascha (Russ), Masha (Russ), Maura, Maure (Ir), Maureen (Ir), Maurita, May, Meriel, Meryl, Mimi, Minette, Minnie, Minny, Miriam, Mitzi, Moira (Scots), Moire (Scots), Mollie, Molly, Moyra (Scot).

Examples: Mary Pickford (Gladys Mary Smith), 1893–1976, Canadian/US film star.
Mary McCarthy, US writer.
Marya Mannes, US novelist and poet.

MARY-ANN(E)
Origin/meaning: Hebrew 'bitter' plus Hebrew 'graceful'.

A combination of two of the most popular English names ever. This double name was fashionable in the late 18th and early 19th centuries and was sometimes 'translated' into the French Marianna or the Italian Mariana, which are in fact the equivalent of the English Marion.

Examples: Mary Ann (later Marian) Evans, real name of novelist George Eliot, 1819–1880.
Mary Ann Clarke, 1776–1852, mistress of George IV's brother, the Duke of York.

MATILDA
Origin/meaning: Old German 'battle strength'.

This is the Latin form of an Old German name, introduced into England by the Normans. Matilda was the name of William the Conqueror's wife and many other relations and descendants. By the 16th century Matilda was almost obsolete. It was, however, one of the most successful revivals of the Romantic Movement which began at the end of the 18th century. Although Matilda, which appears on Latin documents, and Maud were the main forms revived in the 19th century, there are a great many authentic variations on the name, including Mathila, Mauld, Mahhild and Mahault.

Variations and abbreviations: Mahault (Med Fr), Maitilde (Ir), Majalda (It/Port), Matelda (It), Mathilda, Mathilde (Fr/Ger), Matilde (Sp), Mattie, Matty, Maud, Maude, Maudie, Mawt (Med Eng), Mechtilde, Tilda, Tillie, Tilly.

Examples: The Empress Matilda (Maud), 1102-1167, daughter of Henry I of England. Married Geoffrey of Anjou and founded the Angevin dynasty.
Mathilda, d.1115, countess of Tuscany. Supported Pope Gregory VII against the Holy Roman Empire.

MATTEA
Origin/meaning: Hebrew 'gift of Jehovah'.

An Italian feminine form of Matthew q.v.

See also Dieudonnée, Dorothy, Theodora.

MATTIE
Origin/meaning: Old German 'battle strength'.

The usual pet form of Matilda q.v.

Variations and abbreviations: Matt, Matty. See also Matilda.

MAUD
Origin/meaning: Old German 'battle strength'.

A medieval form of Matilda. The two names were used interchangeably for the same person, Matilda tending to be the form used in documents. When medieval names were revived in the 19th century Maud became a great favourite in England. Tennyson's poem 'Maud', 1855, may have contributed to its popularity, although it was not his most successful work.

Variations and abbreviations: Maude, Maudie, Mawt. See also Matilda.

Example: Queen Maud of Norway, 1869-1938, daughter of Edward VII and Queen Alexandra.

MAUREEN
Origin/meaning: uncertain. Possibly Hebrew 'bitter' or 'wished for child'.

This is the Irish diminutive of Mary (Maire) and means 'little Mary'. It is an extremely popular name in Australia, Canada and the US, among people of Irish descent. It has been introduced back into Britain from the US perhaps because of the influence of film stars like Maureen O'Sullivan and Maureen O'Hara.

Variations: See Marion and Mary.

Examples: Maureen Lipman, British actress.
Maureen Duffy, English writer.

MAVIS
Origin/meaning: French 'song thrush'.

A modern name which first appeared in the 19th century. Marie Corelli, 1855-1924, used it in one of her romantic novels, *The Sorrows of Satan*, 1895.

See also Merle.

Example: Mavis Nicholson, British broadcaster.

MAWUSI (pron. Mawusée)
Origin/meaning: Ewe 'in the hands of God'.

A name from Ghana.

MAXINE
Origin/meaning: Latin 'little great one'.

A French feminine diminutive of Max, the short form of Maximilian *q.v.* It dates from the 19th century. There is also a clumsier German form Maximiliana.

Example: Maxine Audley, British actress.

MAY
Origin/meaning: Sanskrit 'growth' 'burgeoning'. The name of the fifth month of the year.

In the 20th century this name has usually been given as the name of the month, like April or June. May is widely considered a special month in the year and is associated with festivity in many countries. In the 18th and 19th centuries May was often used as a familiar form of Mary or, less commonly, of Margaret. May has occasionally been used as an English equivalent of the Italian Maia, a Roman goddess whose name is popular in Germany and Scandinavia. The month is said by some to have been named after her.

Variations and abbreviations: Mae, Mai (Fr/Ger/Scand), Maye. See also Maia, Margaret, Mary.

Examples: Mai Zetterling, Swedish actress and film director.
Mae West, 1892-1982, US film actress.
Queen Mary, 1867-1953, wife of George V, was typical of her generation in being known to her family as May.
May Sinclair, 1863-1946, English novelist.

MEAVE
Origin/meaning: Old Irish 'joy'.

A name from Irish legend, Meave was considered the equivalent of the English Mab, the fairy who manipulated men's dreams.

MEENA
Origin/meaning: Sanskrit, either from meen (fish) or meena (enamel work which shines like fishes' scales).

MEENAKSHI (pron. Meenakshée)
Origin/meaning: Sanskrit 'eyes like a fish'.

This is the equivalent of the English expression 'doe's eyes' and is a flattering description.

MEENAKUMARI
Origin/meaning: Sanskrit 'fish-girl'.

Related to the names Meena and Meenakshi. Kumari is a feminine suffix the equivalent of the masculine kumar.

Example: Meenakumari, Indian film actress famous for her role in *Pakeeza*.

MEERA (pron. Meeráh)
Origin/meaning: from the Rajasthan area, meaning obscure.

Meera was one of the most famous Hindu Saints. She was a devotee of Krishna and wrote many poems about him. Gandhi gave this name to Jane, his adopted English daughter. She was called Meeraben, the addition of the suffix -ben in West India is a form of politeness, as is -bai in North India.

MEGAN
Origin/meaning: Persian?/Greek/Latin 'pearl' or French/English 'daisy'.

This is a comparatively recent Welsh pet form of Margaret *q.v.* The full Welsh versions of Margaret are Margred and Marged. However Megan, which seems to have been used first for Lady Megan Lloyd-George, 1902–1966, daughter of David Lloyd-George, is now the preferred form. It has recently been surprisingly popular in Australia.

Variations and abbreviations: See Margaret.

MEHETABEL

Origin/meaning: Aramai 'God is doing good' or 'God treats us well'.

A Biblical name (Genesis ch.36) popular with the early Puritans but rare today. The US comic writer Don Marquis, 1878–1937, gave the name to a cat in one of his social satires.

Variations and abbreviations: Hetty, Mehitabel.

MELANIE

Origin/meaning: Greek 'black', 'dark-haired'.

This is the French form of the Italian/Latin Melania. St Melania the younger, 383–439, was a rich woman who converted her husband to Christianity. Husband and wife then emancipated their slaves and gave away their wealth to the poor. St Melania the Elder was her grandmother. The name was not used in Medieval England but was common in France. The French version was introduced in the 17th century by Huguenot refugees who fled to England. After being comparatively rare in English-speaking countries it has become extremely fashionable since the Second World War. This may be due in part to the amazing success of the novel *Gone With The Wind* in which Melanie is one of the main characters.

Variations and abbreviations: Mel, Mela, Malania (It), Mélanie (Fr), Melinda, Melloney, Melly, Melony.

MELINDA

Origin/meaning: uncertain. Sometimes given as 'loved' or 'dark-haired'.

This is a name which has appeared from nowhere in the 20th century. It seems to be a combination of several names which are favourites in the US such as Melissa, Melanie and Linda. Some attempt is made to give it a 'history' by referring back to Amelinda which sounds convincingly similar to 17th century pastoral names like Amanda, Amarantha and Araminta. It is sometimes given as a form of Melanie *q.v.*

Variations and abbreviations: Linda, Lynda, Malinda, Melinde.

MELISSA

Origin/meaning: Greek 'bee' or 'Melissa officianalis' the Latin name for the herb lemon balm.

This name has the same meaning as Deborah *q.v.* It was used in

218

pre-Christian Greece and by the 16th and 17th century poets who wished to evoke that era. In the 20th century it has become very popular in North America and has spread to other English-speaking countries. It is also much used in Italy probably because Ludovico Ariosto, 1474–1533, used the name in his epic poem *Orlando Furioso*, 1516, a continuation of the Roland epic. In the poem Melissa is a prophetess who lives in Merlin's cave and is able to metamorphose herself into many different shapes.

Variations and abbreviations: Lisa, Lissa, Malissa, Mel, Melisa, Melitta, Milly, Missie, Missy.

MELITTA
Origin/meaning: Greek 'bee' or 'Melissa officianalis' Latin name for the herb lemon balm.

A version of Melissa *q.v.*

MELODY
Origin/meaning: Greek 'a song being sung'.

This name is used from time to time as much for its pleasant sound as for its meaning.

MELUSINA
Origin/meaning: in French legend Melusina was a fairy doomed to be turned into a serpent from the waist down every Saturday as a punishment for entombing her father in a mountain. She forced her mortal husband, Robert Count of Lusignan, to promise never to visit her on a Saturday. Unfortunately his curiosity overcame his vow and he saw his wife's transformation. He thus doomed her to existence as a wandering spirit, for in marrying a mortal she had gained an immortal soul. Her cry of despair on realizing she was discovered entered the French language as a byword for a sudden scream a '*cri de Mélusine*'.

Variations: Melesina, Mélusine (Fr).

MELVINA
Origin/meaning: Scots Gaelic 'fair loveliness'.

A form of Malvina *q.v.* Also a feminine form of the masculine Melvin which derives from a surname.

MERCEDES
Origin/meaning: Spanish 'mercies'.

This is part of a standard Spanish description of the Virgin Mary. Maria de Mercedes – Mary of Mercies. The main word became a name in its own right which was understood to encompass the entire phrase. Although generally assumed to be a Catholic name it is more familiar in English-speaking countries than comparable epithets such as Pilar or Consuelo. This may be because of its similarity to the English name Mercy or the popularity of the Mercedes Benz car which was named after the designer's daughter.

See also Consuelo, Dolores, Mercy, Pilar.

Example: Mercedes McCambridge, US actress.

MERCIA
Origin/meaning: Old English 'from Mercia'.

The name of Mercia, one of the seven British Kingdoms, comes from the old word mearc or mark, meaning a boundary. It has the same meaning as marches used to describe the border area known as the Welch marches. Mercia was the kingdom in the centre of England. The name was used in the 19th century when there was a great deal of interest in Britain's early history.

MERCY
Origin/meaning: Medieval Latin 'pity'.

This name, which has a similar meaning to Clemency q.v. was one of the abstract virtue names popular with the 17th century Puritans. Although still a viable name, it has survived less well than others such as Faith and Hope.

Variation: Merry.

MEREDITH
Origin/meaning: Welsh 'great?/lord'.

This is a Welsh masculine first name, properly spelt Maredudd and with the accent on the second syllable. It became almost exclusively a surname but as a family name it is now having a new life as a first name, this time mainly for girls. It is particularly popular in North America, and in the Southern US where 'masculine' family names are characteristically used for girls.

Variations and abbreviations: Bedo (Wel), Maredudd (Wel), Meredudd (Wel), Merry.

See Meredith(m).

MERIEL
Origin/meaning: Old Irish 'bright sea'.

An old form of Muriel *q.v.*

Example: Meriel Forbes-Robertson, English actress wife of Sir Ralph Richardson.

MERIERID
Origin/meaning: Latin 'pearl'.

A Welsh name derived from the same root as Margaret *q.v.*

Variation: Mererid.

MERLE (pron. Merrl or Murl)
Origin/meaning: French 'blackbird'.

This is a French surname which may indicate an ancestor who was fond of whistling. Henry James had a character called Madame Merle in his book *The Portrait of a Lady*, 1881. It is a family name of an actress called Estelle O'Brien Merle Thompson who used it to create the stage name Merle Oberon. Her popularity in the films of the 1930s and 40s brought the name into use in the US.

MERRY
Origin/meaning: a form of Mercy *q.v.* As Cherry is a familiar form of Charity.

Recently used as a short form of Meredith *q.v.* This is sometimes given as an independent name on the assumption that it is the word meaning cheerful.

Example: Merry Anders, US actress.

MERYL
Origin/meaning: Hebrew 'bitter' and Latin 'famous in war'.

A familiar form of the common double name Mary Louise, brought to prominence by the US actress Meryl Streep. Where the spelling is Merrell it is a family name derived from the medieval first name Muriel *q.v.*

MHONUM
Origin/meaning: Tiv 'mercy'.

This is a Nigerian name.

MIA
Origin/meaning: uncertain. Possibly Hebrew 'bitter' or 'wished for child'. Sometimes Italian 'mine'.

A European short form of Mary (Maria) made familiar by the US actress Mia Farrow.

Variations and abbreviations: See Mary.

MICHELLE (pron. M'shell)
Origin/meaning: Hebrew 'Who is like the Lord?'.

A French feminine form of Michael *q.v.* adopted in English-speaking countries where there is no native feminine form, and often mispronounced Meeshell. It became common in the 1960s after the success of the Beatles song 'Michelle'.

Variations and abbreviations: Michaela (It), Michela (It), Michèle (Fr), Micheline (Fr), Mick, Mickie, Micky.

Example: Michelle Morgan, French film actress.

MILDRED
Origin/meaning: Old English 'mild strength'.

This was the name of a Saxon Saint who died about 700. The daughter of King Merewald of Mercia she was an abbess renowned for her gentleness. Like the name Etheldreda (the early form of Audrey) Mildred survived the influx of new names at the Norman Conquest because of the Saint's great following. After the Reformation it went into decline, along with most Catholic saints' names. In the 19th century Mildred came back into favour when the fashion was for medieval and pre-Conquest names. Although now regarded as old-fashioned it is still a viable name.

Variations and abbreviations: Meldred (Med Eng), Mil, Mildrid, Millie, Milly.

MILLICENT
Origin/meaning: Old German 'work-strong'.

This is the usual modern form of a name which goes back to the time of the Emperor Charlemagne, 742–814. He named his daughter Melisendra which was a popular name of the period. Melisendra married his nephew Don Gwyferos who rescued her

222

after seven years of imprisonment by the Moors. When the name first came to England it was in the Medieval French form Melisant. The modern French form Melisande is sometimes confused with Melusina q.v. a legendary spirit, as in the opera by Maeterlinck, *Pelléas et Mélisande*.

Variations and abbreviations: Lissa, Mel, Melicent, Mélisande (Fr), Melisenda (Sp), Melisendra, Mellicent, Mellisent, Mellie, Melly, Milicent, Milli, Millie, Millisent, Milly.

Example: Millicent Martin, English singer and dancer.

MILLIE

Origin/meaning: a common short form of Millicent q.v. Sometimes found as a short form of Mildred, Emily, Camilla, Melissa, etc.

MIMI

Origin/meaning: uncertain. Possibly Hebrew 'bitter' or 'wished for child'.

A European familiar form of Mary and Miriam, similar to the US Mamie.

MINERVA

Origin/meaning: Greek 'wisdom'.

Minerva was the Roman equivalent of the Greek Athena, goddess of Wisdom, after whom the city of Athens was named. Although rare it has been used occasionally since the Renaissance revived interest in classical names.

MINNA

Origin/meaning: Old German 'helmet of resolution'.

The German short form of Wilhelmina. It has been an established independent name in Germany for many years and consequently also in the US and Australia which had many German immigrants.

Example: Minna Canth, 1844–1897, Finnish playwright and femininist.

MINNIE

Origin/meaning: Hebrew 'bitter' or Old German 'helmet of resolution'.

A Scottish familiar form of Mary q.v. now used as an

independent name, or a short form of Wilhelmina *q.v.* like the German Minna.

Variations and abbreviations: Min, Mina, Minna, Minne, Minni, Minka (Slav). See also Mary and Wilhelmina.

Example: Minnie Haskins, 1875–1957, British poet and lecturer.

MIRA
Origin/meaning: Latin 'wonderful'.

A short form of Miranda or Mirabel. Sometimes used as an independent name when it is probably confused with the separate name Myra *q.v.*

MIRABEL
Origin/meaning: Latin 'wonderful'.

A name found occasionally since the Middle Ages. Mirabel was used for boys or girls but the more recent Mirabella and Mirabelle are for girls only.

Variations and abbreviations: Mira, Mirabella, Mirabelle (Fr).

MIRABELLA
Origin/meaning: Latin 'wonderfully beautiful'.

A modern development of the old name Mirabel *q.v.* to include the idea of beauty.

Variations and abbreviations: See Mirabel.

MIRANDA
Origin/meaning: Latin 'admirable'.

This name was probably invented by Shakespeare who used it for the heroine of his play *The Tempest*, 1611. Never widely used it has become slightly less rare over the last 20 years.

Variations and abbreviations: Mira, Myra. See also Evangeline, Fiona, Lorna, Pamela, Perdita, Stella, Vanessa, Wendy.

Example: Miranda Seymour, English novelist.

MIRIAM
Origin/meaning: uncertain. Possibly Hebrew 'bitter' or 'wished for child'.

This is a translation of the name which appears in Hebrew as MRYM and is translated elsewhere as Mary. The two translations have come to be accepted as totally independent names. Miriam is the translation used in the Old Testament as the name of the sister of Moses (Exodus ch.15.). Always a popular Jewish name it was also used by Puritans in the 17th and 18th centuries when they revived many Biblical names. It is consistently found in English-speaking countries but has never achieved great popularity.

Variations and abbreviations: Mariamne, Mimi, Mirjam (Ger), Miryam (Fr), Mitzi (US), Myrjam (Ger).

Examples: Miriam Stoppard, British writer.
Miriam Karlin, British actress.

MITZI
Origin/meaning: uncertain. Possibly Hebrew 'bitter' or 'longed for child'.

A familiar form of Miriam *q.v.* Sometimes used as an independent name.

Example: Mitzi Gaynor, US/Hungarian film actress.

MODRON
Origin/meaning: a goddess of Welsh Celtic legend, mentioned in the collection of Welsh folk tales, *The Mabinogion*.

MODWENNA
Origin/meaning: uncertain.

The name of a 7th century saint whose shrine was at Burton-on-Trent in the North of England. Her story is not authenticated and her name is sometimes confused with the Irish St Monenna and the Welsh St Morwenna.

MOIRA
Origin/meaning: uncertain. Possibly Hebrew 'bitter' or 'wished for child'.

This is a Scots version of Mary *q.v.* now used as an independent name. It reflects the pronunciation of the Celtic versions Maire, Mair and Moire.

Variation: Moyra. See also Mary.

Examples: Moira Lister, South African-British actress.
Moira Anderson, Scottish singer.

MOLLY

Origin/meaning: uncertain. Possibly Hebrew 'bitter' or 'wished for child'.

A familiar form of Mary, often used as an independent name and popular in Ireland.

Variation: Mollie.

Example: Molly Keane, Irish novelist.

MONA

Origin/meaning: Old Irish 'little noble one'.

This is a native Irish equivalent of the German Adela q.v. At the beginning of the 19th century it became more widespread as people became interested in native Irish language and culture.

Example: Mona Washbourne, English actress.

MONA

Origin/meaning: Arabic 'hope'.

A muslim name quite unconnected with the Irish name above.

MONICA

Origin/meaning: uncertain. Sometimes given as Latin 'monk' or 'adviser'.

St Monica, 331–387, was the mother of St Augustine. In his writings he explains how she contributed to his conversion to Christianity, at one point being reassured by her Bishop: 'It is not possible for the son of so many tears to be lost'.

Variations and abbreviations: Mona, Monika (Ger), Monique (Fr).

Example: Monica Dickens, English writer, grand-daughter of Charles Dickens.

MORAG

Origin/meaning: Scots Gaelic 'sun'.

A popular Scots name.

MOROWA

Origin/meaning: Akan 'queen'.

A Ghanaian name. Other African names meaning 'queen' are Thema (also used in Ghana) and Torkwase (used in Nigeria). See also Queenie, Regina.

MORWENNA
Origin/meaning: Old Welsh 'wave', 'of the sea'.

A familiar Welsh name because of the comparative ease of pronunciation. St Morwenna was a 6th century saint, the patron of Morwenstow in Cornwall and the name was used in Cornwall as well as Wales. According to legend a well sprang up where she placed a boulder she had brought up from the foot of the cliff on her head. On the site where she eventually placed the stone the church of Morwenstow was built.

Variations and abbreviations: Morwen, Morwinna, Mwynen.

MUKTA (pron. Mookta)
Origin/meaning: Sanskrit 'pearl'.

A name found throughout India. It honours Muktabai, a saintly Hindu woman, the mother of another saint, Dnyaneshwar. Their stoy is found among the collection of stories of the Great Saints of the Maharashtra, which is an area of Northern India. The addition of -bai to a feminine name in North India indicates respect, as does -ben in West India.

See also Margaret, Pearl.

MURIEL
Origin/meaning: Old Irish 'bright sea'.

This is the Norman version of a Celtic name. The Normans brought their version to England from Brittany but it existed independently in Ireland. It was one of many names such as Emma and Alice which died out at about the end of the 15th century and came to be viewed as unsophisticated country names. In the 19th century Muriel was revived along with these and many other medieval and pre-Conquest names.

Variations and abbreviations: Meriel, Miriel, Murial, Muriella, Murielle.

Example: Muriel Spark, English novelist.

MUTETELI (pron. Mutetáyli)
Origin/meaning: Rwanda 'dainty'.

A name used in the Central African Republic of Rwanda.

MYFANWY (pron. Mivvánwee)
Origin/meaning: Welsh 'my rare one'.

A popular Welsh first name which has become known outside Wales. It was sometimes 'translated' into the English Fanny.

Variations and abbreviations: Fanny, Myfi, Myvanwy.

MYRA
Origin/meaning: a coined literary name used in the 17th and 18th centuries when such names were popular. Myra was the name of a city in Asia-Minor. It was used by, among others, Sir Fulke Greville (Lord Brooke), 1554–1628, who may have originated it, and George Crabbe, 1754–1832. It is also used as a short form of Miranda, Miriam and Muriel q.v.

Variations and abbreviations: Mira, Myrrah.

Example: Dame Myra Hess, 1890–1966, English pianist, known for organizing concerts during the Second World War.

MYRTLE
Origin/meaning: Greek. The name of a sweet-smelling flowering shrub.

One of the many flower names which became fashionable in the latter half of the 19th century. There are several legends and superstitions surrounding the myrtle tree. These include the belief that eating myrtle leaves conferred the power to detect witches and that a lover would prove faithful if the glossy myrtle leaves crackled in the hand. The myrtle was associated with Venus the Greek goddess of love. Myrtle leaves were also used by the Greeks as a symbol of victory. The name is now considered rather old fashioned.

Variations and abbreviations: Mertle, Mirtle, Myrrha, Myrta, Myrtah, Myrtice, Myrtilla. See also Esther.

N

NABULUNGI (pron. Nabulongée)
Origin/meaning: Luganda 'beautiful one'.

A name from Uganda in East Africa.

See also Belle, Nomble.

NADIA (pron. Nárdeea)
Origin/meaning: Russian 'hope'.

This is the typical familiar form of the Russian name Nadezhda. Since Russians rarely use the full version of their name (cf Lenka for Helena), Nadia is the name that became most familiar to other Europeans through the popularity of 19th century Russian novels and plays.

Variations and abbreviations: Nada, Nadina (It), Nadine (Fr), Nadja. See also Hope, Speranza.

Example: Nadia Comaneci, Rumanian Olympic gymnast.

NADINE
Origin/meaning: Russian 'hope'.

This is a French form of the Russian name Nadezhda – hope. It is occasionally used in English-speaking countries, as is the Russian familiar form of Nadia.

Variations and abbreviations: See Nadia.

Example: Nadine Gordimer, South African novelist.

NANCY
Origin/meaning: Hebrew 'graceful'.

A derivative of Hannah and Ann *q.v.*

Examples: Nancy Reagan, wife of US President Ronald Reagan. Nancy Mitford, 1907–1973, English writer.

NAJMA (pron. Naíma)
Origin/meaning: Arabic 'benevolent'.

A popular Muslim name.

Variation: Naeemah.

NANETTE
Origin/meaning: Hebrew 'graceful'.

A diminutive of Nan, a familiar form of Ann *q.v.* now found as an independent name. It enjoyed a short vogue in the wake of the musical *No, No, Nanette*.

Example: Nanette Newman, British screen actress.

NAOMI (pron. Nayóhmee)
Origin/meaning: Hebrew 'joy', 'delight'.

This name is the equivalent of the medieval name Pleasance. At about the time that Pleasance was becoming obsolete Naomi came into use. It was used in the 17th century by Puritans who turned away from Catholic saints' names and used the Bible as their main source. Naomi was the mother-in-law of Ruth *q.v.* whose story is told in the Book of Ruth.

Examples: Naomi Mitchison, British writer.
Dame Naomi James, British yachtswoman.

NARELLE
A name with a typical feminine ending confined almost totally to Australia.

NATALIA
Origin/meaning: Latin 'birth', ie Christmas day.

This is a name derived from the phrase 'natale domini' (birth of the Lord). It used to be given to girls born at the Christmas season and is an exact equivalent of Noël/Noelle *q.v.* Natalia is the form used in Italy, Spain and Russia, where the familiar form Natasha has developed. It is now used irrespective of the time of year.

Variations and abbreviations: Natalie (Fr), Natalina (It), Natalja, Natalya, Nathalia, Nathalie, Natasha (Russ), Natty, Nettie.

Example: Nathalie Sarraute, French writer.

NATALIE
Origin/meaning: Latin 'birth', ie Christmas day.

The French and German form of Natalia *q.v.* currently popular in English-speaking countries, especially Australia.

Variations and abbreviations: See Natalia.

Example: Natalie Wood, 1938-1982, US film actress.

NATASHA
Origin/meaning: Latin 'birth', ie Christmas day.

The Russian diminutive of Natalia. It has been used since the 19th century in Britain when Russian novels were popular. It is currently a vogue name in Britain and Australia.

Abbreviation: Tasha

Example: Natasha Parry, British actress.

NELLIE
Origin/meaning: Greek 'bright' or 'light'.

A familiar form of Eleanor or Helen, both of which have the same meaning, and occasionally of Cornelia *q.v.* Sometimes used as an independent name, particularly in the latter half of the 19th century.

Variations and abbreviations: Nell, Nelly.

Examples: Nell (Elinor) Gwyn, 1650-1683, mistress of Charles II. Dame Nellie Melba, 1859-1931, Australian opera singer.

NERINE
Origin/meaning: Greek 'sea nymph'.

In Greek mythology Nerine was one of the Nereids who were daughters of the god Nereus.

Variation: Nerina (It). See also Nerissa, Nerita, Nyse.

NERISSA
Origin/maning: Greek 'sea nymph'.

Nerissa was one of the Nereids who were the daughters of the sea god Nereus. Shakespeare used the name for Portia's waiting maid in *The Merchant of Venice*.

See also Galatea, Nerita, Nerine, Nyse.

NERITA
Origin/meaning: Greek 'sea nymph'.

Nerita was one of the Nereids, a daughter of the sea god Nereus.

See also Galatea, Nerine, Nerissa, Nyse.

NERYS (pron. Néh-rees)
Origin/meaning: Welsh 'lord'.

Example: Nerys Hughes, Welsh actress.

NESSA
Origin/meaning: Greek 'pure', 'chaste'.

An English familiar form of Agnes *q.v.* similar to the Welsh version, Nesta.

Variation: Nessie.

NEST
Origin/meaning: Greek 'pure', 'chaste'.

The Welsh version of Agnes *q.v.* The most famous example is Nest, wife of Gerald of Windsor. Extremely beautiful, she was abducted from Pembroke Castle and became the mistress of Henry I.

Variation and abbreviations: Ness, Nessie, Nesta.

NETTA
Origin/meaning: this is a familiar form of names ending in -et (such as Janet and Annette).

Variations: Nettie, Netty, Nita (Sp).

NICOLA
Origin/meaning: Greek, 'victory of the people'.

This is the Latinized feminine form of Nicholas *q.v.* It has recently become extremely popular in Britain. Although Nichola appears in English medieval documents women in those days would probably have used the masculine form Nicholas, or Nicol, as they did with other names such as Peter, Paul and Eustace.

Variations and abbreviations: Colette, Nichola, Nicole (Fr), Nicoletta (It), Nicolette (Fr), Nikol (Ger/Dut), Nikoline (Ger).

Example: Nicola Pagett, English actress.

NICOLE
Origin/meaning: Greek 'victory of the people'.

232

The French feminine form of Nicholas. It is used in many other countries and is particularly popular in Australia.

Variations and abbreviations: See Nicola.

NICOLETTE
Origin/meaning: Greek 'victory of the people'.

A diminutive of Nicole, the French feminine form of Nicholas q.v. It is occasionally used in English-speaking countries.

Variations and abbreviations: See Nicola.

NIGELLA
Origin/meaning: Old Irish 'champion'.

A rare feminine form of Nigel q.v. It is the Latin feminine form of the Latin Nigellus. By a happy coincidence, it is also the Latin name for Love-in-the-Mist.

NKOSAZANA (pron. 'Nkosazáhna)
Origin/meaning: Xhosa 'princess'.

This name, the equivalent of the Hebrew Sarah, is used by the people living in the South of Africa.

NINA
Origin/meaning: Hebrew 'graceful', or Spanish 'small girl'.

A Russian diminutive of Ann, this name came into use in England along with other Russian names like Natasha and Nadine. In the US it is sometimes given with its Spanish meaning.

Example: Nina Bawden, English novelist and children's writer.

NITA
Origin/meaning: a Spanish diminutive of names like Juanita and Anita.

Now used as an independent name. The English equivalent is Netta q.v.

NOËLLE
Origin/meaning: French 'Christmas'.

This is a modern French feminine form of Noël created on the pattern of a French adjective. Noel, which used to be used for boys and girls has become an exclusively masculine name.

Noëlle has become well established in English-speaking countries.

Variations: Noëlla. See also Natalia.

Example: Noelle Gordon, British actress.

NOMBLE (pron. Nómblay)
Origin/meaning: Xhosa 'beauty'.

A name used in the South of Africa.

See also Belle, Nabulung.

NONA
Origin/meaning: Latin 'ninth'.

A name given to a ninth child or girl when people had large families. It is occasionally used today without any consideration of its meaning but for its pleasant easy sound.

NORA
Origin/meaning: Latin 'honour' or 'beauty'.

An Irish short form of Honora q.v. which has been popular since the Middle Ages. It may also be used as a short form of Eleanor and Leonora.

Variations and abbreviations: Norah, Noreen.

Example: Nora Ephron, US writer.

NORAH
Origin/meaning: Latin 'honour' or 'beauty'.

An alternative spelling of Nora q.v.

NOREEN
Origin/meaning: Latin 'honour' or 'beauty'.

A diminutive of Nora which is an Irish short form of Honora, q.v. The ending -een is a typical Irish one and is found in names like Maureen and Kathleen.

NORMA
Origin/meaning: Latin 'rule'.

This Latin word seems first to have been 'borrowed' as a name by Bellini for his opera *Norma*, 1831. Its main usage has been in the US but it has definitely established itself in all English-speaking countries as a bona fide name. It is sometimes used as a feminine equivalent of Norman but there is no real connection between the two.

Example: Norma Shearer, US film actress.

NUALA
Origin/meaning: Old Irish 'white shoulders'.

An Irish short form of Fenella *q.v.* through the form of Finnuala.

NUR JEHAN
Origin/meaning: Sanskrit 'light of the world'.

This was the name of the wife of Jehangir *q.v.*, 1569–1627, the third Mogul Emperor of India. Unlike Akbar *q.v.* his father Jehangir was idle and pleasure-loving. Because of his weakness Nur Jehan was the effective controller of the Mogul empire. She is said to have relaxed by playing polo and shooting tigers. Nur Jehan is a popular Muslim name.

Variation: Nur Jahan.

NURU
Origin/meaning: Swahili 'in the daylight'.

This name is used in East Africa.

See also Lucy, Lucinda.

NYSE
Origin/meaning: Greek 'sea nymph'.

In Greek mythology Nyse was one of the Nereids.

See also Galatea, Nerissa, Nerita, Nerine.

O

OCTAVIA
Origin/meaning: Latin 'eighth'.

A name given to an eighth girl or eighth child. Rare in the 20th century. Sometimes given independently of its meaning perhaps to honour Octavia, d. 11 BC, sister of the Emperor Augustus and second wife of Mark Antony, who deserted her for Cleopatra.

Example: Octavia Hill, 1838–1912, British housing reformer and co-founder of the National Trust.

ODA
Origin/meaning: Old German 'of the fatherland' or 'rich'.

The feminine form of Odo and Otto *q.v.* The name from which several more familiar names derive eg Odette, Odile, Ottilia *q.v.* and their variations.

Variations and abbreviations: Ode (Fr), Odette (Fr), Odile, Odo, Ota, Ottilia, Ottilie, Uta, Ute.

ODELIA
Origin/meaning: Old German 'of the fatherland' or 'rich'.

A form of the French names Odile and Odette *q.v.*

Variation: Delia.

ODETTE
Origin/meaning: Old German 'of the fatherland', 'rich'.

The German and French diminutive form of the Old German name Oda *q.v.* It is now the most familiar form in all European countries, including Britain. One of the other variations is Odile *q.v.* and in the ballet *Swan Lake*, the black swan and the white swan, danced by the same dancer, have in effect the same name; one is Odile, the other Odette.

236

Variations and abbreviations: Oda, Odetta (It), Odile, Ottillie.
Example: Odette Hallowes GC, French resistance heroine.

ODILE (pron. Odéel)
Origin/meaning: Old German 'of the fatherland' or 'rich'.

A French name derived from the German Oda *q.v.* It is closely related to Odette and Ottillie *q.v.* and their variations.

Variations and abbreviations: Oda, Ode, Odelia, Odella, Odilia, Odilie, Odille, Odine.

OLGA
Origin/meaning: Old Norse 'holy'.

The root of this name is the Norse word helga – holy – and is found in Russia because the founder of the Russian monarchy was a Viking called Rurik. The same race invaded Scotland (and incidentally brought the name Rurik with them, which developed into Roderick *q.v.*). The masculine version of Olga is Oleg, which is virtually unknown in English-speaking countries. Olga on the other hand became popular in the 19th century along with other Russian girls' names like Natasha and Vera. This may have been due to the large number of royal princesses, duchesses, etc who flourished in the 19th century and who sported Slavic names.

Examples: St Olga, d. 969, wife of Prince Igor, she introduced Christianity into Russia and paved the way for its conversion by her grandson, St Vladimir.
Olga Korbut, Russian Olympic gymnast.

OLIVE
Origin/meaning: Latin 'olive tree', 'olive branch'.

The olive, so vital to the southern European way of life, became a symbol of peace because in war the enemy would destroy the precious olive trees. The name may have been given to honour St Olivia, who because of the sound of her name became patron saint of olive trees. It was used in England in the Middle Ages, usually in the form of Oliff or Oliva, which suggests it may sometimes have been given as a feminine of Oliver *q.v.* The name eventually developed into the more familiar Olive. An Italian version, Olivia, became fashionable during the Renaissance period in about the 16th century and again in the 18th century when Latinized names were considered preferable to the home-grown version. In the 19th century when plant and flower names were often used, Olive began to creep back into favour and eventually became a vogue name during the 1920s and 30s in Britain. In the US Olivia has remained the preferred form.

Variations and abbreviations: Liva, Livia, Livie, Livy, Nola, Nollie, Olivia, Olivette, Ollie, Olva.

OLIVIA

Origin/meaning: Latin 'olive tree'.

The Italian version of Olive q.v. It was popular during the 16th century when Shakespeare used it for the beautiful countess in *Twelfth Night*, and in the 18th century when many names were embellished with a Latin ending. In England Olive has become the standard form but in North America Olivia is more usual.

Variations and abbreviations: See Olive.

Examples: Olivia de Havilland, US film actress.
Olivia Newton-John, Australian singer.

OLWEN

Origin/meaning: Old Welsh 'white footprint'.

In *The Mabinogion*, the collection of Welsh Celtic folk tales, Olwen was the daughter of a giant. Her beauty was so great that white trefoils appeared on the ground where she trod. She was wooed by Prince Culhwch, who needed the help of King Arthur and his knights to accomplish the tasks her father set him in order to win her hand in marriage. The linguist Lady Charlotte Guest made a translation of the tales into English between 1838 and 1849. The new version was immensely successful and brought the name Olwen into popular currency in Wales.

Variation: Olwyn.

OLYMPIA

Origin/meaning: Greek 'from Olympia'.

Olympia was a religious centre in Ancient Greece and the site of the Olympic Games. The name is sometimes given as 'from Olympus', the mountain home of the gods and therefore 'celestial'. Olympia was the name of the mother of Alexander the Great. Christians adopted it because of St Olympias, 366–408, a rich widow famous for her generous benefactions. It became a vogue name in Renaissance France and Italy because of its classical connections.

Variations and abbreviations: Olimpe (Fr), Olimpia (It), Olympe (Fr), Olympias.

Example: Olympia Morata, 1526–1555, Italian scholar and poet.

ONDINE (pron. Ondeen)
Origin/meaning: Latin 'water sprite'.

The French form of Undine *q.v.*

ONI
Origin/meaning: Benin 'desired'.

A Nigerian name.

OONAGH (pron. Oohnar)
Origin/meaning: Old Irish, uncertain, possibly 'lamb'.

This name is also found in Scotland, another Celtic area. Because of its supposed meaning it has sometimes been Anglicized to Agnes, which is similar to Agnus, the Latin word for a lamb. Alternatively it has been translated to the similar sounding Winnie and so eventually to Winifred. However since the revival of interest in Old Irish at the beginning of this century it has stood again in its own right as a true Irish name. It is sometimes written as Una, which is a quite separate name. Another variation, Juno, has been wrongly confused with the Roman goddess of the same name.

Variations and abbreviations: Juno, Ona, Oona, Una.

Example: Oona Chaplin, wife of Charles Chaplin and daughter of Eugene O'Neill, the Irish-American playwright.

OPAL
Origin/meaning: Sanskrit 'precious stone'.

This is one of the jewel names which have been used since the 19th century. It has been less commonly used than others, particularly Ruby and Pearl.

239

OPHELIA

Origin/meaning: uncertain. Possibly Greek 'help' or 'serpent'.

This name seems to have been a literary name coined in the 16th century when classical Greek influence was strong. It was first used by an Italian writer but the best known example is Hamlet's rejected lover Ophelia, in Shakespeare's *Hamlet*, c. 1600. It has been used very occasionally since then.

See also Evangeline, Fiona, Morna, Miranda, Pamela, Perdita, Vanessa, Wendy.

ORALIE

Origin/meaning: Latin 'golden'.

A form of Aurelia *q.v.*

ORIANA

Origin/meaning: Latin 'risen', 'dawn'.

A name coined in the 16th century as a flattering title for Queen Elizabeth I and the new era which she symbolized. It was used in her praise by poets and writers of madrigals and has been used occasionally since then. It is the title of one of the Victorian poet Tennyson's best known poems, *The Ballad of Oriana*. The name was used because it belonged to two friends of Tennyson's, which shows it had not become totally obsolete by the 19th century.

Aurora *q.v.* is a close equivalent.

ORIEL

Origin/meaning: uncertain, possibly Old German 'fire-strife' or Latin 'golden'.

This name was found in the Middle Ages and it probably has origins in a pre-Conquest name. Aurelia, the Latin name meaning golden, did not become popular until the 16th century. Nowadays Auriol, a version of the Latin Aurelia, and Oriol, are considered interchangeable because of their similar sound despite the fact that they may well be quite separate names.

Variations and abbreviations: Auriol, Oriole.

ORSOLA

Origin/meaning: Latin 'little she bear'.

An Italian variation of Ursula *q.v.*

OTTILIE

Origin/meaning: Old German 'of the fatherland' or 'rich'.

One of the main variations, with Odile and Odette, of the Old German name Oda.

Variations and abbreviations: Otti, Ottilia (It), Ottoline.

Example: Lady Ottoline Morrell, 1873–1938, English socialite and writer.

P

PAMELA (pron. Pámela or Paméela)
Origin/meaning: this name has no real meaning, although it is sometimes given as 'all-honey' because of a similarity to these Greek words.

This was an invention of Sir Philip Sidney's for his pastoral romance *Arcadia*, 1590. The great popularity of *Arcadia* helped to establish Pamela as a name. In 1740 Samuel Richardson used the name for his novel *Pamela*. This too was widely read and spread the name still further. Pamela was a vogue name in Britain and the US in the 1950s.

Variations and abbreviations: Pam, Pamella, Pammie, Pammy. See also Evangeline, Fione, Lorna, Miranda, Perdita, Ophelia, Wendy, Vanessa.

Example: Pamela Stephenson, Australian actress/comedienne.

PADDIE
Origin/meaning: Latin 'patrician', ie aristocratic.

A familiar Irish form of Patricia *q.v.* and Patrick. More usual for a man than a woman.

PARVATI
Origin/meaning: Hindi 'mountain dweller'.

Parvati is a Hindu goddess wife of Lord Shiva, one of the two major gods of modern Hinduism. She had previously been incarnated as Sati *q.v.* who died on a sacrificial fire, thus giving us the word suttee. She was later reincarnated as Uma.

PARVIN (pron. Parrvín)
Origin/meaning: Persian or Arabic. Meaning uncertain.

This Moslem name is found in both Pakistan and India.

Example: Parvin Babi, Indian film actress.

PASCALE

Origin/meaning: Hebrew/Latin 'of the Passover' or 'of Easter'.

A primarily French name. It used to be given to girls born at the appropriate time of year. However it is now given without regard for the time of year and has been one of the most popular names in post-war France.

Variations and abbreviations: Pascaline (Fr), Pasqua (It).

PAT

Origin/meaning: Latin 'patrician' ie aristocratic.

One of the most popular short forms of Patricia q.v. May also be used as a short form of Patrick q.v. or Patience q.v.

Example: Pat Phoenix, English actress.

PATIENCE

Origin/meaning: Latin/Old French 'calm endurance'.

One of the abstract virtues used as names by 17th century Puritans in England and New England. In England it was sometimes used for men as well as women. Like Faith and Hope it has survived into the 20th century while more outlandish Puritan names, such as Mahershalalhashbaz were soon rejected.

Abbreviation: Pat.

Examples: Patience Collier, English actress.

PATRICIA

Origin/meaning: Latin 'patrician', ie aristocratic.

The feminine form of Patrick q.v. This Latin name probably began as a written form only (just as Eustacia was for the name Eustace), to denote a female holder of the name Patrick. Feminine Latinized names were very popular in the 18th century and Patricia came gradually into use as a spoken form then. The name was given an additional impetus by the popularity of Princess Patricia of Connaught, who was born on St Patrick's day 1886. She epitomized for many the independent spirit of the new generation of women, especially when she renounced her royal title on her marriage.

Variations and abbreviations: Paddie, Pat, Patrice (Fr), Patrizia (It), Patsy, Patti, Pattie, Patty, Tricia, Trish, Trisha.

Example: Patricia Routledge, English actress.

PATSY

Origin/meaning: Latin 'patrician', ie aristocratic.

A short form of Patricia. Used by Princess Patricia of Connaught, 1886–1974, who made the name fashionable. Occasionally used as a short form of Patrick q.v.

PAULA

Origin/meaning: Latin 'small'.

A German feminine version of Paul q.v. It has been used occasionally in England since the Middle Ages, probably to honour the Roman St Paula, 347–404. She was a follower of St Jerome who accompanied him to Bethlehem where she helped him run his religious foundations.

PAULETTE

Origin/meaning: Latin 'small'.

A French diminutive of Pauline q.v.

Example: Paulette Goddard, US film actress, star of *Modern Times* and once married to Charlie Chaplin.

PAULINE

Origin/meaning: Latin 'small'.

A French feminine form of Paul and Paulinus q.v. often given to honour St Paulina. It has been fairly popular in English-speaking countries during the 20th century. Pearl White, a Hollywood actress and stuntwoman, had a tremendous success with her 1914 film serial *The Perils of Pauline* in which the heroine performed amazing feats to escape the clutches of a villainous guardian. The early box office hit undoubtedly helped to spread the name.

Variations and abbreviations: Paola (It), Paolina (It), Paule (Fr), Paulene, Pauletta, Paulette (Fr), Paulina (Sp), Paulyn, Polly.

Examples: Pauline Kael, US critic.
Pauline Frederick, 1883–1938, US film actress.

PEARL

Origin/meaning: Latin 'pearl'.

One of the gem names (others include Ruby, Crystal, Emerald) which came into use at the end of the 19th century and are now considered rather old-fashioned. It is sometimes used as a familiar form of Margaret *q.v.* which derives from Margaritis, the Greek word for Pearl.

Variations and abbreviations: Pearle, Pearlie, Perla, Perry.

Examples: Pearl Buck, 1892–1973, US novelist.
Pearl White, 1889–1938, US silent film star.

PEGGY
Origin/meaning: Persian?/Greek/Latin 'pearl' or French/English 'daisy'.

One of the English short forms of Margaret, probably the result of childish attempts to say Meggy. The same transference is found when Polly becomes a familiar form of Mary through Molly. Peggy was occasionally given as an independent name.

Variations and abbreviations: Peg, Pegeen (Ir), Peggotty.

Examples: Dame Peggy Ashcroft, English actress.
Peggy Guggenheim, d.1979, US art collector and philanthropist.

PENELOPE (pron. Pen-êll-opee)
Origin/meaning: uncertain. Possibly connected with the Greek word for a bobbin.

This is a name from Homer's poem *The Odyssey*. Penelope was the wife of Odysseus. During the ten years he was away at the Trojan wars she was pestered by suitors. To keep them at bay she said she would make her choice when she had finished weaving her father-in-law's shroud. However what she wove in the day she unravelled at night until at last Odysseus returned and sent them all packing. Penelope was thus the epitome of the dutiful, faithful wife. It may have been because of her virtues that her name came into use in England in the 16th and 17th centuries when people were turning away from saints' names to Biblical names and abstract virtues like Clemency and Charity. In Ireland it has sometimes been used to 'translate' the native Fionnghuala. It is used in English-speaking countries and, of course, Greece.

Variations and abbreviations: Pen, Penny, Poppy.

Examples: Penelope Mortimer, English novelist.
Penelope Keith, English actress.

PENNY
A short form of Penelope *q.v.* used as an independent name in the 20th century.

PENTECOST
Origin/meaning: Greek 'fiftieth day' ie Whitsun.

Like Noel, Easter, Theophania etc, this name marks the season of a child's birth. It is still occasionally used today for men or women.

PERDITA
Origin/meaning: Latin 'lost'.

This is a name made up by Shakespeare for his play *A Winter's Tale*. The baby girl is abandoned by her father Leontes who suspects her mother, Hermione, of being unfaithful. It is occasionally used today. The Prince Regent's first mistress, Mrs Mary Robinson, was nicknamed Perdita, because of her success in Shakespeare's play.

See also Fiona, Lorna, Miranda, Ophelia, Pamela, Vanessa, Wendy.

PERPETUA
Origin/meaning: Latin 'continuous' or 'universal'.

The meaning of this name is similar to Constance. St Perpetua was martyred with St Felicity at Carthage in 203. Unlike some of the early martyrs the history of their ordeal is well documented and their names are recited during Mass. This name is almost exclusively used by Catholics.

PERSIS
Origin/meaning: Greek 'Persian woman'.

This is one of the many Biblical names which came into use in the 17th century when Puritans rejected Catholic saints' names. St Paul mentions the name in his Epistle to the Romans.

Example: Persis Ghambetta, US film actress.

PETA
Origin/meaning: Greek 'stone'.

An occasional feminine form of Peter *q.v.*

PETRA
Origin/meaning: Greek 'stone'.

This is the feminine form of Petrus, the Latin form given to the name Peter in medieval documents. Its use in English-speaking countries began in the 20th century.

Variations and abbreviations: Peta, Piera, Petrina, Pierina. See also Petronella.

Example: Petra Davis, English actress.

PETRONELLA
Origin/meaning: Latin, from Petronius, a Roman family name.

In the Middle Ages this name was mistakenly believed to be the name of St Peter's daughter, a mythical St Petronilla who was honoured as a saint. Because of the similarity in sound it was also given as a feminine form of Peter. Although its associations made it very popular in the Middle Ages and its short form, Parnell, gave rise to several surnames, the name went quickly out of favour after the Reformation. This eclipse may have been hastened by the fact that another short form, Pernel, became a slang word for a priest's mistress. It is not uncommon for very popular names to take on slang meanings. Other examples include Dolly the short form of Dorothea, which became the word for a toy baby, and Tommy, the short form of Thomas, which became a slang word for a British army private. The modern feminine form of Peter is Petra.

Variations and abbreviations: Petronel, Petronia (It), Petronilla (It).

Example: Petronella Ford, English actress.

PETULA
Origin/meaning: Latin 'pert' or 'seeker'.

A name made familiar by the English singer and actress Petula Clark.

Abbreviation: Pet.

PHEBE
Origin/meaning: Greek 'shining one'.

An alternative spelling of Phoebe q.v. This is the spelling used in the Authorized Version of the Bible (Romans ch.16, v.1). The name was therefore used in this spelling by 17th century Puritans.

PHILADELPHIA
Origin/meaning: Greek 'brotherly love'.

This is a Greek city name called after its founder Attalus Philadelphus. Americans named one of their cities after it because of their admiration, as a newly independent nation, for the independent democracy of the Greek city states. Puritans, both in England and New England, adopted it as a name because it appears in the New Testament. It is now rare.

PHILIPPA
Origin/meaning: Greek 'lover of horses'.

The Latin feminine form of Philip *q.v.* This form was probably confined to documents in the Middle Ages. Like Eustace and Peter for example, the masculine and feminine probably shared one spoken form. However in the 19th century after the 18th century vogue for names with the Latin feminine -a endings, Philippa, pronounced as it is written, came into vogue.

Variations and abbreviations: Filippa (It), Filippina (It), Phil, Philipine, Pippa, Pippy.

Examples: Philippa Pullar, English writer.
Philippa Carr, British novelist – also writes under the name Victoria Holt.

PHILOMENA
Origin/meaning: Greek 'love of song'.

St Philomena was the name of two early Roman martyrs. In 1802 the supposed remains of one of them were discovered at Rome and a cult grew up around her although there is no authentic evidence of her life or martyrdom. The renewed veneration of St Philomena brought about a revival of her name particularly in Italy.

Variations and abbreviations: Filippa (It), Filippina (It), Phil, Philomela (Ger), Philomene (Fr).

PHOEBE (pron. Feebee)
Origin/meaning: Greek 'shining one'.

In Greek mythology Phoebe was another name for Artemis (Roman–Diana) the goddess of the moon. Her counterpart, Apollo, god of the sun, was also known as Phoebus. This was one of many originally Greek pagan names adopted as Christian names because they appear in the New Testament. The usual Christian spelling was Phebe *q.v.*

Variations: Febe (It), Phebe. See also Cynthia.

Example: Phoebe Nicholls, English actress.

PHYLLIDA
Origin/meaning: Greek 'leafy'.

A literary form of Phyllis *q.v.* much used in the 17th century.

Variations and abbreviations: Filada, Filide (It), Fillida, Philida, Phillada, Phillida.

Example, Phyllida Law, English actress.

PHYLLIS
Origin/meaning: Greek 'leafy'.

Phyllis was a Greek maiden who thought she had been forsaken by her lover and hanged herself. The gods pitied her and turned her into an almond tree. The name was used by Greek and Roman poets to signify an unspoiled country girl. When Renaissance poets imitated the classical masters they used the same names. Phyllis (and its variation Phyllida) became popular for a while but the country bumpkin implications eventually sent it out of fashion. The name was successfully revived at the turn of the century, although since the Second World War it has been regarded as rather old-fashioned.

Variations and abbreviations: Fillis, Phillis, Phyl. See also Phyllida.

Examples: Phyllis Diller, US comedienne.
Phyllis Bottome, 1882–1963, British novelist.

PIA (pron. Péeya)
Origin/meaning: Latin 'devout'.

This is an Italian and Spanish name occasionally used in English-speaking countries. The masculine, Pius, is almost never used, although it has been the name of twelve Popes.

Example: Pia Zadora, US actress.

PILAR
Origin/meaning: Spanish 'pillar'.

This is one of the standard descriptions of the Virgin Mary,

Nuestra Señora del Pilar, which has become a popular name in its own right. It refers to St James's vision of a marble column during his supposed stay in Spain. It is a rare name in English-speaking countries.

See also Dolores, Consuelo, Mercedes.

PIPPA
Origin/meaning: Greek 'lover of horses'.

An Italian short form of Phillipa *q.v.* now used in Britain and found as an independent name. It became popular in the 19th century after Browning, following a visit to Italy, wrote his popular poem *Pippa Passes*, 1841.

PLACIDA (pron. Plassida)
Origin/meaning: Latin 'calm'.

An adjective occasionally used as a girl's name.

PLAXY
Origin/meaning: Greek 'busy'.

An old Cornish name said to be a form of the Greek name Praxedes *q.v.*

PLEASANCE
Origin/meaning: Old French 'pleasure' or 'delight'.

A rare feminine name found since the Middle Ages. Naomi *q.v.* has the same meaning.

Variations and abbreviations: Pleasant, Pleasaunce.

PLEASANT
Origin/meaning: Old French 'pleasing'.

A rare feminine name found since the Middle Ages.

POLLY
Origin/meaning: uncertain. Possibly Hebrew 'bitter' or 'wished for child'.

A familiar form of Mary, through Molly. Currently enjoying a minor vogue as an independent name. For some insufficiently explained reason, it has been used for hundreds of years as a synonym for a parrot.

Variation and abbreviation: see Mary.

Examples: Polly Toynbee, English journalist.
Polly Elwes, English journalist.

POLLYANNA
Origin/meaning: Hebrew 'bitter' plus Hebrew 'graceful'.

A double name equivalent of Mary-Anne (Polly is a familiar form of Mary). It was made familiar by the Pollyanna books written by Eleanor Porter, 1868–1920. Polyanna, a little girl who always looks for the glad side of life became a by-word for a child who is too good to be true.

POPPY
Origin/meaning: either a flower name or the Greek short form of Penelope.

Poppy has enjoyed a minor vogue in Britain in the 1970s and 80s.

PORTIA (pron. Pórsha)
Origin/meaning: either Latin 'sharing' or from Porcius, a Roman family name which may take its meaning from the word pig.

Portia is a Shakespearean name, used for the heroine of *The Merchant of Venice*.

Variation: Porzia (It).

PRAXEDES
Origin/meaning: Greek 'busy'.

This is a Greek name, borne by one of the Roman martyrs.

Variations and abbreviations: Plaxy (Cornish), Prassede (It).

PRIMA (pron. Préema)
Origin/meaning: Latin 'first'.

A name given to a first child or a first girl.

PRIMROSE
Origin/meaning: Latin 'earliest rose'.

Flower names were a new fashion at the end of the 19th century. Primrose, being such a popular flower and associated with the beginning of spring, was one of the most frequently used. It is still used today.

PRISCILLA

Origin/meaning: Priscus was a Roman family name. Probably meaning 'strict' or 'correct'.

This is a pre-Christian name adopted as a Christian name by 17th century Puritans because it is found in the Bible. Prisca was the feminine form and Priscilla its diminutive 'little Prisca'. The name occurs in Acts 18 v.2 and as Prisca in the second Epistle to Timothy. Both forms of the name were used but Priscilla has survived best and is currently popular in France.

Variations and abbreviations: Prisca (Ger/It), Priscille (Fr), Priska (Ger), Prissy, Cilla.

Example: Cilla Black (real name Priscilla White), English singer.

PRITI (pron. Préetee)

Origin/meaning: Sanskrit 'love'.

Found throughout India.

See Amanda, Amy.

PRUDENCE

Origin/meaning: Latin 'prudence', 'discretion'.

Because of its meaning, which tied in with their liking for virtue names like Mercy and Temperance, the Puritans revived this medieval name. It became very common and has survived into the 20th century although it is now regarded as fairly unusual.

Variations and abbreviations: Pru, Prudentia (Lat/Ger/Dut), Prudenzia (It), Prudenziana (It), Prudie, Prue.

Examples: Prue Leith, South African/British cookery writer. Prudence Glynn, English journalist.

PRUNELLA

Origin/meaning: Latin/French 'plum coloured'.

This is a rare name.

Variation: Prunelle (Fr).

Example: Prunella Scales, English actress.

Q

QUEENIE
Origin/meaning: English 'little Queen'.

A late 19th, early 20th century girl's pet name, sometimes at the height of its popularity, given as an independent name. It was originally given as a pet name for girls called Regina *q.v.* (the Latin word for Queen). In the 19th century girls named Victoria *q.v.* after the Queen, were also given Queenie as a nickname. Occasionally the name Queen has been given, particularly in the US, rather as Duke, Earl or Baron have been given to boys, as a baptismal boost up the social scale.

Variations and abbreviations: Queen, Queena, Queeny, Quenie. See also Reine, Regina, Victoria.

QUERIDA
Origin/meaning: Spanish 'beloved'.

QUINTA
Origin/meaning: Latin 'fifth', 'fifth born'.

The female equivalent of Quentin *q.v.* usually used either for a fifth daughter or a fifth child. Quintilla may also mean a girl born in July, the fifth month of the Roman calendar. Rare in English-speaking countries but current in Italy.

Variations and abbreviations: Quintilla (It), Quintina (It).

R

RABIA (pron. Rabéea)
Origin/meaning: Arabic 'spring'.
This is a popular Muslim name.
Variation: Rabiah, Rabiyyah.

RACHAEL
Origin/meaning: Hebrew 'ewe'.
17th century spelling of Rachel, still used occasionally today.
Example: Rachael Heyhoe-Flint, English woman cricketer.

RACHEL
Origin/meaning: Hebrew 'ewe'.

Always a popular Jewish name this became a Christian name as well in the 17th century when Biblical names were used by Protestants as a reaction against Catholic saints' names. Rachel was the beautiful daughter of Laban. Jacob worked for his uncle Laban for fourteen years in order to have Rachel as his wife (Genesis ch.5, 29–35). She became the mother of Jacob's favourite sons Joseph and Benjamin. In the 17th century Rachael was the usual spelling and that old-fashioned spelling is again popular today.

Variations and abbreviations: Rae, Rachael, Rachele (It), Rachelle (Fr), Rahel (Ger), Rakel (Swed), Raquel (Sp), Raquela, Ray, Rey, Shelley, Shelly.

Examples: Rachel Billington, British novelist.
Rachel Kempson, British actress.

RAE
Origin/meaning: Hebrew 'ewe'.

Short form of Rachel q.v. Occasionally short form of Raymonde, a feminine form of Raymond q.v.

Variation: Ray.

Example: Ray Tannahill, British writer.

RAINE (pron. Rane)

Origin/meaning: Latin 'queen'.

An English variation of Regina q.v. through the French Reine.

Variation: Raina (pron. Raheena).

Example: Countess Raine Spencer, stepmother of the Princess of Wales.

RAJNI (pron. Rjni)

Origin/meaning: Sanskrit 'night'.

Found throughout India.

See also Rajnikant(m) and Leila.

RAMONA

Origin/meaning: Old German 'strength protection', 'counsel protection', ie 'strong', or 'wise protector'.

The Spanish feminine form of Raymond q.v. The best known feminine form, perhaps because of the song of the same name.

Variations and abbreviations: Raimonda (It), Raimunde (Ger), Raymonde (Fr), Reimunde (Ger).

RAPHAELA

Origin/meaning: Hebrew 'God has healed'.

A feminine form of Raphael q.v. used in Europe and occasionally found in English-speaking countries.

Variation: Raffaella (It).

RAQUEL

Origin/meaning: Hebrew 'ewe'.

Spanish form of Rachel q.v. given wider popularity because of Raquel Welch, the US film actress.

This is a Muslim name.

Variations: Radhiya (E African), Raziya.

REBA

Origin/meaning: a diminutive of Rebecca *q.v.*

REBECCA

Origin/meaning: uncertain. Probably originates in a language of people neighbouring Israel. Sometimes given as 'faithful wife' or 'strongly bound'.

Rebekah is one of the well-known personalities of the Old Testament. She appears in Genesis as the wife of the Patriarch Isaac and mother of the twins Jacob and Esau (Genesis ch.25). It was an immensely popular name in the 17th century period of Biblical names, especially in Puritan New England. The New Testament spelling was preferred then, as it is today. Rebecca has become a vogue name in all the English-speaking countries in the past ten years.

Variations and abbreviations: Becca, Beckie, Becky, Bekki, Reba, Rebeca (Sp), Rebeka, Rebekah, Rebekka (Ger), Rivkah (Heb).

Example: Rebecca West (Cicely Fairchild), 1892–1983, British novelist.

REGINA (pron. Rejéena)

Origin/meaning: Latin 'queen'.

This is an unusual name in English-speaking countries, although it is familiar in various forms in Europe. Because of its meaning it has the unusual form Queenie. Its use, which began in the Middle Ages, was probably originally to honour the Virgin Mary, one of whose titles is Queen of Heaven.

Variations and abbreviations: Gina, Raina, Raine, Regan, Reggie, Régine (Fr), Reina (Sp), Reine (Fr). See also Stella.

Example: Régine, French night club owner.

REHEMA
Origin/meaning: Swahili 'compassion'.
An East African name.
See also Clemency.

REINE (pron. Renn)
Origin/meaning: Latin 'queen'.
A French form of Regina *q.v.* which is a direct translation into French of the original Latin word.

RENATA
Origin/meaning: Latin 'reborn'.
Not very usual in English-speaking countries although it has been used since the 17th century Puritan period because of its religious meaning. Renata remains popular in Spain and Italy. In the 20th century the French forms René and Renée have been preferred.
Variations and abbreviations: Rena, Renate (Ger), René (Fr), Renée (Fr).
Example: Renata Tebaldi, Italian opera singer.

RENE (pron. Réenee)
Origin/meaning: Greek 'peace'.
Short form of Irene *q.v.* sometimes given as an independent name. Popular at the turn of the century.
Variation: Renie.

RENE(É) (pron. R'náy)
Origin/meaning: French 'reborn'.
The French equivalent of the Latin Renata, found in Italy and Spain. Theoretically the version with the two e's is correct, the other being the masculine form. However both are used for girls in English-speaking countries. Very popular in the 1940s and 50s in North America and in the 1970s in Australia. Without an accent it is a separate name, a short form of Irene *q.v.*

257

RHEA (pron. Raya)
Origin/meaning: in Greek mythology one of the Titans. Wife of Cronus she was the original earth mother for she gave birth to the gods Zeus, Demeter, Poseidon and Hades.

This name is rarely used.

Variations and abbreviations: Rea, Ria.

RHODA
Origin/meaning: either Greek 'from Rhodes' (the isle of roses) or 'rose bush'.

This is one of the pre-Christian Greek names found in the Bible (Acts, ch.12) which was adopted as a Christian name by 17th century Protestants. A quite separate Arabic name, Roda, means 'to be satisfied'.

Variations and abbreviations: Rhode, Rhody. See also Rose.

RHONA
Origin/meaning: uncertain. Possibly Old Welsh Rhonwen 'slender, fair' or Old German Ronalda 'power might'.

This is probably a short form of the Old Welsh name Rhonwen, and possibly related to the Saxon name Rowena.

RHONDA
Origin/meaning: uncertain. Possibly connected with the Rhondda area of Wales.

A name found almost exclusively in the US.

Example: Rhonda Fleming, US film actress.

RHONWEN
Origin/meaning: Old Welsh 'slender, fair'.

A name sometimes considered to be the origin of the supposedly Saxon name Rowena q.v. Geoffrey of Monmouth, the chronicler who wrote the history of the Saxon invasion of Britain and gave the name of the Saxon princess (Rowena or Ronwen) was himself Welsh.

RIA

Origin/meaning: either a short form of Maria meaning 'bitter' or a variation of the name of the goddess Rhea *q.v.*

RICHARDA

Origin/meaning: Old English 'rule hard', ie 'strong king'.

A feminine form of Richard *q.v.* Although the masculine Richard has been one of the most popular names since the Middle Ages the feminine has been rarely used and has several differing forms.

Variations and abbreviations: Ricarda, Riccarda (It), Richenda, Richenza, Rickie, Ricky.

RICHENDA

Origin/meaning: Old English 'peaceful king'.

A feminine form of Richard *q.v.*

Variation: Richenza. See also Richarda.

RICKIE

Origin/meaning: a short form of either Frederica (Old English 'peaceful king') or Richarda (Old English 'strong king').

Variations: Ricky, Rikkie, Rikky.

RITA

Origin/meaning: Persian?/Greek 'pearl'.

The short form of Margarita, the Spanish form of the name Margaret. Rita was popular from the 1920s until immediately after the Second World War, a period when many Spanish sounding names were fashionable.

Examples: Rita (Marguerite) Hayworth, US film actress and dancer.
Rita Moreno, Puerto Rican actress and dancer.

RIVA

Origin/meaning: uncertain. Possibly 'faithful wife' or 'strongly bound'.

A short form of Rebecca from the Hebrew form Rivkah.

259

ROANNA
Origin/meaning: a combination of Rose and Anna. A variation of Rosanna q.v.

ROBERTA
Origin/meaning: Old German 'fame bright'.

A feminine form of Robert q.v. found mainly in Scotland and also in Italy.

Variations and abbreviations: Bobbie, Roberte (Fr).

ROBINA
Origin/meaning: Old German 'fame bright'.

A feminine form of Robin q.v. Found mainly in Scotland. In the US Robin is used for girls, although in Britain it is regarded as exclusively masculine.

Variations: Robbie, Robby, Robena, Robin, Robinia, Robyn.

Example: Robin Astaire, dancer wife of Fred Astaire.

ROIS
Origin/meaning: Latin 'rose'.

The Irish form of Rose q.v.

Variation: Roisin.

ROKEYA
Origin/meaning: Arabic 'she rises on high'.

This is a Muslim name.

Variation: Rukiya.

ROLANDA
Origin/meaning: Old German 'famous man of the land'.

A feminine form of Roland q.v. formed on the Latin pattern for feminine words. It is used mainly in Italy.

ROMA
Origin/meaning: Italian, the city of Rome.

Occasionally used as a girl's name. A modern fashion.

ROMANA
Origin/meaning: Latin 'from Rome'.

An Italian saint's name occasionally used in other countries.

ROMOLA
Origin/meaning: Latin 'of Rome'.

This is a feminine version of the name of Romulus, the supposed founder of Rome. It is the name of one of the early Virgin martyrs and was used by George Eliot for her novel *Romola*, 1863.

Variations and abbreviations: Romella, Romula.

RONA
Origin/meaning: uncertain. Possibly Old Welsh Rhonwen 'slender, fair' or Old German Ronalda 'power-might'.

The popularity of this name in Scotland suggests it is considered a feminine form of the Scottish masculine name Ronald and is a quite separate name from Rhona.

Example: Rona Jaffe, US novelist.

RONALDA
Origin/meaning: Old German/Old English 'power-might'.

A modern feminine form of Ronald *q.v.*

Variations and abbreviations: Rona (Scots), Ronalde (Fr), Ronnie.

RONNIE
Origin/meaning: a familiar form of names such as Veronica, Rosanna, Ronalda and Rowena.

ROSA
Origin/meaning: Latin 'rose'.

This Latinized version of Rose *q.v.* was introduced in the 18th century when Latinized versions of names, eg Augusta, Amelia, Sibylla, were fashionable. Its popularity was maintained throughout the 19th century.

Variations: See Rose.

Examples: Rosa Luxemburg, 1871–1919, German revolutionary. Rosa Lewis, 1867–1952, British hotelier.

ROSABEL
Origin/meaning: Latin 'beautiful rose'.

An 18th century variation of Rose q.v. The ending was typical of many other slightly contrived names of the period such as Claribel and Dulcibel. Sir Walter Scott gave it as the name of Mary Queen of Scots' favourite palfrey in his novel *The Abbot*, 1820.

Variations and abbreviations: Ros, Rosabella, Rosabelle, Rozabel, Rosie, Rosy, Rozabella, Rozabelle.

ROSALBA
Origin/meaning: Latin 'white rose'.

A medieval name, rarely found today. Thackeray used it in his children's story *The Rose and the Ring*, 1855.

Example: Rosalba Carriera, 1675–1757, Italian painter.

ROSALIE
Origin/meaning: uncertain. Either Latin 'roses and lilies' or possibly Latin 'rosalia' a festival of flowers.

The original form Rosalia is still current in Italy but the name came to English-speaking countries via France and in the French form Rosalie. It was a name firmly established in Europe by the 12th century because of the fame of St Rosalia. She was born in Palermo and became its patron saint. Angels were said to have carried her to an inaccessible mountain where she lived the life of a recluse devoted to prayer. The name is popular among Catholics in Ireland.

Variations and abbreviations: Ros, Rosaleen (Ir), Rosalia (It), Rose, Rozalie, Roz.

Example: Rosalie Crutchley, English actress.

ROSALIND
Origin/meaning: Old German 'horse serpent'. Usually given as Spanish 'beautiful rose'.

The original Old German name was taken (like Roderick/Rodrigo) to Spain by the Goths. Despite the meaning the Old German is a flattering name since a serpent was considered a sacred creature (see Belinda). However in Spain it was naturally re-interpreted as the Spanish words Rosa – rose, and linda – beautiful. Shakespeare with his liking for Romance names, popularized Rosalind in England by using it for the heroine of his play *As You Like It*. Being a pretty name with a pretty meaning and impeccable credentials, it has been used ever since.

Variations and abbreviations: Ros, Rosalinda (Sp), Rosaline, Rosalyne, Rosalynd, Roseline, Rosie, Roslindis, Rozalind.

Example: Rosalind Russell, 1911–1976, US film actress.

ROSALINE
Origin/meaning: Old German 'horse serpent'. Usually given as Spanish 'beautiful rose'.

A form of Rosalind *q.v.*

Variation: See Rosalind.

ROSAMOND
Origin/meaning: Old German 'horse protection', Latin 'pure rose'.

A popular alternative spelling of Rosamund *q.v.*

Example: Rosamond Lehman, English novelist.

ROSAMUND
Origin/meaning: Old German 'horse protection', Latin 'pure rose'.

Like Rosalind *q.v.* this Old German name was re-interpreted in the Middle Ages, in this case using the Latin Rosa – rose and munda – pure. Its Italian sound ensured its survival when many Saxon names became obsolete and Latin-based names, especially saints' names, flourished. It has been consistently used since the 12th century when it is found as the name of the mistress of Henry II, 'Fair Rosamund', who was poisoned by his formidable wife Eleanor of Aquitaine.

Variations and abbreviations: Ros, Rosamund, Rosamunda (Sp), Rosamunde (Ger), Rosemonde (Fr), Rosmunda (It), Roz, Rozamond, Rozamund.

Example: Rosamund John, English film actress.

ROSANNA
Origin/meaning: a combination of the names Rose and Anna.

This name has been found in various spellings since the Middle Ages. In legend Rosana was a daughter of the Queen of Armenia. She aided the three sons of St George to extinguish the seven lamps of the Knight of the Black Castle. Until the lamps were extinguished everyone who entered the castle fell into a deep sleep from which they could not be roused. A name popular with the Victorians.

Variations and abbreviations: Roanna, Ronnie, Rosanne, Roseanna, Roseann, Rozanna, Rozanne, Zanna, Zanny.

ROSE
Origin/meaning: Old German 'horse', Latin 'rose'.

This name was probably derived originally from the Old German Hros, meaning horse. The horse, like the serpent, was considered a god by the Saxons, as the white horses cut into chalk hillsides testify. In the Middle Ages almost all people who could read and write used Latin and not surprisingly the old names with the root word hros were gradually 'translated' into the language of literacy. So the name Rose was given in Latin as Rosa and this became the accepted meaning of the name and its variations such as Rosamund and Rosalind.

   In the 19th century flower names including Rose were at the height of their popularity and much significance was placed on the language of flowers. For example a yellow rose symbolized infidelity, white rosebuds a girl who was too young to love and the musk rose capricious beauty. Rose is one of the old-fashioned names enjoying a revival in the 1980s.

Variations and abbreviations: Ffion (Wel), Rhoda, Rosa, Rosie, Rosy, Roze.

Examples: Lady Rose Windsor, daughter of the Duke of Gloucester.
Rose Macaulay, 1881–1958, English writer.
Rose Kennedy, US matriarch, mother of President Kennedy.

ROSEMARY
Origin/meaning: either a combination of two names Rose and Mary (Hebrew 'bitter') or a plant name. The herb Rosemary takes its name from the Latin words ros – dew and marinus – of the sea.

This name became popular in the 20th century which suggests it was influenced by the Victorian liking for flower names with their symbolic meanings. Rosemary has traditionally been taken as a token of remembrance and of fidelity in love. The occasional use of the name in the previous two centuries probably came about as a combination of Rose and Mary. The French version

Rosemarie is certainly a combination of two names as the French word for rosemary is romarin.

Variations and abbreviations: Mary Rose, Romy, Rosemarie (Fr), Rose Marie, Rosie, Rosy.

Example: Rosemary Ann Sissons, British novelist.

ROSETTA
Origin/meaning: Latin 'little rose'.

An 18th century diminutive of Rose q.v.

ROSIA
Origin/meaning: Old German 'fame'.

An unusual girl's name, the feminine equivalent of the masculine Ross q.v.

ROSIE
Origin/meaning: Latin 'rose'.

A diminutive of all the names beginning with Rose.

Variation: Rosy.

ROSINA
Origin/meaning: Latin 'little rose'.

Italian diminutive of Rose q.v. similar to the Spanish Rosita.

ROSITA
Origin/meaning: Latin 'little rose'.

A Spanish diminutive of Rose q.v. Popular among Catholics as the pet name of St Rose of Lima, 1586–1617.

ROUSHAN
Origin/meaning: Arabic 'dawn'.

A Muslim variation of Roxane q.v.
Variation: Roshanna.

ROWENA
Origin/meaning: uncertain. Possibly Old English 'fame friend' or Old Welsh 'slender, fair'.

This is supposedly a Saxon name and was used by Sir Walter Scott for the Saxon heroine of his novel *Ivanhoe*, 1819. Since then it has been given from time to time. The name originally occurs in the rather fanciful history of Britain written by the Welsh chronicler Geoffrey of Monmouth, 1100–1154. He relates the story of Rowena or Ronwen, a 5th century princess, the daughter of the Saxon king Hengist. Vortigern, the ruler of South East Britain, married her. He invited the Saxons to England to help him fight off the Picts and so sparked off the Saxon invasion of Britain. Since the entire story is unsubstantiated the name may not be genuine Saxon at all but Geoffrey of Monmouth's own invention, and a version of the Welsh name Rhonwen.

Variations and abbreviations: Rhonwen, Rona, Ronwen, Rhona.

ROXANE (pron. Rocksahn)
Origin/meaning: Persian 'dawn'.

This is a well-established name in the US. It was the name of the wife of Alexander the Great and has been used from time to time in literature.

Variations and abbreviations: Rossana (It), Roushan (Arabic), Roxana, Roxanna, Roxanne, Roxy. See also Aurora, Dawn, Zarah.

Example: Roxanne Pullitzer, US socialite.

RUBY
Origin/meaning: Latin 'red'. A rare and precious stone.

One of the 19th century jewel names like Pearl or Beryl. Now unfashionable.

Example: Ruby Keeler, US film actress in the 1940s.

RUPERTA
Origin/meaning: Old German 'fame bright'.

A feminine form of Rupert q.v. which is itself a form of Robert. First used as a name for the daughter of the 17th century soldier and inventor, Prince Rupert.

RUTH
Origin/meaning: obscure. Sometimes given as Hebrew 'vision of beauty', also Medieval English 'compassion'.

Since Ruth was a Moabite it is unlikely this is a Hebrew name. A book of the Old Testament is given over to her story. She was the loyal daughter-in-law of the Jewess Naomi. Both women being widows they returned to Naomi's homeland where Ruth married Boaz.

The Puritans took up the name in the 17th century both because of its Biblical origin and its meaning in English since virtue names were also popular with them.

Variations and abbreviations: Ruthann, Ruthe, Ruthie.

Examples: Ruth Prahwar Jhabvala, Polish-born English novelist author of *Heat and Dust*.
Ruth Draper, 1889–1956, US variety artist.

S

SABIAH
Origin/meaning: Arabic 'morning'.

This is a popular Muslim name.

Variations: Sabah (East African), Sabera.

SABINA (pron. Sabeena)
Origin/meaning: Latin 'Sabine woman'. The Sabines were an ancient tribe whose lands bordered on Rome.

This Roman name survived because it was the name of several saints. There were also male saints with the name Sabinus, which is now obsolete in English-speaking countries but still found in Germany, France and Italy.

In Britain Sabin became both a masculine and feminine variation in the Middle Ages. Sabina is now rare in England, though found in Italy and Germany.

Variations: Sabin, Sabine (Ger/Fr), Sabyn, Savina (It), Savine (Fr).

Example: Sabina Franklyn, British actress.

SABRINA
Origin/meaning: the Latin name for the River Severn.

Milton in his play *Comus* retells the supposed Old British legend that Queen Guendolen, spurned by her husband Locrine, raised an army, defeated him and forced his mistress and his daughter Sabre to fly. In her panic Sabre jumped into the Severn but Nereus, a sea god, pitied her and changed her into a nymph. She became the goddess of the river which took its name from her.

Variation: Sabrin.

Example: Sabrina Guiness, British socialite, former girlfriend of HRH Prince Charles.

SACHA
Origin/meaning: Ancient Greek – 'defender of men'.

Short form of Alexander or Alexandra *q.v.* frequently found recently as an independent name for both boys and girls.

Variations and abbreviations: Sascha, Sasha.

SADIE
Origin/meaning: Hebrew 'princess'.

A familiar form of Sarah *q.v.* more popular in the US than Britain.

Variations: Sadye, Saidee.

Example: Sadie Thompson, the title character of one of W. Somerset Maugham's most popular collections of short stories, 1921.

SALLY
Origin/meaning: Hebrew 'princess'.

A form of Sarah *q.v.* which involves a typical change of letter from r to l. In the present century it has been given as a totally independent name.

Variations and abbreviations: Sal, Sallee, Sallie.

Examples: Sally Oppenheim, British politician.
Sally Rand, US fan dancer.

SALLY ANN
Origin/meaning: Hebrew 'graceful princess'.

This is an increasingly popular combination of two well-established names. It is found with or without a hyphen and with the variations in spelling of both names.

Example: Sally Ann Howes, British actress.

SALMA
Origin/meaning: Arabic 'safe'.

A very popular Muslim name.

Variation: Solama.

SALOME (pron. Sallóhmay)
Origin/meaning: Aramaic 'peace'.

This is a Greek form of the Hebrew word Shalom, and in the Middle Ages the pronunciation imitated the original word so that the name was pronounced Salohm. Although the Bible does not say so, it is the name given by tradition to the daughter of Herodias who danced before Herod in return for the head of John the Baptist. Despite this it was a fairly popular Biblical name among Puritans who probably gave it in honour of the follower of Jesus referred to in Mark's Gospel, ch.15 and 16.

Variations: Saláma (Arabic), Salomé (Fr), Salomi, Salomy. See also Solomon.

SAMANTHA
Origin/meaning: uncertain, possibly Aramaic 'listener' or feminine of Samuel ('name of God').

Although there are rare examples of this name in the last two centuries Samantha appears to be a mainly 20th century name 'manufactured' by films and television. Particularly influential have been the characters of Tracy Samantha Lord played by Grace Kelly in the film *High Society*, 1956, and Samantha the young attractive witch in the widely distributed television series *Bewitched*, 1960. The name quickly achieved great popularity and in the 1970s was among the top 50 girls' names in Britain, Australia and Canada.

Variations and abbreviations: Sam, Samanta (It), Samanthy, Sammie, Sammy. See also Darren, Tracy, Kelly.

Example: Samantha Eggar, British film actress.

SAMUELA
Origin/meaning: Hebrew 'name of god'.

An uncommon feminine form of Samuel *q.v.*

Variations and abbreviations: Sam, Sammie, Samuella, Samuelle. See also Samantha.

SANCHIA
Origin/meaning: Latin/Spanish 'holy'.

This name is rare today. It was introduced to England by the marriage in 1243 of the Earl of Cornwall to Sanchia, daughter of the Count of Provence, rather as Blanca was introduced into France by marriage (see Blanche). Its masculine equivalent is Sancho.

Variations: Sancha, Sanche, Sancia.

SANDHYA (pron. Sandayéah)
Origin/meaning: Sanskrit 'evening'.

SANDI
Origin/meaning: Greek 'defender of men'.

A familiar form of Alexandra q.v. Occasionally given to a red-head, although this is more usual with men.

Variations: Sandie, Sandy.

Example: Sandi Shaw, English singer and actress.

SANDRA
Origin/meaning: Greek 'defender of men'.

Italian short form of Alexandra (Alessandra) q.v. now often found as an independent first name.

Variations and abbreviations: Sandi, Sandie, Sondra, Zandra.

Examples: Sandra O'Connor, first US woman judge of the Supreme Court.
Sondra Locke, US film actress.

SAPPHIRA (pron. Safféera)
Origin/meaning: Greek 'sapphire'.

This is a Biblical name which has been used occasionally since the Middle Ages. Sapphira and her husaband Ananias lied to St Peter.

Variations: Sapphire, Sephira.

SARAH
Origin/meaning: Hebrew 'princess'.

This Biblical name was given to Abraham's wife, Sarai q.v. (Genesis ch.17) by God. Although known in the Middle Ages, not being a saint's name it was not popular. It became widespread during the 17th century period of Biblical names. With fluctuations it has remained popular ever since and is currently among the top ten girls' names in Britain, US and Australia.

The spelling Sara is the Greek version. In Ireland Sarah is sometimes used to 'translate' the native names Sorcha and Saraid, although less so in the 20th century as Gaelic names are again becoming popular. Variations which have become independent names include Sally and Sadie.

Variations and abbreviations: Sadie, Sal, Sally, Sara, Saraid (Ir), Sari (Hung), Sarina, Sarita, Sarra, Sharai, Shari (Hung), Sorcha (Ir), Zara, Zarah, Zaria. See also Sharon, Soraya.

Examples: Sarah Bernhardt, 1844–1923, French actress.
Sarah Miles, English actress.
Lady Sarah Armstrong-Jones, daughter of HRH Princess Margaret.

SARAI
Origin/meaning: uncertain. Possibly Hebrew 'quarrelsome'.

The original name of Abraham's wife Sarah *q.v.* Sarai was probably a non-Hebrew name and this is the reason it was changed. Because of its supposed meaning it is now rare.

SARAID
Origin/meaning: Old Irish 'excellent' or Hebrew 'princess'.

Like Sorcha this native Irish name is also used as an equivalent of Sarah and therefore claims two meanings.

SARSWATI (pron. Sarraswatti)
Origin/meaning: Hindu, the Goddess of Education, wife of Brahma.

A long-established name found throughout India. Sarswati is credited with the invention of Sanskrit. She is always portrayed as extremely beautiful.

See Athene and Minerva.

SATI
Origin/meaning: Sanskrit 'virtuous wife'.

This was the name of the first incarnation of Parvati, wife of Shiva. When her father refused to accept her husband she threw herself on to a sacrificial fire and committed suicide. Her ashes blew all over the world and where they fell marked her shrines. From this myth developed the Hindu custom of the ritual suicide of a wife by throwing herself onto her husband's funeral pyre.

SCARLETT
Origin/meaning: Middle English 'rich red'.

This word is assumed to have come from a Persian word for a rich cloth, usually deep red in colour, called Saqirlat. Made famous by the heroine of Margaret Mitchell's book *Gone With the Wind*, 1936, it may possibly have been in use in the Southern US before then.

Variation: Scarlet. See also Amber.

SCHOLASTICA
Origin/meaning: Latin/Greek 'scholar'.

This was the name of St Scholastica, 480–543, sister of St Benedict, the founder of the Benedictine religious Order. She was an extremely popular saint and her name was common throughout Europe in the Middle Ages. It went out of fashion along with most other saints' names, after the Protestant Reformation. It has never regained its former popularity in English speaking countries.

Variations and abbreviations: Scholastika (Ger), Scholastique (Fr), Scolastica (It).

SEBASTIANA
Origin/meaning: Greek 'venerable', Latin 'from Sebastia'.

A feminine form of Sebastian *q.v.* found in Italy but rare in English-speaking countries.

Variations: Sebastiane (Ger), Sebastiénne (Fr).

SECUNDA
Origin/meaning: Latin 'second'.

A name sometimes given to a second daughter.

Variations: Secunda (It), Secondilla (It), Secondina (It).

SELINA
Origin/meaning: probably Latin 'heavenly'. Sometimes given as Greek 'moon'.

This comes from the French name Céline which derives from the Latin caelum meaning heaven or sky. The Greek word for Moon (Seléeny) sounds similar.

A third possibility is that it is from Céline the shortened form of the French Marceline, 'little cloth seller'. It first appeared as an English name at the end of the 17th century when French influence was very strong.

Variations and abbreviations: Celene, Celia, Celina, Céline, Selena, Selene, Selia, Seline. See also Celeste, Celia, Chandra, Urania.

Example: Selina Scott, British TV presenter.

SELMA
Origin/meaning: Old German 'helmet of God'.

A short form, popular in the US of the rare Old English name Anselma q.v.

Variation: Zelma.

SELMA
Origin/meaning: Arabic 'secure'.

A popular Muslim name quite unrelated to the European name.

SENGA
Origin/meaning: Greek 'pure', 'chaste'.

A Scottish name, thought to be simply a reversed spelling of Agnes.

SEPTIMA
Origin/meaning: Latin 'seventh'.

A name given to a seventh daughter or seventh child.

SERAPHINA
Origin/meaning: Hebrew 'burning', 'ardent'.

The name of one of the early saints, it became popular in Spain and Italy, and was occasionally used in Britain and the US in the 19th century when such names enjoyed a vogue.

Variations: Serafina (It), Seraphite (Sp).

SERENA (pron. Seréena)
Origin/meaning: Latin 'calm', 'serene'.

A name found occasionally since the Middle Ages and currently enjoying a minor revival.

See also Placida.

SHAKIRA
Origin/meaning: Arabic 'be grateful'.

A Muslim name.

Variations: Shakila, Shakura (East African).

Example: Shakira Caine, wife of actor Michael Caine.

SHARI
Origin/meaning: Hebrew 'princess'.

A Hungarian form of Sarah *q.v.*

Example: Shari Lewis, US ventriloquist.

SHARON
Origin/meaning: Hebrew place-name. Possibly also Hebrew 'princess'.

The phrase 'rose of Sharon' appears in the Song of Solomon. This name may therefore have begun as a variation on the popular name Rose, like Roseanna and Mary Rose. Rose-of-Sharon became abbreviated to simple Sharon and as such was a vogue name in English-speaking countries in the 1950s and 1960s.

Sharon is sometimes given as a variation of Sarah through the form Sharai.

Variations and abbreviations: Sharai, Shari, Sharron, Sharry, Sharyn.

Example: Sharron Davies, British Olympic swimmer.

SHEILA
Origin/meaning: Latin 'blind'. From the aristocratic Roman Caecilius family.

The Anglicized form of Shelagh/Sighile, which is itself the Irish form of Cecilia *q.v.*

Variations: Sheela, Sheelah, Sheilah, Shelly.

Example: Sheila Scott, British aviatrix.

SHELAGH
Origin/meaning: Latin 'blind'. From the aristocratic roman Caecilius family.

This is the Irish form of the name Cecily. It comes from the Gaelic version Sighile (pron. Sigealay) which is also occasionally found.

Variations: Sheela, Sheelagh, Sheelah, Sheila (Eng).

Example: Shelagh Delaney, Irish playwright.

SHELLEY
Origin/meaning: Old English 'clearing on a bank'.

A surname sometimes used as a feminine first name, perhaps encouraged by the vogue for similar names such as Kerry and Kelly. Also a familiar form of names such as Michelle, Sheila, Shirley, Rachel.

Variation: Shelly.

Example: Shelley (Shirley) Winters, US film actress.

SHENA
Origin/meaning: Hebrew 'Jehovah has favoured'.

Scots form of Joan or Jane, a phonetic spelling of the Scots Gaelic Sìne.

Variations: Sheena, Sìne.

Example: Sheena Easton, Scottish singer.

SHERRY
Origin/meaning: a familiar form of names like Chérie, Sharon, Charlotte, etc.

Sometimes given as an independent name.

SHERYL
Origin/meaning: a variation on names such as Cheryl q.v. Charlotte q.v. Chérie q.v. and Shirley.

SHIRLEY
Origin/meaning: Old English 'bright clearing'.

An English place-name, found in several areas, which became a surname. Unlike most 19th century surnames used as first names, this became a girl's name and not a boy's name. It seems to be a direct result of Charlotte Brontë's novel *Shirley*, 1849, in which the heroine, having no brothers, was given a family surname as a first name so that the name would not be lost on her marriage. In the 19th century when surnames were popular first names, it was also given to boys but soon became firmly fixed in the public imagination as an exclusively feminine name. Its popularity was greatest in the United States, especially in the South where women were frequently given family names as first names. The popularity of child film star Shirley Temple in the 1930s brought the name to its peak. Since 1950 its decline has been fairly rapid.

Variations and abbreviations: Sher, Shir, Shirl, Shirlee, Shirleen, Shirlene, Shirline.

Examples: Shirley MacLaine, US film actress and dancer. Shirley Williams, British politician.

SHOBHA
Origin/meaning: Hindu 'decoration', 'beauty'.

A name found throughout India.

See Belle.

SHOSHANA
Origin/meaning: Hebrew 'lily'.

Hebrew form of Susannah and Susan *q.v.*

Variation: Shushannah.

SIÂN (pron. Sharn)
Origin/meaning: Hebrew 'Jehovah has favoured'.

This is the native Welsh form of Jane *q.v.* Siwan, another variation, is slightly nearer to the English Joan.

Variations: Siani, Sìne (Scots), Sinéad (Ir), Sioned, Siwan (Wel). See also Joan.

Example: Siân Phillips, Welsh actress.

SIBYL
Origin/meaning: Greek. The name given to the women who put the prophecies of the oracles into words.

Christians adopted this pagan belief and agreed that sibyls could be the mouthpieces of divine revelation. Sibyl and in particular its Latin form, Sibylla, became accepted Christian names. The name was introduced into England by the Norman Conquest. It became popular but, like many non-Biblical names, lost ground after the Reformation. In the 19th century Disraeli's novel *Sybil*, 1845, revived interest in the name, although mistakenly spelt with the vowels reversed. It has been used consistently ever since but has not become common.

Variations and abbreviations: Cybil, Cybill, Sib, Sibelle, Sibbie,

277

Sibby, Sibel, Sibella, Sibilla (It), Sibylla, Sibylle (Fr/Ger), Sybil, Sybilla, Sybille.

Examples: Dame Sybil Thorndike, 1882–1976, English actress.
Cybill Shepherd, US film actress.
Sibilla Aleramo, 1876–1960, British novelist.

SIDONY (pron. Sidónee)
Origin/meaning: Greek/Latin 'fine cloth'.

The medieval word sendal, or sendon, which came from a Greek word, was used to describe a fine cloth and by implication in some cases, a winding sheet. Girls born on or about the date of the Feast of the Holy Sendon (winding sheet) were sometimes called Sidony. The surnames Siddons and Siddel may come from the same source. Nowadays it is almost always used by Catholics, and is popular in Ireland where it is sometimes rendered as Sidney. In Italy the masculine version Sidonio is current.

Variations and abbreviations: Sid, Sidney, Sidonia (It), Sidonie (Fr/Ger), Sindonia, Zdenka (Slav).

Example: Sidonie Gabrielle Colette, 1873–1954, the French novelist known as Colette.

SIDNEY
Origin/meaning: Greek/Latin 'follower of Dionysios'.

An aristocratic surname, a contraction of St Denis. Usually used as a masculine name q.v. It may also be a version of Sidony q.v.

Variations and abbreviations: Sid, Syd, Sydney.

SYLVIA
Origin/meaning: Latin 'of the woodland'.

This is the feminine alternative of Silvester (Silvius) q.v. Its use dates from the Renaissance period when classical allusions were popular. Rhea Silvia was the mother of Romulus and Remus, the legendary joint founders of Rome. The name spread to England from Italy mainly as a result of its use in Shakespeare's play The Two Gentlemen of Verona, c.1548, in which occurs the famous line 'Who is Sylvia, what is she?' From then it was used frequently in literature as a name for a fresh, young country maid.

Variations and abbreviations: Silva, Silvana (It), Silverie (It),

Silvestra (It), Silviana (It), Silvie, Sylvia, Sylviane (Fr), Sylvie (Fr), Sylvetta, Zilvia.

Examples: Sylvie Vartan, French singer.
Silvana Mangnano, Italian film actress.
Sylvia Sims, British film actress.

SIMONE (pron. Séemon)
Origin/meaning: uncertain. Usually given as Hebrew 'hearkening'.

This is the French feminine form of Simon *q.v.* sometimes used in English-speaking countries and currently popular in Australia.

Variations and abbreviations: Simona (It), Simonetta, Simonette, Simonne (Fr).

Examples: Simone de Beauvoir, French writer.
Simone Signoret, French film actress.

SÌNE (pron. Sheenay)
Origin/meaning: Hebrew 'Jehovah has favoured'.

Scots Gaelic form of Jane, usually written Shena, *q.v.*

Variations and abbreviations: Sheena, Sheenagh, Shena, Siân (Wel), Sinéad (Ir).

SINEAD (pron. Shináyd)
Origin/meaning: Hebrew 'Jehovah has favoured'.

This is the feminine form of Sean, the Irish form of John. Since the beginning of the 19th century when native Irish culture enjoyed a revival this name has become increasingly familiar. It approximates to the English Jane. Siobhan (see below) is the equivalent of the English Joan.

Variations: Siân (Wel), Sine (Scots), Sinéidín (dim.). See also Joan.

Example: Sinead Cusack, Irish actress.

SIOBHÁN (pron Shiváwn)
Origin/meaning: Hebrew 'Jehovah has favoured'.

The Irish form of Joan *q.v.*

Example: Siobhan McKenna, Irish actress.

279

SISSY

Origin/meaning: Latin 'blind'.

A familiar form of Cecily *q.v.*

Example: Sissy Spacek, US film actress.

SITA

Origin/meaning: Hindu. Mythological. An incarnation of Lakohmi, the wife of Vishnu.

Sita was the wife of Rama, himself one of the incarnations of the god Vishnu. Vishnu had taken the form of Rama in order to destroy the terrible demon Ravana. The exciting adventures of Rama and Sita are told in many poems and stories including the famous epic poem *The Ramayana.*

SONIA

Origin/meaning: Greek 'wisdom'.

This is a Slavic familiar form of Sophie *q.v.* It is particularly popular in Russia and is frequently found in Scandinavia.

Variations and abbreviations: Sonja, Sonnie, Sonya.

Examples: Sonia Bannerman, British athlete.
HRH Crown Princess Sonja of Norway.

SOPHIA

Origin/meaning: Greek 'wisdom'.

The Italian form of Sophie *q.v.* This Latinized form was fashionable in England in the 18th and 19th centuries.

Variations and abbreviations: See Sophie.

Examples: Sophia Loren, Italian film actress.
Sophia Jex-Blake, 1840–1912, English pioneer of women's medical studies.

SOPHIE

Origin/meaning: Greek 'wisdom'.

This is the English and French form of the name Sophia. The name Sophia has long been popular in the areas covered by the Orthodox church because of the former importance of the cathedral of Hagia Sophia (Holy Wisdom) in Constantinople, which is now a museum. There were also several Ss Sophia who were popular in the Eastern church, including the mother of SS

Faith, Hope and Charity. The name came to England with the Hanoverians at the beginning of the 18th century. They popularized many of their traditional family names, including Charlotte, Augusta and Amelia. Sophie, the name of George I's daughter, became fashionable very rapidly, often being spelt Sophy. It remained popular for nearly two centuries, but by the beginning of the 20th century had become neglected. In the 1970s it was revived and has become a vogue name in France and Britain.

Variations and abbreviations: Sofia (Ger/It/Russ), Sofie, Sonia (Slav), Sonja, Sonya, Sophia (It), Sophy.

Example: Sophie Tucker, 1885–1966, US variety star.

SOPHRONIA
Origin/meaning: Greek 'prudence'.

A rare name, similar to Sophie, q.v.

SORAYA
Origin/meaning: Sanskrit/Persian 'good princess'.

An Arab name made more generally familiar by Queen Soraya, former wife of the late Shah of Persia.

Example: Soraya Kashoggi, English socialite.

SORCHA
Origin/meaning: Old Irish 'bright' or Hebrew 'princess'.

This native Irish name has come to be used as the Irish equivalent of Sarah and therefore has two meanings.

Example: Sorcha Cusack, Irish actress.

SPERANZA
Origin/meaning: Latin/Italian 'hope'.

This is the Italian equivalent of the English Hope and Russian Nadia q.v. It is very popular in Italy.

STACEY
Origin/meaning: Greek 'resurrection'.

A short form of Anastasia q.v. which has become more popular than the original, particularly in the US.

Variations and abbreviations: Stace, Stacy.

281

Example: Stacy Dorning, British actress.

STELLA
Origin/meaning: Latin 'star'.

This name was used from time to time in the Middle Ages to honour the Blessed Virgin Mary, one of whose titles is Stella Maris 'Star of the Sea'. Jonathan Swift, 1667–1745, who coined the name Vanessa q.v. for one of his friends, gave the name Stella to another, Esther Johnson. It is a direct translation of Esther which is the Persian word for star. It has since become a well-established name.

Variations: Estella (It/Sp), Estelle (Old Fr), Estrella (Sp).

Examples: Stella Benson, 1892–1933, English writer and traveller. Stella Gibbons, author of *Cold Comfort Farm*.

STEPHANIE
Origin/meaning: Greek 'wreathed', 'crowned'.

This is the feminine form of Stephen q.v. Now increasingly popular in English-speaking countries, it was originally a French name, spelt Stéphanie.

Variations and abbreviations: Etiennette (Fr), Stef, Stefania (It), Stefanie (Ger), Steffie, Steph, Stephana, Stephani, Stephie, Stevana, Stevena.

Examples: Stephanie Powers, US actress.
Stephanie Beacham, English actress.

SUDHA (pron. Soo-thoh)
Origin/meaning: Hindi 'moon', 'nectar'.

See Chandra, Diana, Selina.

SUNITA
Origin/meaning: Hindi 'good morals'.

Found mainly in West India but also in Central India.

SUKEY
Origin/meaning: Hebrew: 'graceful white lily'.

Old-fashioned familiar form of Susan q.v. popular in the 18th century. Now becoming viable as an independent name.

Variation: Suki.

SUSAN

Origin/meaning: Hebrew 'graceful white lily'.

A short form of Susannah *q.v.* used in the 18th century and which, by the 19th century had overtaken the original in popularity. After a period of decline in the early 20th century the name came back into favour in the 1940s and 50s and remains one of the most popular girls' names in English-speaking countries. More fanciful variations like Suki and the French Suzanne are also fashionable.

Variations and abbreviations: See Susannah.

Examples: Susan George, British actress.
Susan Hayward, US film actress.

SUSANNAH

Origin/meaning: Hebrew 'graceful white lily'.

This name, originally Shushannah, has the same meaning as Shushan, the royal city of Assyria. It is a very ancient name yet is one of the most popular names of the mid-20th century. The (now apocryphal) story of Susannah and the Elders in the Old Testament made the name familiar in the Middle Ages and she was regarded as something of a heroine. The beautiful wife of Joachim she was falsely accused of adultery by the Jewish elders. Condemned to death she was proved innocent by the Prophet Daniel and her accusers were put to death in her place. Another Biblical Susanna is referred to in the New Testament (Luke 8, v.3). The name therefore became increasingly popular in the period of Biblical names after the Protestant Reformation. By the 18th century the short form Susan had overtaken the original in popularity and is currently one of the most popular names in all English-speaking countries. In Spain there is a masculine version, Susano.

Variations and abbreviations: Siusan (Scot), Sosanna (Ir), Sue, Sukey, Suki, Susana (Sp), Susana, Susanna (It), Susanne (Fr/Ger), Susette, Susi, Susie, Susy, Suzanna, Suzanne (Fr), Suzette (Fr), Suzi, Suzy, Zsa Zsa (Hung), Zusi.

Examples: Susannah York, English actress.
Suzy Knickerbocker, US journalist.

SUSIE

Origin/meaning: Hebrew 'graceful white lily'.

A popular modern short form of Susan or Susannah.
Variations: Susy, Suzie, Suzy.
Example: Susie Orbach, US writer.

SUZANNE/SUZETTE/SUZAN
Origin/meaning: Hebrew 'graceful white lily'.
French forms of Susannah *q.v.*
Example: Suzanne Lenglen, 1899–1938, French tennis champion.

SYDNEY
Origin/meaning: Greek/Latin 'follower of Dionysios'.
Alternative spelling of Sidney *q.v.* an unusual feminine name.
See also Sidonie.

SYLVIA
See Silvia.

T

TABITHA
Origin/meaning: Aramaic 'antelope', 'gazelle'.

This is the translation of the Greek name Dorcas *q.v.* and both versions are given in the Acts of the Apostles ch.IX. The name was one of the many Biblical names which came into use after the 16th century Protestant Reformation. It is currently unfashionable.

TACE
Origin/meaning: English 'be silent'.

A popular 17th century name when all the virtues, including Silence, were used as names. Its use declined as Puritan influence waned.

Variations: Tacey, Tacy.

TACITA (pron. Tássita)
Origin/meaning: Latin 'silent'.

Feminine of the Old Roman name Tacitus, still viable today, especially in Italy.

TADDEA (pron. Taddáya)
Origin/meaning: uncertain, possibly Hebrew 'praise'.

Feminine form of Thaddeus *q.v.* Mainly used in Italy.

TAMARA
Origin/meaning: Hebrew 'palm tree'.

A popular name in Eastern Europe but rare in English-speaking countries.

Variations and abbreviations: Tamar, Tammie, Tammy.

Example: Tamara Ustinov, actress daughter of Peter Ustinov.

TAMMY
Origin/meaning: Aramaic 'little twin'.

This is a pet form of the feminine versions of Thomas, Tamsin and Thomasina. It is now frequently given as an independent name, particularly in the US where it was among the top fifty girls' names of 1975. It may occasionally be a short form of Tamara.

Variations: Tam, Tammi, Tammie.

Example: Tammy Wynette, US country singer.

TAMSIN
Origin/meaning: Aramaic 'twin'.

A feminine version of Thomas *q.v.* popular in Tudor times. It went out of fashion in the 18th and 19th centuries when Thomasina was more popular, although it continued to flourish in Cornwall. It is currently enjoying a revival in popularity.

Variations and abbreviations: Tam, Tamasin, Tamasine, Tammy, Tamzin, Thomasin, Thomasina.

TANYA
Origin/meaning: uncertain. Possibly 'little queen'.

A Russian short form of Tatiana *q.v.* now used as an independent name.

Variations and abbreviations: Tanhya, Tania, Tonya.

TATIANA
Origin/meaning: uncertain, sometimes given as 'little father', 'little queen'.

One of the five most popular girls' names in Russia. The meaning is not really known but it is sometimes said to derive from an ancient Roman tribe named after Tatianus, a Sabine king. It may also be derived from a childish word for father, tata, which gave the masculine Tatianus of which Tatiana is the feminine. The short form Tanya, has recently become popular in English-speaking countries.

Variations and abbreviations: Tanhya, Tania, Tanya, Tonya.

Example: St Tatiana, 3rd century Roman martyr.

TERRIE
Origin/meaning: obscure, possibly Greek 'from Tharasia' or 'reaper'.

A short form of Theresa *q.v.*
Variations: Terri, Terry.

TESS
Origin/meaning: uncertain, possibly Greek 'from Tharasia' or 'reaper'.

An English short form of Theresa *q.v.* now used as an independent name. May sometimes be given to a fourth child because of the Greek word tessara – four.

Variations: Tessa, Tessie, Tessy.

Example: Tessie O'Shea, British comedienne.

THEA
Origin/meaning: Greek 'goddess'.

This may be used as an independent name or as a short form of names beginning or ending with Thea such as Theodora and Theadora. See also Dora.

Examples: Thea Musgrave, British composer.
Thea Porter, British fashion designer.

THEKLA
Origin/meaning: Greek 'divine fame'.

This is the name of an early saint, St Thekla of Iconium. According to the Acts of St Paul, a document written c. 170 she was a convert of St Paul who wished to dedicate her life to God and refused to marry. This led to her persecution and she eventually found safety in what is now Syria. At the age of 90 she again faced persecution but was saved when the rock-face of her cave opened up to receive her. Her memory was widely venerated, especially in the Eastern church, and an 8th century English nun of the same name was also canonized. In the 19th century it came into occasional use as an English first name, perhaps because of the High Church movement.

Variations: Tecla (It), Thecla.

THELMA (pron. Thelma or Telma)
Origin/meaning: literary, invented by Marie Corelli for her novel *Thelma: a Norwegian Princess*, 1887.

Sometimes given as 'will' or 'intention' because of the Greek word thelima or 'nurseling" because of the Greek word thilazo, which means to nurse a baby.

This name became popular in Britain in the 1920s.

See also Wendy, Vanessa, Mavis, Amanda.

Example: Thelma Ritter, US actress.

THEODORA
Origin/meaning: Greek 'gift of God'.

The feminine form of Theodore *q.v.* used in the 18th century and still found occasionally today.

Variations and abbreviations: Dora, Fedora (Russ), Fjodora (Russ), Teodora (It), Thea, Theo.

THEODOSIA
Origin/meaning: Greek 'gift of God'.

A rare feminine form of Theodosius which is now almost obsolete.

Variations and abbreviations: Theo, Teodosia (It).

THEOPHANIA
Origin/meaning: Greek 'manifestation of God'.

Theophany was another name given to the festival of the Epiphany, when traditionally Christ is said to have first manifested himself to the Gentiles represented by the three Magi. The Greek meaning of the festival's name was forgotten but in the Middle Ages it was sometimes given to girls born on January 6th (Epiphany). In France Theophania was shortened to Tiphaine from which the English short form of Tiffany developed. This is still found as a surname and its use as a first name may sometimes be as a family name, not as a short form of Theophania. A well-known example of the surname is Tiffany's, the New York jeweller. The occasional use of this rare first name may be the result of the film which featured Tiffany's store *Breakfast at Tiffany's* (1961).

Variations and abbreviations: Theo, Theofania, Tiffany, Tyffany.

See also Bertha.

THEOPHILIA
Origin/meaning: Greek 'loved by God', 'lover of God'.

A rare 17th century name from the period when Biblical names were common. It is the feminine form of Theophilus *q.v.* which was better known and more enduring.

THERESA (pron. Terráyza)
Origin/meaning: obscure, possibly Greek 'from Tharasia' or 'reaper'.

This name first took root in Spain and did not spread further until the 16th century. Its sudden introduction to the rest of Catholic Europe was due to the popularity of St Teresa of Avila, 1515-1582, the Spanish nun who was both a mystic and a highly efficient administrator of her own reformed branch of the Carmelite nuns. The name did not reach Protestant England until the 18th century. In Catholic Ireland it has been immensely popular. Since the name was used to translate the native name Treasa it is pronounced there as Terreeza. In the 19th century the name received an additional boost to its popularity because of the French St Thérèse of Lisieux, 1873-1897. She was a simple nun who died of tuberculosis at the age of 24 but whose autobiography showed that sainthood is not confined to 'special' people but is possible for the very ordinary as well.

Variations and abbreviations: Teresa (Sp/It), Terese, Theresita (Sp), Teressa, Terri, Terrie, Terry, Tess, Tessa, Tessie, Tessy, Thérèse (Fr), Theresia (Ger), Tracey, Tracy.

Examples: Maria Theresa, 1717-1780, Empress of Austria.
Mother Theresa of Calcutta.

THIRZA (pron. Thurza)
Origin/meaning: uncertain. Possibly Hebrew 'acceptance' or 'pleasantness' or a place name.

This name occurs in the Book of Numbers ch.26 'and the names of the daughters of Zelophehad were Mahlah and Noah, Hoglah, Milcah and Tirzah'. Zelophehad had no sons and after his death his daughters approached Moses about the inheritance. As a result Moses received from God the important law that daughters and not male kin should be next in line of inheritance after sons. A popular 18th century narrative poem *The Death of Abel*, gave Tirzah as Abel's wife and the name enjoyed a period of popularity in various forms which lasted into the 19th century. Now rare.

Variations: Thyrza, Tirzah.

THORA
Origin/meaning: Old Norse 'strength', 'thunder'.

This is a Scandinavian feminine name from Thor, the Norse god of war and thunder. Its use is comparatively recent in English-speaking countries.

Variations: Thorina, Thyra, Tora (Swed), Tyra.

Examples: Thora Hird, British actress.
Princess Thyra of Denmark, 1853–1953, sister of Queen Alexandra.

TIFFANY
Origin/meaning: Greek 'manifestation of God'.

Medieval English form of Theophania q.v.

TILLY
Origin/meaning: Old German 'battle strength'.

A pet form of Matilda.

Variations and abbreviations: Tillie. See also Matilda.

Example: Tilly Losch, English singer and dancer of the 1920s and 30s renowned for her beauty.

TIMOTHEA
Origin/meaning: Greek 'honour to God'.

A feminine form of Timothy. Very rare.

TINA
Origin/meaning: a short form of names ending in -tine or -tina, eg Clementine, Christine.

Examples: Tina Brown, British journalist.
Tina Turner, US singer.

TONI
Origin/meaning: Latin. From Antonius, one of the great Roman families.

This is a popular short form of Antonia q.v.

Variations: Tonia, Tonie.

Example: Tonia Berg, English singer.

TOTTIE

Origin/meaning: uncertain, possibly Greek 'from Tharasia' or

A common familiar form (like Lottie) of Charlotte, one of the feminine versions of Charles.

Variations: Tot, Totty.

TRACEY

Origin/meaning: uncertain, possibly Greek 'from Tharasia' or 'reaper'.

This is an English familiar form of Theresa. However its upsurge in popularity in the 1960s and 70s has sometimes been attributed to the popularity of the US film actor Spencer Tracy, 1900–1967. Another film influence may have been *High Society*, 1956, in which Grace Kelly played Tracy Samantha Lord.

Variations: Tracie, Tracy. See also Samantha, Kelly.

Example: Tracy Austin, US tennis player.

TRICIA

Origin/meaning: Latin 'patrician'.

A popular short form of Patricia, often used as an independent name.

Variations: Trish, Trisha.

TRIXIE

Origin/meaning: Latin 'bringer of happiness'.

A popular familiar form of Beatrix or Beatrice frequently used as an independent name.

Variations: Trix, Trixy.

TRUDY

Origin/meaning: Old German 'strength' or 'spear strength'.

This is a short form of Gertrude which in the second half of the 20th century has been more popular than the original. In Scandinavia and Germany it may refer back to Thrudhr, one of Thor's daughters, who was one of the twelve Valkyries.

Variations: Druda, Traude (Ger), Traute (Ger), Trude (Den), Trudel, Trudi, Trudie.

TRYPHENA

Origin/meaning: Greek 'dainty' or 'delicate'.

Found in the 17th century like many other Biblical names, which are now rare. The names Tryphena and Tryphosa occur in ch.16 of St Paul's Epistle to the Romans.

Variations and abbreviations: Triffie, Tryphosa.

U

ULLA
Origin/meaning: Latin 'little she bear' or Old German/Old English 'wolf ruler'.

A short form of either Ursula or Ulrike used as an independent name. It is most popular in Scandinavia where it is often used in combination with another name, eg Ulla-Brit. The Scandinavian influence brought the name to Scotland while it is rare in the rest of the British Isles.

Example: Ulla Hyde Parker, Danish biographer of her cousin Beatrix Potter.

ULRIKE (pron. Óolreeka)
Origin/meaning: Old German/Old English 'wolf ruler'.

The feminine of Ulrich, this common German name is rare in English-speaking countries.

Variations and abbreviations: Ulla, Ulrica (It), Ulricha, Ulrika (Scand).

UMA
Origin/meaning: Hindu. A goddess, one of the incarnations of Parvati, wife of the great god Shiva.

UNA (pron. Yéwna)
Origin/meaning: Latin 'one'.

A name first used by Spenser in his poem *The Faeri Queen*. Una represented the unchanging oneness of truth as compared to the 'two-faced' representative of evil Duessa. Sometimes, pronounced Oona, it is also used as a variant spelling of the Irish Gaelic name Oonah *q.v.*

Example: Una Stubbs, English dancer and actress.

UNDINE
Origin/meaning: Latin 'water sprite'.

A name invented by the 16th century Swiss alchemist and astrologer Paracelsus from the Latin word *unda*, meaning wave. He used it to describe a water sprite who could gain an immortal soul by marrying a mortal and having a child.

Variation: Ondine (Fr).

UNITY
Origin/meaning: Latin 'oneness'.

Like Charity and Modesty, Unity is a virtue which came into use as a name during the 17th century Puritan period in England and New England.

Example: Unity Valkyrie Mitford, 1914–1948, one of the 'Mitford Girls', daughters of Baron Redesdale.

URANIA (pron. Ooráynia)
Origin/meaning: Greek 'heavenly'.

Urania was the Greek muse of astronomy, whose name was also sometimes used for Aphrodite the goddess of love. Her name came from the Greek word for sky or heaven and because of its universal importance it came to be used for other goddesses of different cultures. The name was given to one of the newly discovered asteriods in the 19th century and the name of the metal uranium comes from the same source.

Variation: Uranie (Fr). See also Celeste, Celia, Chandra, Selina.

URSULA
Origin/meaning: Latin 'little she-bear'.

St Ursula (probably 3rd or 4th century) was one of the virgin martyrs of the Roman Empire. On the basis of very little fact the story was heavily embroidered and she and her companions were venerated in the Middle Ages as St Ursula and the eleven thousand virgins! The romantic legend which grew up around her said that she was a Christian British princess betrothed to a pagan prince. While travelling abroad to postpone the marriage as long as possible, she arrived in Germany. At Cologne she refused to marry yet another pagan prince, whereupon she and her companions were martyred for their Christianity by the Huns. The discovery of a vast cache of bones at Cologne in the 12th century was used to support the story. The cult flourished in Northern Europe and Venice though the Saint and her name were never particularly popular in Britain.

Variations and abbreviations: Orsa, Orsola (It), Ulla, Ursa, Ursala, Ursel, Ursina (It), Ursola (Sp), Ursule (Fr), Ursulina, Uschi (Ger). See also Orson.

Examples: Ursula Andress, Swiss film actress.
Ursula Howells, British actress.
Ursula Bloom, English romantic novelist.

UTA (pron. Oota)
Origin/meaning: Old German 'fatherland'.

A popular short form of the German name Oda and its several French and English variations, such as Odette, Ottilie, Odelia etc. The equivalent of the masculine name Otto or Odo q.v.

Variations and abbreviations: Uda, Ute, Utta.

Examples: Ute Sax, German film actress.

V

VAL
Origin/meaning: short form of names eg Valentina, Valerie *q.v.* which begin with Val.

VALBURGA
Origin/meaning: Old German 'powerful protection'.

The Italian form of Walburga *q.v.*

VALENTINA
Origin/meaning: Latin 'strong', 'healthy'.

The feminine version of Valentine *q.v.* although occasionally girls are also called by the original version.

Variations and abbreviations: Val, Valentine.

Example: Valentina Tereshkova, Russian astronaut.

VALERIE
Origin/meaning: Latin 'strong', 'influential'. From the patrician Roman family of Valerius.

The English feminine form of this name was brought over from France in the 19th century as Valérie. The Latin form Valeria has been popular in Italy for centuries and there are three listed in the official martyrology of the Catholic church. There is a masculine form Valerian *q.v.*

Variations and abbreviations: Val, Valeria (It), Valeriane, Valérie (Fr), Valery, Valerye, Valeska (Slav). See also Antonia, Aurelia.

Example: Valerie Solanis, US feminist.

VALMAI
Origin/meaning: Old Welsh 'may blossom'.

VANESSA
Origin/meaning: a pet name invented by the 18th century writer Jonathan Swift for his friend Esther Vanhomrigh. He amalgamated

the first syllable of her surname with -essa, a short form of Esther.

Vanessa is also the name of one of the butterfly families.

Variations and abbreviations: Nessa, Vanna. See also Fiona, Lorna, Miranda, Pamela, Perdita, Stella, Wendy.

Examples: Vanessa Redgrave, British actress.
Vanessa Bell, 1879–1961, English painter, sister of Virginia Woolf.

VANORA
Origin/meaning: Old Gaelic 'white wave' or 'fair and yielding'.

This is a Scottish variant of the Old Welsh name Guinevere, which gave rise to several other names including Jennifer.

Variations and abbreviations: see Guinevere.

VARINA
Origin/meaning: 'stranger', 'foreigner'.

A Slavic version of Barbara *q.v.* In Slav and Greek languages the letter B is pronounced V. The typical diminutive form is Varinka from which we most probably derive Varina.

VARSHA (pron. Vuhrsháh)
Origin/meaning: Sanskrit 'rain'.

A name found throughout India.

VASHTI
Origin/meaning: Persian 'good'.

A Biblical name from the Book of Esther. The first wife of King Ahasuerus, Vashti was deposed for refusing to come at his command. Esther was appointed in her place.

VEENA
Origin/meaning: Sanskrit 'sitar'

A name found throughout India. In Indian mythology this instrument is used by Narad (pron. Nard) the messenger of the gods.

VELMA
Origin/meaning: Old German 'helmet of resolution'.

A short form, popular in US, of Wilhelmina *q.v.* from the

297

German pronunciation.

VELVET
Origin/meaning: the name (Middle English) of a smooth silky fabric.

Occasionally found as a first name in the US. Rare in England.

VENETIA
Origin/meaning: Latin 'of Venice', sometimes listed as 'blessed' from the Celtic Gwyneth q.v.

A name occasionally used in England since the Renaissance. Disraeli's novel of the same name, published 1837, gave it renewed popularity.

Example: Venetia Stanley, 1600–1633, celebrated beauty, wife of Sir Kenelm Digby.

VENUS
Origin/meaning: Latin 'charm', 'love'.

Venus was the Roman goddess of love. Unlike the name of another Roman goddess, Diana, it is rarely used, perhaps because it sets an impossible standard to live up to.

VERA
Origin/meaning: Latin 'true', Russian 'faith'.

Probably in England a 19th century short form of Veronica q.v. now used as an independent name. It may however be a direct use of the popular Russian name which is pronounced Vyera, and which was used by several 19th century lady novelists such as Ouida (*Moths*, 1860). In France it is also a short form of Véran (Verena).

Variations and abbreviations: Véra (It), Vere, Veria, Verla. See also Faith.

Examples: Vera Miles, US film actress.
Vera Brittain, 1893–1970, British author.
Vera Lynn, the Force's sweetheart, English singer.

VERDA
Origin/meaning: Latin 'green', 'springlike'.

A rare name with a similar meaning to Verna q.v.

VERENA
Origin/meaning: Old German 'defender', 'protector'.

A martyr whose feast falls on the 1st September. A popular name in Switzerland and Italy, its introduction to England was probably through Mrs Yonge's popular novel *The Heir of Redclyffe*. Sometimes used as a short form of Veronica.

Variations and abbreviations: Rena, Véran (Fr), Verina, Verine, Verna.

VERITY
Origin/meaning: Middle English word for 'truth'.

Used since the 17th century when Puritans chose virtues and Biblical names as an alternative to Catholic saints' names.

Variation: Verily.

VERNA
Origin/meaning: Latin 'springlike'.

A Latin word used rarely as a first name. Or it maybe a short form of Verena *q.v.*

Variations: Verne, Vernita, Virna. See also Verda.

Example: Verna Lisi, Italian film actress.

VERONICA
Origin/meaning: Latin 'true icon/image'.

The name traditionally given to the woman who wiped the face of Christ with a cloth while he was walking to Calvary. The image of Christ's face was said to be left on the cloth she used. Not surprisingly perhaps she is Patron Saint of photographers. More popular in Europe, (particularly the French form Véronique) than in England, until the end of the 19th century when it suddenly became fashionable.

Variations and abbreviations: Nicky, Ronnie, Vera, Verena, Veronika (Ger), Véronique (Fr), Vroni.

Example: Veronica Lake, US film actress.

VESTA
Origin/meaning: the name of the Latin goddess of the hearth.

Occasionally found as a first name.

Example: Vesta Tilley (Matilda Powles), 1864–1952, English music hall star and male impersonator.

VICKY
Origin/meaning: Latin 'victory'.

Short form of Victoria *q.v.* now found as an independent name.

Variations: Vicki, Vickie, Vikki, Vikky.

Example: Vicki Baum, 1896–1960, US writer.

VICTORIA
Origin/meaning: Latin 'victory'.

Rare in England before the reign of Queen Victoria, 1837–1901. Victoria was the Queen's second name and had been one of the names of her German mother, the Duchess of Kent. Because of the popularity of the Queen the name was often given to towns and geographical features like Lake Victoria, the largest lake in Africa, Victoria – the capital of British Columbia in Canada and Victoria – one of the Australian states.

Variations and abbreviations: Queenie, Vic, Vicki, Vickie, Vicky, Victoire (Fr), Victorine, Viktoria (Ger), Viktorine, Vita, Vitoria (Sp), Vittoria (It), Vittorina (It).

Example: Victoria Holt, English novelist.
Victoria Principal, US actress.

VICTORINE
Origin/meaning: Latin 'conqueror'.

The French feminine version of Victor *q.v.* sometimes used in English-speaking countries as a diminutive of Victoria *q.v.*

VIDA
Origin/meaning: Hebrew 'beloved'.

A short form of feminine versions of David *q.v.* eg Davida, Davidina. See also Davina.

Example: Vida Scudder, 1861–1954, US writer and reformer.

VILLETTE
Origin/meaning: Old German 'helmet of resolution'.

Regional French feminine version of William *q.v.*

See also Wilhelmina, Minna.

VINCENTIA
Origin/meaning: Latin 'conqueror'.

Feminine version of Vincent q.v.

Variations and abbreviations: Vincenza (It), Vinciane (Fr).

VIOLA
Origin/meaning: Latin 'violet flower'.

This Latin word for a violet was used occasionally during the Middle Ages as a feminine first name, although French and Italian versions of the word were usually preferred. It was chosen by Shakespeare for his heroine in *Twelfth Night*. In the 19th and 20th centuries the English word Violet q.v. has been used instead.

Variations and abbreviations: Vi, Violante, Viole, Vye. See also Iolanthe, Yolande, Violet.

Example: Viola Dana, b.1897, US star of silent films.

VIOLET
Origin/meaning: Latin 'the violet flower'.

During the Middle Ages the original Latin word for a violet – viola – was more or less replaced in England by the French diminutive form Violete from which comes the English word violet. At the same time the name Viola became less popular than the French versions Violette and Violante (see Yolande) and the Italian Violetta. The English word violet is first found as a name in Scotland in the 16th century, but it was not until the 19th century that the name became fashionable in England itself, along with many other flower names. In a relatively short time, it replaced all the other variations which had survived for centuries. They are now rarely used. The Victorians set great store on the language of flowers and Violet was given as a name which implied innocence and love of truth.

Variations and abbreviations: Vi, Violante (Fr), Violetta (It), Violette (Fr), Vye.

See also Ianthe, Iolanthe, Yolande, Viola.

Examples: Violet Trefusis, 1894–1971, English novelist and socialite.
Lady Violet Bonham Carter, 1887–1969, British politician.

VIRGINIA

Origin/meaning: either Latin from the Patrician Roman family Verginius (spring) or Latin 'maidenly', 'virginal'.

The American plantation, (later State) of Virginia, was named by Sir Walter Raleigh to honour Elizabeth I, England's Virgin Queen in 1584. The name from this source has long been a popular one in the United States. In Europe the Latin family name Verginius gave rise to a similar feminine first name Verginia. In the form Virginie it became very popular in France and was introduced into England in the last century, but has now been overtaken by the English/American version, Virginia.

Variations and abbreviations: Ginger, Ginni, Ginnie, Ginny, Jinny, Jinney, Verginia, Virgie, Virginie (Fr).

Examples: Virginia Wade, British tennis player.

Virginia Woolf, 1882–1941, English novelist.
Virginia Dare, b.1587. First child born in America of English parents.

VITA

Origin/meaning: Latin 'life', 'full of life'.

A name with the same meaning as Vivien q.v. and the masculine name Vitalis q.v. This Latin word was not used as a name until comparatively recently. Sometimes it is a short form of similar names, eg Victoria.

Example: Vita (Victoria) Sackville-West, 1892–1962, English writer and gardener.

VIVIEN

Origin/meaning: Latin 'full of life'.

The original medieval version of this name was Viviana, the Latin feminine form of Vivianus. St Viviana (or Bibiana) was one of the early martyrs. In the 19th century Tennyson used Vivien, which is based on the French form Vivienne, for one of his poems of the Arthurian legends, *Vivien and Merlin*. It is possible he may have confused it with the Old Celtic name Ninian when he was looking for names appropriate for that time and area of Britain. Nevertheless the poem helped to popularize the name.

Variations and abbreviations: Bibiana, Viv, Vivian, Viviana (It), Viviane (Ger), Vivianne, Vivie, Vivienne (Fr), Vivyan. See also Vita.

Examples: Vivien Leigh, 1913–1967, English actress.
Vivien Merchant, 1929–1982, English actress.

VOLETTA
Origin/meaning: Old French 'a veil'.

Variations and abbreviations: Volet, Vollet (both pron. vollay).

W

WALBURGA
Origin/meaning: Old German 'powerful protection'.

This Saxon name is now rare in English-speaking countries but was very popular in the Middle Ages because of St Walburga, d. 776. It is still fairly common in German-speaking countries, Scandinavia and Italy.

Variations: Valborg (Scand), Valburga (It), Walburg (Ger), Waldburg, Waldburga, Wali, Walli.

WALLIS
Origin/meaning: Old Scots 'from Wales', 'foreign'.

A surname used as a girl's first name – a common practice in the Southern United States. Established more generally because of the US born Mrs Wallis Simpson who married Edward VIII in 1937 and became the Duchess of Windsor. Occasionally this spelling is used as a masculine name but then the more usual form is Wallace *q.v.*

WANDA (pron. Wonda)
Origin/meaning: uncertain. Possibly Old German 'stem' or 'branch'. Sometimes given as 'wanderer'.

This German name may itself be of Slavic origin for there was an 8th century Polish Princess called Wanda. Very popular in Germany at the end of the 19th century it was introduced into England by the novelist Ouida, who gave the name to the heroine of her book *Wanda*, 1883.

Variations and abbreviations: Vanda (It), Wenda.

Examples: Wanda Ventham, English actress.
Wanda Gág, 1893–1946, US artist and children's writer.
Wanda Ladowska, 1887–1959, Polish pianist and harpsichordist.

WANDER
Origin/meaning: Old Gaelic 'white wave'.

304

A Scottish variant of Guinevere *q.v.* which is a Welsh name with many derivations. Sometimes confused with the Old German name Wanda *q.v.*

WENDY
Origin/meaning: invented by J. M. Barrie for his book *Peter Pan*, 1904. Apparently he had the idea because Margaret Henley, the small daughter of a friend, nicknamed him 'friendy-wendy'.

An immensely popular 20th century name which has already acquired its own variations.

Variations and abbreviations: Wendi, Wendie, Wendye. See also Evangeline, Fiona, Lorna, Miranda, Ophelia, Pamela, Perdita, Vanessa.

Examples: Dame Wendy Hiller, British actress.
Wendy Turnbull, Australian tennis player.

WILHELMINA
Origin/meaning: Old German 'will helmet' ie 'helmet of resolution'.

A feminine form of William *q.v.* brought to England from the Netherlands and Germany during the 18th century partly because of the influence of the Dutch and Hanoverian members of the Royal family. Popular in 19th and 20th centuries in English-speaking countries with large German immigrant populations.

Variations and abbreviations: Billie, Billy, Guglielma (It), Guillema, Guillemette (Fr), Guillelmina (Sp), Guillelmine (Fr), Gullelma, Min, Mina, Minna, Minni, Minnie, Minny, Valma, Velma, Vilhelmina (Slav), Villette (Fr), Vilma, Wilella, Wilhelmine, Willa, Willamina, Williamina, Wilma, Wilmette, Wylma.

Examples: Queen Wilhelmina of the Netherlands.
Williamina Fleming, 1857–1911, US astronomer.

WILLA
Origin/meaning: Old German 'helmet of resolution'.

Short form, popular in US of Wilhelmina, Wilella.

Example: Willa Cather, 1873–1947, US novelist.

WILLOW
Origin/meaning: Old English 'willow tree'.

WILMA
Origin/meaning: Old German 'helmet of resolution'.

A short form of Wilhelmina *q.v.* now a popular independent name in the USA.

Variations: Valma, Vilma, Wylma.

Example: Vilma Banky, Austro-Hungarian born early Hollywood film actress.

WILMOT
Origin/meaning: Old German 'helmet of resolution'.

A medieval first name derived from the same root as William and Wilhelmina *q.v.* It is also found as a boy's first name and a surname.

Variations: Wilmett, Wylmot.

WINIFRED
Origin/meaning: Old German 'peaceful friend', Old Welsh 'blessed reconciliation'.

Although this name is traditionally given the first meaning it is equally likely that it is the English version of the Old Welsh name Gwenfrewi (through the Latin Wenefreda), which means 'blessed reconciliation'. A 7th century Welsh Princess of that name was martyred by Prince Caradoc and became a saint. Because of the spelling, Welsh form Gwenfrewi it is sometimes mistakenly listed as a variation of Guinevere or Gwendolyn which sound similar. Winifred became popular in England in the 16th century but has gone out of fashion in the last 50 years and has been replaced in popularity by the shortened version, Freda.

Variations and abbreviations: Freda, Fredi, Freddie, Venefrida (It), Wenefrede, Wenefride, Winefred, Win, Winnie, Winnifred, Winny, Wyn.

Examples: Winifred Holt, 1870–1945, US social worker, founder of the Lighthouse charity.
Winifred Holtby, 1898–1935, English novelist, author of *South Riding*.

WINONA
Origin/meaning: Sioux Indian 'first born daughter'.
Variation: Wenona.

WINNIE

Origin/meaning: Old German 'peaceful friend' or Old Welsh 'blessed reconciliation', 'white', 'fair'.

Short form usually of either Winifred *q.v.* or Gwendolyn *q.v.* and their variations. Sometimes of other names, eg Gwyneth, which contain the same sound.

Variation: Wynne.

X

XANTHE (pron. Zanthee)
Origin/meaning: Greek 'yellow'.

Rare in English-speaking countries.

Variation: Xantha.

XANTHIPPE (pron. Zantippy)
Origin/meaning: Greek 'light-coloured horse'.

This was the name of Socrates' wife who had a reputation for shrewishness and bad temper! Very rare.

XAVIERA (pron. Sp. Havierra, Eng. Zaviera)
Origin/meaning: Arabic 'bright', 'splendid'.

Feminine form of Xavier *q.v.*

XENIA (pron. Zennia)
Origin/meaning: Greek 'hospitable', 'guest'.

Variations and abbreviations: Xena, Zena, Zenia.

Y

YASMIN
Origin/meaning: Arabic/Persian 'jasmine flower'.

The Arab original of the better known English form Jasmine *q.v.* It is very popular in Arab countries.

Variation: Yamina. See also Jasmine.

Example: Princess Yasmin Khan, daughter of Rita Hayworth and the late Aga Khan.

YETTA
Origin/meaning: Old English 'giver'.

Sometimes used as a short form of Henrietta.

YNEZ
Origin/meaning: Greek 'pure', 'chaste'.

A spelling of Inez, the Spanish form of Agnes *q.v.*

YOLANDE
Origin/meaning: Latin 'violet flower'.

A French name which developed from Violaine, or Violante, Medieval French forms of Viola, the Latin word for violet.

Variations and abbreviations: Iola, Iolande (It), Iolande, Iolanthe (Ger), Jolanda (It), Jolanthe (Ger), Yolanda (Sp), Yolanthe. See also Violet, Ianthe.

Example: Yolande Turner, US actress.

YVETTE
Origin/meaning: Old German 'yew'.

Like Yvonne, a feminine version of Yves, the French form of Ivo.

Variations: Evette, Ivette.

Example: Yvette Mimieux, US film actress.

YVONNE

Origin/meaning: Old German 'yew'.

A French feminine version of Yves, Yvon, the French forms of Ivo q.v. Popular in English-speaking countries in the 20th century.

Variation: Evonne. See also Yvette.

Examples: Yvonne Arnaud, 1892–1958, French actress.
Yvonne de Carlo, US film actress.
Evonne Cawley, Australian tennis player.

Z

ZAINAB
Origin/meaning: Arabic 'beautiful'.
A Muslim name, Zainab was the eldest daughter of Mohammed.
Variation: Zainabu (E African).

ZAKIYA
Origin/meaning: Arab 'intelligent'.
This is a popular Muslim name.

ZANDRA
Origin/meaning: Greek 'defender of men'.
An abbreviation of Alexandra q.v.
Example: Zandra Rhodes, British fashion designer.

ZARAH
Origin/meaning: possibly Arabic 'flower', or Hebrew 'sunrise', 'dawn'. Possibly also a variant of Sarah 'princess'.
Rare, although in the 17th century popular among Puritans.

Variations and abbreviations: Zara, Zariah, Zerah, Zora. See also Dawn, Roxanne.

Example: Zara Phillips, daughter of HRH Princess Anne and Captain Mark Phillips.

ZELDA
Origin/meaning: uncertain. May be a contraction of Griselda q.v. 'grey battle maid'.
A 20th century name.

Example: Zelda Fitzgerald, 1900–1948, wife of US novelist F. Scott Fitzgerald.

ZELIE (pron. Zaylie)
Origin/meaning: Greek 'zealous', 'ardent'.

311

An unusual name, used in Victorian times, probably French in origin. Also a short form of the 19th century flower name Azalea.

Variations and abbreviations: Zele, Zelia (Sp), Zelina.

Example: Zelia Nuttal, 1857–1933, US archaeologist and anthropologist.

ZELINDA
Origin/meaning: Hebrew/Latin 'beautiful dawn'.

A name found in Italian and Spanish-speaking countries.

Variation: Zerlinda. See also Aurora, Dawn, Roxanne, Zarah.

ZELMA
Origin/meaning: Old German 'helmet of God'.

A form of Anselma/Selma *q.v.*

Example: Zelma Hedrick, the real name of US film actress Kathryn Grayson.

ZENA
Origin/meaning: Greek 'hospitable'.

An Anglicized version of Xenia *q.v.*

Examples: Zena Skinner, British cookery writer.
Zena Dare, English actress.

ZENOBIA
Origin/meaning: probably Arabic 'ornament of the father'. Possibly Greek 'gift of Zeus'.

A Greek version of the Arabic original. The best known example is the 3rd century Queen of Palmyra who became such a threat to the Roman Emperor Aurelian that he declared war against her and defeated and captured her in AD 272.

Variation: Zenovia.

ZILIA
Origin/meaning: Latin 'heavenly'.

An unusual spelling of Celia *q.v.*

ZILLAH
Origin/meaning: uncertain. May be Hebrew 'shade'.

A biblical name (Genesis ch.4), one of the two wives of Lamech, (the other was Adah *q.v.*). Sometimes said to be a popular name among gypsies, it is otherwise rare. A folk tale once popular tells the story of Zillah, a young girl from Bethlehem. She rejected a loutish suitor who took revenge by naming her as a witch. As she stood at the stake to be burnt, God diverted the flames. Zillah was saved and the stake became a living rosetree covered with red and white roses. Antonia White used the name for the maid in her novel *Frost in May*. It is also given to the maid in Emily Brontë's *Wuthering Heights*.

ZINNIA
Origin/meaning: a tropical plant.

One of the flower names occasionally used.

ZIPPORAH
Origin/meaning: Hebrew 'sparrow'.

The wife of Moses.

Variations: Zippora, Zipporal.

ZITA (pron. Zeeta)
Origin/meaning: Etruscan 'young girl'. Sometimes given as Greek Zeta the 6th letter of the Greek alphabet. It may sometimes be a short form of names, eg Rosita, which end in Sita or Zita.

Now comparatively rare in English-speaking countries, though still found in Europe especially Italy. The name was popular in medieval times, because of St Zita, 1218–1278, the patron saint of domestic servants who was born and lived at Lucca in Italy.

Example: Empress Zita, b.1892, wife of Charles, last Emperor of Austria.

ZOË
Origin/meaning: Greek 'life'.

Initially used because of its meaning to translate the Biblical Hebrew word for Eve, the mother of mankind, into Greek, Zoë became a name in its own right. A 20th century name in English-speaking countries, it has been popular far longer in countries which adhere to the Greek and Russian orthodox church.

Variations: Zoa, Zoé (Fr).

Examples: Zoë Wanamaker, English actress.

Empress Zoë, 980–1050, daughter of Byzantine Emperor Constantine VIII, wife of Romanus III (whom she murdered), Michael IV (whom she exiled) and Constantine IX.

ZONA
Origin/meaning: Greek 'girdle'.

A comparatively new name in English-speaking countries. More familiar in the US than in Britain.

Variation: Zone.

Example: Zona Gale, 1874–1938, US writer and suffragette.

ZORA
Origin/meaning: Arabic 'sunrise', 'dawn'.

A version of Zarah/Aurora, *q.v.*

Example: Zora Hurston, 1903–1960, US writer and folklorist.

ZSA ZSA (pron. Jhah-Jhah)
Origin/meaning: Hebrew 'lily' or 'princess'.

Hungarian form of Susan or Sarah made familiar by American/Hungarian actress Zsa Zsa (Sari) Gabor.

ZULEIKA (pron. Zoolîka)
Origin/meaning: Arabic 'fair', 'beautiful'.

A favourite Persian name. Max Beerbohm's satirical novel *Zuleika Dobson*, 1911, gave it some popularity in England.

Variation: Suleika (Ger).

PART TWO

Names for Boys

A

AARON
Origin/meaning: Hebrew 'high mountain' or Egyptian (no known meaning).

Aaron was the brother of Moses (Exodus 4) and first High Priest of Israel. It was not used as a first name until after the 16th century Reformation. Aaron has always been more popular in the US than in the UK and is also fairly widespread in Australia.

Variations and abbreviations: Aron (Eng), Aharon (Heb), Haroun (Ar).

Examples: Aaron Burr, 1756–1836, 3rd Vice-President of the US.
Aaron Copland, US composer.

ABBAS
Origin/meaning: Arabic 'stern'.

Abbas, 566–652, was an uncle of Mohammed. At first hostile he eventually became one of the Prophet's most ardent supporters. He was the founder of the Abbasides, Khalifs of Baghdad, 750–946.

Variation: Abasi (Swahili).

Examples: Abbas the Great, 1557–1628, Shah of Persia.
Abbas Pasha, 1813–1954, Viceroy of Egypt.

ABBOTT
Origin/meaning: Old English 'abbey father' from the Hebrew 'abba' – 'father'.

More commonly found as a surname.

Variations and abbreviations: Ab, Abad (Sp), Abba, Abbé (Fr), Abbey, Abbie, Abboid (Gaelic), Abbot, Abby, Abott.

Example: James Abbot McNeill Whistler, 1834–1903, US artist and lithographer.

ABDUL
Origin/meaning: Arabic 'servant of God'.

This is one of the commonest Muslim names, and is found in slightly varying forms in many countries.

Variations and abbreviations: Abdu (worshipper of God) (Swahili). Abdala (Swahili), Abdullah.

Example: Abdullah Ibn (son of) Hussein, 1882–1951, first King of Jordan.

ABE
American contraction of Abel, Abram or Abraham *q.v.*

ABEL
Origin/meaning: Hebrew 'breath' or 'son'. Also a short form of Abelard *q.v.*

Abel was the second son of Adam and Eve, killed by his brother Cain.

Abbreviations: Abe, Abell, Able, Nab.

Examples: Abel Evans, 1679–1737, English poet.
Abel Janszoom Tasman, 1603–1659, Dutch navigator, discoverer of Tasmania and New Zealand.

ABELARD
Origin/meaning: Old German 'noble resolution' from 'adal' – 'noble, hard – resolute'.

The French and best-known version of the name. Now extremely uncommon.

Variations and abbreviations: Adalard (Eng), Adalhard (Old Ger), Alard.

Example: Pierre Abelard, 1079–1142, French Monk and philosopher, whose illicit romance with his pupil Eloïse ended tragically for them both.

ABHAY (pron. Ahbpóy)
Origin/meaning: Sanskrit/Gujerati, 'fearless'.

ABNER
Origin/meaning: Hebrew 'father of light'.

Abner was the cousin of King Saul and the commander of his army. Now a rare name in England, although common for a while after the 16th century Reformation. Still popular in some areas of the US.

317

Variations and abbreviations: Ab, Avner, Eb, Ebner.

ABRAHAM
Origin/meaning: Hebrew: 'father of a multitude' from the Hebrew word 'abba' – 'father'.

The name of the Patriarch of Israel whose name was changed by God from Abram to Abraham (Genesis ch.17). This was one of the names brought into use in the 13th century in England. Like many Biblical names it increased in popularity after the 17th century Reformation. Now more popular in the US than Britain because of President Abraham Lincoln.

The contraction Bram is popular in the Netherlands and US.

Variations and abbreviations: Abe, Abey, Abie, Abrahamo (It), Abrahán (Sp), Abram, Abramo, Avram, Avrom, Bram, Ibrahim (Ar), Ham.

Examples: Abraham Lincoln, 1809–1865, 16th President of the United States.
Abraham Cowley, 1618–1667, English poet.
General Ibrahim Abboud, 1901–1983, former prime minister of the Sudan.

ABRAM
Origin/meaning: Hebrew 'the high father'.

The original name of the Patriarch of Israel, Abraham *q.v.*
He changed his name when he settled in Palestine.

Variations and abbreviations: Abe, Abramo (It), Avram, Bram.

ABSOLOM
Origin/meaning: Hebrew 'father of peace'.

The name of King David's son by Maacah (Samuel I + II). Popular in the 12th and 13th centuries.

Variations and abbreviations: Absolon (Fr), Axel (Ger/Scand).

Example: The Clerk in Chaucer's *The Miller's Tale*.

ACE
Origin/meaning: may be an abbreviation of Acelin *q.v.*

More common in US than in Britain.

Variations and abbreviations: Acey, Acie.

ACELIN
Origin/meaning: Old German 'noble'.

A diminutive of the Old German Azzo and Old French Asce which are both derived from the frequently used root 'adal' – noble.

One of the 13th century influx of Christian names in England.

Variations and abbreviations: Ace, Ascelyn, Ezzelmo (It).

ACHILLES
Origin/meaning: Greek. May mean 'tight-lipped' or be connected with the River Achellos.

Still common in Greece and therefore found frequently in the US and Australia where there are large Greek communities. Extremely rare in the UK.

Variation: Achille (Fr).

Examples: Achilles, the Greek hero of Homer's epic poem *The Iliad*, who slew the Trojan hero Hector.
Claude Achille Debussy, 1862–1918, French composer.

ACKERLEY
Origin/meaning: Old English 'from the oak tree meadow'.

More commonly found as a surname but occasionally used as a first name.

Variations and abbreviations: Ackley, Ack.

ADAIR
Origin/meaning: Gaelic 'from the oak tree ford'.

Found as both first name and surname in Scotland and Scottish communities. Uncommon as a first name.

ADALARD
Origin/meaning: Old German 'noble resolution'.

An English variation of Abelard *q.v.* which is the more usual form.

Variation: Alard.

Example: St Adalard, Saxon saint, c. 751–827.

ADALBERT
Origin/meaning: Old German 'nobly bright'.

319

The original form of Albert *q.v.*

Variation: Adelbert.

ADAM

Origin/meaning: Hebrew 'red (earth)'.

In the Book of Genesis Adam, the first man, was fashioned from the earth and is presumed to have taken his name from its colour. The Jews did not use the name. Although occasionally used by monks before the Conquest Adam became popular in Britain in the 13th century especially in the North. Its popularity has revived in the 20th century. Many surnames derive from it, eg Adams, Adamson, Atkins, MacAdam.

Variations and abbreviations: Ad, Adamh (Ir), Adamnan, Adamo (It), Adan (Sp), Adda (Wel), Addan, Adao (Port), Ade, Edom (Scot).

Examples: Adam Smith, 1723–1790, economist, author of *The Wealth of Nations*.
Adam Lindsay Gordon, 1833–1870, British poet.

ADDISON

Origin/meaning: Old English 'son of Adam'.

Generally found as a surname it is occasionally used as a first name, especially in US.

Variations and abbreviations: Ad, Addie, Addy. See also Adam.

ADE

Origin/meaning: Yoruba 'royal'.

See also Oba, Rex.

ADOLPH

Origin/meaning: Old German 'noble wolf'.

The English version of Adolphus *q.v.* Never very popular in English-speaking countries, it has become even less so because of its association with Adolf Hitler.

Variations and abbreviations: Adolf (Ger), Adolphe (Fr).

Examples: Adolphe Menjou, 1890–1963, dapper American film actor.
Adolph Ochs, 1858–1935, US journalist who invented the saying 'All the news that's fit to print'.

ADOLPHUS

Origin/meaning: Old German 'noble wolf'.

Latin form of an Old German name which was also found in the Old English form Aethelwulf. King Aethelwulf was the father of King Alfred who burnt the cakes. In its present form, it was brought to England by the Hanoverians in the 18th century but never achieved great popularity.

Variations and abbreviations: Adolfus, Adolf (Ger), Adolph, Adolphe (Fr), Dolly.

Example: Adolphus Greely, 1844–1935, US Arctic explorer.

ADRIAN

Origin/meaning: Latin 'from Adria' (the port which gave its name to the Adriatic Sea).

One of the best known holders of this name is the Roman Emperor Hadrianus, who built Hadrian's Wall in the North of England to keep out the Scots. Adrianople was also named after him. Although there are some early English examples of the name it did not become well known until the 12th century when Nicholas Breakespear became the first (and only) English Pope, taking the name Adrian IV.

Variations and abbreviations: Adriaen, Adrien (Fr), Arrien, Arne.

Example: Adrian Mitchell, English poet.

AENEAS (pron. Inéeas)
Origin/meaning: Greek 'the praised one'.

The subject of Virgil's famous poem, Aeneas was one of the heroes of the Trojan Wars, and escaped from Troy to found the city of Rome. The name is now rare in English-speaking countries although it has been used occasionally since the Renaissance revival in classical Greek learning. In Scotland Aeneas is sometimes found quite independently from the Greek name as a transliteration of the Gaelic Aonghus (Angus).

Variations and abbreviations: Angus, Eneas (Sp).

AHMED
Origin/meaning: Arabic 'praiseworthy'.
This popular name is found in all Muslim countries in the same form. It was the name of three Turkish Sultans in the 17th and

early 18th centuries.

Examples: Ahmed Arabi, 1840–1911, Egyptian rebel leader.
Ahmed Shah (Emperor Ahmed), 1724–1773, first monarch of Afghanistan.
Ahmed Zogu, 1893–1961, (King Zog of Albania).

AIDAN
Origin/meaning: Old Irish 'little fire' or 'little fiery one'.

The name of an influential 7th century Irish saint who converted the North of England to Christianity.

Variations: Adan, Eden.

AKBAR
Origin/meaning: Sanskrit 'the great'.

This was the epithet applied to the great Mogul Emperor Jelal-ed-din-Mohammed, 1542–1605. His reign corresponded approximately to that of Elizabeth I of England. In a few years he extended his Empire to the whole of India north of the Vindhya Mountains. He was a wise and humane ruler who practised religious tolerance. His name is now used as a personal name throughout India.

See also Magnus, Maximilian.

AKIIKI (pron. Akee-éekee)
Origin/meaning: Muneyankole 'friend'.

ALAN
Origin/meaning: 'handsome'.

A name originally introduced into England at the time of the Norman Conquest from Brittany, the Celtic area of France. It was originally found in its French form, Alain, but there are now many English variations. Not surprisingly it has remained most popular in the Celtic areas of Ireland and Scotland.

Variations and abbreviations: Ailean (Scot), Ailin (Ir), Al, Alain (Fr), Aland, Alano (It/Sp), Alein, Allan, Allayne, Allen, Alleyn.

Examples: Alan Alda, US actor.
Alan Bennett, English playwright.

ALARIC
Origin/meaning: Old German 'noble ruler'.

The name of one of the Gothic kings, 370–410. He was leader of the army which sacked Rome in 410 and effectively brought the Roman Empire to an end.

See also Ulric.

ALASTAIR
Origin/meaning: Ancient Greek 'defender of men'.

A Scottish form of Alexander *q.v.*

Variations and abbreviations: Al, Alasdair, Alistair, Alister, Allister.

Examples: Alistair Cooke, British/US journalist.
Alastair Sim, 1900–1976, Scottish actor.

ALBAN
Origin/meaning: Latin 'white', 'fair'.

Although never extremely fashionable this name has appeared consistently since at least AD 287 when St Alban was martyred at the Roman town of Verulamium, later named St Albans in his honour.

Variations and abbreviations: Albany, Alben, Albin (Ger), Albion, Alva (Sp), Aubin (Fr).

Example: Alban Berg, 1885–1935, Austrian composer.

Alban Berg, 1885–1935, Austrian composer.

ALBERT
Origin/meaning: Old German 'noble bright' from adal – noble, berhta – bright.

A modern short form of the original German Adalbert. The Old English version Athelbert, and names connected with it, were used both before and after the Conquest of 1066. However its real popularity in the present form is almost entirely due to Queen Victoria's marriage in 1840 to the German Prince Albert. Although Albert was never greatly popular his name caught on immediately.

Variations and abbreviations: Adalbert, Ailbert (Scan), Al, Alberto (It/Sp), Albrecht (Ger), Aubert (Fr), Bert, Bertie, Halbert.

Examples: Albert Schweitzer, 1875–1965, French missionary

and philosopher.
Albert Einstein, 1879–1955, Swiss scientist.
Albert Finney, English actor.
Albrecht Dürer, 1471–1528, German painter.

ALDO
Origin/meaning: Old German 'old'.

Usual American form of Aldous q.v.

Example: Aldo Ray, US actor.

ALDOUS
Origin/meaning: Old German 'old'.

One of the many 13th century additions to the number of English first names. Still rare and usually found both as a first name or a surname on the East Coast of England.

Variations and abbreviations: Aldis, Aldo, Aldus.

Example: Aldous Huxley, 1894–1963, English writer.

ALDRED
Origin/meaning: Old English 'old counsel'.

An Anglo-Saxon name still found occasionally after the Norman Conquest. Similar to Edred q.v. Unlike Edgar and Edwin it was not noticeably helped by the Romantic Movement's love of old names and remains rare.

ALEC
Origin/meaning: Ancient Greek 'defender of men'.

One of the many variations of Alexander q.v.

Variations and abbreviations: Alek, Aleck, Alic, Alick.

Examples: Sir Alec Guinness, English actor.
Alec McCowen, English actor.

ALEXANDER
Origin/meaning: Ancient Greek 'defender of men'.

The name of the famous Greek conqueror Alexander of Macedon, 356–323 BC, it has been popular ever since. Many of its short forms have become independent names eg Alex, Alec, Sandy, and it has given rise to many surnames, eg Allister, McAllister, Saunders, Sanderson. It is particularly popular in

Scotland which has had several kings of that name. In Scotland it frequently takes the form Alastair.

Variations and abbreviations: Al, Alasdair (Scot), Alastair (Scot), Alaster, Alec, Alejandry (Sp), Alek, Aleksandr (Russ), Alessandro (It), Alex, Alexan, Alexandre (Fr), Alexio (Port), Alexis, Alic, Alick, Alisander, Alistair (Scot), Alister, Allister, Sacha, Sander, Sandro (It), Sandy, Sasha, Saunder.

Examples: Alexander Kerensky, 1881–1970, Russian statesman.
Sir Alexander Fleming, 1881–1955, discoverer of Penicillin.

ALEXIS
Origin/meaning: Ancient Greek 'helper' or 'defender'.

Popular in Russia and Greece Alexis has recently become more popular in English-speaking countries. Also a short form of Alexander q.v. Sometimes found as a short form of the girl's name Alexandra q.v.

Variations: Alexei, Alecco (Gr).

Examples: Saint Alexis, who lived in poverty in Syria in the 5th century.
Alexei Sayle, British comedian.

ALFRED
Origin/meaning: Old English 'elf counsellor', 'good counsellor'.

This was the name of one of the Saxon Kings of England, Alfred the Great, 849–901. It was very popular in this Saxon form and also in variations of the Latinized version – Alvredus or Aluredus – which led to the surname Avery.

Variations and abbreviations: Al, Alf, Alfie, Alfredo (It/Sp), Alfy, Alured, Avery, Fred, Freddie, Freddy.

Examples: Alfred, Lord Tennyson, 1809–1892, English poet.
Alfred Hitchcock, 1899–1980, film director.
Alfred Nobel, 1833–1896, Swedish inventor and philanthropist.

ALGERNON
Origin/meaning: Norman French 'bearded', 'with whiskers'.

This name began as a nickname some 900 years ago at a time when most men were clean-shaven. In Tudor times it was adopted by several aristocratic families and it enjoyed a period of more general popularity in the 19th century. It has now become rare again and regained its aristocratic overtones.

Abbreviations and variations: Algie, Algy.

Examples: Algernon Moncrieff in Oscar Wilde's play *The Importance of Being Earnest*, 1895.
Algernon Charles Swinburne, 1837–1909, English poet.

ALI
Origin/meaning: Arabic 'exalted'.

Ali, d.661, was the cousin of the Prophet Mohammed, and the first convert to Mohammedanism. He married the Prophet's youngest daughter, Fatima *q.v.* He was fearless in his devotion to the Prophet and became Khalif, but was assassinated six years later. Ali may be used as a personal name or as a religious name in conjunction with another name, in which case the two should always be spoken together.

Examples: Ali Pasha (the lion), 1741–1822, ruler of Albania.
Mohammed Ali (formerly Cassius Clay), US boxer.

ALISON
Origin/meaning: Old German 'nobility' or 'Alice's son'.

Rarely found as a masculine name, more common as a feminine name (from Alice *q.v.*) or as a surname.

Variations and abbreviations: Al, Allison.

ALONZO
Origin/meaning: Old German 'noble and ready'.

A form of Alphonso *q.v.*

ALOYSIUS (pron. Allowíshus)
Origin/meaning: Old German 'glorious battle'.

This is an old form of the French name Louis *q.v.* It developed as the Latin, written form of the Provençal name Aloys meaning son of Loys (Louis). A 16th century St Aloysius, one of the early Jesuits, popularized the name in Catholic Europe. It is still a name used almost exclusively by Catholics.

Variations and abbreviations: Alois (Ger), Aloisio (It), Aloisius, Aloys. See also Louis.

ALPHONSO
Origin/meaning: Old German 'adal-funs' – 'noble and ready'.

Now a comparatively rare name except in Spain where it was introduced in the 8th century.

Variations and abbreviations: Affonso (Port), Alfons (Ger), Alfonso (Sp/It/Scand), Alonzo, Alphonse (Fr), Alphonsus (Lat/Ir), Fons, Fonsie, Fonz, Fonzie.

Examples: Alphonse Daudet, 1840–1897, French writer.
Alphonse (Al) Capone, 1899–1947, US gangster.

ALVIN
Origin/meaning: Old German 'noble friend'.

A form of the Old English name Aylwin q.v. which is more usually found in America.

Variations and abbreviations: Aloin (Fr), Aluin, Alvan, Alwin (Ger).

Example: Alvin Stardust, British pop singer.

AMADEUS
Origin/meaning: Latin 'beloved of God'.

Uncommon in English-speaking countries.

Variations and abbreviations: Amadeo (Sp/It), Amadis, Amado, Amando, Amédé (Fr)

Examples: Wolfgang Amadeus Mozart, 1756–1791, Austrian composer.
Amadeus I, 1845–1890, elected King of Spain 1870–1873.

AMBROSE
Origin/meaning: Greek 'divine', 'immortal'.

The Greek gods fed on Ambrosia which ensured their immortality. St Ambrose a 4th century saint, made the name popular and it is still in use, particular in Ireland and among Catholic families.

Variations and abbreviations: Ambie, Ambrogio (It), Ambros (Ir/Ger), Ambrosi, Ambrosio (Sp), Ambrosius (Ger/Scand), Amby, Emrys (Welsh). See also Iolo.

Example: Ambrose Bierce, 1824–1914, American writer and journalist.

AMOS
Origin/meaning: Hebrew 'burden' or 'bearer of burdens'.

A minor prophet of the Old Testament. Amos became popular

during the 17th century Puritan period in England and among the Puritan settlers of New England. It remains more popular in the US than in other English-speaking countries.

Example: Amos Aricha, former head of Israeli police force.

AMYAS
Origin/meaning: French/Latin 'beloved'.

A medieval masculine form of Amy this name was never very common. Kingsley's use of it for the hero of his novel *Westward Ho* brought about a minor revival in the 19th century. With the similar feminine name Amice, it is the root of several surnames.

Variations and abbreviations: Amias, Amis, Amiot, Esmé.

ANASTASIUS
Origin/meaning: Greek 'resurrection'.

More common in Greece and Russia than in English-speaking countries, although sometimes found in Ireland. A masculine form of Anastasia *q.v.*

ANCEL
Origin/meaning: Old German 'of God'

A popular Norman name in the early Middle Ages. The diminutive Ancelot was sometimes confused with Lancelot *q.v.*

Variations and abbreviations: Anseau (Fr), Ansel, Ansell.

ANDERS
Origin/meaning: Greek 'manly'.

A Scandinavian form of Andrew *q.v.*

ANDRÉ
Origin/meaning: Greek 'manly'.

A French form of Andrew *q.v.*

Examples: André Previn, American musician.
André Gide, 1869–1951, French writer.

ANDREW
Origin/meaning: Greek 'manly'.

St Andrew, one of Jesus's Apostles (Luke 6 : 14), was an

immensely popular saint who was Patron Saint of Scotland and Russia. Versions of this name have been popular in many different countries. In England it came into use after the Conquest. The old Scottish short form Dandy, became synonymous with a man who is over-interested in his appearance.

Variations and abbreviations: Anders (Scand), Andie, André (Fr), Andrea (It), Andreas (Ger/Dut), Andres (Sp), Andy, Drew.

Examples: HRH Prince Andrew.
Andrew Lloyd Webber, English composer.

ANEURIN (pron. An-eye-rin)
Origin/meaning: Latin 'honourable'.

A common name in Wales though rarely heard elsewhere. There was a 7th century Welsh bard of that name whose poem *Y Gododdin* describes a famous Welsh attack on the English at Catterick.

Variations and abbreviations: Aneirin, Neirin, Nye.

Example: Aneurin Bevin, 1897–1960, British Socialist minister.

ANGEL
Origin/meaning: Greek 'messenger'.

The word used to translate the Biblical Hebrew word for God's messengers. In English-speaking countries this name is almost obsolete in the masculine form except among communities of Greek or Italian origin.

Variations and abbreviations: Ange (Fr), Angelo (Gk/It).

ANGUS
Origin/meaning: Old Gaelic 'one choice'.

A common name in Scotland but rare elsewhere. It is found in early legends and was the name for a 9th century saint. During the Renaissance it was sometimes confused with the name of the Trojan hero Aeneas and this is still found in Scotland as an alternative to Angus. It has an Irish Gaelic equivalent – Aonghus, pronounced the same way.

Variations and abbreviations: Aonghus (Or), Aeneas, Gus.

Examples: Angus Ogilvie, husband of HRH Princess Alexandra.
Angus Stirling, British Director-General, National Trust.

ANSELM

Origin/meaning: Old German 'helmet of God'.

A Lombard name similar to Ancel *q.v.* brought to England after the Norman Conquest. The name of a 12th century saint, who was Archbishop of Canterbury. Never common it enjoyed a brief revival in the 19th century among religious enthusiasts.

Variations and abbreviations: Anseaume (Fr), Anselmo (Ir), Elmo.

ANTHONY – see ANTONY

ANTONY

Origin/meaning: Latin – Antonius. The name of one of the great families of Rome. Meaning uncertain but is sometimes given as 'beyond price'.

The best known early holder of this name was Mark Antony, the famous Roman soldier and lover of Cleopatra. Two saints – saint Antony the Great, 4th century, and St Antony of Padua, 13th century, helped to establish the popularity of the name. The alternative spelling, Anthony, appeared at the end of the 16th century, when it was thought that, like Anthea, the name had its origin in the Greek word for flower. As a result in the United States, the name is sometimes pronounced with a soft 'th' sound instead of a hard 't'.

Variations and abbreviations: Anthony, Antoine (Fr), Anton (Ger/Scand), Antoni, Antonio (It/Sp/Port), Antonius, Tony.

Examples: Anton Dolin, 1904–1983, British ballet dancer.
Sir Anthony Eden, 1897–1977, British Prime Minister.

APOLLONIUS

Origin/meaning: from the name of Apollo, Greek god of the sun.

A name associated with masculine beauty. Rare in English-speaking countries. Both Apollo and Apollonio are found in Europe. Polonius in Shakespeare's *Hamlet* may be a short form.

Variations and abbreviations: Apollo, Apollinarius.

ARCHIBALD

Origin/meaning: Old German 'genuinely bold'.

Despite its meaning this name has become unfashionable except in parts of Scotland, perhaps because it has often been given by writers to dim-witted characters and members of the aristocracy.

Variations and abbreviations: Archaimbaud (Fr), Archambault (Fr), Archibaldo (Sp), Archibold, Archie, Archy.

Examples: Archibald Wavell, 1883–1959, British Field Marshal. Archibald MacLeish, US poet.

ARCHIE
Origin/meaning: Old German 'genuinely bold'.

An abbreviation of Archibald found as an independent name especially in the US.

ARLEN
Origin/meaning: Gaelic 'a pledge'.

Rare masculine equivalent of Arlene *q.v.* More commonly found as a surname.

Variation: Arlin.

ARMAND (pron. Ar-mon)
Origin/meaning: Old German 'a soldier'.

A French variation of the Old German name Herman. When used in English-speaking countries the 'd' is often pronounced to make 'ar-mond'.

Variations and abbreviations: Arman, Armando (It/Sp), Armin (Eng), Hermann (Ger).

ARMIN
Origin/meaning: Old German 'a soldier'

An English 17th century version (now rare) of Armand *q.v.*

ARNOLD
Origin/meaning: Old German 'eagle-power'.

This name has absorbed the similar but obsolete English name Arnulf (eagle-wolf) although originally they were separate. The name-day for Arnold in Europe is celebrated on St Arnulf's day. Brought to England by the Normans at the time of the Conquest Arnold was very popular for several centuries, often in the French form Arnaud.

Many surnames derived from it, eg Arnott, Arnett, Arnell. After a period of relative obscurity it is again becoming popular in the 20th century.

Variations and abbreviations: Arnoldo (Sp), Arnaud (Fr), Arni, Arnie, Arnoldo (It), Arny.

Examples: Arnold Bennett, 1867–1931, English novelist.
Arnold Wesker, British playwright.
Arnold Palmer, US golf champion.

ARON
Origin/meaning: Hebrew 'high mountain' or Egyptian (no known meaning).

A variation of Aaron.

ARRAN
As in the Isle of Arran. Occasionally used as a male name on the same basis as Florence, Paris and other place names.

ARTHUR
Origin/meaning: Old Welsh 'bear' or Old Irish 'stone' or Latin 'Artorius' (one of the patrician Roman families).

Early versions of the name 'Arter' and 'Artar' are generally found in Celtic areas. The 'h' appears around the 16th century. It did not become popular until the 19th century, when the general revival of interest in Medieval history and the legend of King Arthur and his Knights of the Round Table was coupled with the popularity of the victor of Waterloo, Arthur Wellesley, Duke of Wellington.

Variations and abbreviations: Art, Artair (Scot), Arte, Arttois (Fr), Artie, Artur (Ir), Arturo (Sp/It), Artus (Fr), Arty.

Examples: Artur Rubinstein, 1885–1982, Polish/US pianist.
Arthur Millar, US playwright.
Arthur, Prince of Wales, d.1502, elder son of Henry VII.
Arturo Toscanini, 1867–1957, Italian conductor.
Arthur Negus, British antiques expert.

ASA
Origin/meaning: Hebrew 'physician', 'healer'.

A Biblical name, one of the Kings of Judah, I Kings 15. Popular among 17th century Puritans.

Example: Asa Briggs, English historian.

ASHER
Origin/meaning: Hebrew 'happy'.

Asher was one of the sons of Jacob by Zilpah, the maid of his wife Leah (Genesis 30 ch.13). He was the founder of one of the tribes of Israel. The name is found both as a surname and first name among Jewish people.

ASHLEY
Origin/meaning: Old English 'ash tree wood' or 'clearing'.

A widespread English surname which became popular, especially in the United States, during the 19th century when many surnames were adopted as Christian names, eg Howard, Courtenay. Now popular in Australia.

Variations and abbreviations: Ash, Ashlin.

Examples: Ashley Wilkes, in Margaret Mitchell's novel *Gone With The Wind*.
Anthony Ashley Cooper, 1st Earl of Shaftesbury, 1621–1683.

ASHOK (pron. Assówk)
Origin/meaning: Sanskrit 'tree'.

Ashok, 269–233 BC, was one of the most famous Indian Emperors. His symbol is incorporated into the modern Indian flag. During his reign Buddhism became widespread. He encouraged builders to use stone so their buildings would last.

Variations: Ashoka, Asoka.

ATHOL
Origin/meaning: Old Scots 'new Ireland'.

The name of an area of Scotland found both as surname and first name.

Variation: Atholl.

Example: Athol Fugard, South African playwright.

AUBERON (pron. Oberon)
Origin/meaning: Old German 'little elf-ruler'.

Diminutive English form of the German Alberich, from its French version Auberi. It was not unusual in Medieval England. Shakespeare used the alternative spelling Oberon as the appropriate name for the King of the Fairies in *A Midsummer Night's Dream*. It is rare today.

Variations and abbreviations: Oberon, Bron.

Example: Auberon Waugh, English journalist and critic.

AUBREY
Origin/meaning: Old German 'elf-ruler'.

The English form of the German Alberich comes from its French version Auberi, as does Auberon q.v. Common in Medieval England, when it gave rise to a number of surnames, it is now comparatively rare.
Variations: Alberich (Ger), Alberik, Albery, Avery.

Example: Aubrey Beardsley, 1872–1898, English artist.

AUGUSTINE
Origin/meaning: Latin 'venerable', 'majestic'.

A diminutive of Augustus q.v. it was the name of the first Archbishop of Canterbury, St Augustine, who brought Roman Christianity to Britain. Probably because of this Saint, or perhaps because of the fame of the great Doctor of the Church, St Augustine of Hippo, the name was popular in medieval England. It was often found in its typical English contraction, Austin q.v.

Variations and abbreviations: Aguistin (Ir), Agustin, Augie, Augustin (Fr/Ger), Augy, Austen, Austin, Gus.

AUGUSTUS
Origin/meaning: Latin 'venerable', 'majestic'. A title given to Roman emperors.

Augustus was used by Renaissance princes, especially in Germany, in conjunction with their own names, to imitate the rulers of classical times quickly became an independent name. Brought to England by the Hanoverians in the 18th century, it was popular for about a century and was the second name of Queen Victoria's husband Albert. It is now out of favour and, like Algernon, Archibald etc considered rather old-fashioned and pompous. Still popular in Europe.

Variations and abbreviations: Agosto (It), Aguistin (Ir), Agustin, Augie, August (Ger), Auguste (Fr), Augustin, Augustine, Augusto (Sp), Austen, Austin, Augy, Gus.

Examples: Augustus John, 1878–1961, British painter.
Pierre Auguste Renoir, 1841–1919, French painter.
Johann August Strindberg, 1849–1912, Swedish playwright.

Auguste Rodin, 1840–1917, French sculptor.

AURANGZEB
Origin/meaning: Sanskrit 'ornament of the throne'.

This Muslim name is given in honour of Aurangzeb, 1618–1707, the last Muslim Emperor of the Indian Mogul empire. He was the third son of Shah Jehan. Aurangzeb was a ruthless man who kept his father a prisoner for the last seven years of his life and put to death three of his brothers. His reign of half a century was outwardly the most magnificent of all the Mogul emperors, but the atmosphere of treachery and the Emperor's harshness to his Hindu subjects sowed the seeds for the overthrow of the Mogul dynasty. Dryden's *Aureng-Zebe*, 1676, is about his treatment of Shah Jehan.

Variations: Aurangzebe, Aurangzib.

AURELIAN
Origin/meaning: Latin 'golden', 'beautiful'.

Aurelius was the name of one of the great families of Rome. Aurelianus is a diminutive of the name and is the root of the English version. Like the feminine Aurelia it was rediscovered as part of the Renaissance interest in classical names and has been used occasionally since the 17th century.

Variation: Aurelius.

Example: Aurelian Townshend, 17th century English poet.

AUSTIN
Origin/meaning: Latin 'venerable', 'majestic'.

An English variation of Augustus and Augustine *q.v.* found both as first name and surname.

Variation: Austen.

Example: Austin Mitchell, English MP and journalist.
Austin Chamberlain, 1863–1937, British politician.

AVENEL
Origin/meaning: Old French 'hay merchant'.

A name which appeared in Britain at the time of the Norman Conquest and which was popular in the early Middle Ages. Sometimes considered the masculine version of Eveline *q.v.*

AVINASH (pron. Aveenass)
Origin/meaning: Sanskrit 'indestructible'.

This is a Hindu name.

AXEL
Origin/meaning: Hebrew 'father of peace'.

The Scandinavian and German form of Absalom *q.v.*

Examples: Axel Munthe, 1857–1949. Swedish writer.
Count Axel Oxenstierna, 1583–1654, Swedish statesman.

AYLMER
Origin/meaning: Old English 'Aethelmaere', 'noble and famous'.

The Old German name Ailemar was brought over to England by the Normans and became indistinguishable from the Old English original. A popular variation in the US is Elmer *q.v.*

Variations and abbreviations: Aylmar, Aymar, Elmer.

AYLWIN
Origin/meaning: Old German 'noble friend'.

The Old English original of Alvin *q.v.* A pre-Conquest name it has never been common but is the root of several surnames, eg Alwin, Elwin.

Variations and abbreviations: Ailwin, Alvin, Alwin, Alwyn.

AZARIAH
Origin/meaning: Hebrew 'whom God aids'.

A Biblical name, principally one of the Kings of Judah, although it occurs many times in the Old Testament. Rare in the 20th century but popular in 17th century among Puritans of England and New England. Occasionally listed and used as a girl's name, perhaps because of its 'feminine' sound.

Variations and abbreviations: Azaria, Zaria.

AZIKIWE (pron. Azeekiwi)
Origin/meaning: Ibo 'vigorous'.

This is a name found in Nigeria.

Abbreviation: Zik

Example: Nnamdi Azikiwe, Nigerian nationalist politician. First President of the Nigerian republic.

AZIZ
Origin/meaning: Arabic 'precious'.
This name is popular among Muslims.
Variation: Azizi (Swahili).

B

BABAR
Origin/meaning: Sanskrit 'tiger'.

This Muslim name was first used as an epithet applied to Zahir-ud-Din-Mohammed, 1493–1530. He was the first of the Moslem Mogul (Mongol) Emperors of India. The empire which he established in 1526 when he captured Delhi and Agra reached the height of its power at the end of the 16th century under Akbar q.v. The character in French children's literature, Babar the elephant, is named after him.

Variation: Babur. See also Shere.

BADHUR
Origin/meaning: Arabic 'born at the full moon'.

A popular Muslim name.

Variations: Badar, Badr, Badru (Swahili).

BALDWIN
Origin/meaning: Old German/Old English 'bold friend'.

A popular name before and after the Conquest. Initially it was used as a first name when it became customary to have a surname as well as a given name. Later it became more familiar as a surname, together with its variations such as Bowden. Its use as a first name now is usually as a result of being a family surname.

Variations and abbreviations: Balduin, Baudouin (Fr), Win.

BARDOLPH
Origin/meaning: Old German 'bright wolf'.

Popular after the Conquest this name, like Baldwin, became more familiar as a surname than a first name.

Variations and abbreviations: Bardolf, Bardy.

Example: Bardolph, drinking companion of Falstaff in Shakespeare's plays *Henry IV, Henry V* and *Merry Wives of Windsor*.

BARNABAS

Origin/meaning: Hebrew 'son of consolation'.

A popular medieval first name, especially in its typical English form Barnaby. Barnabas was the friend and travelling companion of St Paul 'a good man full of the Holy Ghost and of faith' (Acts xi, 24). Currently popular in England.

Variations and abbreviations: Barnaby, Barny, Barnie.

Example: *Barnaby Rudge*, Charles Dickens' novel, 1841.

BARNET

Origin/meaning: Old German 'bear-hard', Old English 'noble and strong'.

A typically English contraction of Bernard through the form Barnard. It became common as a surname and has been re-introduced as a first name since the last century. This use of family names as first names is common in the US.

Variations and abbreviations: Barnett, Barney.

Example: Barnet Newman, US painter.

BARRY

Origin/meaning: Old Irish 'spear'.

An exclusively Irish name until 19th century when Irish emigrants spread it further afield. As a surname it may indicate an ancestor from Barry Island, where a Welsh hermit of that name used to live.

Variation: Barrie.

Examples: The hero of Thackeray's novel *Barry Lyndon*, 1844.
Barry Manilow, US singer.
Barry Humphries, Australian actor and comedian.
Barry Owen Jones, Australian politician and writer.

BARTHOLOMEW

Origin/meaning: Hebrew 'son of Tolmai', 'son of a farmer'.

This is the patronymic (father's name) of the Apostle Nathanael, and the name by which he is best known. St Bartholomew was immensely popular in Medieval England. Numerous churches and religious foundations were dedicated in his honour including St Bartholomew's Hospital in London which was founded by a monk in the 12th century. The popularity of the name made it widespread and many common surnames such as Batt, Bateson and Bateman, derive from it. Not popular in the 20th century.

Variations and abbreviations: Bart, Bartelmy, Barthel (Ger), Barthelemy (Fr), Bartholomé (Fr), Bartolome (Sp), Bartholomeus (Scand/Dut), Bartholomeo (It), Bat.

Examples: Bartholome Diaz, Venezuelan guitarist.
Bartholomew Newsam, d.1593, Clockmaker to Queen Elizabeth I.

BARUCH
Origin/meaning: Hebrew 'blessed'.

The name of the companion of the prophet Jeremiah. Popular in the 17th century like many other Biblical names.

BASIL
Origin/meaning: Greek 'kingly'.

A popular name in the Eastern Christian Church because of St Basil the Great, 330–379, who instituted the orthodox church's ideas of monastic life. The name was probably brought to Western Europe by the Crusaders. It has been consistent but never common although the High Church movement in 19th century England brought about a temporary upsurge in its popularity.

Variations and abbreviations: Baz, Basile (Fr), Basilio (It/Port/Sp), Basilius (Dut/Ger/Scand), Vasilis, Vassily (Slav/Russ).

Examples: Cardinal Basil Hume, head of the Catholic church in England.
Basil Rathbone, 1892–1967, British-US actor.

BEAU
Origin/meaning: French 'handsome'.

Also a short form of Beauregard or Beaumont. Rarely found outside US.

Variation: Bo.

Examples: Beau (George) Brummell, 1778–1840, Regency man of fashion.
Beau Bridges, US film actor.

BEN
Origin/meaning: Hebrew 'son'.

Used by Jewish people in combination with other names, or a short form of names such as Benedict and Benjamin. Occasionally used as an independent name.

Examples: Ben Jonson, 1574-1637, English playwright and poet. Ben Nicholson, 1894-1982, British painter.

BENEDICT
Origin/meaning: Latin 'blessed'.

A common name in England after the Norman Conquest, usually in the typically English abbreviation Benet/Bennett, which shows the influence of the French form Benoit. Another old form now out of use is Benedick, used by Shakespeare in *Much Ado About Nothing*. Throughout Europe the name is found in various forms and its original popularity was largely due to the honour in which St Benedict, 480-547, the founder of the Benedictine Order, was held. In England the fame of St Benedict (Benet) Biscop, founder of influential monasteries at Wearmouth and Jarrow, contributed to the name's popularity.

Variations and abbreviations: Ben, Bendix, Bendt (Dan), Benedetto (It), Benedicht (Swiss), Benedick, Benedicto (Sp), Benedikt (Ger/Scand), Benet, Bengt (Swed), Bennet, Bennett, Benito (It/Sp), Bennie, Benny, Benoit (Fr)

Examples: Benedetto Crose, 1766-1852, Italian Statesman. Benedict Spinoza, 1632-1677, philosopher.

BENET
Origin/meaning: Latin 'blessed'.

An English short form of Benedict. More widespread in the Middle Ages than the original, it gave rise to several surnames. In the US it is as a family name that it is now used as a first name. It is sometimes pronounced Benay, like the surname of Stephen Benét, 1898-1943, the US poet.

Variations and abbreviations: Ben, Benett, Bennet, Bennett.

Example: Bennett Cerf, US writer.

BENJAMIN
Origin/meaning: Hebrew 'son of my right hand'.

In the Book of Genesis ch.35, Rachel, Jacob's second wife, died giving birth to a son whom she called Ben-oni 'son of my sorrow'. He was then renamed by his father Benjamin 'son of the south' or 'son of my right hand'. The name Benjamin has come to be synonymous with a much loved youngest son. In the Middle Ages Benjamin was regarded as an exclusively Jewish name. Since the 16th century Protestant Reformation when Biblical names were preferred to Catholic saints' names, Benjamin has been far more widespread. It was particularly popular in the Puritan settlements in 17th century New England. After a period of unpopularity since the beginning of the century it is once more becoming common.

Variations and abbreviations: Ben, Beniamino (It), Benji, Benjie, Bennie, Benny.

Examples: Benjamin Franklin, 1706–1790, US scientist and statesman.
Benjamin Britten, 1913–1976, English composer.
Benjamin Disraeli, 1804–1881, British Prime Minister.

BERNARD
Origin/meaning: Old German 'bear-hard', Old English 'noble and strong'.
A common European name, popular in England for several centuries after the Norman Conquest. Often used to honour St Bernard of Clairvaux, 1091–1153, founder of the Cistercian Order of Monks. The name was revived in Britain by High Church enthusiasts in the 19th century. It is the origin of several surnames.

Variations and abbreviations: Barnard, Barnet, Barney, Bearnard (Ir/Scot), Berend (Ger/Dan), Bern, Bernardo (It/Sp), Bernd (Ger), Berne, Bernhard (Ger), Bernt (Swed), Bernie, Berny, Burnard, Burnhard.

Examples: St Bernard of Montjoux, 996–1081, Founder of hospices for Alpine travellers – after whom St Bernard dogs are named.
Bernard Law Montgomery, Viscount Montgomery of Alamein, 1887–1976, British Field Marshal.
Bernardo O'Higgins, 1778–1842, Irish–Chilean rebel and patriot.
Prince Bernhard of the Netherlands.

BERN
Origin/meaning: Old German 'bear'.
A German name sometimes found in English-speaking countries. Also a short form of Bernard.

Variations and abbreviations: Berin, Birin, Björn (Scand).

BERT
Short form of names Albert, Herbert, Bertram, Osbert etc
q.v. Sometimes used as an independent name.

Variations: Bertie, Berty, Burt.

Examples: Burt Lancaster, US film actor.
Burt Reynolds, US film actor.
Bert Lahr, US actor.

BERTOLD
Origin/meaning: Old German 'brilliant ruler'.

A popular German name occasionally found in Britain and the
US.

Variations and abbreviations: Bartel, Barthold, Bartold, Bert,
Berthold (Ger), Berthoud (Fr), Bertoldo (It), Bertolt.

Example: Bertolt Brecht, 1898-1956, German playwright.

BERTRAM
Origin/meaning: Old German 'brilliant raven'.
One of many names brought to England at the time of the
Norman Conquest. The raven was the device of Odin, Norse
god of war.

Variations and abbreviations: Bart, Bartram, Beltrame (It),
Beltrán (Sp), Bert, Bertie, Bertran, Bertrand (Fr), Bertrando (It),
Berty.

Examples: Bertram Mills, 1873-1935, British founder of Bertram
Mills Circus.
A. Bertram Chandler, US novelist.

BERTRAND
Origin/meaning: Old German 'brilliant raven'.

The French form of Bertram *q.v.*

Variation: Bertran.

Example: Beverley Nichols, 1888-1983, English author and

BEVERLEY
Origin/meaning: Old English 'from the beaver stream'.

A surname used as a first name for both boys and girls.

Variations and abbreviations: Bev, Beverly.

Example: Beverley Nichols, 1888–1983, English author and journalist.

BEVIS
Origin/meaning: Old French, meaning uncertain. May be 'boy' or 'young calf'.

A name brought over by the Normans in 1066. Never widely popular.

Example: Bevis Hillier, English writer, authority on antique furniture.

BHARAT (pron. B'rat)
Origin/meaning: Sanskrit 'the sustainer'.

This is one of the names of the Hindu god of fire Agni. It is also the name of a brother of Rama *q.v.* He became a famous king and gave to the country the name (pron. Bhaar't), which many Indians still use today instead of India.

BILL
Origin/meaning: Old German 'will helmet' ie 'helmet of resolution'.

A popular short form of William *q.v.* sometimes given as an independent name.

Examples: Bill Oddie, English actor and comedian.
Bill Tidy, British cartoonist.

BJÖRN
Origin/meaning: Old German 'bear'.

The Scandinavian form of Bern, one of the short forms of Bernard. Now widely known in English-speaking countries because of the Swedish tennis champion Björn Borg.

Variation: Beorn (Med Eng).

BLAKE
Origin/meaning: Old English 'pale' or 'black'.

An English family name not uncommon as a first name in the US perhaps because of its short 'masculine' sound.

Example: Blake Edwards, US film producer.

BLASE

Origin/meaning: Latin 'stammerer' or possibly French 'from Blois'.

This name seems to go back to the martyr St Blaise, d.316. Because of some of the miracles attributed to him he was the patron saint of wool carders and invoked for protection against diseases of the throat. The popularity of his name in Medieval England may well be due to the great importance of the wool industry at that time.

Variations and abbreviations: Biagio (It), Blaise (Fr), Blas (Sp), Blasien (Ger), Blasius (Ger/Latin), Blayze, Blaze.

Example: Blaise Pascal, 1623–1662, French mathematician and philosopher.

BOB

Origin/meaning: Old German 'fame bright'

Popular short form of Robert *q.v.*

Variations: Bobbie, Bobby.

Examples: Bobby Riggs, US tennis player.
Bob Willis, English cricket captain and fast bowler.

BORIS

Origin/meaning: Old Slav 'fighter', 'warrior'.

A popular Russian name, short for Borislav. Occasionally used in English-speaking countries since the 19th century.

Examples: Boris Karloff, US film actor.
Tsar Boris Godunov, d.1605.
Boris Pasternak, 1890–1960, Russian writer and Nobel prize-winner.

BRAD

Origin/meaning: a short form of many surnames used in US, and occasionally in other English-speaking countries, as given names, eg Bradford, Bradley, Brady.

BRADLEY

Origin/meaning: Old English 'broad clearing'.

An English place-name used as a surname. One of many surnames used in the US as given names. Also popular in Australia.

345

Abbreviation: Brad.

BRAM
Origin/meaning: Hebrew 'father of a multitude'

An abbreviation of Abraham *q.v.* Popular as a name in its own right in the US and the Netherlands.

Example: Bram Stoker, 1847–1912, author of *Dracula*.

BRENDAN
Origin/meaning: Old Irish 'dweller by the flame' or 'dweller by the beacon'.

An Irish name, correctly pronounced without the d, as in the modern Irish spelling Brenainn. St Brendan was a 6th century Irish saint and according to legend the first discoverer of America.

Variations and abbreviations: Brandan, Brandon, Brendin, Brenainn (Ir Gaelic) Brennan.

Examples: Brendan Behan, 1923–1964, Irish playwright.
Brendan Foster, British athlete.
Brandon Thomas, 1857–1914, English writer (*Charley's Aunt*)

BRETT
Origin/meaning: Old English/Old French 'Breton'.

Not uncommon, particularly in the US, probably because of its simplicity and 'masculine' sound.

Example: Bret Harte (Francis Brett Harte), 1836–1902, US writer.

BRIAN
Origin/meaning: Celtic (probably Old Irish) from the word 'strength' or 'hill'.

A Celtic (probably Irish) name introduced to England from Celtic Brittany at the time of the Conquest. Although popular for several centuries it fell out of favour in England from the 16th century and was re-introduced from Ireland at the end of the 19th century. The Irish surname O'Brien comes from it.

Variations and abbreviations: Briano (It), Briant, Brien, Brion, Bryan, Bryant, Bryon.

Examples: Brian Boru, 11th century Irish king and folk hero.

Bryan Ferry, English singer.
Bryan Brown, Australian actor.
Brian Aherne, US actor.

BRIGHAM
Origin/meaning: Old English 'house by the bridge'.

An English surname used as a first name. Made current by Brigham Young, 1801–1877, Mormon leader and founder of Salt Lake city.

BRODERICK
Origin/meaning: Old Welsh 'son of Roderick'.

A surname used, particularly in the US, as a first name.

Example: Broderick Crawford, US actor.

BRODY
Origin/meaning: Old Irish 'ditch'.

A surname used as a first name for both boys and girls.

Variation: Brodie.

BROOK
Origin/meaning: Old English 'brook'.

A common surname used as a first name, particularly in the US.

Variations: Brooke, Brooks.

BRUCE
Origin/meaning: a place name, Braöse/Brieuse (modern) in Normandy.

This was brought over to Britain as a surname – de Braöse or de Bruce – at the time of the Norman Conquest. The family was very influential and widespread. One member, Robert de Bruce, or Robert the Bruce, 1274–1329, became King of Scotland and defeated the English at Bannockburn. It came into use as a given name in the 19th century as part of a fashion for using aristocratic surnames, eg Howard, Vernon. Naturally it was most popular in Scotland and also in Australia which has a large population of Scottish descent.

Variation: Brucie.

Examples: Bruce Forsyth, English entertainer.

347

Bruce Jay Friedman, US writer.

BRUNO
Origin/meaning: Old German/Old English 'brown'.

Used in the Middle Ages to honour St Bruno, 1033–1101, the founder of the Carthusian Order of Monks. Still occasionally used in English and German speaking countries, it remains most popular in Italy.

Example: Bruno Bettelheim, US psychiatrist and writer.

BRYN
Origin/meaning: Old Welsh 'hill'.

Rare outside Wales.

BUD
Origin/meaning: US familiar term for 'brother'.

Usually a nickname but sometimes used as a given name.

Variations and abbreviations: Budd, Buddie, Buddy.

Examples: Buddy Holly, 1938–1959, US singer.
Bud (William) Abbott, US comedian.

BYRON
Origin/meaning: Old English 'at the cowsheds'.

A place name from the north of England from which the name of Lord Byron, the English Romantic poet, derived. The surname is not uncommon in the north of England and its use as a first name may be as a family name or occasionally to honour the poet.

Variations: Byram, Byrom.

Example: Byron Haskin, US film director.

C

CADELL
Origin/meaning: Old Welsh/Old Scots 'spirit of battle'.

Found as a first name in Wales and a surname in Scotland.

Variation: Cadel.

CADWALLADER (pron. Cadd-wóll-edda)
Origin/meaning: Old Welsh 'battle leader'.

Rare outside Wales, although sometimes found in areas with a population of Welsh descent.

Variations: Cadwaladr, Cadwalladr.

Example: Cadwaladr, d.1172, a Welsh prince, blinded by Irish pirates. He fought against Henry II of England.

CAI (pron. Kay)
Origin/meaning: from the Roman family name Gaius which is derived from the verb 'to rejoice'.

This Roman name is still used today in Wales, just as Emrys is used for Ambrose. It is more familiar in England as Kay q.v. who was one of the Knights of the Round Table.

Variations and abbreviations: See Kay.

CALEB
Origin/meaning: Hebrew 'dog'.

A Biblical name popular in Puritan England and New England in the 17th century when such names were common. Still found occasionally today.

Example: Charles Caleb Colton, 1780–1832, British clergyman and writer

CALVIN
Origin/meaning: Latin 'bald'.

John Calvin, 1509–1564, the French Protestant religious reformer, was a hero figure among Puritans, especially those who went to America from England in the 17th century. By the 18th century his surname was being used as a first name in the US and it is still current today.

Variations and abbreviations: Cal, Calv, Vin, Vinny.

Example: Calvin Coolidge, 1872–1933, 30th President of the United States.

CAMERON
Origin/meaning: Old Scots 'crooked nose'.

A Scottish clan-name used as a first name. Popular among people of Scottish descent in Australia and Canada.

Abbreviation: Cam.

Example: Cameron Mitchell, US actor.

CARADOC (pron. Carúddock)
Origin/meaning: Old Welsh 'amiable', 'nice'.

An almost exclusively Welsh first name. Like many Celtic names it has a Latin version Caractacus, which dates from the Roman occupation of Britain.

Variations: Caractacus (Lat), Caradawg (Wel), Craddock (Eng).

Example: Caradoc Evans, 1878–1945, Welsh novelist.

CARL
Origin/meaning: Old German 'man'.

This is a German form of Charles q.v. but in North America and later in other English-speaking countries the spelling Carl was preferred to Karl. It therefore survived the periods of the two World Wars, when German names were unpopular, and became accepted as a quite separate name from Charles.

Variations: Karl, Carlo (It)

Examples: Carlo Ponti, Italian film producer.
Carl Maria von Weber, 1786–1826, German composer.
Carl Davis, US composer and conductor.

CAROL
Origin/meaning: Old German 'man'.

350

A form of Charles from the Latin version Carolus. It is used as a masculine name and more commonly as a feminine name.

Variations and abbreviations: Carrol, Carroll, Carolus, Caryl, Karel (Cz), Karol (Pol).

Example: King Carol I, 1839-1914, First king of Rumania.

CARY
Origin/meaning: Old English place name from the Somerset area.

A surname used as a first name. Popularized by film star Cary Grant. Sometimes Cary is used as a familiar form of Charles *q.v.*

Example: Cary Harrison, playwright son of actor Rex Harrison.

CASIMIR
Origin/meaning: Polish 'command of peace'.

The English and French version of a Polish name. It is found in areas of the US and Australia with immigrant Polish populations.

Variations and abbreviations: Casimiro (It), Kasimir (Ger), Kazimierz (Pol), Kazmer.

Examples: Casimir Delavigne, 1773-1843, French writer.
St Casimir, 1458-1484, Prince, Patron Saint of Poland.

CASPAR
Origin/meaning: uncertain, possibly Persian. Sometimes, because of the legend of the three wise men, said to mean 'treasurer'.

Jasper *q.v.* is the more usual form of this name in English-speaking countries.

Variations and abbreviations: Casper, Cass, Cassie, Kaspar (Ger), Kasper. See also Jasper.

Example: Caspar Weinberger, US Republican politician.

CASSIUS
Origin/meaning: Latin 'vain'.

Cassius is the name of one of the men who plotted against Julius Caesar in Shakespeare's play. In America after the War of

Independence it was used because it symbolized revolution, just as small American towns were given the names of independent city states, eg Carthage, Syracuse.

Variations and abbreviations: Cass, Cassie, Cassy.

Example: Cassius Clay (now Mohammed Ali), US boxer.

CECIL
Origin/meaning: Latin – Caecilius – one of the patrician families of Rome. Probably from the Latin word for 'blind'.

This was rarely used as a masculine first name until the 19th century. It was one of many aristocratic surnames (Cecil is the family name of the Marquis of Salisbury) which were adopted in that period as first names. It is uncommon in other European languages. The feminine forms eg Cecilia, Cecily q.v. have a much longer history.

Variation: Cécilio (It).

Examples: Cecil Beaton, 1904–1980, English photographer and designer.
Cecil Rhodes, 1835–1902, English explorer and administrator.

CEDRIC
Origin/meaning: uncertain. Possibly Old Welsh 'war chief'.

Used by Sir Walter Scott for one of his characters 'Cedric the Saxon' in *Ivanhoe*, 1820, it is sometimes supposed that he misspelt Cerdic, the Anglo-Saxon name of the founder of Wessex. Like many names from that period of history it was popularized by the Romantic Movement of the 19th century. Its use for the hero of Frances Hodgson Burnett's popular book *Little Lord Fauntleroy*, 1886, reinforced its popularity. It has gone out of favour in the 20th century.

Example: Sir Cedric Hardwicke, 1893–1964, British actor.

CEREDIG
Origin/meaning: a character from Welsh legend. Ceredig was the son of Cunedda. He gave his name to the area Ceredigion.

CHAD
Origin/meaning: Old Welsh 'battle'.

St Chad (Ceadda), d.672, was bishop of Mercia. His life is described in the Venerable Bede's *History of the English Church and People*. The name went out of use until the 19th century High Church movement revived interest in it. It is found in the United States but often as a short form of surnames such as Chadwell or Chadwick, when they are used as given names.

Example: The Rev Chad Varah, founder of the Samaritan movement.

CHANDRA (pron. Chandr')
Origin/meaning: Sanskrit 'moon', 'brother'.

When used as a male name this is never used on its own but is added to the end of another name as a mark of politeness or respect, eg. Dinesh Chandra. It is very important to leave the last *a* silent, or otherwise it sounds like the feminine name Chandra and becomes meaningless. The Sikh name Singh *q.v.* is used in much the same way and so is the name Kant *q.v.*

Example: Bankim Chandra Chatterji, 1838-1894, Indian writer.

CHAPMAN
Origin/meaning: Old English 'merchant'.

A surname now sometimes used as a given name.

Example: Chapman Pincher, British journalist.

CHARLES
Origin/meaning: Old German 'man'.

This was the name of the Holy Roman Emperor Charlemagne – Charles the Great, 742–814. The German form of the name was Karl which was Latinized in documents as Carolus. From this Latin form we get the adjective Caroline to describe something originating in the reign of a King Charles. The Holy Roman Empire split into separate areas more or less corresponding to France and Germany today. In the Eastern area the name Karl survived. In the Western (French) area it developed from Carolus into Charles (pronounced Sharle) and many French kings carried the name. The French were constantly at war first with the Normans, who later invaded England, and then with the English. So the name was never used in England in the Middle Ages as it had too many associations with the enemy. The Scots and the French however were on good terms and Mary Queen of Scots, 1542–1587, who was brought up in France, named her son Charles James. He came to the English throne in 1603 as James I but named his second son Charles. This son came to the throne as Charles I and from that time the name has enjoyed considerable popularity in England and English-speaking countries. The Puritan settlers of New England who had opposed Charles I in the Civil War at home, naturally did not use the name. However Charles has become a well established name in the United States in the 19th and 20th centuries. The US short form is Chuck.

Variations and abbreviations: Carl, Carlo (It), Carlos (Sp), Carrol, Carroll, Cary, Caryl, Charley, Charlie, Chick, Chuck, Karel, Karl, Karol (Pol).

Examples: Charles Lindbergh, 1902–1974, US aviator.
Charles Dickens, 1812–1870, English novelist.
Charles Chaplin, 1889–1979, English actor and director.
HRH The Prince of Wales.

CHAUNCEY
Origin/meaning: a French place name which became an English surname.

Used in the 19th century particularly in the United States, when there was a fashion for using surnames as given names, particularly if they had historic or aristocratic connotations.

Variations and abbreviations: Chance, Chaunce.

Example: Chauncey Jerome, 1793–1860, American clock-maker.

CHESTER
Origin/meaning: Latin/Old English 'fortified camp'.

The Latin word Castra – camp became integrated into many English place names as Chester. It therefore became a common surname now found, mainly in the US, as a given name. Its popularity may have been helped by Scott's use of the name in his poem *Marmion*, 1808.

Abbreviation: Chet.

Example: Chester Arthur, 1830–1886, 21st President of the USA.

CHICK
Origin/meaning: 'man'.
US familiar form of Charles q.v.
Variations: Chic, Chicky.

CHRIS
Origin/meaning: Latin 'Christian' or 'Christ bearer'.
A short form of Christian or Christopher, sometimes used as an independent name.
Variations: Cris, Kris.
Example: Chris Bonnington, English mountaineer.

CHRISTIAN
Origin/meaning: Latin 'Christian'.

This is the masculine equivalent of the much more widespread feminine names Christina and Christiana. Found since the early Middle Ages, it has always been rare in English-speaking countries. It is also used as a surname. It has long been popular in Denmark which has had several Kings of that name.

Variations and abbreviations: Chrétien (Fr), Chris, Chrissy, Christiano (It/Sp), Kristian (Sp).

Examples: Hans Christian Andersen, 1805–1875, Danish poet and storywriter.
Christiaan Huygens, 1629–1695, Dutch physicist and astronomer.
Christiaan Barnard, South African heart surgeon.
Chrétien de Troyes d.1183, French poet who wrote many of the Arthurian romances.

CHRISTMAS
Origin/meaning: English 'Christmas'.

Name given to boys born on Christmas day. Now largely superseded by the French Noel.

Example: Christmas Humphreys, 1901–1983, English judge and leading Buddhist.

CHRISTOPHER
Origin/meaning: Greek 'Christ bearer'.

This is one of the earliest Christian names and proclaimed that the person believed in Christ. However, because of the meaning, it was applied to a legendary saint who was supposed to have carried the infant Christ across a river. St Christopher thus became the Patron Saint of all travellers. It has been steadily popular in England and English-speaking countries since the 16th century. Its equivalent in the other European languages is also widespread. The surnames Christie/Christy derive from it.

Variations and abbreviations: Chris, Chrissie, Chrissy, Christie, Christoffer (Dan), Christoforo (It), Christoph, Christophe (Fr), Christophonis (Ger), Christy, Chrystal, Cris, Cristóbal (Sp), Cristoforo (It), Cristoval (Sp), Kester, Kit, Kristoff (Scand).

Examples: Christopher Columbus, 1451–1506, explorer, discoverer of America.
Christopher Marlowe, 1564–1593, English dramatist.
Christopher Lewis, New Zealand tennis player.

CHRYSTAL
Origin/meaning: Greek 'Christ bearer'.

A Scottish short form of Christopher, increasingly rare, particularly since the use of Crystal as a feminine name.

CHUCK
Origin/meaning: 'man'.

US familiar form of Charles q.v.

Example: Chuck Berry, US rock singer.

CLARENCE Origin/meaning: Latin 'bright', 'famous'.

An English Royal title. Lionel, son of Edward III, was given the title Duke of Clarence in 1362, because his wife was heiress of the Clare family. Occasionally used for Royal princes since then, the last time when the eldest son of the Prince of Wales was created Duke of Clarence in 1890. The name then reached the height of its popularity as one of the fashionable aristocratic surnames such as Percy, Sidney etc which were being adopted as given names. Less popular in the 20th century.

Variations and abbreviations: Clare, Claire.

Example: Clarence Darrow, 1857–1938, US Attorney.

CLARK
Origin/meaning: Old French 'scholar'.

An extremely common and widespread English surname which has become a first name, particularly in the US. Its simplicity has probably contributed to its popularity.

Variations: Clarke, Clerk.

Example: Clark Gable, 1901–1961, US film actor.

CLAUD
Origin/meaning: Latin 'lame'. The name of a patrician Roman family.

The feminine forms of this name are better established in England than the masculine version. The masculine Claud did not appear in England until it was introduced from France in the 16th century. It has never been as popular in English-speaking countries as in France.

Variations and abbreviations: Claude (Fr), Claudian, Claudianus (Ger), Claudio (It/Sp), Claudius (Ger/Dut), Klaudius (Ger). See also Anthony, Cecil.

Examples: Claude Debussy, 1862–1918, French composer.
Sir Claude Auchinleck, 1884–1981, British Field Marshal.
Claude Monet, 1840–1926, French Impressionist painter.
Claudio Monteverdi, c.1567–1643, Italian composer.

CLEM
Origin/meaning: Latin 'gentle', 'merciful'.

A short form of Clement q.v. sometimes found as an independent name, particularly in the US.

CLEMENT
Origin/meaning: Latin 'gentle', 'merciful'.

Considered the first of the Apostolic fathers because of his letter to the Corinthians, Clement was the third successor to the See of Rome after St Peter. Many other Popes were named in his honour and Clement was a popular name in the Middle Ages. Its popularity was revived among some groups in the 19th century by the High Church movement.

Variations and abbreviations: Clem, Clemens (Dan/Ger), Clément (Fr), Clemente (Ir/Sp), Clementius (Dut), Clemmie, Clim, Klemens (Ger).

Examples: Clement Attlee, 1883–1967, British Prime Minister.
Clement Freud, British politician.
Clément Delibes, 1836–1891, French composer.
Prince Klemens Metternich, 1773–1859, Austrian statesman.

CLIFF
Origin/meaning: Old English 'ford at a cliff'.

Short form of Clifford and occasionally of other surnames, eg Clifton, which begin with that syllable. Frequently used as an independent name.

Variation: Clif.

Examples: Cliff Richard, British singer.
Cliff Young, Australian marathon runner.

CLIFFORD
Origin/meaning: Old English 'ford at a cliff'.

An English surname, the family name of Baron Clifford of Chudleigh. It has been used as a first name since the 19th century fashion for using aristocratic surnames as given names.

Abbreviations: Clif, Cliff.

Example: Clifford Odets, 1906–1963, US playwright and actor.

CLIFTON
Origin/meaning: Old English 'settlement on a cliff'.

A family name sometimes used as a given name. It shares its short form with Clifford q.v.

Abbreviations: Clif, Cliff.

Example: Clifton Fadiman, US writer.

CLINTON
Origin/meaning: Old English 'from the headland farm'.

An English surname used as a given name.

Abbreviation: Clint.

Examples: Clint Walker, US film actor.
Clint Eastwood, US film actor.

CLIVE
Origin/meaning: Old English 'at the cliff'.

The surname of Robert Clive, 1725–1774, the English soldier and statesman largely responsible for annexing India for the East India Company. He was consequently known as Clive of India and his surname was used as a first name, particularly by families with Indian connections.

Example: Clive James, Australian journalist.

COLAN
Origin/meaning: Old Cornish 'dove'.

Cornwall was one of the Celtic areas (along with Wales, Scotland, Ireland and Northern France) whose languages were very similar. Colan is the Old Cornish version of the Latin Columba q.v. and is therefore the equivalent of the Old Irish names Colum and Colman. Colin is sometimes given as a Scottish equivalent.

COLE
Origin/meaning: Old English 'swarthy' or Greek/Old French 'victory of the people'.

Either an English surname used as a first name or a diminutive of Nicholas q.v. similar to the French Colin. It may also be a short form of names like Colman.

Examples: Cole Lesley, 1911–1980, writer, secretary to Noel Coward.
Cole Porter, 1893–1964, American song writer.

COLIN
Origin/meaning: Greek/Old French 'victory of the people' or Old Scots 'young man'.

This name came to England from France in the Middle Ages as a diminutive of Nicholas. It has been more popular in this century than ever before. The identical sounding Scottish name has a totally different meaning and is sometimes considered to be yet another variation on the name Columba, 'dove' *q.v.*

Variations and abbreviations: Cailean (Scots), Col, Colán (Ir), Cole, Collin.

Examples: Colin Cowdrey, English cricketer.
Colin Chapman, 1928–1982, Founder of Lotus cars.

COLMAN
Origin/meaning: Latin 'dove'.

One of several Irish names deriving from the Latin name Columba. There were several pre-Conquest saints of that name. When surnames as well as given names came into use in the Middle Ages Colman came to be used primarily as a surname rather than a first name. The comparatively recent fashion, particularly in the US and Australia, of using surnames as given names, has brought it back into use as a first name.

Variations and abbreviations: Cole, Coleman, Coley.

COLUM
Origin/meaning: Latin 'dove'.

This Irish name is one of several Celtic forms of Columba *q.v.* Their popularity resulted from the great prestige of St Columba among people in Celtic areas. The name is almost never found outside Ireland.

Variations and abbreviations: Col, Cole, Colm. See also Colan, Colin, Colman, Malcolm.

Example: Colm Connolly, Irish novelist.

COLUMBA
Origin/meaning: Latin 'dove'.

The Latin name from which several Celtic names eg Colum, Malcolm, Colman, derive. St Columba, 521–597, was an Irish monk who took the teachings of Christ to the North of Scotland, earning the title 'The Apostle of the Picts'. He founded monasteries at Iona and Lindisfarne.

CON
Origin/meaning: frequently used short form of popular Irish names such as Cornelius, Connor, Conal. Sometimes used as an independent name.

Variation: Conn.

CONAL
Origin/meaning: Old Irish 'high'.

From the same root word as Conan it is used almost exclusively in Ireland.

Variations and abbreviations: Con, Conn, Conny.

Example: Conal Gregory, British wine expert and writer.

CONAN (pron. Eng. Cóe-nan, Irish, Connáwn)
Origin/meaning: Old Irish 'high', 'mighty' or 'intelligent'.

A widely found Celtic name it came to England from Ireland via Celtic France after the Norman Conquest. In the 13th century it gave rise to many surnames, including Conning and Channing, but almost died out as a first name.

Variations and abbreviations: Con, Conn, Conny, Kynan.

Example: Sir Arthur Conan Doyle, 1859–1930, creator of Sherlock Holmes.

CONNOR
Origin/meaning: Old Irish 'high desire'.

An extremely popular Irish name which gave rise to the surname O'Connor.

Variations and abbreviations: Con, Connaire (Ir), Conn (Ir), Conor.

Example: Conor Cruise O'Brien, Irish politician and journalist.

CONRAD
Origin/meaning: Old German 'bold counsellor'.

A German name found in the US, Canada and Australia but rare in Britain.

Variations and abbreviations: Con, Conn, Connie, Conrade (Fr), Corrado (It), Corradino (It), Cort (Dan), Curt, Koenraad (Dut), Konrad (Ger/Scand), Kurt.

Examples: Conrad Hilton, US hotel owner.
Konrad Bartelski, Polish-British ski champion.

CONSTANT
Origin/meaning: Latin 'constant', 'faithful'.

An English form of Constantine q.v.

Example: Constant Lambert, 1905–1951, British composer.

CONSTANTINE
Origin/meaning: Latin 'constant', 'faithful'.

Constantine was the first Christian Roman emperor. Not surprisingly his name recurred as a Christian name and in England was usually found in the typically shortened form Costin, which in turn produced the surnames Costin and Costain. The other English form Constant is probably a direct use of the English adjective.

Variations and abbreviations: Con, Conn, Connie, Conny, Constantin (Fr), Constantina (Sp), Costa (Grk), Costánte (Ir), Costantino (It), Costin, Konstantin (Ger/Scand/Slav).

Examples: Ex-King Constantine of Greece.
Constantine Fitzgibbon, British novelist.

CONWAY
Origin/meaning: Old Welsh 'holy water' or Old Irish 'hound of the plain'.

The origin of this name is obscure but it may be from the place-name Conway in Wales. Generally a surname its easy sound has made it a regularly used first name.

Variations and abbreviations: Con, Conn, Connie, Conny.

CORBETT
Origin/meaning: Old French 'raven'.

A surname probably denoting black hair. Occasionally used as a given name, usually because of family connections.

Variations and abbreviations: Corbet, Corbin, Corby, Cory.

Example: Corbett Woodall, British newscaster.

CORMAC
Origin/meaning: Old Irish 'charioteer'.

An Irish surname and first name, it features in many of the pagan Irish myths and legends.

Variations and abbreviations: Cormack, Cormick, Mac.

CORNELIUS
Origin/meaning: the Cornelius family, one of the great families of Ancient Rome. The name may come from the Latin 'horn' which implied kingship.

The Cornelian family produced many famous Romans including the dictator Sulla and the historian Tacitus. The name remained popular after the fall of the Roman Empire because there were several saints of the name. One of these, a 3rd century Pope, was martyred and his remains eventually taken to the Low countries. The cult surrounding him made the name popular in the Netherlands to this day, and also among descendants of the early Dutch settlers in the United States, such as the Vanderbilt family. The name is also given to honour St Cornelius in other Catholic countries and in Ireland in particular where it was found a convenient substitute for the native Irish name Conchubhar, 'high desire'.

Variations and abbreviations: Con, Conn, Connie, Connor, Conny, Cornel, Cornelis (It/Sp), Cornell, Corny, Cory.

Examples: Robert Cornelius, Lord Napier, 1810–1890, British Field Marshal.
Cornelius Vanderbilt, 1794–1877, US financier.

COSMO
Origin/meaning: Greek 'order', 'harmony', 'the universe'.

SS Cosmas and Damian, two of the early Christian martyrs, are Patron Saints of Milan. They were, according to legend, twin brothers, who practised as doctors without charging money. Their fame from the 5th century onwards in Italy was very great. The Medici family, Dukes of Florence, adopted the form Cosimo as a family name which popularized it further. It was introduced into Scotland in the 18th century by the Gordon family, the 3rd Duke being named after Cosimo III, Duke of Tuscany. It has recurred spasmodically in Britain since then.

Variations and abbreviations: Cos, Cosimo (It/Sp), Cosmé (Fr).

Example: (William) Cosmo Gordon Lang, 1864–1945, Archbishop of Canterbury.

COSTIN
Origin/meaning: Latin 'constant', 'faithful'.

An English shortened form of Constantine q.v. popular in the Middle Ages.

COURTENAY
Origin/meaning: either Old French 'short nose' or de Courtenay, an aristocratic family from Courtenay in France.

The family name of the West Country Earls of Devon, this aristocratic surname was one of many used as given names in the 19th century which have retained their popularity. It was particularly successful in the United States where it is usually found in the slightly shortened form of Courtney.

Variations and abbreviations: Court, Courtnay, Courtney, Curt.

Example: Courtney Brandreth, US wild-life artist.

CRADDOCK
Origin/meaning: Old Welsh 'amiable', 'nice'.

English version of the common Welsh name Caradoc. More usually found as a surname.

Variations and abbreviations: Caradoc (Wel), Cradock.

CRAIG
Origin/meaning: Old Scots/Old Welsh 'crag'.

One of the most common Scots surnames, based on several place names and popular as a given name because of its simple, easy sound. It is found especially in Australia and Canada where there are many people of Scottish descent.

Examples: Craig Claiborne, US cookery writer.
Craig Sheppard, US pianist.

CRISPIAN
Origin/meaning: Latin 'curled'.

Crispinianus was one of two shoemakers who were both martyred for their Christianity, probably in the 3rd century. The other was Crispinus (see Crispin). They were the patron saints of shoemakers. One legend says that they fled from persecution to Faversham in Kent. Certainly both names were extremely popular in the Middle Ages in their English forms. Crispinian was shortened still further to Crispian in a typical English fashion just as Benedict was shortened to Benet and Constantine to Costin. The names were, not surprisingly, often considered to be one and the same.

Variations and abbreviations: Crispinian, Crispinianus, Crispin.

CRISPIN
Origin/meaning: Latin 'curled'.

Crispinus and Crispinianus were two early Christian martyrs, the Patron Saints of shoemakers. The English forms of the names, Crispin and Crispian *q.v.* were popular in the Middle Ages and Crispin has survived to the present time as representative of both.

Variations and abbreviations: Crispian, Crispinus.

Example: Crispin Fuller, c.1778–1827, London silversmith.

CURT
Origin/meaning: a short form of names like Conrad, Courtney, Curtis. Used as a given name, particularly in the US.

Variation: Kurt.

Example: Curt Jurgens, German film actor.

CURTIS
Origin/meaning: Old English 'short hose' or 'courteous'.

With either meaning this is undoubtedly a nickname which became a surname in the Middle Ages. It has become well used as a given name particularly in the US.

Variations and abbreviations: Curt, Curtiss.

Example: Curtis Mayfield, US singer.

CUTHBERT
Origin/meaning: Old English 'famous – bright'.

The popularity of the Anglo-Saxon St Cuthbert, 634–687, whose miracles were many and well known, ensured that this old English name survived the influx of new names after the Norman Conquest. Like many non-Biblical 'Saints' names, it went out of favour after the Protestant Reformation. The 19th century High Church movement revived its popularity to some extent but it is now rare, perhaps because during the First World War it was used as a slang term for someone seeking to avoid military service.

Variations and abbreviations: Bert, Cudbert, Cuddy.

Examples: Cuthbert Mayne, d.1577, executed for 'treason' ie being a Catholic.
Cuthbert Tunstall, 1474–1559, Bishop of Durham.

CYPRIAN (pron. Sípprean)
Origin/meaning: Latin 'from Cyprus'.

St Cyprian, 200–258, was Bishop of Carthage. He was martyred during the Emperor Valerian's persecution of the Christians. Never very common in England the name was revived by the High Church movement of the 19th century when several churches were dedicated to St Cyprian.

Variations and abbreviations: Cipriano (It/Sp), Cyprianus (Ger/Dut), Zyprian, Zyprianus.

CYRIL
Origin/meaning: Greek 'lordly'.

There have been several saints of this name which made it popular in the Middle Ages. St Cyril, 827–869, with his brother St Methodius, took Christianity to the Slavic people of Central Europe, their success being in part due to their knowledge of Slav languages. The alphabet they devised to enable these languages to be written down was based on the Greek alphabet. It is known as Cyrillic after St Cyril, and is still used today for the Russian language. The name Cyril was one of many early saints' names revived by the 19th century High Church movement and one of the most successful. There has been a sharp down-turn in its popularity since the Second World War.

Variations and abbreviations: Cirille (Fr), Cirillo (It), Cirilo (Sp), Cyrill (Ger), Cyrillus (Dut), Kyrill (Ger), Kyrillus (Ger).

Examples: Cyril Smith, English politician.
Cyril Fletcher, English comedian.
Cyril Cusack, Irish actor.

CYRUS
Origin/meaning: Persian/Greek 'throne'.

Cyrus the Great, 560–629, first Persian king was a powerful ruler surrounded by fable and legend. He is mentioned in the Bible and is historically well documented, so his name therefore came to be used in the West. It is particularly popular in the US.

Variations and abbreviations: Ciro (It/Sp), Cirus, Cy, Russ.

Example: Cyrus Vance, former US Secretary of State.

D

DAI
Origin/meaning: Hebrew 'darling', 'friend'.

A popular Welsh short form of David q.v. from Dewi and Dafydd.

DALE
Origin/meaning: Old English 'from the valley'.

An English surname used as a first name for both boys and girls.

Variations and abbreviations: Dael, Dal.

Example: Dale Robertson, US actor.

DAMIAN
Origin/meaning: Greek 'tamer'.

Damian and Cosmas were two early Christian martyrs who probably died in Syria. They became a cult and many legends and additional embellishments were added to their story, including the fact that they were twin physicians. The discovery of their supposed relics by St Ambrose in Milan led to their being declared Patron Saints of the city. Damian was used in England in the Middle Ages but fell out of favour after the Protestant Reformation. It is usually used by Catholics but recently seems to have become a little more widespread.

Variations and abbreviations: Dami, Damiano (It), Damien (Fr), Damyan.

DAMON
Origin/meaning: Greek 'tamer', 'guide'.

This name is sometimes confused with Damian q.v. In Greek and Roman legend Damon and Phintias were two Syracusans who were very close friends. Phintias was accused of murder. Damon had stood bail for his friend and when Phintias failed to return from putting his affairs in order, it seemed he would die in his place. However Phintias returned at the last minute and saved him. Their loyalty so impressed the tyrant Dionysius that

367

he pardoned them both. The name Phintias was mistakenly rendered as Pythias in English and for a long time 'like Damon and Pythias' was a common expression to describe a very close friendship.

Example: Damon Runyan, 1880–1946, US humorist and writer.

DAN
Origin/meaning: Hebrew 'God has judged' or Old Irish 'dark-haired' or Scandinavian/German 'Danish'.

A short form of Daniel q.v. sometimes used as an independent first name. In Germany and Scandinavia it is used as an independent name meaning Danish, the equivalent of the feminine Dana.

Variations and abbreviations: Dana, Danni, Dannie, Danny.

Example: Dana Andrews, US actor.

DANDY
Origin/meaning: Greek 'manly'.

Old Scottish short form of Andrew. It has come to mean a man excessively fond of fashion.

DANIEL
Origin/meaning: Hebrew 'God has judged' or Old Irish 'dark-haired'.

Daniel was a Hebrew prophet who was delivered from the lions' den where he had been thrown by the Persian king Darius. Although it was used before the Conquest by monks and priests this name did not come into general use until the early Middle Ages. The 17th century Puritan liking for Biblical names gave it an extra boost. In the Book of Susannah Susannah herself is proved innocent of adultery by Daniel. The name is therefore sometimes used to describe someone of wise judgement. The name is currently enjoying a revival in Australia, Britain and North America. In Ireland Daniel was used to Anglicize the native name Domnall, which means dark-haired.

Variations and abbreviations: Dan, Daniele (It), Danilo (Slav), Danni, Dannie, Danny, Deiniol (Wel).

Examples: Daniel Defoe, 1660–1731, English journalist and novelist.
Danny Kaye, US entertainer.
Daniel Massey, English actor.

DANTE

Origin/meaning: 'lasting'.

An Italian diminutive of Durante, the Italian version of Durand *q.v.*It is occasionally given to honour the great Italian poet Dante Alighieri, 1265–1321. See also Beatrice.

Example: Dante Gabriel Rossetti, 1828–1882, English poet.

DARBY

Origin/meaning: Old Irish 'free from envy' or English 'from Derby'.

Darby may sometimes be a development of the Irish Diarmaid/ Dermot or it can be an English place-name/surname used as a given name. The use of Darby in the phrase Darby and Joan, meaning an inseparable old married couple, dates back to 1735. It is therefore more likely to have the first meaning as surnames were not commonly used as first names until the 19th century.

Variation: Derby.

DARCY

Origin/meaning: Old French 'from Arcy', Old Irish 'dark man'.

This is a name that came to England as a surname, D'Arcy, with William the Conqueror. It became an Irish first name after a branch of the family settled there in the late Middle Ages and was used to Anglicize the Old Irish name Dorchaide. Now found in North America and Australia where surnames are popular.

Variations and abbreviations: D'Arcy, Darsey, Darsy.

DARIUS

Origin/meaning: uncertain. Probably Persian, possibly ' preserver' or 'possessor of riches'.

Darius the Great was king of Persia from 521–485 BC. His army was beaten by the Greeks at the battle of Marathon. The use of this name, which is rare, is probably due to occasional references to Darius in the Bible. The Roman martyrology also lists a St Darius.

Variation: Dario (It).

Example: Darius Milhaud, 1892–1974, French composer.

DARREN

Origin/meaning: uncertain. Sometimes given as Old Irish 'little

369

one' or Greek 'from Doris'.

This name which seems to have come from nowhere in the 1960s and 70s is a surname used as a first name in the typical US fashion. However it is not a popular name in the US while in Australia and Britain it has become one of the front runners of the last two decades. It may have been because of the influence of an American television series of the early 1960s in which the main character's name was Darren, reinforced by the concurrent popularity of US singer Bobby Darin. Certainly it has an easily acceptable sound with no embarrassing short forms, and it is similar to two well-established though uncommon names – Darryl *q.v.* and Dorian *q.v.* Indeed it is sometimes given as a variation of Dorian. So for various, not totally understood reasons, Darren is now a totally bona fide new name which seems likely to retain its place alongside more conventional favourites, like John and Michael.

Variations: Daren, Daron, Darrin.

Example: Darren McGavin, American actor.

DARYL
Origin/meaning: Old English 'little dear', 'darling'.

A very old name still used occasionally today and popular in Canada. There is a modern feminine equivalent Darlene *q.v.*

Variations and abbreviations: Darrel, Darrell, Darryl, Daryll.

Examples: Darryl Zanuck, 1902–1979, US film producer.
Daryl Hall, US singer.

DATUS
Origin/meaning: Latin 'given'.

Probably a short form of the Latin Deodatus 'God given' and therefore similar to the Hebrew Nathan, or the Greek Theodore. Unlike these two Deodatus/Datus seems in England to have been almost entirely confined to monks or priests. Deodato is still used in Italy and Dieudonné and Deodat are found in France.

Variations and abbreviations: Deodat (Fr/Ger), Deodata (Ir), Deodatus, Deodonatus, Donat, Donatus. See also Dorothy, Dieudonnée, Jonathan, Theodore, Nathaniel.

DAUD
Origin/meaning: Arabic 'beloved'.

370

A widespread Muslim name similar to David *q.v.*

Variations: Daudi (E Africa), Dauvud.

DAVID
Origin/meaning: Hebrew 'darling' or 'friend'.

Probably, like many Hebrew names, this started out as a pet name. Its world-wide popularity is hardly surprising since King David, who slew Goliath and is reputed to have written the Psalms, is one of the outstanding characters in the Bible. The 6th century Welsh saint Dewi was Primate of Wales. He founded many monasteries, chief among them being at Mynyw, now known as St David's. His monastic rule was very strict and his monks were known as the 'water men' as they were allowed no alcohol. When his fame spread to England he was called St David and he is now known in Wales as St Dafydd, the usual Welsh version of that name. The Scots had their own St David, 1084–1153, who was also their king, David I. The name was therefore well-established in both Scotland and Wales before it was introduced into England at the time of the Norman Conquest in 1066. It was immediately popular and therefore gave rise to many surnames, eg Deacon, Davy, Dawes, Dawson. In Scotland it gave rise to the surname McTavish, the D being easily changed to a T as in the English attempt at the Welsh pronunciation, Taffy. In Ireland David was used to Anglicize the native name Dathi. The name David was not highly regarded by Puritans in England or North America during the 17th century because of King David's many sins. Since that hiatus it has been consistently used and over the last 30 years has been one of the most popular boy's names in Britain, North America and Australia.

Variations and abbreviations: Dai (Wel), Dafydd (Wel), Dave, Davidde, Davide (Fr/It/Sp), Davie, Davin, Davy, Deio (Wel), Dewey (Wel).

Examples: David Bowie, British singer.
David Niven, 1910–1983, British actor and film star.

DAVIS
Origin/meaning: Middle English 'son of David'.

An English surname derived from David, sometimes used as a given name, particularly in the US.

DEAN
Origin/meaning: 'from the valley'.

An English surname used as a first name, perhaps because of its simplicity and similarity to Dan. There is a more artificial feminine version, Dena. In the US the Italian Dino is used as an alternative.

Variations and abbreviations: Deane, Dene, Dino.

Example: Dean Martin, US singer and actor.

DECIMUS
Origin/meaning: Latin 'tenth'.

A name used for a tenth son or tenth child. Rare today.

DEMETRIUS
Origin/meaning: Greek 'follower of Demeter'.

Demeter was the ancient Greek goddess of the fertile earth and of agriculture. There were two Saints who bore the name, an early martyr who popularized the name in the area of the Greek orthodox church and St Demetrius, Bishop of Rostov, 1651–1709. A great scholar and much loved by the people, his influence accounts for the great popularity of the name in Russia in the form Dmitri.

Variations and abbreviations: Demetre (Fr), Demetri, Demetrio (It), Dimitri, Dmitri (Russ).

Example: Dmitri de Grunwald, Russian/British film producer.

DENIS
Origin/meaning: Latin/Greek 'follower of Dionysos'.

The Greek name Dionysius was a common one because of the popularity of the god of fertility and wine, Dionysos. Many early saints, converts to Christianity, bore the old pagan name, including Dionysos the Areopagite, an early convert of St Paul, and Dionysius the Great, Bishop of Alexandria. A St Dionysius who took Christianity to the Gauls (in what is now France) was beheaded at Montmartre (the hill of the martyr) in Paris in 258. He was eventually adopted as the Patron Saint of France and known as St Denys. Like many Saints' names it came to England in the early Middle Ages and was popular enough to produce several surnames eg Dennison and Tennyson. As a Catholic saint's name it went out of fashion at the time of the 16th/17th century Protestant Reformation. It enjoyed a revival of popularity in Britain, Australia and the US from the 1920s but now seems to be on the wane.

Variations and abbreviations: Den, Denness, Dennet. Denney, Dennis, Denny, Denys (Fr), Dion, Dionisio (It/Sp), Dionys (Ger), Dionysius (Ger).

Examples: Denny Lane, British musician.
Denis Healey, British politician.
Denis Price, English actor.

DENZIL
Origin/meaning: uncertain, possibly Latin/Greek 'follower of Dionysos'.

A Cornish surname used as a first name, principally in Cornwall, since the 17th century.

Variation: Denzell.

Example: Denzil Bachelor, British writer.

DEREK
Origin/meaning: Old German 'ruler of the people'.

This name, which was most popular in Britain just before and after the Second World War, is from the Old German Theodoric q.v. In the Middle Ages Theodoric and the Old English Theodric were found in England in the shortened from Terry (from the French version Thierry). However in the late Middle Ages trade with Holland introduced the Dutch forms Diederick (similar to the modern German form Dietrich) and Dirk, from which we get Derrick and the 20th century spelling Derek. In the US the name was introduced independently by Dutch settlers in New Amsterdam (now New York), but it has never been a great favourite in the US.

Variations and abbreviations: Dedrik, Deric, Deryk, Derrick, Diederich (Ger), Diederick (Dut), Dietrich (Ger), Dirk.

Examples: Derek Jacobi, English actor.
Derek Tangye, British writer and traveller.

DERMOT
Origin/meaning: Old Irish 'free from envy'.

This is an Anglicized form of the Irish Diarmaid. Diarmaid, in Irish legend ran off with Grainne, Queen of Tara. Her husband caught up with them and forced Diarmaid to fight with a wild boar which killed him. The name, with its short form Darby, came early to England with Irish immigrants. The English spelling Dermot reflects the Irish pronunciation.

Variations and abbreviations: Darby, Derby, Dermott, Diarmid, Diarmit.

Example: Dermot Walsh, Irish actor.

DESMOND
Origin/meaning: Old Irish 'from South Munster'.

This is an Irish surname which came into general use as a first name in the 19th century, although it has no obvious aristocratic connections. It is found now in England and, less often, in Australia and North America.

Abbreviation: Des.

Examples: Desmond Morris, British zoologist and writer.
Des O'Connor, British singer and comedian.

DEXTER
Origin/meaning: Old English 'dyer'. Sometimes given as Latin 'right-handed' 'dexterous'.

An English surname sometimes used as a first name.

DHRUVA (pron. Dhroov)
Origin/meaning: this is the Hindu name for the pole-star.

Dhruva is a character from Indian mythology. Rejected by his father, King Uttanpada, he went into the forest and gradually achieved spiritual perfection through meditation. As a result the gods favoured him and he eventually became king himself. On his death the gods transformed him into Dhruva-Loka, the pole star.

DICK
Origin/meaning: Old English 'hard ruler'.

The most common modern short form of Richard q.v. Sometimes given as an independent name. It is a short form of the original medieval form, Diccon.

Examples: Dick Francis, English thriller writer.
Dick van Dyke, US actor/comedian.
Dick Gregory, US comedian.

DIGBY
Origin/meaning: Old English 'settlement by a ditch'.

An English place name which became a surname and has been occasionally used as a given name.

Example: One of the Geste brothers in P. C. Wren's *Beau Geste* was named Digby.

DIGGORY
Origin/meaning: French 'lost', 'strayed'.

An old-fashioned name, possibly Cornish, rare nowadays.

Example: Diggory, the farm labourer used as a butler by the Hardcastles on special occasions in *She Stoops to Conquer* by Oliver Goldsmith, 1773.

DILLON
Origin/meaning: Old Irish 'faithful' or Old German 'destroyer'.

An Irish surname sometimes used as a first name.

DION
Origin/meaning: Latin/Greek 'follower of Dionysus'.

A form of Denis *q.v.* It is a short form of the Italian version Dionisio and is used in areas with people of Italian descent.

DINESH
Origin/meaning: Hindi/Gujerati 'helper of the poor'.

DIRK
Origin/meaning: Old German 'ruler of the people'.

A Dutch form of Theodoric *q.v.* from which the German Dietrich and English Derek *q.v.* are derived. It is found in England since the late Middle Ages when England was engaged in the wool trade with Holland.

Variations: Dierk (Ger), Derk.

Example: Dirk Bogarde, English film actor (of Dutch descent).

DOMINIC
Origin/meaning: Latin 'of the Lord'.

A name either intended to dedicate a child to God or to indicate he was born on a Sunday, the Lord's day. Used by monks before the Conquest it gained wider acceptance in the Middle Ages when it was used to honour St Dominic, 1170–1221, founder of the Dominican Order of Preaching Friars. After the Protestant Reformation the name was used in Britain only by Catholics. Very recently it has become more widely used.

Variations and abbreviations: Dom, Domenic, Domenico (It), Domingo (Sp), Dominick, Dominique (Fr), Nick, Nickie, Nicky.

Examples: Dominic Behan, Irish journalist and poet.
Domenico Scarlatti, 1685–1757, Italian composer.

DONALD
Origin/meaning: Old Scots 'world ruler'.

The name of six Scottish kings Donald is, not surprisingly, one of the commonest Scottish names. The Irish name Donal, from the Old Irish of the same meaning, is also popular. It has sometimes been used to translate Daniel although the meanings are different. The short form Don/Donen has the independent meaning 'dark' and is found in several Irish/Scots surnames which are sometimes used as given names, such as Donovan, Donnelly and Donahue.

Variations and abbreviations: Don, Donal (Ir), Donalt, Donn, Donnie, Donny.

Examples: Don McLean, US singer.
Donald Smith, Lord Strathcona, 1820–1913, Canadian statesman.
Donald Sutherland, US actor.

DONATUS
Origin/meaning: Latin 'given', 'God-given'.

A name similar to Datus q.v. which dates back to the Roman period in Britain.

Variations and abbreviations: Don, Donat (Ir), Donato (It). See also Nathaniel, Theodore.

DONOVAN
Origin/meaning: Old Irish 'dark warrior', 'brown warrior'.

One of many Irish and Welsh names containing the Celtic word for dark. This is still mainly found as an Irish surname.

Abbreviation: Don.

Example: Donovan, British singer/songwriter.

DORIAN

Origin/meaning: Greek 'from Doris' (one of the famous areas of classical Greece).

This is the male version of Doris and Doria *q.q.v.* Made famous by Oscar Wilde's novel *The Picture of Dorian Gray*, 1891. See also Dylan.

DOUGAL (pron. Doogal)
Origin/meaning: Old Irish 'dark stranger'.

Used by the Irish as a term for Scandinavian invaders it became a general Celtic term used by Irish, Scots and Bretons for strangers. For example the Bretons used it for the French and the Scots for the English or even for people from a different area of Scotland. It became a widespread first name and is still common in Scotland.

Variations and abbreviations: Doug, Doyle (Ir), Dug, Dugald, Duggie.

DOUGLAS
Origin/meaning: Old Irish/Old Scots 'from the dark water'.

This is a common descriptive place or river name, the equivalent of Dawlish in England and Duvas in Welsh. A well-known example is Douglas in the Isle of Man (a Celtic area). The famous Scottish clan Douglas was clearly named after a local river or loch. Their surname developed as a first name through inter-marriage with the family, when it was given as a name to both male and female children. At the end of the 19th century, it was introduced more generally as one of those aristocratic surnames (of the Earl of Morton and Marquess of Queensberry) which became fashionable first names for boys. Its popularity is greatest in Scotland and areas of Australia and Canada with populations of Scottish origin.

Variations and abbreviations: Doug, Dougie, Douglass, Dougy, Dug, Duggie.

Examples: Douglas Fairbanks, 1883–1939, swashbuckling American film actor.
General Douglas MacArthur, 1880–1964, US general.

DOYLE
Origin/meaning: Old Irish 'dark stranger'.

The Irish version of Dougal *q.v.* found as both surname and first name.

DREW

Origin/meaning: Old German 'bearer' or Old French 'vigorous'.

This is the Medieval English form of the name Drogo, by way of the French form Dru. It was introduced in both German and French forms at the time of the Norman Conquest. Being a fairly common name it became a surname, and there are several place names which refer back to the overlordship of a man named Drogo or Drew, which have separately given rise to surnames. Drogo lost its popularity after the 17th century but Drew survives, possibly because it has found new life, in the US particularly, as a surname used as a given name.

Variations and abbreviations: Drogo, Dru.

DUANE (pron. Dwayne)

Origin/meaning: Old Irish 'small and dark'.

A 'new' first name popular in the US in the 1950s and 60s perhaps because of the guitarist Duane Eddy and also its similarity to another 60s favourite, Wayne. It spread to Britain in the 70s but is not yet popular in Australia.

Variation: Dwayne.

Example: Duane Eddy, US guitarist.

DUDLEY

Origin/meaning: Old English 'Dudda's clearing'.

Dudda was a Saxon nobleman, and Dudley is a town in Worcestershire. The place name became a surname and the Dudley family was one of the fastest rising families in Tudor England, eventually being granted the Earldom of Leicester. Apart from occasional use because of family intermarriage, the surname was not used as a first name until the 19th century when aristocratic surnames became fashionable as first names for boys.

Abbreviation: Dud.

Examples: Dudley Moore, English musician and film actor. Charles Dudley Warner, 1829–1900, US writer.

DUGALD (pron. Doogal)

Origin/meaning: Old Irish 'dark stranger'.

An alternative spelling of Dougal q.v.

DUKE

Origin/meaning: English 'duke' or Old Irish/Welsh 'servant of Madoc'.

This name used to be found only as a short form of Marmaduke and therefore had the second meaning. However since the 19th century it has been a given name directly from a family surname and more rarely it has been used deliberately to bestow a 'title' on a child.

Example: Duke Ellington, 1899–1974, US musician.

DUNCAN

Origin/meaning: Old Irish 'brown headed'.

Like many names of Irish origin this was quickly adopted by its neighbour Scotland whose language was so similar. There were two Scottish kings of that name, the first of whom is the Duncan, 1034–1040, murdered by MacBeth and well-known from Shakespeare's play. Duncan, with Donald, Douglas and Ian, is one of the commonest Scottish names but has not spread as readily as the others. The Irish version is now usually 'translated' to the English Denis.

Abbreviations: Dun, Dunc, Dunk.

Example: Duncan Goodhew, English Olympic swimmer.

DUNSTAN

Origin/meaning: Old English 'stone-hill'.

A name given in England in the Middle Ages to honour St Dunstan, 909–988, who re-organized monastic life in Britain. As the archbishop of Canterbury who crowned King Edgar, he is mainly responsible for devising the Coronation ceremonial still followed in the 20th century. The name was dropped after the Protestant Reformation because of the disapproval of non-biblical, saints' names. The 19th century High Church movement re-introduced it, along with other saints' names, like Cyril and Basil, but it remains uncommon.

DURAND

Origin/meaning: Latin 'lasting'.

Introduced at the time of the Norman Conquest this name has lasted better as a surname than as a first name. Dante q.v. is the short form of the Italian form Durante.

Variations and abbreviations: Dante, Durand (Fr), Durant, Durante (It), Durrand, Durrance.

DWIGHT
Origin/meaning: uncertain, possibly Old French 'from the Isle of Wight' or Old Flemish De Witt, 'from Witt'.

A common surname in the New England area of the US where the first immigrants from England settled. The short 'masculine' sound of the surname combined with its long association with the US made it an obvious choice in the 19th century when surnames became fashionable as given names.

Example: Dwight D Eisenhower, 1890–1969, 34th President of the US.

DYLAN (pron. Dúllan)
Origin/meaning: Old Welsh 'dark' often given as 'from the sea'.

This is a character from Welsh legend whose father was the God of the Sea. The US singer Bob Dylan (pron. Dillon) may account for some use of the name pronounced incorrectly. The use of the spelling Dillon may come directly from another surname meaning possibly 'destroyer'.

Variations and abbreviations: Dill, Dillan, Dillon, Dullan. See also Dorian.

Example: Dylan Thomas, 1914–1953, Welsh poet.

E

EAMON
Origin/meaning: Old English 'prosperous protector'.

The Irish form of Edmund *q.v.*

Variation: Eamonn.

Examples: Eamon Andrews, Irish broadcaster.
Eamon de Valera, 1882–1975, Irish statesman.

EARL
Origin/meaning: Old English 'nobleman' or 'warrior'.

This is an English surname which probably indicates an ancestor was in the service of an earl rather than an earl himself. Since the 19th century when surnames became popular as first names, this family name has been used in the US. It was most popular there before the Second World War and is curretly unfashionable. In other English-speaking countries it is rare.

Variations: Earle, Erle.

Examples: Earl Derr Biggers, 1844–1933, US novelist.
Erle Stanley Gardener, 1889–1970, US detective fiction writer.

EASTER
Origin/meaning: this name was given to both boys and girls born around the time of the festival of Easter.

See also Christmas, Noel, Pascal.

EBEN
Origin/meaning: Hebrew 'stone of help'.

A short form of Ebenezer *q.v.* used as an independent name in the US.

Example: Eben Rexford, 1848–1916, English song-writer.

EBENEZER

Origin/meaning: Hebrew 'stone of help'.

This is a Biblical place name referred to in the 7th chapter of the first Book of Samuel. It was popular among the 17th century Puritans who rejected Catholic saints' names. Although the English Puritans used it it was most popular among the Puritans of New England. Being refugees in search of religious freedom they found the quotation it came from particularly apt: 'Then Samuel took a stone, and set it between Mizpeh and Shen, and called the name of it Ebenezer, saying, Hitherto hath the Lord helped us'. In the 19th century the name declined in popularity and become synonymous with unattractive simpletons. In England the decline of the name was accelerated by the unattractive character Ebenezer Scrooge in Charles Dickens' *A Christmas Carol*.

Variations and abbreviations: Benezer, Eben.

Examples: Ebenezer Moulton, 1768–1824, US silversmith. Ebenezer Cobham Brewer, 1810–1897, English compiler of the *Dictionary of Phrase and Fable*.

EBNER

Origin/meaning: Hebrew 'father of light'.

A variation of Abner *q.v.*

ED/EDDIE

Short forms of Edgar, Edmund, Edward and Edwin.

Examples: Eddie Cantor, 1892–1964, US actor/comedian. Ed McBain, US crime writer.

EDEN

Origin/meaning: Hebrew 'delight'.

A family name occasionally used as a personal name.

Example: Eden Phillpotts, 1862–1960, English novelist, dramatist and poet.

EDGAR

Origin/meaning: Old English 'rich spear'.

Edgar (Eadgar) was one of the names used by the royal house of

Wessex, whose best known king was Alfred the Great, 849–899. Alfred's grandson was King Edgar, 944–975, who united the English kingdom. Edgar Aetheling the last heir of Edward the Confessor did not die until 1125. Its royal usage together with hopes of a Saxon revival, may account for the survival of the name for several centuries after the Norman Conquest. After 500 years in abeyance it was revived in the Romantic Movement at the turn of the 18th century. It has now become rather unfashionable.

Variations and abbreviations: Eadgar, Ed, Edgard (Fr).

Examples: Edgar Allan Poe, 1809–1849, US poet and story writer.
Edgar Degas, 1834–1917, French artist.
Edgar Rice Burroughs, 1875–1950, US novelist.

EDMOND
Origin/meaning: Old English 'rich protection'.

French form of Edmund q.v. introduced into England in the Middle Ages and used with equal frequency.

Example: Edmond Halley, 1656–1742, English astronomer.

EDMUND
Origin/meaning: Old English 'rich guardian'.

As in Edward, Edgar and Edith the first syllable of this name indicates it was used by the royal house of Wessex before the Conquest. Edmund Ironside, 981–1016, was a son of Ethelred the Unready. He ended the wars with the Danes by sharing the kingship of England with Canute. The main reason why the name survived the Conquest was probably the fame of St Edmund, 841–870, after whom the town of Bury St Edmunds is named. A king of the East Angles he was defeated by the Danes in 870, and shot to death with arrows because he refused to renounce his Christianity. Another influential saint was St Edmund Rich, 1170–1240, an archbishop of Canterbury who supported the church against Henry III. The name has never completely gone out of fashion.

Variations and abbreviations: Eamon (Ir), Ed, Eddie, Edmond (Fr), Edmondo (It), Edmundo (Sp), Ned, Nedely, Ted, Teddy.

Examples: Sir Edmund Hillary, New Zealand explorer and

mountaineer.
Edmund Spenser, 1552–1599, English Renaissance poet.
Edmund Purdom, British/US film actor.
Sir Edmund Goss, 1849–1928, British poet and critic.

EDRED

Origin/meaning: Old English 'rich counsel'.

An Anglo-Saxon name which did not survive the influx of new names with the Norman Conquest. It was revived in the 19th century along with many other pre-Conquest names but like the similar sounding Aldred q.v. it never achieved great success.

EDWARD

Origin/meaning: Old English 'rich guardian'.

Like most names beginning with Ed- this is closely connected with the royal house of Wessex. Edward the Elder, 870–924, succeeded his father Alfred the Great and greatly increased the influence of Wessex over the other British kingdoms. Edward the Martyr, 963–978, succeeded his father King Edward and was murdered by his stepmother Elfrida. Edward the Confessor, 1003–1066, was the last of the Anglo-Saxon kings. He founded Westminster Abbey and was made a Saint shortly after his death. Because of the fame of these three the name survived the influx of new names at the time of the Norman Conquest.
Three Plantagenet kings, Edward I, Edward II and Edward III between them ruled England from 1272–1377, which did much to establish the name as an unshakable favourite in England, and eventually in the rest of Europe. Of the remaining five kings who bore the name, Edward VII gave it most popularity. After over a thousand years of use it is as popular today as ever.

Variations and abbreviations: Duarte (Port), Ed, Eddie, Eddy, Edouard (Fr), Eduard (Ger/Dut), Eduardo (It/Port/Sp), Edvard (Scand), Ned, Neddie, Neddy, Ted, Teddie, Teddy.

Examples: Edward Kennedy, US Senator.
Edouard Manet, 1832–1883, French painter.
Edvard Grieg, 1843–1907, Norwegian composer.

EDWIN

Origin/meaning: Old English 'rich friend'.
Edwin, King of Northumbria, 585–633, who eventually gained

overlordship over the whole of England except the kingdom of Kent, was the best known bearer of the name in Anglo-Saxon times. Northumbria at that time extended into Scotland and Edwin gave his name to Edinburgh (Edwinsburgh). He was a convert to Christianity and was canonized after his death in battle. The name lost favour after the Norman Conquest but never died out completely.

In the 19th century it was successfully revived along with many other Old English and Medieval names such as Alice, Ermintrude and Edgar.

Variations and abbreviations: Ed, Eddie, Eddy, Eduino (It/Sp), Edwyn, Ned, Neddie, Neddy, Odwin, Otwin, Ted, Teddie.

Examples: Sir Edwin Landseer, 1802–1873, English painter.
Edwin (Buzz) Aldrin, US astronaut.

EGBERT
Origin/meaning: 'bright sword'.

A popular Anglo-Saxon name borne by the first real king of England, d.839, and by a Northumbrian saint, 639–729, who was influential in Ireland. It was revived in the 19th century but without the same lasting success as Edgar and Edwin.

ELI (pron. Éelie)
Origin/meaning: uncertain. Possibly Hebrew 'God' or 'high'.

This is a Biblical name which achieved some popularity in the 17th century when Puritans rejected Catholic saints' names. Eli was the High Priest who brought up the prophet Samuel when he was a child. The name is not much used now.

Variation: Ely.

Examples: Eli Wallach, US actor.
Eli Whitney, 1765–1825, US inventor of the cotton gin.

ELIAS
Origin/meaning: Hebrew 'Jehovah is God.'

The Greek form of Elijah q.v. This was a common first name in the Middle Ages, together with the variation Ellis. Its popularity was revived in the 17th century Puritan period both in England and New England, but it has become rare since the 19th century.

Elia was the pseudonym of the English essayist Charles Lamb, 1775–1839.

Variations and abbreviations: El, Eli, Elia (It), Elias (Sp), Elie (Fr), Elliott, Ellis, Ilja (Slav).

Examples: Elias Ashmole, 1617–1692, English antiquarian.
Elia Kazan, US film director.
Elias Canetti, Bulgarian writer.

ELIJAH
Origin/meaning: Hebrew 'Jehovah is God'.

A popular Old Testament name both in the Middle Ages and in the 17th/18th centuries when Puritans favoured Biblical names. It was often found in the Greek form Elias q.v. Elijah was a Hebrew Prophet who lived about 900 BC. He was fed by ravens at the brook Cherith and miraculously brought back to life the son of Zeraphath. See I Kings ch.17 v.2, and 2 Kings.

ELISHA
Origin/meaning: Hebrew 'God is generous'.

A Biblical name. Elisha was a Hebrew prophet who was a disciple of Elijah.

Example: Elisha Kent Kane, 1820–1857, US Arctic explorer.

ELLIOTT
Origin/meaning: Hebrew 'Jehovah is God'.

An English surname derived from Elijah q.v. through the Greek form Elias q.v. which was a popular name in the Middle Ages. Elliott is the familiar or diminutive form. It has been used as a first name since the 19th century particularly in the US where it is currently very fashionable.

Variations and abbreviations: Eli, Eliot, Elliot. See also Ellis.

Example: Elliott Gould, US actor.

ELLIS
Origin/meaning: Hebrew 'Jehovah is God'.

This is a form of Elijah q.v. through its Greek form Elias q.v. Both Elias and Ellis were common first names in the Middle Ages, but

Ellis eventually developed primarily as a surname. Its use as a first name in the 19th and 20th centuries is usually as a family name being used as a personal name. Emily Brontë, 1818–1848, used the name Ellis Bell as her pseudonym.

Variation: Ellison.

Example: Sir Ellis Ashmead-Bartlett, 1849–1902, US-born British MP and supporter of the Turkish cause.

ELMER

Origin/meaning: Old English 'noble and famous'.

An English surname which developed from the Old English name Aylmer *q.v.* It has been popular as a first name in the US since surnames became common as first names in the 19th century. This popularity is sometimes attributed to the Elmer brothers who were prominent in the American Revolution. However the name is less popular in their native area of New England than in the rest of the US. Elmer is almost never used in other English-speaking countries.

ELMO

Origin/meaning: Greek 'beloved'.

A short form of Erasmus *q.v.* Used primarily in Italy and by people of Italian origin to honour St Elmo.

ELVIS

Origin/meaning: Old Norse 'all wise'.

This is probably a typical American use of a surname as a first name. Recent use is almost totally due to the fame of the US singer Elvis Presley.

Example: Elvis Aaron Presley, 1935–1977, US singer.

EMANUEL

Origin/meaning: Hebrew: 'God with us'.

A name used in the Old Testament to describe the promised Messiah (Isaiah ch.7 v.14). This is the Greek/Latin form of Immanuel. It was a popular name in the Eastern church and later spread to Italy and Spain in slightly varying forms including the

387

shortened form Manuel. Although it was used in the 17th century by Puritans in England and New England, who favoured Biblical names, its use in English-speaking countries has been confined mainly to Jewish people. In France the name was very popular in the inter-war period.

Variations and abbreviations: Emanuele (It), Emmanuel (Fr), Immanuel (Ger), Mannie, Manny, Manoel (Port), Manuel (Sp).

Examples: Emanuel I, 1469–1521, King of Portugal.
Immanuel Kant, 1724–1804, German philosopher.

EMILE
Origin/meaning: Latin: from the Roman clan name, Aemilius. Meaning sometimes given as 'zealous' or 'bronze beater'.

This is the masculine equivalent of Emily q.v. It is rare in English-speaking countries but frequently used in Germany and France.

Variations and abbreviations: Aemilius, Emil (Ger), Emilio (It/Sp), Emlyn (Wel).

Example: Emile Zola, 1840–1902, French novelist.

EMLYN
Origin/meaning: Latin: from the Roman clan name, Aemilius. Meaning sometimes given as 'zealous' or 'bronze beater'.

This is the Welsh form of the name which is found in Europe as Emile or Emil. Many Roman names which were lost in England when the Germanic tribes invaded survived in Wales which remained comparatively untouched by Saxon influence.

Variations and abbreviations: see Emile.

Example: Emlyn Williams, Welsh actor and writer.

EMRYS
Origin/meaning: Greek 'divine' or 'immortal'.

The Welsh form of Ambrose q.v. Ambrosius Aurelianus was a legendary 5th century Welsh petty king whose resistance to the Saxons may have given rise to the legends of King Arthur.

Example: Emrys James, Welsh actor.

ENOCH
Origin/meaning: uncertain. Possibly Hebrew 'mortal' or 'skilled'.

This is one of many Biblical names used by 17th century Puritans. It became virtually obsolete in the 19th century. Enoch was a Hebrew patriarch, father of Methuselah (who was said to have lived 969 years) and grandfather of Noah (Genesis ch.5).

Variation: Enos (Greek).

Examples: Enoch Powell, British politician.
Enoch Arnold Bennett, 1867–1931, English novelist.

EÓIN (pron. 'Yon)

Origin/meaning: Hebrew 'Jehovah has favoured'.

The Irish Gaelic form of John *q.v.* almost identical to the Scottish form Iain *q.v.* Its use has grown steadily since the revival in Irish Gaelic culture at the turn of the century. Before that it was virtually obsolete and had been overtaken by another Irish form – Sean *q.v.* Eóin was sometimes 'translated' by the English as Eugene.

EPHRAIM

Origin/meaning: uncertain. Sometimes given as Hebrew 'very fruitful'.

This is a Biblical name. Ephraim was the grandson of Jacob and gave his name to one of the tribes of Israel. It was used by 17th century Puritans, particularly those living in New England. It consequently remained in use in the US far longer than in Britain.

Variations: Efrem, Ephraem, Ephrem.

Examples: Efrem Zimbalist Jnr, US actor.
St Ephraem of Syria, 306–373, Doctor of the early church.

ERASMUS

Origin/meaning: Greek 'beloved'

This name was used in the Netherlands and Germany in the Middle Ages, probably to honour St Erasmus, a 4th century martyr who was the Patron Saint of Sailors. Corposant, an electrical discharge sometimes occurring round the masts of ships in a storm, was popularly called St Elmo's fire and taken as an indication of the Saint's protection. Erasmus came into use in England in the late Middle Ages because of trading between the

Low countries and England. It was boosted by the reputation of Desiderius Erasmus, 1466–1536, the eminent Dutch scholar and reformer who spent much of his life in England. The name is now rare in English speaking countries.

Variations and abbreviations: Asmus, Elmo, Erasme (Fr), Erasmo (It), Telmo.

Example: Erasmus Darwin, 1731–1802, English radical, grandfather of Charles Darwin.

ERIC
Origin/meaning: Old Norse. Ric means ruler (as in Richard). The meaning of the first syllable is uncertain but may be 'ever'. Therefore usually given as 'ever ruling'.

This is a popular Scandinavian name, borne by seven Danish and fourteen Swedish kings. Notable among them was (St) Eric VIII of Sweden, d.1160, who tried to conquer Finland and convert it to Christianity. The name was brought to England and Scotland by the Scandinavian invaders who followed the fall of Roman rule. When the Normans invaded in 1066 the name died out. It was revived in England at the beginning of the 19th century because of the influence of the Romantic Movement. In the US, Canada and Australia the name was introduced by Scandinavian settlers in the mid-19th century. It was a popular name in England in the 1920s and in France in the 1950s and 60s.

Variations and abbreviations: Aic, Erich (Ger), Erick, Erico (It), Erik (Swed/Dan), Eirik (Nor), Jerik (Dan), Rick, Rickie, Ricky.

Examples: Eric Heffer, English politician.
Eric Clapton, English rock musician.
Erich von Stroheim, 1885–1957, Austrian actor and director of early Hollywood films.
Eric the Red, 10th century Norwegian hero, subject of Icelandic sagas.

ERNEST
Origin/meaning: Old German 'earnestness' or 'vigour'.

This was introduced into Britain in the 18th century by the Hanoverian royal family. In the 19th century its popularity quickly increased probably because of its aristocratic associations but in the latter half of the 20th century its popularity has waned. Oscar Wilde used the name in his play *The Importance of Being Earnest*, 1895.

Variations and abbreviations: Earnest, Ern, Ernesto (It), Ernestin (Fr), Ernestus, Ernie.

Examples: Ernest Hemingway, 1898–1961, US novelist.
Ernest Rutherford, 1871–1937, New Zealand/British nuclear physicist.
Ernst Lubitsch, early Hollywood film director.

ERROL
Origin/meaning: Old English/Old Norse 'army power'.

A variation of the name Harold *q.v.* from one of its earliest forms, Eral. Sometimes given as a variation of Earl *q.v.* a popular US first name.

Example: Errol Flynn, 1909–1959, Irish-American film actor.

ESMÉ
Origin/meaning: French/Latin 'beloved'.

Used both as a masculine and a feminine name. Like the masculine Amyas it is a variation of the more popular Amy.

Variations and abbreviations: Aimé, Amyas.

Example: Esmé Stuart, 1542–1583, cousin of King James I. First example of the name in Britain.

ESMOND
Origin/meaning: Old English 'grace protection'.

This Old English name survived for a while after the Norman Conquest. It more or less died out as a first name by the end of the 14th century but survived as a comparatively unusual surname. In the 19th century, when surnames became fashionable as first names, Thackeray's highly successful novel *The History of Henry Esmond*, 1852, brought the name back into currency as a personal name. It is still used occasionally today.

Example: Vere Harold Esmond Harmsworth, Viscount Rothermere, Chairman of the Associated Newspapers Group.

ETHELBERT
Origin/meaning: Old English 'noble bright'.

One of the pre-Conquest names revived at the time of the Romantic Movement but without lasting success.

Abbreviation: Bertie.

Example: Ethelbert, King of Kent, 552–616, who introduced the first written English laws.

ETHELRED
Origin/meaning: Old English 'noble counsel'.

A pre-Conquest name, held by two of the early English kings including Ethelred the Unready, 968–1016. It was revived as a result of the Romantic Movement but with no lasting success.

ETIENNE
Origin/meaning: Greek 'wreathed', 'crowned'.

A French form of Stephen *q.v.*

EUAN
Origin/meaning: Old Scots/Irish 'young warrior'.

This is probably from the same root as the common Welsh name Owen *q.v.* Both Owen and Euan were often 'translated' by the English as Eugene. This is more understandable in the case of Euan which has the Gaelic spelling Eoghain.

Variations and abbreviations: Evan, Ewan, Owain (Wel), Owen.

EUGENE
Origin/meaning: Greek 'noble', 'well-born'.

This name was used in the Middle Ages to honour St Eugenius, one of the four Popes who bore the name. Later the name was popularized among the British and their allies by the exploits of Prince Eugene of Savoy, 1663–1736. A French-born Austrian who was insultingly treated by Louis XIV he fought against the French with several countries. His most notable battles were his victories with the Duke of Marlborough at Blenheim, 1704, Oudenarde, 1708 and Malplaquet, 1709. The name was popular in the US at the end of the 19th century and is still used there today, especially in its short form Gene.

Variations and abbreviations: Eugen (Ger), Eugène (Fr), Eugenio (It/Sp), Eugenius (Ger/Dut), Yevgeny (Russ).

Examples: Eugene O'Neill, 1888-1953, US playwright.

Yevgeny Yevtushenko, Russian poet.
Eugene Ionesco, Rumanian/French playwright.

EUSTACE
Origin/meaning: Greek 'fruitful'.

This is the name of two early, though unauthenticated, Saints. One was supposedly a General under the Emperor Trajan. He was converted to Christianity while out hunting, by a vision of a stag with a luminous cross between its antlers. The soldier was later martyred and became one of the Patron Saints of huntsmen. The name came to England with the Normans and has been used ever since, though it has never been popular.

Variations and abbreviations: Eustache (Fr), Eustachius (Ger), Eustasius (Ger/Dut), Eustatius (Dut), Eustazio (It), Eustic, Stacy.

Examples: Eustache Le Sueur, 1617–1655, French painter.
Eustace and Hilda, novel by L. P. Hartley, 1947.

EVAN
Origin/meaning: Old Scots/Old Irish 'young warrior' or Hebrew 'Jehovah has favoured'.

An English form of the Scots name Euan *q.v.* and the Welsh names Owen *q.v.* and Ifan. Owen is sometimes considered the Welsh form of John in which case the Hebrew meaning applies.

EVELYN (pron. Eevlyn)
Origin/meaning: diminutive of the Old German name Avi, or Old French 'hazel tree' or Old Celtic 'pleasant'.

Evelyn has been used as a masculine first name since the 16th century. It was used as a first name in families which had married into families with the surname Evelyn. The original surname probably developed from Avi, an Old German name introduced to England at the time of the Norman Conquest as Aveline. Not often used for boys in the 20th century since the same spelling has been taken over as a popular variation of the feminine name Eveline *q.v.*

Example: Evelyn Waugh, 1903–1966, English novelist.

EVERARD
Origin/meaning: Old German 'strong as a boar'.

393

This is the form of the name introduced into England by the Normans who adapted many of the Teutonic names to the sounds of their own language. Although used as a first name in the Middle Ages it survived more successfully as a surname.

Variations: Everett, Ewart.

Example: Sir John Everett Millais, 1829–1896, English painter.

EWAN
Origin/meaning: Old Scots/Old Irish 'young warrior'.

An English form of the Scots name Euan *q.v.*

EZEKIEL
Origin/meaning: Hebrew 'God is strong'.

This is the name of one of the Old Testament prophets and also of one of the Books of the Old Testament. It came into use in the 17th century among Puritans who rejected the names of Catholic saints. It is now rare even in the US, where it was once popular. However the short form, Zeke, is now well-established there as an independent first name, though it is uncommon in other English-speaking countries.

Variations and abbreviations: Ezechiel (Fr/Ger/Dut), Ezechiele (It), Ezequiel (Sp), Zeke.

EZRA
Origin/meaning: Hebrew 'help'.

A Biblical name used by 17th century Puritans in England and New England. Ezra was a prophet who lived in the 5th century BC. His name was given to one of the Books of the Old Testament. It never came into general use.

Variations: Esra (Ger).

Example: Ezra Pound, 1885–1972, US poet.

F

FABIAN
Origin/meaning: Latin. Fabius was a Roman family name, possibly meaning 'bean grower'.

Fabian was mainly used as a surname in England in the Middle Ages, though it presumably started as a Christian name, like surnames of similar origin. It was probably given to honour St Fabiano, one of the early Popes. Shakespeare used the name for a servant of the Countess Olivia in *Twelfth Night*, 1601. The feminine forms are Fabiola, Fabia and Fabiana.

Variation: Fabius.

FARAMOND
Origin/meaning: Old German 'journey protection'.

This name was used by the Normans who introduced it into Britain after 1066. Faramond was said to have been the first King of France.

Variations and abbreviations: Farman, Faramund, Pharamond.

FARQUHAR (pron. Fárkar)
Origin/meaning: Old Scots 'friendly man'.

This is used as a first name and, more commonly, as a surname in Scotland. Fearchur was an early Scottish king.

FELIX
Origin/meaning: Latin 'fortunate'.

This is the name of over 50 saints, not all of whom are well documented. However four Popes bore the name as well as St Felix of Dunwich, d.648. He was the apostle of East Anglia who gave his name to the East Anglian town of Felixstowe. It is probably his fame which accounts for the use of the name in the Middle Ages. It is still used today although it is rather unusual.

Variations and abbreviations: Félicité (Fr), Félix (Fr), Felice, Feliciano (It).

Examples: Félicité de Lamennais, 1782-1854, French philosopher.

Felix Mendelssohn, 1809-1847, German composer.

Felix Aylmer, 1889-1979, English actor.

FERDINAND

Origin/meaning: Old German 'journey venture' ie. 'adventurer'.

This Teutonic name was taken to Spain by the invading Goths, where it became a firm favourite. It was strongly associated with royalty, an example being Ferdinand of Aragon, 1452-1516, husband of Isabella of Castile and joint founder of a united Spain. Other royal Ferdinands included the Holy Roman Emperors Ferdinand I, 1503-1564, Ferdinand II, 1578-1637, and Ferdinand III, 1608-1657. In England in the Middle Ages the form Ferrand was sometimes used and gave rise to several surnames. Ferdinand itself was never popular. After the 16th century, Protestant Reformation, the name was too closely associated with the Catholic monarchies to ever become widespread.

Variations and abbreviations: Ferd, Ferdi, Ferdy, Fernand (Fr), Fernando (It/Sp), Ferñao (Port), Ferrante (Sp), Hernando (Sp).

Examples: Ferñao Magalhães (Ferdinand Magellan), 1480-1521, Portuguese navigator.

Ferdinand de Lesseps, 1805-1894, French engineer of the Suez Canal.

Fernando Rey, Spanish actor.

FERGUS

Origin/meaning: Old Irish/Old Scots 'choice of man'.

This is generally considered a Scottish name, although there is an Irish version. It gave rise to the Scottish surname Ferguson and is the name of ten Saints.

Variations and abbreviations: Fergie, Feargus (Ir).

Example: Feargus O'Connor, 1794-1855, Irish chartist.

FERRAND

Origin/meaning: Old German 'journey venture' ie. 'adventurer'.

The Medieval English form of Ferdinand *q.v.*

FLORENCE

Origin/meaning: Latin 'in bloom' or 'prosperous'.

Although Florence is now most familiar as a girl's name, in the Middle Ages it was used equally for both boys and girls. In Europe it is still not uncommon for boys but in English-speaking countries it is virtually obsolete, except in Ireland where it continues to flourish. This is because in Ireland it was long used to 'translate' native names such as Fingthin and Flaithri into the acceptable saint's name Florentius. It is therefore used in Ireland as an indigenous name with the variations Flo, Florry and Flurry.

Variations and abbreviations: Fiorenzo (It), Flo, Florens (Ger), Florenz (Ger), Florent (Fr), Florentius (Lat/Dut), Florry.

Example: Florenz Ziegfeld, 1869-1932, US showman, Creator of the Ziegfeld Follies, 1907-1931.

FLORIAN
Origin/meaning: Latin 'flowering'.

A masculine name approximating to Flora or Florence. It was used occasionally in the Middle Ages to honour St Florian, one of the many early Roman martyrs of whom little or nothing is known. By tradition he was the patron Saint of Mercers. Florian is often the name given to Prince Charming in the story Cinderella.

Variations and abbreviations: Florin, Florestan, Floriano (It). See also Florence.

FLOYD
Origin/meaning: Old Welsh 'grey'.

This is an English adaptation of the common Welsh name Lloyd. It is sometimes used as a first name derived from the family name.

Variation: Lloyd.

Example: Floyd Paterson, US Heavyweight Boxer.

FRANCIS
Origin/meaning: Old German 'a Frank'. Medieval Latin 'from France' or 'free'.

The Franks were a Teutonic race who took their name from the franca, a type of javelin. They controlled the area of central Europe which approximates to France and Germany and were at the height of their power when their Emperor Charlemagne was crowned in Rome in 800. They were proud of their independence and their name became synonymous with free-dom. So in the Middle Ages the Latin word for free was francus. The personal name Frank was used throughout Europe in various forms. It described a Frank or someone with Frankish ancestry. The feminine equivalent was Franka. Eventually the Franks split into two separate nations. Those in the area now known as France retained the name and the Latin adjective Franciscus came to mean a Frenchman. This adjective gave rise to a separate name, Francis, which in England superseded Frank as a name, and which used Frank as a familiar form. The name first came into use in Italy in the form Francesco. An early example is the Italian St Francis of Assisi, 1182–1226. Francesco was his nickname (his real name was Giovanni). It was given to him because in his youth he had been pleasure-loving and fond of the songs of French troubadours. The example of his reformed life and the order of mendicant friars which he founded spread rapidly throughout Europe. His nickname soon became accepted as an established saint's name and therefore acceptable as a baptismal name, for he was canonized only two years after his death. The influence of St Francis consolidated a name that had already existed, for others had been given it as a nickname, most probably to indicate French ancestry. Among those who may have contributed to the name's popularity were the magnificent French king, Francis I, 1494–1547, and St Francis Xavier, 1506–1602. However, since both were notable Catholics they may partially account for the fact that in Protestant England it was not much used after the 16th century. It was not until the 19th century that Francis became a popular English name. It is now used consistently in all English-speaking countries.

Variations and abbreviations: Chico (It), Ffransis (Wel), Fran, Francesco (It), Francisco (Sp/Port), François (Fr), Frank, Frankie, Frannie, Frans (Swed), Frants (Dan), Franz (Ger), Franziskus (Ger), Pancho (Sp).

Examples: Sir Francis Drake, 1540–1596, English navigator.
Francisco Franco, 1892–1975, Spanish head of State.
Francesco Petrarch, 1304–1374, Italian poet.
Francis Bacon, Irish Painter.
François Mitterand, French President.

FRANK
Origin/meaning: Old German 'a Frank' Medieval Latin 'from France' or 'free'.

This was a name used well before Francis, to indicate someone of Frankish ancestry or connections. The Franks were the people who settled in the middle of Europe after the collapse of the Roman Empire and gave their name to France (see Francis). Once Francis had become fashionable in England in the 16th century Frank was rarely given as an independent name, but was used as a short form of Francis. The feminine form in documents was Franka, but in practice the usual feminine form was also Frank and it was used as a short form of the feminine Frances. Frank has recently come back into favour as an independent name.

Variations and abbreviations: Franc (Fr), Franco (Ir/Sp), Franck (Ger/Fr), Frankie, Franklin (Ger/Fr), Franz (Ger).

Examples: Franco Zeffirelli, Italian film director.
Frank Wedekind, 1864-1918, German dramatist.
Frank Lloyd Wright, 1869-1959, US architect.

FRANKLIN
Origin/meaning: Old German 'a Frank' Medieval English 'free citizen'.

The Frankish tribes prided themselves on their liberty and independence. Their name became a Latin word for free (francus) and Franklin, a diminutive of Frank, was the medieval word for a free man. One of Chaucer's Canterbury Tales is *The Franklyn's Tale*, c.1390. The word became a surname and has in the last 100 years come full circle as a first name given because it is a family name. It is particularly popular in the US where it honours Benjamin Franklin, 1706-90, the US statesman who helped formulate the Declaration of Independence.

Variations and abbreviations: see Frank/Francis.

Example: Franklin D. Roosevelt, 1884-1945, 32nd President of the US.

FRANZ
Origin/meaning: Old German 'a Frank' or 'free'.

A German familiar form of Frank and Francis (Franziscus) used frequently as an independent name.

Examples: Franz Kafka, 1883-1924, German writer.
Franz Liszt, 1811-1886, Hungarian-born composer.

FLETCHER

Origin/meaning: Old French 'arrow-maker'.

This is a family name sometimes used as a first name.

Example: Fletcher Christian, ringleader of the mutiny on the Bounty, 1789.

FRASER

Origin/meaning: French 'strawberrier'.

This common Scottish surname comes from the Norman surname de Fresel, a place in France. Since this sounds like 'fraise' the French word for strawberry, the name took on the pun meaning. The name came into use as a first name in the 19th century when aristocratic surnames were fashionable. It is the surname of several Scottish aristocratic families.

Variation: Frazer.

Example: Frazer Hines, English actor.

FRED

Origin/meaning: Old German 'peace'.

A short form of names beginning or ending with Fred, eg Frederick *q.v.* or Alfred.

Examples: Fred Zimmerman, US film producer.
Fred Trueman, English cricketer.

FREDERICK

Origin/meaning: Old English/Old German 'peace-rule'.

The -rick part of this name is the same word that is found in Richard and in words like *rex* (the Latin word for king), and *reich* (the German word for kingdom). Although the name is found in its Latin form Fredericus, before the Norman Conquest, it was not popular in Britain until the 18th century. It was brought to England by the Hanoverians from Germany, where it had long been popular. George II gave the name to his eldest son. Its royal credentials were impeccable; it was the name of three kings of Prussia including Frederick the Great, 1712–1786, who was the founder of Prussia's and Germany's military might. Four other Prussian kings bore the double name Frederick-William. Nine Danish kings were also called Frederick. One, Frederick VIII, 1843–1912, was the brother of Alexandra the popular wife of the Prince of Wales, later Edward VII. This may have boosted the popularity of the name in Britain, together with the marriage of Queen Victoria's daughter the Princess Royal, to Frederick III of Prussia, who had progressive liberal ideas. It therefore became one of the most common English names but since the Second World War has been regarded as rather old-fashioned.

Variations and abbreviations: Federico (It), Federigo (Sp), Ferry (Med Eng), Fred, Freddie, Freddy, Frédéric (Fr), Frederic, Frederich, Frederik (Dan/Dut), Fredric, Fredrick, Friedrich (Ger), Fritz (Ger), Rick, Rickie, Ricky, Rik.

Examples: Frederick Forsythe, English novelist.
Frédéric Chopin, 1810–1849, Polish composer and pianist.
Fred Astaire (Frederic Austerlitz), US dancer and actor.
Frederic Raphael, British writer.

FRITZ
Origin/meaning: Old German 'peace-rule'.

A German short form of Frederick *q.v.* frequently given as an independent name.

Example: Fritz Lang, 1890–1976, German film-maker.

FULKE
Origin/meaning: Old German 'the people'.

This was a name brought to England from Europe by the Normans, who adapted many Teutonic names. Although not uncommon in the Middle Ages it became virtually obsolete from the 17th century. It is still used by the Greville family and the Earls of Warwick.

Variations and abbreviations: Fawke, Fulcher, Fulk.

Example: Sir Fulke Greville, 1554–1628, English poet.

G

GABRIEL
Origin/meaning: Hebrew 'strong man of God'.

In the Book of Enoch it says there are seven archangels. Gabriel, with Michael and Raphael is one of the three actually named in the Bible. He was the one chosen to announce the coming birth of John the Baptist to his father, Zacharias the Priest, and to announce to the Virgin Mary the coming birth of Christ. The name was used in the Middle Ages but survived more successfully as a surname. In the 18th century the short form Gaby, was used to mean a simpleton. In Europe it was always more popular as a feminine name, especially in Germany and Austria. Gabriella and Gábrielle are now becoming increasingly popular feminine names in English-speaking countries.

Variations and abbreviations: Gabby, Gabe, Gabriele (It), Gavrilo (Russ).

Examples: Gabriel Fauré, 1845–1924, French composer.
Gabriele D'Annunzio, 1863–1938, Italian poet.

GAIUS
Origin/meaning: from the Roman family name Gaius/Caius, derived from the verb 'to rejoice'.

Rare today in English-speaking countries, this name is still found in Wales as Cai or Kay.

Variations and abbreviations: see Kay.

GALAHAD
Origin/meaning: uncertain. Usually given as Welsh 'battle hawk' to tie in with the similar Gawain q.v.

It may also be from another, unknown source since the tale of Sir Galahad unlike many other Arthurian legends, did not originate in Wales. Sir Galahad was the son of Elaine and Sir Lancelot, who deserted her (see Elaine). He grew up to be the

402

only knight pure enough in thought and deed to successfully complete the search for the Holy Grail. The name has occasionally been used since Tennyson rewrote the Tales of King Arthur as *Idylls of the King*, 1859–1872.

Variation: Galaad. See also Guinevere.

GANESH (pron. Ganess)

Origin/meaning: Sanskrit 'head of the Ganas'. (The Ganas are demi-gods who wait on Shiva.)

This is a very popular name in India because the god it honours is very popular. He is the god of wisdom and patron of the arts, more or less the equivalent of the Greek goddess Athena. Businessmen and bankers also honour him and he is frequently invoked to take away difficulties. Ganesh is the second son of Shiva *q.v.* and Parvati *q.v.* According to legend he died and Shiva ordered him to be given the head of the first animal to appear, in order to bring him back to life. That animal chanced to be an elephant and so he is always depicted as elephant-headed. Along with his new head Shiva gave him the name Ganesh.

Variations: Ganapati, Ganesha.

GARETH

Origin/meaning: either Old German 'hard-spear' (from Gerard) or Welsh 'gentle'.

Gareth is yet another character from the tales of King Arthur and his Knights of the Round Table. Since the source of many of these adventures was in the tales handed down by the Welsh bards and collected in *The Mabinogion* it is usually assumed the name is Welsh in origin. However the story of Gareth may equally have originated in Celtic France. It was never a common name even in the Middle Ages. Tennyson used it for Gareth and Lynnet, 1872, in one of the episodes of his *Idylls of the King*, based on the Arthurian legends. It has been used from time to time since, usually in a Welsh context. A more modern Welsh name, Garth, is assumed to be a short form.

Variations and abbreviations: Garrett, Garth, Gary, Gerard. See also Guinevere.

Examples: Gareth Edwards, Welsh Rugby player.
Gareth Thomas, Welsh actor.

GARMON (pron. with a hard 'G')
Origin/meaning: Latin 'a German'.

The Welsh form of the name German/us *q.v.* St Garmon is the patron saint of Powys.

Variations and abbreviations See German.

GARRET
Origin/meaning: Old German 'spear-hard'.

This is both a first name and surname form of Gerard *q.v.* It is most common in Ireland.

Variations and abbreviations: See Gerard.

Example: Dr Garret Fitzgerald, Prime Minister of Eire.

GARTH
Origin/meaning: Welsh 'high-land' or a form of Gareth *q.v.*

This is the name of several mountains in Wales and is used as a Welsh name. It may also be a modern short form of Gareth *q.v.* The name was used in Florence Barclay's novel *The Rosary*, 1909, and was the name of a comic strip hero who appeared for many years in the *Daily Mirror*. Both of these may have accounted for its use in recent years.

GARY
Origin/meaning: Old German 'spear'.

A short form of Gerald and Gerard *q.v.* through the form Garret. Also used as a form of Gareth (Welsh 'high mountain').

Examples: Gary Cooper, 1901–1961, US film star.
Gary Crosby, entertainer son of Bing Crosby.
Gary Player, South African golfer.

GASTON
Origin/meaning: French 'from Gascony'.

This name was not infrequent in the Middle Ages, when areas of France often shared the same ruler as England and many names were common to both countries. The name was famous because of Gaston, Lord of Claros. Like Roland and Oliver he was a

Frankish hero and one of the Paladins of the Holy Roman Emperor Charlemagne, 742–814. The name is still common in France but is now rare in English-speaking countries.

Variations and abbreviations: Gascon, Gastone (It).

Example: Gaston Doumergue, 1857–1937, first Protestant President of France.

GAVIN
Origin/meaning: uncertain. Usually given as Welsh 'hawk of the plain'.

A medieval form of Gawain *q.v.* still used in Scotland. It is currently very popular in Australia and North America.

Example: Gavin Maxwell, 1914–1969, British author (*Ring of Bright Water*).

GAWAIN
Origin/meaning: uncertain. Usually given as Welsh 'hawk of the plain' – 'little hawk'. Possibly also Old German 'tribute' or 'partition of land'.

Sir Gawain is one of the best established of the characters in the Tales of King Arthur and his Knights of the Round Table. He appears in all the early sources, including the collection of Welsh folk tales *The Mabinogion*. This has reinforced the idea that the name is Welsh and was originally Gwalchmai, with gwalch meaning hawk. Sir Gawain was nicknamed 'the courteous'. His famous adventures with the Green Knight are found only in the English version of the stories. The name is currently popular in the form Gavin.

Variations and abbreviations: Gauvaine, Gavin, Gawayne, Gawen, Gawin, Gwion.

GAYLORD
Origin/meaning: Old French 'merry', 'high-spirited'.

This is a surname derived from the French word gaillard. In the US it has become an established first name which is used without any family connections.

Variations and abbreviations: see Eugene.

Example: Gaylord Hauser, US nutritionist and cookery writer.

GENE

Origin/meaning: Greek 'noble', 'well-born'.

This is the usual short form of Eugene q.v. in the US, where it is frequently found as an independent name.

Variations and abbreviations: see Eugene.

Examples: Gene Kelly, US dancer/actor.
Gene Wilder, US actor.

GEOFF

Origin/meaning: Old German 'district-peace' or 'traveller-peace'.

A short form of Geoffrey (Jeffrey) sometimes used as an independent name.

GEOFFREY

Origin/meaning: Old German. Uncertain. Probably 'district-peace'. Sometimes given as 'traveller-peace'.

A common medieval name, similar to Godfrey and often used interchangeably with it, although they have slightly different meanings. The alternative spelling is Jeffrey. Its early popularity is evident from the many surnames such as Jeffreys, Jepherson, Jepson, Jeeves, which derive from it. Like many other medieval names it was revived in the 19th century after several centuries of comparative obscurity.

Variations and abbreviations: Geoff, Geoffroi (Fr), Geoffroy (Fr), Jeff, Jeffrey.

Examples: Geoffrey Chaucer, 1345–1400, English poet.
Geoffroi de Villehardouin, 1160–1213, French historian of the Crusades.
Geoffrey Household, English novelist.

GEORDIE

Origin/meaning: Greek 'farmer'.

A diminutive form of George used in parts of the North of

England and Scotland. It has come to mean a native of the area round Newcastle-on-Tyne.

GEORGE

Origin/meaning: Greek 'farmer'.

St George was a Roman officer martyred at Lydda in 303 for his adherence to the Christian faith. He was venerated throughout the Eastern church (he is the Patron Saint of Greece as well as England) and the centre of his cult was in Palestine where he was martyred. Norman English Crusaders, returning from the Holy Land, introduced his cult into England, especially since they believed he had interceded on their behalf at the battle at Antioch, 1089. Many Medieval English churches were dedicated in his honour, but surprisingly the name was not much used on a personal level. In 1349 Edward III dedicated his new order of chivalry, the Order of the Garter, to St George, thus more or less officially designating him as the Patron Saint of England. In 1415 he was proclaimed Protector of England and the English flag is the red cross of St George. However it was not until the accession of the Hanoverian King George I in 1714 that the name started to become generally popular. By 1830 when George IV died there had been a King George on the British throne for 116 years, and George had become a standard name to rank with Thomas, John, William and Henry. In the US it might have been expected that George would be an unacceptable name because of the revolution against George III, but of course one of the chief architects of that revolution, and the first US President, was George Washington, so the name flourished there as well. Since the Second World War George has declined rapidly along with other familiar names like Frederick, Albert and Ernest.

Variations and abbreviations: Dod, Doddy, Geordie, Georg (Ger), Georges (Fr), Georgie, Georgy, Giorgio (It), Jöran (Swed), Jorge (Sp), Jörgen (Dan), Seiorse (Ir), Siôr (Wel), Yorick, Yuri (Russ).

Examples: George Bernard Shaw, 1856–1950, Irish writer.
George Frederick Handel, 1685–1759, German–English composer.
George Harrison, English musician, member of the Beatles.
Yuri Gagarin, 1934–1968, Russian cosmonaut.

GEORGIE

Origin/meaning: Greek 'farmer'.

A diminutive of George.

Example: Georgie Fame, English musician.

GERAINT (pron. Gerrighnt or Jerrighnt)
Origin/meaning: Greek 'old'.

Like several other Welsh names this is based on a Roman name and dates from the Roman occupation of Britain. It survived in the Celtic areas, especially Wales and Cornwall, which were unconquered by the Saxons who invaded most of England bringing their Teutonic names with them. The original is probably the Roman name Gerontius. The name is found in the collection of Welsh Celtic tales, *The Mabinogion*, on which many of the tales of King Arthur and his Knights of the Round Table are based. Tennyson used the tale of Enid and Geraint as one of the episodes in his own blank verse re-telling of those tales – *Idylls of the King*, 1859. This made the name Geraint known outside Wales although it is still a primarily Welsh name.

Example: Geraint Evans, Welsh opera singer.

GERALD

Origin/meaning: Old German, 'spear-rule'.

This Teutonic name was adopted by the Normans who introduced it into England in 1066. It was used in the Middle Ages in England but eventually died out. It survived better in Ireland where it was the surname of one of the best-known families, the Fitzgeralds, Earls of Kildare. The name was re-introduced into England in the 19th century when there was a revival of interest in medieval names. Gerald is now well-established in all English-speaking countries. It is sometimes confused with Gerard *q.v.* which is similar in meaning and origin.

Variations and abbreviations: Gary, Gearalt (Ir), Géralde (Fr), Gerold (Ger), Gerrie, Gerry, Giraldo (It), Giraud (Fr), Jerold, Jerrie, Jerry.

Examples: Gerald du Maurier, 1873–1934, British actor-manager.
Gerald Kaufmann, British politician.
Gerald Durrell, British zoologist and writer.

GERALLT

Origin/meaning: Old German 'spear-rule'.

This is the Welsh form of Gerald *q.v.* It is pronounced with a hard G. Gerallt Cymro (Gerald the Welshman) was a grandson of Nest *q.v.* He helped raise Welsh volunteers for the Third Crusade.

Variations and abbreviations: See Gerald.

GERARD
Origin/meaning: Old German 'spear-hard'.

This is a similar name to Gerald and the two are often confused. It was more popular than Gerald in the Middle Ages and gave rise to several surnames including Garrard and Garret. The latter is also used as a first name variation. In Wales the name is sometimes confused with the native Gareth. It shares the same short forms as Gerald including Gary, which has become one of the most popular post war names in Britain and the US.

Variations and abbreviations: Gary, Garry, Garret, Gearard (Ir), Geraud (Fr), Gerardo (Sp/It), Gerhard (Ger/Scand), Gerhardt (Ger), Gerrard, Gearoid, Gerry, Jerry.

Examples: Gerard Manley Hopkins, 1844–1889, English poet. Dr Gerard Vaughan, British politician.

GERMAN
Origin/meaning: Latin 'a German'.

Although used by one or two English priests before the Conquest, this name was widely introduced into England by the Normans. It was given in the Middle Ages to honour three saints: Germanus of Auxerre, 378–448, a French saint who helped the Britons in a battle against the Picts and Saxons; St Germanus of Paris, 496-576, who, like Saint Genevieve attempted to prevent the Franks from being excessively cruel to the natives of Paris, and St Germanus of Constantinople, 634–733. The surname form Jarman is still common today and sometimes used as a first name. The name has survived most successfully in France where it takes the form Germain.

Variations and abbreviations: Garmon (Wel), Germain (Fr), Germano (It), Germanus (Latin), Jarman, Jermyn.

GERSHOM
Origin/meaning: Hebrew 'bell'. Sometimes given as 'stranger'.

A Biblical name given to the first born child of Moses and Zipporah. Nowadays it is used mainly by Jewish people but in the 17th century it was popular with Puritans who mined the Bible for names untainted by Catholic associations.

Variation: Gersham.

GERVASE
Origin/meaning: uncertain. Possibly Old German 'spear' plus Celtic 'servant' (as in vassal).

St Gervase was an early martyr whose remains with those of St Protase, were discovered in Milan in 386 after St Ambrose had received a vision which prompted him to search for them. Because of the circumstances of their discovery a cult grew up around them and Gervase became a popular name which was brought to England by the Normans in 1066. Nowadays it is an unusual name.

Variations and abbreviations: Gervais, Gervaise (Fr), Gervasio (It), Gervaso (It), Gervasius (Ger), Jaruis.

GIDEON
Origin/meaning: Hebrew 'destroyer', 'tree feller'.

A Biblical name of one of the Judges of Israel. It was a popular Puritan name and still survives in the US and France.

Variations and abbreviations: Gedeon, Gédéon (Fr), Gedeone (It).

GILBERT
Origin/meaning: Old German 'bright pledge'.

The Normans introduced this name into England and it was a great favourite in the Middle Ages. Like all popular names it led to many surnames including Gibbon and Gibson, from the short form Gib. In Scotland it 'translated' the native Gilbride which means servant of St Bridget. St Gilbert of Sempringham, 1085-1189, was the founder of the only English religious order, the Gilbertines, which was disbanded by Henry VIII.

Variations and abbreviations: Bert, Bertie, Berty, Gib, Gibb, Gil, Gilberto (It), Gilbrecht (Ger), Gill, Giselbert (Ger), Giselbrecht (Ger).

Examples: Gilbert (G.K.) Chesterton, 1874-1936, English writer. Gilbert Bécaud, French singer.

GILES

Origin/meaning: uncertain. Usually given as Greek 'kid' therefore 'youthful'.

This name has a rather complicated history. The Latin name Aegidius was said to be taken from the Greek word for a kid. The name reached France early on, probably before the 9th century because of St Aegidius, a Greek hermit so named because he wore a goat skin. He was said to have fled to France to pursue a solitary life. The French adapted the name to Gide and then Gilles which is the form in which it reached England in the 12th century. By that time St Gilles (Aegidius) was the centre of a flourishing cult based around Saint-Gilles, near Arles, where he had lived. The main story attached to him was saving the life of his pet hind, which was being hunted by King Wamba, by taking it in his arms and being shot himself. St Giles was the Patron Saint of beggars and cripples. Many churches in Britain and Europe were dedicated to him, including the Cathedral of Saint Giles in Edinburgh. The name itself has not been used as much as might have been expected given the Saint's following. For a long time it had a distinctly rustic image and country people were often given the joke title 'Farmer Giles'.

Variations and abbreviations: Aegidius, Egide (Fr), Egidio (It), Egidius (Dut), Gide, Gil (Sp/Ger), Gill (Ger), Gilles (Fr), Gyles.

Examples: Giles Fletcher, 1588–1623, English poet.
Giles Cooper, 1918–1966, English playwright.

GLENN

Origin/meaning: Celtic 'valley', 'glen'.

This, like the Welsh form Glyn, is a name which has become increasingly popular in all English-speaking countries since the Second World War. It probably began in the US as a family name used as a first name. It has also been used to honour John Glenn, the first American to orbit the earth in the Mercury space capsule in 1962.

Variations: Glen, Glyn (Wel), Glynn.

Example: Glenn Miller, 1904–1944, US bandleader and composer.

GLYN

Origin/meaning: Welsh 'valley' or possibly a short form of Glyndwr (Glendower).

A popular Welsh name now also fairly common outside Wales, probably because of its short 'masculine' sound.

Variations: Glenn (Scots/Ir), Glynn.

Examples: Glyn Thomas, Welsh writer.
Glyn Houston, Welsh actor.

GODFREY
Origin/meaning: Old German/Old English 'God's peace'.

The original English form of this name was absorbed by the version introduced by the Normans in the 11th century. It is similar to Geoffrey *q.v.* with which it is often confused.

Variations and abbreviations: Godefroi (Fr), Godofredo (Sp), Golfredo (It), Gottfrid (Scand), Gottfried (Ger).

Examples: Godfrey Tearle, 1884–1953, British actor.
Godfrey of Bouillon, 1061–1100, Crusader.
Sir Godfrey Kneller, 1646–1723, German-born painter.

GODWIN
Origin/meaning: Old English 'God friend'.

One of the handful of Old English names which survived the influence of Norman names, after the Conquest. The best known example was Godwin, Earl of Wessex, whose daughter Edith married Edward the Confessor.

Variations: Godin, Goodwin.

GORDON
Origin/meaning: uncertain. Possibly Scots Gaelic 'by the great hill'.

A Scottish place name which became the surname of one of the most famous Scottish clans, the Gordons. It came into use as a first name in the 19th century when aristocratic surnames were fashionable as personal names. In Britain it was often given to honour General Gordon, 1833–1885, a distant relative of the Scottish Dukes of Gordon. He was remembered as the hero who died defending Khartoum against the troops of the Mahdi. In North America and Australia the name has been much used by families of Scottish descent.

Variations and abbreviations: Gorden, Gordie, Gordy.

Examples: Gordon Jackson, Scottish actor.

George Gordon Noel, Lord Byron, 1788–1824, English poet.

GORONWY (pron. Gorónwee)
Origin/meaning: Welsh 'hero'.

A popular Welsh first name, but rarely used outside Wales.

Variations and abbreviations: Gronow, Gronw, Ronw.

GRAHAM
Origin/meaning: Old English 'gravelly homestead' or 'from Grantham'.

This name was taken to Scotland in the Middle Ages by an Anglo-Norman nobleman and is now fundamentally a Scottish surname. It came into use as a first name in the 19th century when many surnames were adopted as first names. It has proved most popular in Britain and Australia but is rare in the US.

Variations and abbreviations: Graeme, Grahame, Grame.

Examples: Graham Greene, English writer.
Graham Sutherland, 1903–1980, English painter.

GRANT
Origin/meaning: French 'tall'.

This is a surname which began as a nickname. It came into use as a first name in the 19th century when surnames were much used as first names. In the US it was used to honour General Ulysses S. Grant, 1822–1885, the 18th President and hero of the Civil War.

GRANVILLE
Origin/meaning: French 'from the large town'.

A surname based on a French place name in Normandy. It became widespread in the 19th century when surnames were popular as first names, probably because of its aristocratic connections (the Earls of Granville).

Variations: Grenfell, Grenville.

Example: Harley Granville Barker, 1877–1946, English actor and playwright.

GREG
Origin/meaning: Old Scots 'fierce' or Greek 'watchful' (a short form of Gregory q.v.).

413

Greg(g) is not only a first name but a surname which can be derived from either the Scottish or Greek source. Modern use as a personal name may well be the result of the tendency, particularly in the US, to use family names as personal names.

Variations: Gregg, Greig, Griff.

Example: Greg Chappell, Australian cricketer.

GREGOR
Origin/meaning: Greek 'watchman'.

A Scots form of Gregory q.v. which also developed into the surname MacGregor. It is also the German form of the name Gregory.

Variation: Gregour (Med Eng). See also Gregory.

GREGORY
Origin/meaning: Greek 'watchman'.

This is a name which has many associations with the Orthodox and Catholic churches. In the East it was given particularly to honour St Gregory of Nazianzen, 329–389, a prominent theologian and St Gregory of Nyssa, 335–395, a bishop and theologian. These two were instrumental in defeating the Arian heresy. In the Western church there were sixteen Popes who used the name. The best known in England is the first, St Gregory the Great, 540–604, who sent St Augustine to England to convert the Anglo-Saxons after having seen fair-haired Saxon boys on sale in the Slave market of Rome.

The Normans introduced Gregory as a Christian name into England but its strong Catholic connections caused it to lose favour after the 16th century Reformation.

It was fairly common in the US and Australia after the Second World War.

Variations and abbreviations: Greer (Eng), Greg, Gregg, Grégoire (Fr), Gregor (Scots/Ger), Greggor (Dut), Gregorio (Sp/It), Gregorius (Dut/Ger), Grigori (Russ).

Examples: Gregory Peck, US actor.
Grigori Rasputin, 1871–1916, Russian monk who held sway over the Tsarina before the revolution.

GRIFFITH
Origin/meaning: Old Welsh 'lord'.

414

This is the English spelling of the Welsh Gruffudd q.v. Often found as a surname outside Wales it has also become more usual as a first name because of the increasing tendency to use family names as personal names.

Variations and abbreviations: Griff, Griffin. See also Gruffudd.

Example: Griffith Jones, Welsh actor.

GROVER
Origin/meaning: Old English 'dweller in the grove'.

An English surname used as a first name in the US because of Stephen Grover Cleveland, 1837–1908, who was twice President.

GRUFFUDD (pron. Griffuth)
Origin/meaning: Welsh 'lord'.

This is popular in Wales and is also a common surname. It has been Anglicized as Griffith.

Variations and abbreviations: Griff, Griffin, Griffith (Eng), Gruffydd, Gutun, Guto.

Example: Griff Rhys Jones, Welsh actor.

GÜNTER
Origin/meaning: Old German 'hardy in war'.

A name introduced into England by the Normans and now more familiar in English-speaking countries as a surname. A vogue name in German-speaking countries in the 20th century.

Variations and abbreviations: Gunnar (Scan), Gunner, Gunt (Fr), Gunther (Ger).

Examples: Gunther Sachs, German socialite.
Günter Grass, German-born writer.

GUSTAVE
Origin/meaning: Old German 'staff of the Goths'.

This name was never much used in England but was introduced into the US in the 19th century by Swedish immigrants. The powerful Swedish King Gustavus Adolphus (Gustaf Adolf), 1594–1632, made the name well known in Europe through his successes in the Thirty Years War.

Variations and abbreviations: Gus, Gustav (Ger), Gustave (Fr), Gustavo (It), Gustaf (Swed), Gustaff (Dut).

Examples: Gustav Mahler, 1860–1911, Czech–Austrian composer.
Gustave Courbet, 1819–1877, French painter.

GUY
Origin/meaning: Old German, uncertain, possibly 'wood' or 'wild' or Latin 'life'.

The Latin meaning was added in the Middle Ages because there was no St Guy to make it an acceptable Christian name. Guy was therefore associated with St Vitus because of the similar sound to the German form of Guy – Wido. The meaning of Vitus is 'alive'. In France St Vitus's dance is known as St Guy's dance. Guy, Earl of Warwick was a legendary hero of the Middle Ages, in love with Phelis the Fair. He had to succeed in many doughty deeds to win her hand. Among his exploits were rescuing the daughter of the Emperor of Germany, slaying the giants Amarant and Colbrand and killing a black dragon in Northumberland. He ended his days as a hermit. From the 12th century to the 15th century the name was popular, perhaps because of the legendary Earl, and was often found in the forms Guido and Wido. Many surnames developed from it including Guise, Gyatt and Wyatt. However the attempt by Guy Fawkes, 1570–1606, to blow up James I in the Houses of Parliament placed the name firmly out of fashion in Britain. In the 19th century it was reintroduced by writers of the Romantic Movement such as Sir Walter Scott in his novel *Guy Mannering*, 1815, and has survived, although it has never been particularly common.

Variations and abbreviations: Guido (Fr/Ger/It/Sp), Vito (It), Vitas, Wido (Ger).

Examples: Guido Gezelle, 1830–1899, Flemish poet.
Guy Carleton, 1st Baron Dorchester, 1724–1808, British administrator and Governor of Quebec.
Guy de Maupassant, 1850–1893, French writer.
Guido di Pietri (Fra Angelico), 1387–1455, Italian painter.

GWALLTER
Origin/meaning: Old German 'rule-people'.

The Welsh form of Walter *q.v.*

GWERN
Origin/meaning: Old Welsh 'alder trees'.

This is the name of the son of Branwen *q.v.* and the Irish king Matholwch. His story is told in the collection of Welsh bardic tales *The Mabinogion.* He was thrown onto the fire by Efnisien.

GWILYM
Origin/meaning: Old German 'helmet of resolution'.

The Welsh form of William *q.v.* It is used as a first name and as a surname.

GWYN
Origin/meaning: Welsh 'white/fair' or 'good'.

A short form of names like Gwynfor or an independent name. It may also be used as a surname. The feminine is usually differentiated by the spelling – Gwen.

Variations and abbreviations: Gwynn, Gwynne, Wynne.

H

HABIB
Origin/meaning: Arabic 'beloved'.

A name found in all Muslim countries.

HACON
Origin/meaning: Old Norse 'useful'.

This is a pre-Conquest name introduced into England by the Danish invaders. It survived into the Middle Ages. It is now rare in Britain but familiar in Scandinavia, especially Norway where it has been used by seven kings.

Variations and abbreviations: Haakon, Hakon (Ger), Håkon (Scand).

Example: Haakon VII of Norway, 1872–1957, leader of Norwegian war-time resistance.

HAL
Origin/meaning: Old German 'home-ruler'.

This was the most usual pet form of Henry for many hundreds of years. King Henry VIII was known to his people as Good King Hal. It is still used today but less frequently than in the Middle Ages.

Variations and abbreviations: See Henry.

HALDANE
Origin/meaning: Old English 'half-Dane'.

A name which recalls the Danish invasions of Britain in the 9th and 10th centuries. It is most common as a surname but occasionally used as a first name.

HALLAM
Origin/meaning: Old Norse 'from the rocky place'.

A surname from the North of England, this was introduced as a first name by Tennyson. His greatest friend had been Arthur

Hallam, after whom he named his own son Hallam. Arthur Hallam's early death in 1843 prompted one of Tennyson's greatest works *In Memoriam*, 1850. The success of the poem caused others to use the name. Hallam is still a name used by the Tennyson family.

Example: Hallam Tennyson, English producer and broadcaster.

HAM
Origin/meaning: Hebrew 'hot'.

The name of Noah's second son (Genesis 10:1) Occasionally used since the 17th century period of Biblical names.

HAMISH
Origin/meaning: uncertain. Usually given as 'supplanter'.

The English spelling of Seumas, the Scottish form of James *q.v.* The equivalent of the English spelling Shamus for the Irish Seamus.

Variations and abbreviations: See James.

HAMO
Origin/meaning: Old German 'home'.

A name introduced by the Normans and still used occasionally today. The common surname Hammond derives from it. Shakespeare's only son Hamnet, b.1585, was named after a godfather whose surname it was. However the play *Hamlet* is based on a quite separate name, Amleth, who features in a 12th century history of Denmark by Saxo Grammaticus. The fact that Hamlet is also an English surname derived from Hamo is purely coincidental.

Variations and abbreviations: Hamlet, Hamnet, Hamon.

Example: Sir Hamo Thornycroft, 1850–1925, English sculptor.

HANIF
Origin/meaning: Arabic 'true believer'.

This is a Muslim name, found in North Africa.

HANK
Origin/meaning: Old German 'home ruler'.

A familiar form of Henry confined almost entirely to the US.

Variations and abbreviations: See Henry.

Example: Hank Marvin, British guitarist, with 'The Shadows'.

HAROLD
Origin/meaning: Old English/Old Norse 'army power'.

This Old English name died out in its original form after the influx of new names which arrived with the Normans in 1066. Symbolically it was King Harold who was killed by William the Conqueror's invaders at the battle of Hastings. However the name survived successfully in its other native land, Norway, where three kings bore the name. When, as a result of the Romantic movement, old names were revived in the 19th century, Harold appeared in a form similar to the native Norwegian Harald.

Variations and abbreviations: Araldo (It), Errol (Eng), Harald (Scand), Harry, Herold (Dut).

Examples: Harold Robbins, US writer.
Harold Macmillan, former British Prime Minister.
Harold Lloyd, 1893–1971, US silent film comedian.

HAROUN
Origin/meaning: Arabic 'exalted'.

A common Muslim name in North Africa.

Variation: Harun.

Example: Haroun Al Raschid, 763–809, Caliph of Baghdad. His court was the centre of Muslem culture and attracted scholars throughout the world. Legends about him were perpetuated through the *Tales of the Arabian Nights*.

HARRY
Origin/meaning: Old German: 'home-ruler'.

In the last 100 years this has been used as a familiar form of Henry. However in the Middle Ages Harry and Henry were equally correct versions of the name. In the last few years Harry has again been used in England as an independent name and not as a pet name. The wide use of the name can be deduced from the expression 'every Tom, Dick and Harry' meaning everybody.

Variations and abbreviations: See Henry.

Examples: Harry Belafonte, US singer and actor.
Sir Harry Lauder, 1870–1950, Scottish comic singer.
HRH Prince Harry (Henry) second son of the Prince and Princess of Wales.

420

HARTLEY
Origin/meaning: Old English 'deer meadow'.

This is an English surname which comes from several places called Hartley. In the 19th century it was one of many surnames which were adopted as first names.

Example: Hartley Coleridge, 1796–1849, English writer, son of S. T. Coleridge.

HARVEY
Origin/meaning: Celtic French 'battle worthy' or Old German 'warrior in battle'.

This is a name introduced by the Normans. It may have been accepted because of its similarity to a Saxon name Harvig. Harvey developed most successfully as a surname when these became common in the 13th and 14th centuries. In the 19th century it was one of many surnames which were revived as first names. There is a German, feminine form, Herwiga.

Variations: Herve (Fr), Hervey, Herwig (Ger).

Example: Harvey Smith, British showjumper.

HASAN
Origin/meaning: Arabic 'handsome'.

A version of this name is found in all Muslim countries.

Variations: Hasani, Husani (E Africa).

HECTOR
Origin/meaning: Greek 'steadfast'.

In Greek legend Hector was a Trojan hero, the son of Priam and Hecuba. He was killed by the Greek Achilles, who added unnecessary insult to the injury by dragging his body three times round the walls of Troy. Although the name is a familiar one it is rare in English-speaking countries. In Scotland it is sometimes used to 'translate' the native Eachdonn (horseman).

Variations: Ector (Fr), Ettore (It).

Example: Hector Berlioz, 1803–1869, French composer.

HEMCHANDRA (pron. Hemchandr)
Origin/meaning: Sanskrit 'golden moon'.

The last *a* is silent. This is the masculine equivalent of Hema.

HENRY

Origin/meaning: Old German 'home-ruler'.

This name was introduced into England by the Normans in the form Henri. In England Henry and Harry developed simultaneously but, although Harry was probably more used, Henry is usually assumed to be the slightly more formal version. It has never gone completely out of fashion in any European country and is well established in North America and Australia.

Variations and abbreviations: Arrigo (It), Enrico (It), Enrique (Sp), Hal, Hank, Harry, Heindrick, Heinrich (Ger), Heinz (Ger), Hendrik (Dut/Scand), Henne (Scand), Henri (Fr), Henrik (Scand).

Examples: Henry Kissinger, US politician.
Henry James, 1843–1916, US novelist.
Henrik Ibsen, 1828–1906, Norwegian dramatist.

HERBERT

Origin/meaning: Old English/Old German 'bright army'.

This Saxon name was a favourite of the Normans who brought over their own version of it after the Conquest. Like many early names it was rediscovered in the 19th century. Its popularity was also aided by the fact that Herbert was the aristocratic surname of a family which had arrived with the Conqueror. So the name also fell into the same category as Howard, Percy and Cecil which were then becoming fashionable. It has been regarded as old-fashioned since the Second World War.

Variations and abbreviations: Aribert (Fr), Ariberto (It), Bert, Bertie, Berty, Erberto (It), Harbert, Haribert, Hebert, Herb, Herbiberto (Sp), Herbie.

Examples: Herbert Hoover, 1874–1964, 31st US President.
Sir Herbert Beerbohm Tree, 1853–1917, English actor-manager.
Herbert (H.G.) Wells, 1866–1946, English writer.

HEREWARD

Origin/meaning: Old English 'army protection'.

This Saxon name survived beyond the Norman Conquest because of the fame of Hereward the Wake. He was a Lincolnshire nobleman who held the Isle of Ely against the advance of William the Conqueror in 1070–1071. The name was one of those revived in the 19th century because of the influence of the Romantic Movement. Charles Kingsley's novel *Hereward the Wake*, 1866, helped to make it widely known but it is a rare name today.

HERMAN

Origin/meaning: Old German 'army man'.

This name was introduced into England by the Normans. It is unusual today in English-speaking countries but still popular in Germany where it was one of many medieval names revived in the 19th century. Armin is one of the forms which developed in England.

Variations and abbreviations: Armand (Fr), Armin (Eng), Ermanno (It), Haro, Hermann (Ger).

Examples: Herman Melville, 1819–1891, US novelist (*Moby Dick*).
Herman Hesse, 1877–1962, German writer.

HEW

Origin/meaning: Old German 'understanding' or 'thought'.

A form of Hugh *q.v.*

HEZEKIAH

Origin/meaning: Hebrew 'God is strong'.

Hezekiah was an 8th–7th century BC king of Judah. The name was used by Puritans on both sides of the Atlantic in the 17th–18th century period of Biblical names. It is now rare.

HILARY

Origin/meaning: Medieval Latin 'cheerful'.

This medieval name shares the same form as the feminine version as many masculine names did in the Middle Ages. It was popular enough in England to become a surname. However its popularity was greatest in France where it was given to honour St Hilary (Hilaire) of Poitiers, 315–367. He was a leading opponent of the Arian heresy which said that Christ was not God. His feast day is January 14th and the first law and university term of the year is known as the Hilary term because of this (see Michael). Hilary was revived in the 19th century with many other medieval names but has been more successful as a girl's name in the 20th century.

Variations and abbreviations: Hilaire (Fr), Hilar (Ger), Hilario (Sp/Port), Hilarius (Dut/Ger/Scand), Ilario (It).

Example: Hilaire Belloc, 1870–1953, Anglo-French writer.

HILDEBRAND
Origin/meaning: Old German 'war sword'.

This was the real name of Pope Gregory VII, 1020–1085, who struggled to free the Church from political interference. He was hounded by the Emperor Henry IV and died in exile. The name was revived in the 19th century by the High Church Movement which favoured the names of early saints. It is still used occasionally today and is fairly common in Germany.

Variations and abbreviations: Hilbrand, Ildebrando (It).

HILTON
Origin/meaning: Old English 'the place on the hill'.

A surname from the North of England occasionally used as a first name.

HIPPOLYTUS
Origin/meaning: Greek 'unfettered horse'.

This was the name in Greek mythology of the son of Theseus, King of Athens and Hippolyta, the queen of the Amazons. He was dragged to death when the horses pulling his chariot bolted and later restored to life by Esculapios. Its occasional use as a Christian name is due to St Hippolytus of Rome, d.235, a theologian and martyr. It has never been common but seems to have been most successful in France.

Variations and abbreviations: Hippolyt (Ger), Hippolyte (Fr), Ippolito (It).

Example: Hippolyte (Paul) Delaroche, 1797–1856, French painter.

HIRAM
Origin/meaning: uncertain. Sometimes given as Hebrew 'my brother is high'.

Hiram was the king of Tyre, the Lebanese sea-port. Lebanon was famous for its cedars which Hiram supplied to King David and King Solomon, to build the temple in Jerusalem. The name was popular in the US in the 19th century but is now regarded as old-fashioned.

Abbreviations: Hi, Hy.

Example: Sir Hiram Maxim, 1840–1916, English-US inventor (of a machine gun and a flying machine).

HOB
Origin/meaning: Old German 'fame bright'.

An old short form of Robert q.v. from which surnames like Hobbes and Hobson developed.

HOMER
Origin/meaning: Greek 'pledge' or 'hostage'.

The name of the Greek epic poet, author of the *Odyssey* and the *Iliad*, is occasionally used as a first name.

Variations and abbreviations: Homère (Fr), Homerus (Dut/Ger), Omero (It).

HORACE
Origin/meaning: Latin, from Horatius, the name of a famous Roman clan.

This French form of Horatius became an alternative form of the name in England, together with Horatio. It is now the more usual form.

Variations and abbreviations: See Horatio.

Examples: Horace Walpole, 4th Earl of Orford, 1717–1797, English writer, son of Sir Robert Walpole, Prime Minister.
Horace Mann, 1796–1859, US educationist.
Horace Greeley, 1811–1872, US editor and politician, founder of the *New Yorker* and *New York Tribune*.

HORATIO (pron. Horáysheeo)
Origin/meaning: Latin, from Horatius, the name of a famous Roman clan.

This is a form of the name more familiar in English-speaking countries as Horace. The two forms are directly interchangeable and were often used for the same person. Horatio probably arrived in England from Italy in about the 16th century when the Renaissance had stimulated interest in classical culture and therefore in classical names. Shakespeare has a character called Horatio in his play *Hamlet*, 1600. The Roman family produced many remarkable people, including Publius Horatius Cocles, a hero who defended single-handed the bridge across the Tiber into Rome against the invading Etruscans; and the poet Quintus

Horatius Flaccus, better known in England as Horace, 65–8 BC. The name was used by the distinguished Walpole family. One of these was godfather to Admiral Nelson, 1758–1805, the hero of the Battle of Trafalgar, who was named Horatio after his godfather.

Variations and abbreviations: Hod, Horace (Fr/Eng), Horacid (Sp/Port), Horas, Horatius, Horaz (Ger), Horry, Orazio (It).

Examples: Horatio Greenough, 1805–1852, US sculptor.
Horatio Kitchener (Kitchener of Khartoum), 1850–1916, English soldier and statesman.

HOWARD
Origin/meaning: either Old German 'brave thought' or Middle English 'hayward' (the guardian of the animal enclosure).

This name developed in the Middle Ages into a surname, most notably of the Earls of Norfolk, hereditary Earls Marshal of England. When aristocratic surnames came to be adopted as personal names in the 19th century, Howard proved an immediate favourite. It has remained popular probably because of its simple 'manly' sound when others, such as Percival, have waned.

Variations and abbreviations: Howey, Howie.

Examples: Howard Keele, US actor/singer.
Howard Hughes, 1905–1976, eccentric US business tycoon and film-producer.

HOWELL
Origin/meaning: Welsh 'eminent'.

An Anglicized spelling of the Welsh Hywel q.v. now like Powell (ap Hywel) a not uncommon surname in England.

Variations and abbreviations: See Hywel.

HUBERT
Origin/meaning: Old German/Old English 'bright thought'.

Hubert is similar in meaning to Hugh and Howard. It was a popular medieval name, perhaps because of St Hubert, d.727. A legend grew up about him that he was converted to Christianity by finding a stag with a cross between its antlers. He therefore came to be considered the Patron Saint of hunters and trappers. One English form of the name, Hubbard, is recalled in the children's rhyme, Old Mother Hubbard. Hubert was revived in the 19th century when medieval names again became popular. It is still used today but is uncommon.

Variations and abbreviations: Bert, Bertie, Berty, Hubertus (Dut/Ger), Huberto (Sp/It), Hugbert (Ger), Oberto (It), Uberto (It).

Examples: Hubert van Eyck, 1370–1426, Flemish painter.
Hubert Horatio Humphrey, 1911–1978, US Vice-President.

HUGH

Origin/meaning: Old German 'understanding' or 'thought'.
This was a name introduced by the Normans into Britain, although a similar Celtic name, Huw q.v. already existed. The original German Hug(o) was both an independent name and an element of several other common German names (Hugbald, Hugdietrich). The English Hugh is pronounced like the Medieval French Hue but the spelling reflects the German/Latin Hugo.

In France the name had become popular because of Hugh Capet, 938–996, founder of the 3rd Frankish dynasty, and two saints, Hugh of Cluny, 1024–1109, and Hugh of Grenoble, 1053–1132. In England the name was given to honour St Hugh of Lincoln, 1135–1200, a vigorous supporter of the common people against injustice. The name is still much used today and the old form Hugo is currently back in favour.

Variations and abbreviations: Hew, Huey, Hughie, Hugo (Ger/Latin), Hughes (Fr), Huw (Wel), Ugo (It).

Examples: Ugo Betti, 1892–1954, Italian dramatist.
Sir Hugh Casson, British artist and architect
Gerald Hugh Tyrwhitt-Wilson, 14th Baron Berners, 1883–1950, British composer and novelist.

HUGO

Origin/meaning: Old German 'understanding' or 'thought'.

This German Latin form of Hugh was used in England in the Middle Ages and is coming back into favour in the 1980s.

Example: Hugo Morley-Fletcher, British antiques expert.

HUMBERT

Origin/meaning: Old German 'bright (famous) son'.

Although occasionally used in Germany and England this name

427

is most popular in Italy in the form Umberto.

Variations and abbreviations: Humbrecht (Ger), Umberto (It).

Examples: Umberto Nobile, 1885–1980, Italian airman and explorer.
Umberto I, 1844–1900, King of Italy.
Humbert Humbert, hero of Nabokov's novel, *Lolita*, 1959.

HUMPHREY
Origin/meaning: Old German 'peace-son' usually given as 'protector'.

This was an extremely popular medieval name. The German Hunfried came to England with the Normans in the form Onfroi but the Medieval English spelling was usually Humfrey. A familiar form was Dumphrey and Humphrey Dumphrey is the origin of the nursery rhyme character Humpty Dumpty. Having once been an aristocratic name it went into decline and when used was usually associated with peasants and farmers. In the 19th century it was one of many medieval names revived as part of the general interest in medieval culture.

Variations and abbreviations: Humfrid (Scand), Humfried (Ger), Humfry, Humph, Hunfredo (Sp), Onfroi (Fr), Onofrio (It).

Examples: Humphrey Atkins, British politician.
Humphrey Bogart, 1899–1957, US film actor.

HUNTER
Origin/meaning: Old English 'huntsman'.

A common Scottish surname, used since the 19th century as a first name, especially in the US.
Example: Hunter Davies, English journalist.

HUW
Origin/meaning: Celtic 'fire'.

This Welsh name is now usually assumed to be the same as the Old German. Hugh *q.v.* The two names are now used interchangeably although their origins and meanings are really separate.

HYACINTH
Origin/meaning: Greek 'hyacinth flower' or 'a red precious stone'.

In Greek mythology, Hyacinth was a beautiful boy loved by the

428

sun god Apollo and Zephyr the West wind. Because Hyacinth preferred Apollo, Zephyr, in a fit of jealous rage, blew Apollo's quoit at the boy's head and killed him. However Apollo assured his immortality by turning the drops of his blood into the flowers which bear his name. Hyacinth is also the name given to a blood red precious stone such as a zircon or garnet. Although a pre-Christian name it was used as a baptismal name to honour the Roman St Hyacinth, martyred by fire with St Protus. Hyacinth was never much used in England but was more common in other European countries and had a minor revival after the discovery of the tomb and charred remains of St Hyacinth in the cemetery of Basilla in 1845. In English-speaking countries Hyacinth has recently been used as a girl's name as a result of the 19th century fashion for flower names. The original feminine form was Jacintha *q.v.*

Variations and abbreviations: Giacinto (It), Hyacinthe (Fr), Hyazint, Hyazinth (Ger), Hyacinthus (Dut), Jacinto (Sp).

Examples: Hyacinthe Rigaud, 1659–1743, French portrait painter. Jacinto Benavente, 1866–1954, Spanish playwright.

HYMAN
Origin/meaning: Hebrew 'life'.

This is primarily a Jewish name. It is the English form of Chaim and in English-speaking countries is often found as a surname.

Variations and abbreviations: Chaim, Hayyim, Hy, Hymie, Mannie, Manny.

HYWEL (pron. Howell)
Origin/meaning: Welsh 'eminent'.

A popular Welsh first name. Hywel Dda (Hywel the Good), d.950, was one of the most famous Welsh Kings. Through marriage his rule extended over the whole of South Wales. On the death of his cousin Idwal, 943, he became ruler of North Wales as well. During his reign Welsh law was first codified. In Medieval Wales this original code of law was expanded and known as the Law of Hywel the Good. Hywel has given rise to several surnames which are found in English-speaking countries. One of these, Powell, is a contraction of Ap Hywel, which means son of Hywel.

Variations and abbreviations: Hoel (Celtic Fr), Howel (Eng), Howell (Eng), Powell.

Example: Hywel Bennet, British actor.

I

IAGO
Origin/meaning: uncertain. Possibly Hebrew 'supplant'.

The Spanish and Welsh form of Jacob/James q.v. from the Latin version Jacobus. Iago causes the destruction of Othello in Shakespeare's play.

IAIN
Origin/meaning: Hebrew 'Jehovah has favoured'.

An alternative, and slightly more authentic spelling of Ian, the Scots form of John. Unlike Ian this version is still found mainly in Scotland.

Variations and abbreviations: See John.

Example: Iain Cuthbertson, Scottish actor.

IAN
Origin/meaning: Hebrew 'Jehovah has favoured'.

The Scottish form of John q.v. often used without any Scottish connection. The more correct spelling is Iain.

Variations and abbreviations: See John.

Examples: Ian Smith, former Prime Minister of Rhodesia (now Zimbabwe).
Ian Carmichael, English actor.

IDRIS
Origin/meaning: Old Welsh 'fiery lord'.

Id- is a part of many Welsh names such as Idno and Idwal. It means lord and derives from the older form iud. It is the same word that is found as -udd on the end of other Welsh names like Gruffudd. Idris is one of the most popular Welsh names but it does not have an English form. In Wales there has been increasing interest in names which have no English forms. Others such as Ifan (English version Evan) and Gruffudd (English version Griffith) are less highly regarded by people who wish to nurture Welsh culture. In Welsh legend Idris Gawr (the giant) was a magician, philosopher and astronomer who had his observatory on the mountain Cader Idris (seat of Idris). Where piles of stones and rocks are found for no apparent reason they are said to have been dropped by giants like Idris or Rhitta Gawr, who is said to have been killed by King Arthur because he had tried to take his beard!

IFOR (pron. Eevor)
Origin/meaning: Old Celtic 'lord'.

A name related to other Welsh names beginning with Id- or ending with -udd, both of which mean lord in Welsh. Ifor is the Welsh Celtic version of a name found in slightly different forms in the other Celtic areas, including Cornwall and Brittany. The Cornish Saint Ifor gave his name to the little town of Saint Ives. Sometimes confused with Ivo *q.v.*

Variations and abbreviations: Ifar, Ives, Ivor (Eng).

IGNATIUS
Origin/meaning: uncertain. Possibly Latin 'fiery'.

This was originally a Greek name which may have been interpreted as fiery because of the similarity to the Latin word ignis- fire. In the Eastern Church it was popular because of St Ignatius, Bishop of Antioch who was martyred about AD 114. The name was also found in Spain and belonged to a vigorous leader of the counter-reformation St Ignatius Loyola. He was the founder of the Jesuits and because of him the name became widespread. Since it is often given to honour him it is still regarded as a predominantly Catholic name.

Variations and abbreviations: Enesco, Enego, Ignace (Fr), Ignacio (Sp), Ignaz (Ger), Ignazio (It), Inigo.

Example: Ignace Paderewski, 1860–1941, Polish pianist and patriot.

ILLTYD
Origin/meaning: Old Welsh 'ruler'.

This name, which is found in several variations, was popularized in Wales because of the fame of St Illtyd who lived about the end of the 5th century. He was a learned abbot who founded a monastic school. Many other saints were his pupils there. His monastery was destroyed at the time of the Norman Conquest.

Variations and abbreviations: Illtud, Illtut.

Example: Illtyd Harrington, British politician.

IMMANUEL
Origin/meaning: Hebrew 'God with us'.

The Old Testament spelling of Emanuel q.v.

Example: Immanuel Kant, 1724–1804, German philosopher.

INGMAR
Origin/meaning: Old Norse/Old German 'famous Ingvi'.

A Scandinavian name, one of many containing the name of the hero-god Ing orIngvi. Ingmar is rarely found outside Scandinavia and areas with a large population of Scandinavian origin.

Variations and abbreviations: Ingemar, Ingo. See also Ingram and the feminine names Inge and Ingrid.

Example: Ingmar Bergman, Swedish film director.

INGRAM
Origin/meaning: Old Norse/Old German 'Ingvi's raven'.

Ingvi or Ing was a hero of the Teutonic (Germanic) tribes who spread throughout Northern Europe including Britain. He may have given his name to the Angles who were one of the tribes which invaded Britain, and he therefore may be the source of the name England. The raven was considered a mystical bird. The name Ingram was brought to England by the Normans and eventually established itself as a surname rather than a first name. It is again being used as a first name now that family names are commonly used as personal names. Names beginning Ing are common in Germany and Scandinavia.

INIGO
Origin/meaning: uncertain. Possibly Latin 'fiery'.

A form of Ignatius q.v. familiar because of the first great English architect Inigo Jones, 1573–1652, who introduced the Palladian style of architecture into England.

INNOCENT

Origin/meaning: Latin 'harmless' 'innocent'.

Rare in England-speaking countries but found throughout Europe. It is usually used by Catholics since it was the name of thirteen Popes.

Variations and abbreviations: Innocente (It), Innocentius (Ger/Dut), Innocenzo (It), Innozenz (Ger).

IOLO

Origin/meaning: uncertain, possibly Greek 'downy', ie 'unbearded', 'youthful'.

Commonly assumed to be the Welsh form of Julius *q.v.* The Roman influence in Britain extended to Wales where Roman names became merged with native Welsh names so that it becomes difficult to be sure which came first. Since Wales, like the other Celtic areas of Britain, was relatively free from Anglo-Saxon or Viking influence, the names were not swamped by new names of Teutonic (Old German) origin. Other names which may have survived in Wales from the time of the Romans include Emrys (Ambrosius), Gladys (Claudia) and Owen (Eugenius). Sometimes used as a short form of Iorwerth.

Variations and abbreviations: see Julius and Iorwerth.

Example: Iolo Morgannwg, Welsh bard.

IORWERTH

Origin/meaning: Old Welsh 'worthy lord'.

This is usually used as the Welsh equivalent of Edward *q.v.*

Variations and abbreviations: Iolo, Iorath, Yorath (Eng).

IRA

Origin/meaning: Hebrew 'watchful' or Aramaic 'stallion'.

A Biblical name adopted by the Puritans in the 17th century. It survived most successfully in the US but is now becoming rare and is sometimes assumed to be a girl's name.

Examples: Ira Gershwin, 1896–1983, US lyricist, brother of composer George Gershwin.
Ira Levin, US author.

IRVING

Origin/meaning: uncertain. Possibly Old English 'sea friend' or 'green river'.

A surname derived from an English place-name. It has become a popular 20th century first name in the US, particularly among Jewish people.

Example: Irving Berlin, US song writer.

ISAAC
Origin/meaning: uncertain. Possibly a non-Hebrew name. Usually given as Hebrew 'laughter'.

Abraham's wife Sarah was past the age of child-bearing when she gave birth to Isaac her first child. The name is usually supposed to refer to her laughter of joy. The name was popular for a while with 17th century Puritans when the preferred spelling was Izaak. It is rarely used now.

Variations and abbreviations: Ike, Ikey, Isaak (Ger/Dut), Isacco (It), Izak, Izaak.

Examples: Sir Isaac Newton, 1642–1727, English scientist and mathematician.
Izaak Walton, 1593–1683, English writer (*The Compleat Angler*).
Isak Dinesen, 1885–1962, pen name of Danish novelist, Baroness Kara Blixon.

ISIDOR
Origin/meaning: uncertain. Possibly Greek 'gift of Isis' (an Egyptian god).

This is an ancient Greek name borne by two notable Spanish Saints. One was Isidore the farm servant, 1070–1130, who was canonized for his exemplary life-style and is the Patron Saint of Madrid. The other was Bishop Isidore of Seville, a notable scholar. These two account for the popularity of the name, and its feminine equivalent Isadora, in Spain. Elsewhere the name seems mainly to be used by Jewish people.

Variations and abbreviations: Dory, Isador (Ger), Isidoro (It), Isidro (Sp), Izzy.

Example: Izzy Bonn, British music-hall comedian.

ISRAEL
Origin/meaning: Hebrew 'ruling with the Lord'.

The new name given to Jacob by God when he promised him he

would found a new nation (Genesis ch.35, vs. 10 and 11). The name was taken by the Jewish nation and is now used exclusively by Jewish people although in the 17th and 18th centuries it was sometimes used by Puritans.

Examples: Israel Putnam, 1715–1790, American general at Bunker Hill.
Israel Zangwill, 1864–1926, Jewish writer.

IVAN
Origin/meaning: Hebrew 'Jehovah has favoured'.

The Russian form of John *q.v.* used by six notable Russian Grand Dukes and Tsars.

Variations and abbreviations: *see* John.

Examples: Ivan Lendl, Czech tennis player.
Ivan Turgenyev, 1818–1883, Russian novelist.

IVO
Origin/meaning: Old German 'yew'. Sometimes by connotation 'yew-bow' or 'archer'.

An English name from the Old German word Iv, through the Old French forms Ives and Ivon. It came to England with many other French names at the time of the Norman Conquest. The French form Ives, was particularly popular in the Celtic areas of Normandy and Brittany at that time and is still found in France as Yves *q.v.* Sometimes confused with Ivor *q.v.* because of the variation Ives which the two names share.

Variations and abbreviations: Ia, Ivon, Ives, Yves (Fr), Yvon (Fr).

IVOR
Origin/meaning: Old Welsh 'Lord'.

The English version of the Welsh Ifor *q.v.* a name found, in several forms, in all Celtic areas.

Variations and abbreviations: Ifar (Wel), Ifor (Wel), Ivar, Iver, Ives, Yvor.

Examples: Ivor Novello, 1893–1951, Welsh musical comedy star and writer.
Ivor Emmanuel, Welsh singer.

J

JABEZ

Origin/meaning: uncertain. Possibly Hebrew 'Because I bore him in sorrow'.

This name occurs in the First Book of Chronicles, ch.4. It was a popular Puritan name both because of the meaning and because Jabez is granted great prosperity by God. It has fallen into disuse as Biblical names have gone out of fashion.

JACK

Origin/meaning: Hebrew 'Jevovah has favoured'.

This is a long established familiar form of John from the medieval form Jankin. In the 20th century it has been much used as an independent name.

Variations and abbreviations: Jackie, Jacko (Scots), Jacky. See also John.

Examples: Jack Nicklaus, US golfer.
Jackie Stewart, Scottish motor racing champion.

JACKSON

Origin/meaning: Middle English 'son of Jack'.

An English surname derived from the familiar form of John and therefore the exact equivalent of Johnson. It came into use as a first name along with many other surnames in the 19th century. In the US it was often given to honour General Andrew Jackson, 1767–1845, a military hero and 7th President.

Example: Jackson Pollock, 1912–1956, US surreal and abstract artist.

JACOB

Origin/meaning: uncertain. Possibly Hebrew 'supplanter'.

Both James and Jacob come from the same Hebrew name Aqob. In the Greek translation of the Bible this became Iacobos which was retranslated later into Latin first as Jacobus and then as Jacomus. In several European countries, as well as England, this led to two slightly different versions of the same name. In England Jacob and James, in Italy Jacopo and Giacomo and in Spain Jacobo and Jaime. When the Bible was translated into English in the 16th century, Jacob was used for the Old Testament character to distinguish him from the New Testament apostles St James the Great and St James the Less. (Just as Miriam and Mary are really the same name.) In the Middle Ages Jacob was used almost exclusively by Jewish people. In the 17th century Protestants, anxious to find names without Catholic connotations, brought Jacob into more widespread use. They named their children after the patriarch Jacob who tricked his father Isaac into giving him the elder son's blessing intended for Esau by covering his hands with goat's skin to feel like his hairier brother (Genesis 26-60). Jacob's new name, Israel, was to become the name of the entire Jewish race and eventually of their country. In the 20th century Jacob is less popular in English-speaking countries than James.

Variations and abbreviations: Cob, Cobb, Giacobbe (It), Giacobo (It), Giacopo (It), Jacobo (Sp), Jake, Jakie, Jakob (Ger).

Examples: Sir Jacob Epstein, 1880–1959, British/Russian sculptor.
Jacob Grimm, 1785–1863, German folklorist and writer.
Jacopo Robusti (Tintoretto), 1518–1594, Venetian painter.

JAKE
Origin/meaning: uncertain. Possibly Hebrew 'supplanter'.

A Medieval English form of Jacob/James possibly from the French form Jacques, which the English pronounced Jakes.

Variation: Jaikie.

Example: Jake Thackeray, English singer.

JAMES
Origin/meaning: uncertain. Possibly Hebrew 'supplanter'.

James is the form of the Hebrew name Aqob which was used by translators of the New Testament. Jacob q.v. was used for the Old Testament. The two forms of the name had developed in most European languages because there were two Latin forms, Jacobus and Jacomus. The English version James, was probably based on the Spanish Jaime, itself a development of the Italian Giacomo. It was brought back by pilgrims to the famous shrine at Compostella in Spain where the remains of the apostle St James the Great were said to be buried. By the 13th century it was a well-established name in England and also in Scotland, where it was the name of seven kings. The accession in 1603 of one of these, James I and VI, in succession to Queen Elizabeth brought about a period of great popularity for the name. It is currently one of the most used masculine names in English-speaking countries.

Variations and abbreviations: Diego (Sp), Giacomo (It), Hamish (Anglo-Scots), Iago (Sp/Wel), Jacques (Fr), Jago (Cornish), Jaime (Sp), Jake, Jamey, Jamie, Jay, Jayme (Sp), Jem, Jemmy, Jim, Jimi, Jimmie, Jimmy, Seamus (Ir), Seumas (Scots), Shamus (Anglo-Irish).

Examples: James Joyce, 1882–1941, Irish writer.
Captain James Cook, 1728–1779, English navigator and explorer of Australasia.

JAMIE
Origin/meaning: uncertain. Possibly Hebrew 'supplanter'.

A Scottish familiar form of James q.v. currently popular as an independent name in Britain.

Variations and abbreviations: see James.

JAN
Origin/meaning: Hebrew 'Jehovah has favoured'.

An English regional form of John. Also a form found in European countries such as Holland and Poland and as a short form of the German version of John – Johannes.

JAPHET
Origin/meaning: uncertain. Possibly Hebrew 'extender'.

This is the name of one of the sons of Noah. It has occasionally been used since the 17th century period of Biblical names.

Variation: Japheth.

JARED
Origin/meaning: Hebrew 'descent'.

A Biblical name used occasionally since the 17th century mainly in the US.

JARMAN
Origin/meaning: Latin 'a German'.

This is a form of the name German(us) *q.v.* It is most commonly found as a surname.

JARVIS
Origin/meaning: Old German 'spear' plus Celtic 'servant'.

A form of Gervase *q.v.* usually found as a surname but sometimes used as a first name.

Variations and abbreviations: see Gervase.

JASON
Origin/meaning: uncertain. Sometimes given as Greek 'healer'.

This is a Biblical name, which came into use in the 17th century. It is a rendering of the name Eason which occurs in Acts 17 vs.5-9 and St Paul's Epistle to the Romans ch.16. The English form was presumably influenced by the name of Jason the Greek mythological hero. However since Paul refers to Jason as his kinsman it seems likely that the Biblical name was not the Greek one but a quite different name, and probably Hebrew in origin. It was rather a vogue name in Britain in the 1960s.

Example: Jason Robards, 1893–1963, US actor.

JASPER
Origin/meaning: uncertain. Possibly Persian. Sometimes given as 'treasurer' because of the legend of the three wise men.

The names traditionally given to the three wise men who brought gifts to the infant Jesus are Caspar, Melchior and Balthazar. These names became current in the Middle Ages, although they do not appear in the Bible. Jasper is the English version of Caspar *q.v.* It is rarely heard now but Caspar is beginning to become more common.

Variations and abbreviations: Caspar, Gaspar (Sp), Gaspard (Fr), Gaspare (It), Jesper (Scand).

Example: Jasper Conran, English dress designer.

JAY
Origin/meaning: Old French 'jay'.

The name of this common European bird has been used as an English surname since the Middle Ages. It may have been applied initially to someone with either the jay's beauty or its characteristic of endless chattering. In the 20th century it has been used, mainly in the US, as a first name. Jay is sometimes

used as a short form of names beginning with the letter J.
Example: Bruce Jay Friedman, US writer.

JED
Origin/meaning: Hebrew 'beloved of the Lord'.

This is a short form of the Biblical name Jedidiah, a name used for King Solomon. The original is now obsolete, but Jed has become quite a common independent name in the US.

JEFF
Origin/meaning: Old German 'district peace' or 'traveller peace'.

A short form of Jeffrey (Geoffrey) *q.v.* Sometimes used as an independent name.

In the US Jeff may also be a short form of Jefferson *q.v.*

JEFFERSON
Origin/meaning: Medieval English 'son of Jeffrey.'

This is a common English surname which developed in the surname period of the 13th and 14th centuries from the popular name Jeffrey. It has been given in the US as a first name since the beginning of the 19th century to honour Thomas Jefferson, 1743–1826, the third President.

Abbreviation: Jeff.

JEFFREY
Origin/meaning: uncertain. Probably Old German 'district-peace'. Sometimes given as 'traveller-peace'.

An alternative spelling of Geoffrey *q.v.* a common medieval name which is again popular today.

Example: Jeffrey Archer, English writer.

JEHANGIR
Origin/meaning: Sanskrit 'conqueror of the world'.

A Muslim name. Jehangir, 1569–1627, was the third Mogul Emperor of India. His father was Akbar *q.v.* Jehangir was a weak ruler, who was addicted to opium. His real interests were literature and art and it was he who laid out the famous Shalimar gardens in Kashmir. He is buried in a mausoleum built in the gardens. During his reign the government was effectively run by Nur Jehan *q.v.* his remarkable wife.

Variation: Jahangir.

JEM

Origin/meaning: uncertain. Possibly Hebrew 'supplanter'.

An old short form of James from a medieval form Jeames. The word jemmy (a burglar's tool) is said to derive from it. It has now been superseded by the more modern Jim/Jimmy.

Variation: Jemmy. See also James.

JEREMIAH

Origin/meaning: Hebrew 'God is high'.

This is the name of an Old Testament prophet who lived 650–585 BC. He foresaw the fall of Assyria, the bondage of Judah to Egypt and Babylon and the fall of Jerusalem. A book of the Old Testament is given over to his depressing prophecies. Not surprisingly the word Jeremiah became a synonym for complaint. The name was taken from the Greek form Jeremias when the Authorized version of the Bible was translated in the early 17th century. Both Jeremiah and Jeremias were popular among 17th/18th century Puritans in England and North America and have survived fairly well. The native English form Jeremy *q.v.* which was used in the Middle Ages, was almost unknown until very recently in the US. It is regarded there as a modern variation.

Variations and abbreviations: Geremia (It), Jere, Jeremias (Ger/Dut/Sp), Jérémie (Fr), Jeremy (Eng), Jerry.

Examples: Jeremiah Clarke, 1659–1707, English composer of the Trumpet Voluntary.
Jeremiah Dummer, 1645–1718, American silversmith.

JEREMY

Origin/meaning: Hebrew 'God is high'.

This is the native English form of the name of the prophet Jeremiah. It developed in the Middle Ages from the Greek/Latin Jeremias which was used in documents to render the name later translated in the 17th century authorized version of the Bible as Jeremiah. After the 17th century Jeremy and Jeremiah were both used in England but the form Jeremiah, preferred by the Puritans, became the accepted form in the US. Since the Second World War Jeremy has become a fashionable name in Britain and has become more widely known in North America and Australia.

Variations and abbreviations: see Jeremiah.

Examples: Jeremy Bentham, 1748–1832, English writer on jurisprudence and ethics.
Jeremy Clyde, British actor.
Jeremy Irons, British actor.

JERMYN
Origin/meaning: Latin 'a German'.

A form of German *q.v.*

JEROME
Origin/meaning: Greek 'sacred name'.

Jerome is the English form of the Greek name Hieronymous. This became an acceptable Christian name in the Middle Ages because of St Eusebius Sophronius Hieronymous, 342–420, known in England as St Jerome. He was an ascetic and one of the greatest Biblical scholars. His translations of the Hebrew and Greek writings of the Old and New Testament into Latin formed the main part of the Latin Vulgate Bible, accepted as the orthodox version by the Catholic Church. In the Middle Ages the name was used throughout Europe to honour the great Saint. It is now considered a rather unusual name in English-speaking countries.

Variations and abbreviations: Gerome, Geronimo (It), Gerrie, Gerry, Hieronymus (Dut/Ger), Jérôme (Fr), Jerry.

Examples: Jerome K. Jerome, 1859–1927, English humorous writer, author of *Three Men in a Boat*.
Jerome Kern, 1885–1945, US songwriter.
Hieronymus Bosch, 1460–1516, Dutch painter.

JESSE (pron. Jessy)
Origin/meaning: Hebrew 'Jehovah exists'.

This is a Biblical name brought into general use after the Reformation when Protestants were anxious to use names not associated with Catholicism. Jesse was the father of King David (I Sam. 16), and therefore the first in the direct family tree of Jesus Christ.

Variations and abbreviations: Jess, Jessie.

Example: Jesse James, 1847–1882, US outlaw of the Wild West.

JETHRO
Origin/meaning: Hebrew 'pre-eminence'.

This Hebrew name may well have begun as a title (cf English names Earl and Prince). The name is found in the Old Testament as the father-in-law of Moses. As a Biblical name it was used by Puritans in England and North America. It is still used today but is rather rare.

Example: Jethro Tull, 1674–1741, English agriculturalist.

JEVAN
Origin/meaning: Hebrew 'Jehovah has favoured'.

This is one of several Anglo-Welsh forms of John. The true native Welsh form of John is Siôn.

Variations: Evan, Owen. See also John.

JIM
Origin/meaning: uncertain. Possibly Hebrew 'supplanter'.

The most usual modern short form of James q.v.

Variations: Jimi, Jimmie, Jimmy. See also James.

Examples: Jimmy Connors, US tennis player.
Jimmy Carter, 39th US President.

JOAB
Origin/meaning: Hebrew 'Jehovah is father'.

A Biblical name used by 17th and 18th century Puritans. It is rare today. Joab was the name of King David's military commander.

JOACHIM
Origin/meaning: Hebrew 'Jehovah has exalted'.

By tradition St Joachim was the father of the Blessed Virgin Mary. Because of this the name was used as a Christian name. It was never popular in England but was reasonably well established in Germany and Italy.

Variations and abbreviations: Achim, Akim, Gioacchino (It), Joaquin (Sp), Jochem, Jochen, Jokum (Scand).

Examples: Gioacchino Rossini, 1792–1868, Italian composer.
Jochen Rindt, Austrian racing driver.

JOB
Origin/meaning: uncertain. Usually given as Hebrew 'persecuted'.

This meaning is derived not from the language itself but from the Old Testament story of Job, who retained his faith in God despite endless misfortunes. The name has been used occasionally since the 17th century period of Biblical names.

JOCELYN
Origin/meaning: Old German 'a man of the Goths'.

Jocelyn was one of many Teutonic names brought to England by the Normans. These names were absorbed by and confused with native Anglo-Saxon names which were very similar because of the similarity between the two languages. Jocelyn was also mixed up with Joyce *q.v.* a Celtic name used in the Middle Ages for both men and women but in the 20th century regarded as a feminine name. In the Middle Ages Jocelyn was not an unusual name, and it gave rise to several surnames including Gosling and Joslin. In the 20th century it is rather rare and tends to be given in families where it has become traditional. It is now being used as a feminine rather than a masculine name, particularly in the US.

Variations: Jocelin, Joscelin, Joss.

Examples: Jocelin de Brakelond, 1155–1215, English Benedictine monk and chronicler.
Jocelyn Brooke, 1908–1966, author (*The Orchid Trilogy*).

JOE
Origin/meaning: Hebrew 'May Jehovah increase'.

The usual English short form of Joseph *q.v.* Sometimes used as an independent name. In Australia a joey is a small kangaroo.

Variations: Jo, Joey. See also Joseph.

Example: Joe Davis, 1901–1978, former English snooker champion.

JOEL
Origin/meaning: Hebrew 'Jehovah is God'.

A Biblical name. Joel was a minor Hebrew prophet in the 5th century BC. A Book of the Old Testament contains his prophecies. The Puritans used the name in the 17th century when Biblical names were used in preference to Catholic Saints' names and it is still used today.

Examples: Joel Gray, US entertainer and actor.
Joel Macrae, US actor.

JOHN

Origin/meaning: Hebrew 'Jehovah has favoured' (via the Latin form Johannes).

An important Christian name since almost a hundred early Saints were called John. Chief among them were of course St John the Baptist and St John the Evangelist. Initially a popular name in the area of the Eastern Orthodox Church, it was popularized in Western Europe by returning Crusaders. Like Anne it is a name which has accounted for a large percentage of all given names in English-speaking countries since the 17th century. It has been marginally less popular in the 20th century. It has equivalents in every European language.

Variations and abbreviations: Evan (Anglo-Wel), Ewan (Anglo-Scots), Ewen, Giovanni (It), Hans (Ger), Iain (Scot), Ian, Jack, Jacky, Jan (Dut/Slav), Janesi, Jean (Fr), Jens (Dan), Jevan (Anglo-Welsh), Jock (Scot), Jocko, Johan, Johann, Johannes (Ger), Johnnie, Johnny, Jon, Jonn, Juan (Sp), Owen (Anglo-Wel), Sean (Ir), Shaughn (Ir), Shaun, Shawn (Anglo-Irish), Siôn (Wel), Zane.

Examples: John F. Kennedy, 1917–1963, assassinated US President.
Jean-Jacques Rousseau, 1712–1778, French philosopher.
Johannes Brahms, 1833–1897, German composer and pianist. ·

JOLYON

Origin/meaning: from the Roman family name Julius possibly meaning 'downy'.

A north country English form of Julian given wider currency by John Galsworthy (1867–1933) in his novel sequence *The Forsythe Saga*, 1920–1934.

Variations and abbreviations: see Julian.

JON

Origin/meaning: Hebrew 'Jehovah has favoured' or Hebrew 'Jehovah gave'.

A short form of either John or Jonathan.

Example: Jon Voight, US film actor.

JONAH

Origin/meaning: Hebrew 'dove'.

Jonah is the Old Testament form of the name Jonas. It was the name of a minor Hebrew prophet. God told him to go to Ninevah and prophesy but he grew frightened and fled by ship. God caused the ship to be wrecked and the enraged sailors threw Jonah into the sea where he was swallowed by a large fish and eventually cast out onto land. Jonah therefore became a name for a person who brings bad luck. The name was sometimes used in the period of Biblical names.

Variation: Jonas.

Example: Jonah Barrington, British squash champion.

JONATHAN
Origin/meaning: Hebrew 'Jehovah gave'.

Jonathan is sometimes confused with the separate name John q.v. They share the short form Jon. The name Jonathan came into use in the 17th century with many other Biblical names. Puritans, looking for names unconnected with Catholic saints, used it to honour Jonathan, the son of Saul and friend of David (First Book of Samuel). The expression 'a David and Jonathan' means two inseparable friends. In the US the expression Brother Jonathan means the US people, perhaps because of Jonathan Trumbull, 1710–1785, the US patriot whose views were always closely consulted by George Washington. In the period following the Second World War Jonathan has become a vogue name in English-speaking countries.

Variations and abbreviations: Gionata (It), Jon, Jonathon, Jonty. See also Datus, Dieudonné, Nathanial, Theodore.

Examples: Jonathan Swift, 1667–1745, Irish clergyman, author of *Gulliver's Travels*.
Jonathan Miller, British theatre director and doctor.

JORDAN
Origin/meaning: Hebrew 'flowing down'.

This is the name of the main river in Palestine. It was possibly introduced as a name by Crusaders returning from the Holy Land in the 11th–13th centuries. It may possibly have echoed an older Old German or Anglo-Saxon name which helped it to become established.

Variations and abbreviations: Giordano (It), Jourdain (Fr).

Example: Giordano Bruno, 1548–1600, Italian philosopher.

446

JOSEPH

Origin/meaning: Hebrew 'may Jehovah increase'.

Joseph was a popular name among the people of Israel who probably gave it to honour the patriarch Joseph. He was the favourite son of Jacob and Rachel whose brothers, envying the coat of many colours which was a sign of their father's favour, sold him into captivity in Egypt. (Genesis ch.30-50.) Joseph was also used in the Middle Ages as a Christian name to honour St Joseph, the husband of the Blessed Virgin Mary, and St Joseph of Arimathea who provided the tomb for Jesus. It was Joseph of Arimathea who is traditionally supposed to have come to England and built a church at Glastonbury. In the 17th century in England and New England Joseph became a favourite name among Puritans, despite its popularity among European Catholics, because it occurs many times in the Old Testament. It is still a frequently used name today.

Variations and abbreviations: Beppo (It), Giuseppe (It), Iossif (Russ), Iossip (Russ), Jo, Joe, Joey, José (Sp), Josef (Ger), Josephus.

Examples: Emperor Josef I of Austria, 1678-1711.
Joseph Addison, 1672-1719, English essayist.
Giuseppe Garibaldi, 1807-1882, Italian patriot.
Joseph Conrad, 1857-1924, Polish/British novelist.
Joseph Cotten, US film actor.

JOSH

Origin/meaning: a short form of either Joshua (Hebrew 'Jehovah saves') or Josiah ('Jehovah supports').

This short form is often used as an independent name in the US.

JOSHUA

Origin/meaning: Hebrew 'Jehovah saves'.

Joshua was the successor of Moses. The 6th Book of the Old Testament tells how he conquered Canaan. It is the translation used in the Old Testament for the name which is given as Jesus in the New Testament (cf also Miriam/Mary and Jacob/James). Joshua was much loved as a name by Puritans on both sides of the Atlantic in the 17th and 18th centuries. The name has survived best in the US but is still used in other English-speaking countries. In Spanish-speaking countries Jesus is also used but elsewhere it is considered too sacred to be given as a personal name.

Variations and abbreviations: Giosué (It), Josh, Josua (Ger), Josué (Fr).

Examples: Sir Joshua Reynolds, 1723–1792, English portrait painter.
Joshua Logan, US film producer/director.
Joshua Nkomo, Zimbabwe politician.

JOSIAH
Origin/meaning: Hebrew 'Jehovah supports'.

Josiah was a king of Judah, 647–608 BC, renowned for his religious reforms. As a Biblical name it was much used in the 17th and 18th centuries but is now rather rare.

Variations and abbreviations: Jos, Josh, Josias.

Examples: Josiah Wedgwood, 1730–1795, English potter.
Josiah Spode, 1733–1769, English potter.

JOSS (E)
Origin/meaning: French Celtic 'champion'.

An early form of Joyce q.v. a medieval name used for both men and women until very recently. The Breton St Judoc was usually known in Britain as St Josse. Joss is the form still used for men while Joyce is now considered almost exclusively feminine. Also a short form of Jocelyn q.v. a name confused with Joyce.

Variations and abbreviations: see Joyce.

Example: Joss (Jocelyn) Ackland, British actor.

JOYCE
Origin/meaning: French Celtic 'champion'.

This is the final English form of the name of the Breton St Judoc(us), d.668. Judoc was the son of King Juthael of Brittany but renounced his wealth and was ordained a priest. He lived as a hermit and after his death his followers claimed that his body remained incorrupt. The name was brought to England in 902 when refugees from St Josse sur Mer where his cult was centred, brought his relics to the newly built Minster at Winchester. In later documents the saint was known as St Judocus, but popularly he was known as St Josse. The name was fairly commonly used in his honour for boys and girls and the popularity of the cult may be deduced from the fact that in Chaucer's *Canterbury Tales*, c.1387–1400, the Wife of Bath uses the oath 'By God and by Seint Joce'. There were several medieval spellings of the name but it was the form Joyce which was revived in the 19th century when medieval names were fashionable. Like Vivian, Hilary and Evelyn, it is now primarily considered a girl's name. The name Jocelyn *q.v.* is sometimes confused with it because it also has the short form Joss.

Variations and abbreviations: Joisse (Med Fr), Jooss (Dut), Joost (Dut), Joss, Josse, Jodoc, Judoc, Judocus.

Example: Joyce Cary, 1888–1957, English novelist.

JUDAS
Origin/meaning: Hebrew 'praise of the Lord'.

The Greek form of Jude and Yehudi. Rarely used because it was the name of the disciple who betrayed Christ.

JUDE
Origin/meaning: Hebrew 'praise of the Lord'.

The Anglicized form of the Jewish name Judah. It is used to distinguish the writer of the Epistle of Jude from Judas Iscariot.

Variations and abbreviations: Jud, Judah, Judas, Judd, Yehudi.

Example: The hero of Thomas Hardy's novel *Jude the Obscure*, 1895.

JULIAN
Origin/meaning: from Julius, a Roman family name, possibly meaning 'downy'.

This is a derivative of Julius *q.v.* which is more common in English-speaking countries than Julius itself. In the Middle Ages, when it was already popular, it was used for boys and girls. The feminine form Juliana did not appear in speech until the 18th century. Julian's popularity was due in part to the great number of saints who bore the name. For the most popular of these, Julian the Hospitaller, there are no historical facts. He was said to have accidentally killed his parents and in expiation went to live by a ford where he and his wife helped poor travellers, one of whom was Christ in disguise. He was patron among many things of travellers, ferrymen, innkeepers and circus entertainers.

Julian has been fashionable in Britain since the Second World War.

Variations and abbreviations: Jolyon, Jules, Julyan.

Examples: Julian Slade, English composer of the musical *Salad Days*.

Jules Janin, 1804–1874, French critic and novelist.

Julian Symons, British thriller writer.

JULIUS

Origin/meaning: From Julius, a Roman family name, possibly meaning 'downy'.

This name is fairly unusual in English-speaking countries where Julian is the preferred form. Gaius Julius Caesar (100–44 BC) is the most famous member of the family and it is in his honour that boys are usually named.

Variations and abbreviations: Giulio (It), Jule, Jules (Fr), Julio (Sp).

Examples: Sir Julius Caesar, 1558–1636, English judge, son of an Italian doctor, Casare Adelmare.

John Julius Norwich, English writer and broadcaster, son of Lady Diana Cooper.

JUMOKE (pron. J'mókhi)

Origin/meaning: Yoruba 'everyone loves the child'.

A Nigerian name that can be used for both boys and girls.

JUSTIN

Origin/meaning: Latin 'just'.

A name borne by two 5th century Byzantine Emperors. Always popular in Ireland where it may possibly 'translate' a native name it has become very fashionable in English-speaking countries since the 1970s.

Variations and abbreviations: Giustino (It), Giusto, Justinian, Justino (Sp), Justinus, Justus, Yestin (Wel).

K

KAMUZU

Origin/meaning: Nguni 'medicinal'.

This name comes from the South of Africa.

Variation: Kamazu.

Examples: Dr Hastings Kamazu Banda, President of Malawi and himself a qualified doctor.

KANE

Origin/meaning: Old Welsh 'beautiful' or Manx 'warrior'.

A widespread Irish surname currently popular as a personal name in Australia.

Variation: Caine.

KANT

Origin/meaning: Sanskrit 'lover'.

This is found as a name in its own right, and also as a typical masculine suffix to a name ending in *a, i* or *e*, eg Suryakant.

KANTI (pron. Kantee)

Origin/meaning: Sanskrit 'sun's rays' or 'beauty'.

Found throughout India but less popular than it used to be.

KARL

Origin/meaning: Old German 'man'.

A form of Charles *q.v.*

Variation: Carl.

Examples: Karl Marx, 1818–1883, political philosopher.
Karl Lagerfeld, German couturier.

KASHYAPA

Origin/meaning: unknown.

This is the name of one of the ancient Hindu saints of India.

KAY
Origin/meaning: from the Roman name Gaius or Caius, 'rejoice'.

This is the English spelling of the Welsh name, Cai. Many Roman names survived in Wales, in native forms, while they were being replaced elsewhere in Britain by Saxon and Viking names. Sir Kay was one of the characters from the Tales of King Arthur and his Knights of the Round Table, who was known for his boastfulness and lack of success.

Variations: Cai (Wel), Caius, Gaius, Kai, Kaye, Key.

KEITH
Origin/meaning: Scots Gaelic 'wood'.

This is a Scots surname taken from several Scottish places which have the name. It came into use as a first name in the 19th century when surnames became popular as first names. Its aristocratic connections (it is the family name of the Earls of Kintore) may have contributed to its popularity. Keith was initially a Scottish name but is now found throughout the English-speaking world.

See also Silas and Silvester.

Examples: Sir Keith Holyoake, New Zealand Prime Minister.
Keith Richards, British rock musician.
Sir Keith Joseph, British politician.

KEN
Origin/meaning: Gaelic 'handsome'.

The usual short form of the Scottish name Kenneth *q.v.*

Variations and abbreviations: see Kenneth.

Examples: Ken Russell, British film producer.
Ken Kesey, US writer, author of *One Flew Over the Cuckoo's Nest*.

KENDAL
Origin/meaning: Old English 'at the head of the valley'.

An English place-name from the Lake District which became a surname and is occasionally found as a first name. Also used for girls.

Variations: Kendall, Kendell.

KENELM

Origin/meaning: Old English 'brave helmet'.

This pre-Conquest name survived the Norman invasion because of St Kenelm (Cynhelm), d.821. The name, although never common, was given in the Middle Ages to honour the saint, who was a son of King Coenwulf of Mercia and who died in battle against the Welsh. Over the centuries many unfounded legends grew up around his name, including the story that his sister Quendreda had him murdered when he was seven years old. In reality the maligned Quendreda was a pious abbess at Minster in Kent. The name was used mainly in the Midlands of England, the area which had been Mercia. It is rare today.

Variations and abbreviations: Cynhelm, Ken, Kenhelm.

Example: Sir Kenelm Digby, 1603-1665, English diplomat and writer, one of the founder members of the Royal Society.

KENNETH

Origin/meaning: Scots Gaelic 'handsome'.

This is primarily a Scots name although there are native forms in other Celtic areas such as Wales. Kenneth I (Coinneach) MacAlpine of Scotland was a 9th century king who kept the Danes out of Scotland. He united his people (the Dalriada Scots) with the Picts after defeating them in 846, and greatly increased the power of Scotland. The name has long been given in Scotland but in the 20th century has become so widespread throughout the English-speaking countries that it is now given without any reference to its Scottish origins.

Variations and abbreviations: Canice (Ir), Cennydd (Wel), Ken, Kenny. See also Kevin.

Examples: Kenneth MacMillan, British choreographer.
Kenneth More, 1914-1982, English film actor.
Kenneth McKeller, Scots singer.
Kenneth Williams, English comedian.

KENT

Origin/meaning: Latin 'man from the area or kingdom of Kent'.

An English surname recently used as a first name, probably because of its short easy sound.

KENTIGERN

Origin/meaning: Old Welsh 'head chief'.

St Kentigern, d.612, alson known by his nickname Mungo, was a Scot who brought Christianity to his native area of Lothian. He is the Patron Saint of Glasgow and his symbols, a ring and a fish, appear on the city's coat of arms. The name, although uncommon, is still used but mainly in Scotland.

KESTER

Origin/meaning: Greek 'Christ bearer'.

An 18th century English form of Christopher.

Variations and abbreviations: see Christopher.

KEVIN

Origin/meaning: Old Irish 'handsome at birth'.

This name is similar in sound and meaning to the Scots name Kenneth q.v. Until the 20th century it was almost totally confined to Ireland but is now more widespread having been taken further afield by Irish imigrants. St Kevin (Coemgen), d.618, was, according to tradition, a Leinster nobleman who was ordained as a priest and founded a monastery at Glendelough. He is said to have died at the age of 120.

Variations and abbreviations: Kev, Kevan.

Example: Kevin Keegan, English footballer.

KHAN

Origin/meaning: Sanskrit 'king', 'lord' or 'ruler'.

Khan added to Muslim names indicates respect as for the Aga Khan. Genghis Khan, 1162–1227, changed his name from Temujin to Genghis Khan which means 'very mighty ruler'.

KIERAN

Origin/meaning: Old Irish 'black-haired'.

This is a diminutive of an Old Irish name Ciar, meaning black or black-haired. The Irish place-name Kerry, which has been adopted as a feminine name, means the home of Ciar's people or the home of dark-haired people but the real feminine equivalent of Kieran is Ciaran.

KIM
Origin/meaning: Old English 'royal' from the surname Kimball – 'royal hill'.

This name was introduced by Rudyard Kipling in his book *Kim*, 1901. It is now used equally for boys and girls.

KINGSLEY
Origin/meaning: Old English 'from the king's wood'.

An English surname based on several places of that name. It came into use in the 19th century with many other surnames. It may have been given to honour Charles Kingsley, 1819–1875, the popular Victorian novelist, author of *The Water Babies*.

Examples: Kingsley Amis, English novelist.
Sir Kingsley Wood, 1881–1943, English politician, deviser of PAYE tax system.

KIRK
Origin/meaning: Old Norse 'church'.

In Scotland, which had close connections with Scandinavia, the usual word for a church is still kirk. Kirk is a common surname in the areas of Scotland and the North of England which were invaded by the Vikings. Kirk is now used as a first name, particularly in the US.

Variation: Kirke.

Example: Kirk Douglas, US film actor (real name Issur Demsky).

KIT
Origin/meaning: Greek 'Christ bearer'.

A popular short form of Christopher which has been used for centuries.

Variations and abbreviations: see Christopher.

KNUT
Origin/meaning: Old German 'kin' sometimes given as 'bold'.

A common German and Scandinavian name, familiar in Britain as Canute, the Danish king who ruled Britain from 816–835. It is now a rare name in English-speaking countries.

Variations and abbreviations: Canute (Eng), Kanut, Knud (Dan/Ger).

KRIS
Origin/meaning: Latin 'Christian' or Greek 'Christ-bearer'.

A short form of Christian or Christopher q.q.v.

Example: Kris Kristoffersen, US singer.

KRISHNA
Origin/meaning: Hindu.

Krishna is regarded by most Hindus as the greatest and most complete incarnation of the god Vishnu. His story is found in many stories and poems, most notably the 9th century *Bhagavata Purana*. These stories like those of King Arthur, are probably based on a real person. Krishna was a defender of justice and slew many wrongdoers and evil demons.

Example: Vengalil Krishnan Krishna Menon, 1897–1974, Indian politician.

KURT
Origin/meaning: Old German 'bold counsellor'.

An alternative spelling of Curt, a short form of Conrad q.v.

Variations and abbreviations: see Conrad.

Example: Kurt Vonnegut, US writer.

KUSUM-CHANDRA
Origin/meaning: Sanskrit 'flower'.

The equivalent of the feminine Kusum with the addition of the typical male suffix-chandra. The *a* at the end should not be pronounced or it becomes the female name meaning 'moon'.

KWAME
Origin/meaning: Akan 'born on Saturday'.

Similar names are Kwasi – Born on Sunday; Kwakoa – Born on Wednesday.

Example: Kwame Nkrumah, 1909–1972, first President of Ghana.

L

LACHLAN (pron. Loklan)
Origin/meaning: Scots Gaelic 'from the lake (fiord) land ie 'a Viking'

This is a Scots first name and surname. It is rare outside Scotland and Ireland.

LAMBERT
Origin/meaning: Old German/Old English 'land famous'.

A name made popular in the Middle Ages by St Lambert, 635–705, Bishop of Maastricht in what is now Holland. He was venerated as a martyr because of his violent death possibly at the instigation of Pepin, king of the Franks. The name developed as a surname but became uncommon as a first name. It was revived with other medieval names in the 19th century but without great success.

Example: Lambert Simnel, 1477–1534, who led an unsuccessful rebellion against Henry VII and was put to work in the kitchens. Lambert Hitchcock, 1795–1852, American chair-maker.

LANCE
Origin/meaning: Old German 'land'.

The original French name from which Lancelot (little Lance) developed. In England it is regarded as a short form of Lancelot because of the great fame of Lancelot, one of the Knights of the Round Table. The short form Lance survived into the 20th century after the 19th century rivival of Lancelot.

Variations and abbreviations: see Lancelot.

Example: Lance Percival, British actor.

LANCELOT
Origin/meaning: Old German 'land'.

This is a French diminutive of the name Lance and means 'little Lance'. It became a familiar name in the Middle Ages because it was used in some of the French stories of the legendary King

457

Arthur and his Knights of the Round Table. The tale of Lancelot's illicit love for Guinevere, King Arthur's wife, became one of the best known stories of the Arthurian romance. The name was revived in the 19th century when many other names from the Tales were also revived. Some of these were not French but Welsh in origin eg Eluned, Elaine and Gareth. Lancelot became a popular name in the North West of England where it still survives. The short form Lance, fashionable after the Second World War, is also used as an independent name.

Variations and abbreviations: Lance, Lancelin, Lancelyn, Lando (Ger), Lanslet, Launce, Launcelot.

LARRY
Origin/meaning: Latin 'from Laurentium'.

The usual pet form of Laurence *q.v.* Sometimes used as an independent name.

Examples: Larry Adler, US mouth organist.
Larry Hagman, US actor.

LARS
Origin/meaning: Latin 'from Laurentium' (the city of laurels').

The Scandinavian form of Laurence *q.v.*

Example: Lars Larsson, Swedish composer.

LATIF
Origin/meaning: Arabic 'pleasant'.

A common Muslim name.

Variation: Lateef (E Africa).

LAURENCE
Origin/meaning: Latin 'from Laurentium' (the city of Laurels).

This name probably became popular because laurel leaves were the victor's traditional crown. The name therefore came to be associated with triumph and was considered a good omen for a baby. Like most Latin-based names it was rare in England before the Norman Conquest. During the Middle Ages its popularity increased along with that of many other saints' names. It was usually given to honour St Laurence, a Deacon of Rome, who was martyred in 258. He was said to have been roasted to death on a gridiron for presenting to the Prefect the city's poor and sick when asked to hand over the church's treasure. The name may also have been used in England to honour St Laurence, d.619, the successor of St Augustine as Archbishop of Canterbury. In Ireland it honoured St Laurence O'Toole, 1128–1180, an Archbishop of Dublin, renowned for his simple life and devotion to the people. In English-speaking countries the spellings Laurence and Lawrence are equally valid. Many English and European surnames derive from Laurence, including Lawson, Lauren, Loren, Larkin and Lawrie.

Variations and abbreviations: Lanty (Ir), Larry, Lars (Swed), Lauren, Laurenz (Ger), Laurens (Fut), Laurent (Fr), Laurentius (Ger/Dut), Laurien, Lauritz (Dan), Lauro (It), Lawrence, Lawrie, Lawry, Lonnie, Lonny, Loren, Lorens, Lorenzo (Ger/Dut), Lorenzo (It), Lorin, Lorrie, Lorry.

Examples: Laurence Oliver, English actor.
Laurence Sterne, 1713–1768, English novelist.
Lorenzo de Medici (the Magnificent), 1449–1492, Duke of Florence.

LAWRENCE
Origin/meaning: Latin 'from Laurentium' (the city of laurels).

An alternative English spelling of Laurence q.v. It is the spelling most often used as a surname.

Variations and abbreviations: see Laurence.

Example: Sir Lawrence Alma-Tadema, 1836–1912, Dutch/English painter.

LAZARUS
Origin/meaning: Hebrew 'Jehovah helps'.

Now used only by Jewish people, this was sometimes used by Puritans in the 17th century when Biblical names were much favoured.

LEABUA
Origin/meaning: Sotho 'you speak'.

This name is much used in the South of Africa.

Example: Dr Leabua Jonathan, Lesotho politician.

LEANDER
Origin/meaning: Greek 'lion-like'.

A name occasionally used because of the Greek legend of Hero and Leander (see Hero f). It corresponds to Leonard q.v.

LEE
Origin/meaning: Old English 'meadow'.

An English surname. It came into use as a first name in the US to honour General Robert E. Lee, 1807–1870. It has since spread to other English-speaking countries, helped by the fact that it is simple to say and remember. Like Kim and Kelly it is now used for girls as well as boys. It is sometimes used by Jewish people as a short form of Levi q.v.

Variations and abbreviations: Lea, Leigh.

Examples: Lee Marvin, US film actor.
Lee Montague, British actor.

LEIGH
Origin/meaning: Old English 'meadow'.

An alternative spelling of Lee q.v. It was one of numerous surnames which became personal names in the 19th century.

Example: Leigh Hunt, 1784–1859, English poet and essayist.

LEMUEL
Origin/meaning: Hebrew 'God is bright'.

This is the name of a king who is mentioned twice in the Book of Proverbs. It was brought into use by the Puritans in the 17th century but is rare today. The best known example is Lemuel Gulliver, the hero of Jonathan Swift's *Gulliver's Travels*, 1726.

Example: Lemuel Curtis, 1790–1857, American clockmaker.

LEO
Origin/meaning: Greek/Latin 'lion'.

A pre-Christian name, it was adopted as a Christian name because of the Roman St Leo the Great, 390–461. He was the first Pope to bear the name. The most recent Leo XIII, 1810–1903. The name has long been a popular one in Catholic countries.

See also Leoline, Leon, Leonard, Lionel.

Examples: Leo Sayer, British singer.
Leo Abse, British politician.

LEOLINE
Origin/meaning: Welsh 'lion-like'.

This is an Anglicized form of the Welsh name Llewelyn, which is influenced by an interpretation of the name derived from the Welsh word for lion. It was used in the Middle Ages. It also occurs in Coleridge's poem 'Christabel', 1816, which provoked interest in several half-forgotten medieval names.

Variations and abbreviations: Leo, Leolin. See also Llewelyn and Leonard.

LEON
Origin/meaning: Greek 'lion'.

The original Greek form of the Latin word leo. It is often, but not exclusively, a Jewish name and is popular in France and Spain.

Variations and abbreviations: Léon (Fr), Léonce (Fr), Leone (It), Leonz (Ger), Lyon. See also Leo, Leoline, Leonard, Lionel.

Examples: Leon Brittan, British politician.
Leon Blum, 1872–1950, French socialist statesman.

LEONARD
Origin/meaning: Latin, Old German 'lion-bold'.

In the Middle Ages St Leonard was much-loved particularly among Crusaders, who regarded him as the Patron Saint of prisoners. Typical of the early saints nothing definite is known about him but many, often preposterous, miracles were attributed to him. He is usually described as a 6th century hermit who founded a monastery at what is now Saint Léonard, near Limoges, in France. Although the name never went totally out of fashion it received a boost in the 19th century from the influential fashion for medieval names.

Variations and abbreviations: Leander (Gr), Len, Lenard, Lennard, Lennart (Scand), Lennie, Lenny, Leo, Leon, Léonard (Fr), Leonardo (It), Leonerd, Leonhard (Ger), Leinhard (Swiss). See also Leander, Leo, Leoline, Leon, Lionel, Shehr/Singh.

Examples: Leonardo de Vinci, 1452–1519, Italian painter, sculptor and engineer.
Leonard Bernstein, US composer (*West Side Story*).

LEOPOLD
Origin/meaning: Old German 'people-bold'.

Mainly a German name, Leopold was used in 19th century Britain, because of Queen Victoria's uncle, Leopold I, 1790-1865, King of the Belgians. He had been briefly married to George IV's daughter, Princess Charlotte, who had died in childbirth. He was a sensible moderate man, who was much respected. Queen Victoria named one of her own sons after him.

Variations and abbreviations: Leo, Leobold, Léopold (Fr), Leopoldo (It), Luitpold.

Examples: Leopold II, 1747-1792, Holy Roman Emperor, brother of Marie Antoinette.
Leopold Sacher-Masoch, 1836-1895, Austrian writer.
Leopold Stokowski, 1882-1977, US conductor.

LEROY
Origin/meaning: French 'king'.

This name seems to be confined to the US where it may have been taken from the Northern French surname Le Royer, which means 'wheelmaker'. However it is undoubtedly intended to mean 'le roi' – king, and that is the meaning usually given.

LESLIE
Origin/meaning: Scots Gaelic 'garden by the pool'.

The usual spelling of the Scottish surname when used as a masculine name. (Lesley tends to be the feminine version.) Leslie is derived from a Scottish place-name in Aberdeenshire. It came into use as a personal name in the 19th century when surnames were in vogue. Like Percy, Howard, Sidney etc, it was helped along by its aristocratic connections, being the surname of the Earls of Rothes.

Variations and abbreviations: Lee, Les, Lesley, Lezlie.

Examples: Leslie Howard, 1893-1943, British film actor.
Sir Leslie Stephen, 1832-1904, English writer and philosopher, father of Virginia Woolf.

LESTER
Origin/meaning: Old English 'Leicester'.

This is an English surname derived from the place-name. It has become well established as a personal name since the 19th century.

Examples: Lester Piggott, English jockey.
Lester B. Pearson, 1897-1972, Canadian politician.

LEVI

Origin/meaning: Hebrew 'pledged'.

Leah's third son by Jacob and the ancestor of one of the tribes of Israel. Now used mainly by Jewish people, it was also introduced as a Christian name by 17th century Puritans and did not lose popularity in the US until the 19th century.

LEW

Origin/meaning: Old German 'glorious battle'.

A short form of Lewis/Louis, found particularly in the US, as an independent name.

Example: Lew Ayres, US film actor.

LEWIS

Origin/meaning: Old German 'glorious battle'.

This English name is quite separate from the Welsh name Lewis q.v. It is a form of the French name Louis q.v. which was introduced into England by the Normans. The usual Medieval English forms were Lewis or Lowis but the French spelling is sometimes retained while the English pronunciation is used.

Variations and abbreviations: see Louis.

Examples: Lewis Carroll (pen-name of Charles Lutwidge Dodgson), 1832–1898, English author of *Alice's Adventures in Wonderland*.
Sir Lewis Namier, 1888–1960, British Historian.

LEWIS

Origin/meaning: Welsh 'lion-like' or from the name of the Celtic god Luel.

This is an Anglicized form of Lewys, a short form of the Welsh name Llywelyn. It is quite unconnected with the English name Lewis, which is the English version of the French Louis.

LIAM

Origin/meaning: Old German 'helmet of resolution'.

The Irish version of William q.v.

LINDSAY

Origin/meaning: Old English. Uncertain, possibly 'Lincoln's island'.

A Scottish aristocratic surname adopted as a male and female popularity in the US until the 19th century.

Variations and abbreviations: see Lindsay (f).

Example: Lindsay Anderson, British film director.

LINUS
Origin/meaning: Latin 'flaxen-haired'.

Possibly a name derived from the Latin word for flax. It is well known because of the Peanuts cartoons in which the character Linus appears.

Example: Linus Pauling, US biochemist, twice awarded the Nobel Prize.

LIONEL
Origin/meaning: Latin/French 'little lion'.

The French diminutive of Leon q.v. it has been used in Britain since the Middle Ages.

Variations: Lionello (It), Lyonel. See also Leo, Leoline, Leon, Leonard.

Examples: Lionel Bart, British composer (*Oliver*).
Lionel Barrymore, 1878–1954, US film actor.

LISLE
Origin/meaning: French 'the isle'.

A French or English surname sometimes used as a first name. May be confused with Lyall q.v.

LLEWELYN
Origin/meaning: uncertain. Possibly Welsh 'like a lion' or a reference to the Celtic god Luel.

One of the many forms of Llywelyn q.v.

LLOYD
Origin/meaning: Welsh 'grey' or 'brown'.

This is a common Welsh surname occasionally used as a first name.

Variation: Floyd.

Examples: Lloyd Bridges, US actor.
Lloyd Nolan, US actor.

LLYR
Origin/meaning: Welsh mythology. Llyr was a sea god. He was the father of Branwen and her brother Bendigeidfran, one of the Welsh giants (cf Idris).

The name Lear, used by Shakespeare for his play *King Lear*, 1607, is thought to be based on this Old Welsh name.

Variations and abbreviations: Lear, Leir.

LLYWELYN (pron. Chloowellin)
Origin/meaning: uncertain. May be Welsh 'like a lion' or a reference to the Celtic god Luel.

This is one of the most popular Welsh names perhaps because it was borne by two famous Welsh princes, Llywelyn ap Iorwerth, d.1240, and his less successful nephew Llywelyn ap Gruffydd, d.1282, the last Welsh Prince of Wales. Even among the Welsh the spelling varies and attempts to 'translate' it into English have led to an independent form – Leoline, as well as borrowing the name Lewis, which has a quite different meaning.

Variations and abbreviations: Flewelin, Fluellen, Leoline (Eng), Lewellings, Lewis (Eng), Llelo, Llew, Llewelin, Llowelin, Lyn, Wellings.

LONNY
Origin/meaning: Latin 'from Laurentium'.

A familiar form of Laurence.

Variations and abbreviations: Lonnie. See Laurence.

Example: Lonny Donegan, British singer.

LOUIS (pron. Lóuee or Lóuiss)
Origin/meaning: Old German 'glorious battle'.

The original Teutonic form of this name was Chlodovech. Chlodovech, 465–511, was the first Merovingian king of the Western Franks. The area ruled by him corresponded very approximately to the area now known as France. In Latin documents Chlodovech was known either as Clovis or Ludovicus from the first or second parts of the name. Ludovicus developed into the French name Louis. It has remained a popular French name for over a thousand years. There have been eighteen French kings who have borne the name. The fame of Louis IX, 1215–1270 (St Louis) an ardent Crusader, did much to spread the name beyond France. Louis XIV, 1638–1715, known as the

Sun King, was probably the most magnificent monarch Europe has ever seen. The name Louis was introduced into England by the Normans. It soon developed a native form – Lewis. In Scotland, which had close ties with France, both the French spelling and pronunciation were retained, and the alternative French form Ludovic was also adopted. In the US also the French form is preferred as seen in the pronunciation of the town St Louis. The US state Louisiana, claimed by the French in 1682, was named after Louis XIV. It was sold to the US by France in 1803, but still retains signs of French influence.

Variations and abbreviations: Aloys (Provençal), Aloysius, Lew, Lewes, Lewis (Eng), Lodewig (Ger), Lou, Louie, Louis (Fr/Scots), Lovis, Lowes (Med/Eng), Lowis, Lodovico (It), Ludovic (Scot), Ludovico (It), Luigi (It).

Examples: Louis Pasteur, 1822–1895, French chemist, pioneer of bacteriology.
Ludwig van Beethoven, 1770–1827, German composer.
Louis Jourdan, French film actor.
Louis Hayward, US actor.

LOVELACE
Origin/meaning: Medieval English 'love token'.

A surname best known for the Cavalier poet Richard Lovelace, 1618–1657 who wrote poems to Lucasta and Althea which introduced two new feminine names. The surname is sometimes used as a personal name.

LUCAS
Origin/meaning: Greek 'from Lucania'.

This is a Latin form of the name better known in England as Luke. In France and Germany Lucas is a common form of Luke. In England Lucas developed as a surname rather than a first name. Twentieth century use of Lucas as a personal name in English-speaking countries, such as Australia, where it is not uncommon, probably comes from the use of it as a family name.

Variations and abbreviations: see Luke.

Example: Lucas Cranach, 1472–1553, German painter.

LUCIAN (pron. Lóosean or Lóoshan)
Origin/meaning: Latin 'light'.

An alternative from of Lucius q.v. St Lucian, d.312, was a

466

theologian from Antioch who revised the Greek version of the Old Testament and the gospels. The name was sometimes used in England.

Variations and abbreviations: Lucien (Fr). See also Lucius.

Examples: Lucian, 120-190, Greek Philosopher and writer.
Lucien Freud, English painter.
Lucien Pissarro, 1863-1944, French book illustrator, son of Camille Pissarro.

LUCIUS
Origin/meaning: Latin 'light'.

This name was a pre-Christian Roman name, probably used for a child born at first light of day. It was adopted as a Christian name because of St Lucius, d.259. He was a Bishop of Rome, beheaded with several others, including St Montanus. Two Popes bore the name but it was never greatly used in England. The English feminine form Lucy is currently very popular.

Variations and abbreviations: Lucian, Luciano (It), Lucien (Fr), Lucillio (It), Lucio (It), Luzian, Luzius (Ger).

Example: Luciano Pavarotti, Italian opera singer.

LUCK
Origin/meaning: Greek 'from Lucania' or 'wolf'

A Medieval English form of Luke q.v. now found mainly as a surname.

LUDOVIC
Origin/meaning: Old German 'glorious battle'.

This is a variation of the name Lewis q.v. through one of its Latin forms, Ludovicus. It is used in Italy as an alternative to Luigi, and in France as an alternative to Louis. It is probably because of the former close connections between France and Scotland that in Britain the name is almost invariably confined to Scotland. There is an English spelling Lodowick, which Shakespeare used in his play *Measure for Measure*, 1604. The English spelling is extremely rare today.

Variations and abbreviations: Lodowick (Eng), Lodovico (It), Ludo, Ludovico (It), Ludwig (Ger). See also Lewis.

Example: Ludovic Kennedy, Scottish writer and broadcaster.

LUKE

Origin/meaning: Greek 'from Lucania'. Sometimes given as 'wolf'.

This is the name of one of the four Evangelists, and author of the Acts of the Apostles. He was a Greek and a doctor, called by St Paul 'our beloved Luke, the physician'. He is the Patron Saint of doctors. He is also the Patron Saint of painters because he is supposed, erroneously, to have painted several early portraits of the Virgin Mary. Luke was a common name in the Middle Ages but not as successful a name as John. It was also popular with the early Puritan settlers of North America. It seems to be coming into fashion in Australia and Britain. The hero of the phenomenally successful *Star Wars* film is called Luke Skywalker.

Variations and abbreviations: Loukas (Gr), Luc (Fr), Luca (It), Lucano (It), Lucas (Fr/Eng/Ger), Lucio (Sp), Luck (Eng), Lukas (Ger/Scand).

Examples: Luca Giordano, 1632–1705, Italian painter.
Luc, Marquis de Vauvenargues, 1715–1747, French moralist.

LYALL

Origin/meaning: French 'from Lyons' ('the hillfort') or French 'little lion'.

An English surname not infrequently used as a first name in Britain and the US. Sometimes confused with Lisle *q.v.*

Variations and abbreviations: Lyal, Lyle.

LYN

Origin/meaning: uncertain. Possibly Welsh 'like a lion' or a reference to the Celtic god Luel.

A Welsh male name. A short form of Llewellyn *q.v.* now used as an independent name. It has no connection with the girl's name Lynn which is so popular in North America, although both have Welsh origins.

Example: Lyn Davies, Olympic long-jumper.

LYNDON

Origin/meaning: Old English 'from the lime tree hill'.

An English place-name which became a surname. Used mainly in the US where family names are common as personal names.

Variation: Lindon.

Example: Lyndon B. Johnson, 1908–1973, 36th US President.

M

MADHUKAR (pron. Madtookarr)
Origin/meaning: Sanskrit 'bee'.

The masculine equivalent of Madhuri *q.v.*

MADOC
Origin/meaning: Welsh 'fortunate'.

Found in Wales both as a first name and a surname. According to Welsh folklore a Welsh prince Madoc, son of Owain Gwynedd, discovered America in about 1170.

Variations: Maddock, Maddox, Madog, Madox.

Example: Ford Madox Brown, 1821–1893, English painter.

MAGNUS
Origin/meaning: Latin 'great'.

This adjective, usually applied to rulers, which became a name in its own right. Charlemagne is a corruption of the Latin Carolus Magnus (Charles the Great). Magnus was used as a name by St Olaf of Norway for his son, who became Magnus I 'the Good', 1024–1074. The name was used by six further kings of Norway, and has become popular in the Scandinavian countries as well as Iceland, Scotland and Ireland, which came under their influence. It gave rise to the surnames McManus, Magnusson and Manson. In Britain it is still confined mainly to the North. Rare in North America and Australia.

Variation: Manus (Ir).

Examples: Magnus Magnusson, Scottish/Icelandic writer and broadcaster.
Dr Magnus Pyke, English writer and broadcaster.

MALCOLM
Origin/meaning: Old Scots 'servant of Columba'.

A popular Scottish name for hundreds of years because of the influence of St Columba who brought Christianity to a large part of Scotland. Now used in all English-speaking countries, and particularly in Australia and Canada which have large populations of Scottish descent.

Abbreviation: Mal.

Examples: Malcolm Frazer, Australian Prime Minister.
Malcolm Muggeridge, English writer and broadcaster.

MANFRED
Origin/meaning: Old German 'man-peace'.

A pre-Conquest name adopted by the Normans and introduced by them into England. It was one of many old names revived in the 19th century. Despite Byron's drama *Manfred*, 1819, it was no more successful in 19th century England than it had been in the Middle Ages.

Variations and abbreviations: Manfredo (It), Manfried (Ger).

Example: Manfred, Baron von Richthofen, 1882–1918, German World War I flying ace.

MANNY
Origin/meaning: either a familiar form of Chaim/Hyman (Hebrew – 'life') or a short form of Emanuel (Hebrew – 'God with us')

Variation: Mannie.

Example: Mannie (Emanuel) Shinwell, British politician.

MARC
Origin/meaning: Latin 'of Mars' (the Roman god of war), ie 'warlike'.

The French form of Mark *q.v.* currently enjoying a certain amount of popularity in English-speaking countries.

MARCEL
Origin/meaning: Latin 'little Marcus' from 'Mars' (the Roman god of war) ie 'warlike'.

This is the French form of the Latin Marcellus, a diminutive of Marcus. The name is popular in France and Italy but rare elsewhere.

Variations and abbreviations: Marcello (It), Marcellus, Marzellus (Ger). See also Mark.

Example: Marcel Proust, 1871–1922, French novelist.

Marcel Marceau, French mime artist.

MARCELLUS
Origin/meaning: Latin 'little Marcus' from Mars (the Roman god of war).

The best known form of this name is Marcel. Marcellus has occasionally been used in England since the Renaissance.

Variations and abbreviations: See Marcel. See also Marcus, Mark, Martin.

MARCUS
Origin/meaning: Latin 'of Mars' (the Roman god of war), ie 'warlike'.

This is the Roman name which developed into the Christian name Mark *q.v.* Marcus and Mark were interchangeable in the Middle Ages. Marcellus was the diminutive and Martin and Marius also have the same meaning.

Variations and abbreviations: see Mark.

Examples: Marcus Clarke, 1846–1881, Australian writer.
Marcus Binney, English writer on architecture and conservation.

MARIUS
Origin/meaning: Latin, from the name of the Roman Marius family, probably connected with Mars, god of war.

This name was one of many classical names re-introduced during the 16th century renaissance period. Marius has never been common in English-speaking countries.

Variation: Mario (It). See also Marcus, Mark, Martin.

Examples: Marius Goring, English actor.
Mario Puzo, US novelist (*The Godfather*).

MARK
Origin/Latin 'of Mars' (the Roman god of war), ie 'warlike'.

This name comes from the popular Roman name Marcus. It was widespread in all the countries where Roman influence was strong. It became an established Christian name because of St Mark who wrote one of the four gospels. His history is not certain, but it is thought that after travelling with St Paul to convert Cyprus he became Bishop of Alexandria and was

471

martyred by the Emperor Trajan. St Mark is closely associated with the city of Venice for in 829, after Alexandria had been conquered by the Moslems, his body was stolen from there and brought to Venice. The Moslems refrained from inspecting the baggage containing his remains because they were told it contained pork! St Mark's cathedral is one of the most famous in the world and Marco is a common Italian name. Although its credentials were good Mark was never a common name in medieval England and was found equally with the Latin form Marcus. It was made even less popular by the Protestant reaction against saints' names. In the 19th century both Mark and Marcus were revived when medieval names were fashionable. Since the Second World War Mark has become one of the most frequently used names in English-speaking countries.

Variations and abbreviations: Marek (Slav), Marc (Fr), Marcel (Fr), Marco (It), Marcos (Sp), Marcus, Marko, Markus (Ger/Dut/Scand), Marks, Marx.

Examples: Marco Polo, 1254–1324, Venetian traveller.
Mark Spitz, US Olympic swimmer.

MARMADUKE
Origin/meaning: Old Welsh/Old Irish 'servant of Madoc'.

An English North country name. In the 19th century it developed effete aristocratic overtones which have caused it to be shunned in the 20th century.

Abbreviation: Duke.

MARTIN
Origin/meaning: Latin 'of Mars' (the Roman god of war), ie 'warlike'.

This was a popular name in the Middle Ages when it was given to honour St Martin of Tours, 315–397. A young Roman officer, he gave half his cloak to a poor beggar whom he later recognized as Christ. Following his conversion he left the army to live as a recluse. He became Bishop of Tours and was active in founding monasteries and in missionary work, particularly in Gaul (France). He was a popular saint throughout Europe and in England, where many churches were dedicated in his honour. The best known is Saint Martin-in-the-Fields at Trafalgar Square. Unlike most Catholic saints' names, Martin survived in Protestant countries because it was the name of the foremost Protestant reformer, Martin Luther, 1483–1546. The name has been used consistently to the present day. In the 1960s it was a vogue name in Britain.

Variations and abbreviations: Mart, Martainn (Scots), Marten, Martie, Martinet (Fr), Martino (It/Sp), Marton, Marty, Martyn, Merten, Morten (Dan). See also Marcus, Mark.

Examples: Sir Martin Frobisher, 1535–1594, English seaman and explorer.
Martin Luther King, 1929–1968, US civil rights leader.
Martin Amis, English novelist.

MASUD
Origin/meaning: Arabic 'fortunate'.

This is a common Muslim name found in all Muslim countries.

Variations and abbreviations: Mansur, Masood, Massur.

MATSIMELA
Origin/meaning: Sotho 'roots'.

This name comes from the African state of Lesotho, formerly known as Basutoland, in South Africa.

MATTHEW
Origin/meaning: Hebrew 'gift of Jehovah'.

This is the form of the name Mattathiah used in the English translation of the Bible for the Evangelist. It developed from Matheu, which was introduced into England by the Normans. In the Middle Ages it was given to honour St Matthew, the Apostle and Evangelist. He was called by Christ to leave his job as a tax collector and follow him. Little is known of his life but he is reputed to have been martyred in Ethiopia. The name was much loved throughout Europe. It is found in many forms and has given rise to a large number of surnames. Since the 1970s Matthew has been one of the most consistently popular names in all English-speaking countries.

Variations and abbreviations: Mat, Mateo (Port/Sp), Mathias, Matias, Matt, Matteo (It), Matthaeus, Matthaüs (Swiss), Mattheus, Matthias (Ger), Matthieu (Fr), Mattias, Mattie, Matty.

Examples: Matthew Arnold, 1822–1888, English poet.
Matthew Ridgway, US general.

MATTHIAS

Origin/meaning: Hebrew 'gift of Jehovah'.

The Greek/Latin form of the Hebrew name Mattathiah. This form is used in the English translation of the Bible to distinguish the man chosen by lot to replace Judas (Acts ch.1 vs.15–16) from the Evangelist St Matthew. The 17th century Puritans used it when they favoured Biblical names but it has never been very popular in English-speaking countries. It is the usual form of Matthew in German-speaking countries.

Variations and abbreviations: see Matthew.

Example: Matthias Albani, 1621–1673, Austrian violin-maker.

MAURICE

Origin/meaning: Latin 'a man from Mauretania' (Morocco).

This Roman name was introduced as a Christian name because of the 3rd century St Maurice (Mauritius). He was said to have been the commanding officer of a legion of Christian Roman soldiers who refused to obey orders to take part in heathen rituals. As a result they were all executed for mutiny at Agaunum in Switzerland and earned the collective title The Martyrs of Agaunum. The name is still much used in Switzerland and the ski resort of St Moritz takes its name from the saint. The English form of Mauritius was based on the more general Latin adjective Maurus – a Moor. This gave the French forms Maur and Maurisse which were introduced into England in the early Middle Ages. The predominant English spelling was Moris or Morris but in the 19th and 20th centuries Maurice has become the accepted first name form and Morris the surname. Other surnames which developed include Seymour (St Maur). For some strange reason the English folk dances based on characters from the tales of Robin Hood became known as Morris (Moorish) dances. Maurice is a favourite name among Jewish people.

Variations and abbreviations: Maur (Fr/Ger), Mauricio (Port/Sp), Maurie, Maurise, Mauritius (Ger), Maurits (Dut), Mauriz, Maurizio (It), Mauro (It), Maurus (Ger), Maury, Morie, Moritz (Swiss), Moriz, Morris, Morry.

Examples: Maurice Chevalier, 1888–1972, French entertainer. Maurice Ravel, 1875–1937, French composer.

MAWULAWDE (pron. Mahwoolawdáy)
Origin/meaning: Ewe 'God will provide'.

This name comes from Ghana in West Africa.

MAWULI (pron. Máhwoolee)
Origin/meaning: Ewe 'there is a God'.

A popular name in Ghana.

MAX
Origin/meaning: Latin 'greatest'.

A short form of Maximilian or Maxwell. It has become popular
since the end of the 19th century as an independent name.

Variations and abbreviations: see Maximilian.

Examples: Sir Max (Henry Maximilian) Beerbohm, 1872–1957,
English writer and caricaturist.
Max Planck, 1858–1947, German physicist, formulator of the
revolutionary quantum theory.
Max Beloff, English professor and writer.

MAXIMILIAN
Origin/meaning: Latin 'greatest'.

This is derived from the Latin word maximus. Both Maximus
and Maximilian were saints' names. St Maximus, 580–662,
was an abbot who died, after barbaric punishment, for defying
the Emperor Constans II. Maximilian, d.295, was a martyr who
was beheaded for refusing to join the Roman army. The name
became popular in Germany because of the highly successful
and popular Emperor Maximilian I, 1459–1519. One story goes
that his father, Frederick III, concocted the name as a good
omen from the names of two Roman Generals, Fabius Maximus
and Scipio Aemilianus. However the name had already been in
existence for 1000 years! It is an unusual name in English-
speaking countries, although the short form Max has been
rather successful as an independent name.

Variations and abbreviations: Mac, Massimiliano (It), Massimo
(It), Max, Maxime (Fr), Maximilien (Fr), Maximus.

Examples: Maximilien François Marie Isadoire de Robespierre,
1758–1794, French revolutionary.
Maximilian Schell, Austrian film actor.

MAXWELL
Origin/meaning: Scots/Old English 'Magnus's well'.

This is a Scottish place-name which became a surname. It has been used consistently since the 19th century as a first name, perhaps because it allows for the popular short form Max, which it shares with Maximilian.

Variations and abbreviations: Mac, Max.

Example: (Peter) Maxwell Davies, British composer.

MAYNARD
Origin/meaning: Old German 'strength-hardy'.

A name introduced in England by the Normans.

Variations and abbreviations: Manard, Meinhard (Ger), Ménard (Fr).

Example: John Maynard Keynes, 1883–1946, English economist.

MAYUR
Origin/meaning: Sanskrit 'peacock'.

One of Shiv's sons, Kumara or Skanda, the six-headed god of war, is usually depicted riding on a peacock.

MELCHIOR
Origin/meaning: Hebrew 'The King is light'.

With Caspar and Balthasar this is one of the traditional names of the three kings who followed the star to Bethlehem. It is virtually obsolete today.

Example: Melchior Schildt, 1592–1667, German musician.

MELVIN
Origin/meaning: French/English 'town on a hill' or Old English 'sword friend'.

This is an English surname which has been established since the 19th century as a personal name. It is a version of Melville, the family name of the Earls of Leven and Melville, which may have helped its popularity. Sometimes believed to be a masculine form of the invented Gaelic feminine name Malvina. The interpretation is then given as 'smooth/polished sword'.

Variations and abbreviations: Melvin, Mel, Melville, Melvyn.

Examples: Melvyn Bragg, English novelist and broadcaster.

Mel Brooks, US film director.

MEREDITH
Origin/meaning: Old Welsh 'great? lord'.

This began as a Welsh first name. In Welsh the accent comes on the second, not the first, syllable. Like many medieval names it survived most successfully as a surname and is now being re-introduced as a family name/first name. Although originally a masculine name in North America it is now often used for girls because of family connections.

Variations and abbreviations: Bedo (Wel), Maredudd (Wel), Mereddud (Wel), Merry.

Examples: Mareddud (Meriteut), d.1035, King of Dheubarth (SW Wales).
Meredith Edwards, Welsh actor.

MERLIN
Origin/meaning: Old Welsh 'sea hill'.

This name is still used occasionally in Wales. It is widely known as the name of King Arthur's magician. A great proportion of the Tales of King Arthur and his Knights of the Round Table were based on Welsh legends surrounding a British king who lived after the Romans had departed from Britain. Tales of Merlin can be found in all the sources of the Arthurian Romance and are retold by Spenser in his *Faerie Queene* and Tennyson in his *Idylls of the King*. Merlin was the son of a maiden seduced by a devil. However he was found and baptized so that he was lost to Satan but retained many magical powers. He died while in a trance put on him by his mistress Vivian.

Variation: Merlyn.

Example: Merlyn Rees, British politician.

MERVYN
Origin/meaning: Old English 'famous friend' or Celtic 'fair sea'.

This surname has English and Welsh forms and the two may be quite separate. The name has been used, like most surnames, only since the 19th century. Sometimes given as a form of Merlin q.v.

Variations and abbreviations: Merfyn (Wel), Merv, Mervin. See also Morgan, Murdoch, Murray.

Example: Mervyn Peake, 1911–1968, English writer and illustrator.

MICHAEL

Origin/meaning: Hebrew 'Who is like the Lord?'

Michael is the name of the archangel who led the angels into battle (Rev.12:7) to cast out Satan. Like St George he is usually represented slaying a dragon.

Autumn is still known in some instances, such as the legal year, as Michaelmas because the feast of St Michael and All Angels falls on September 29th. Not surprisingly St Michael was the Patron Saint of Soldiers and his name was popular in war-torn medieval Europe. It came into use in England in the 12th century and has remained in use ever since. The surnames Michell and Mitchell indicate that initially the English pronunciation was similar to the French Michel. The name fell rather out of favour for a while after the Protestant Reformation because of its Catholic connections. Like Mary and Bridget it became correspondingly more popular in Ireland in the 17th century as that country remained faithful to the Catholic Church. Nowadays the short form Mick is almost as common a term for an Irishman as Paddy. Michael has been a favourite in Britain, North America and Australia since the Second World War.

Variations and abbreviations: Meikle, Micah, Michal, Michel (Fr), Michele (It), Mick, Mickey, Mickie, Micky, Miguel (Sp/Port), Mikael (Scand), Mike, Mikel, Mikey, Mikhail (Russ), Mikkel (Dan), Mischa (Russ), Mitch, Mitchell.

Examples: Michael Jackson, US singer.
Miguel de Cervantes, 1547–1616, Spanish writer, author of *Don Quixote*.
Michael Heseltine, British politician.
Michael Palin, British actor.

MICAH

Origin/meaning: Hebrew 'Who is like the Lord?'

A variation of Michael used in the Old Testament for one of the Prophets. Used by Jewish people and by Puritans in the 17th and 18th centuries.

Variations and abbreviations: see Michael.

MILES

Origin/meaning: Old German. Uncertain, possibly 'merciful' or Latin 'soldierly'.

A popular medieval name, which was successfully revived in the

19th century and is still in use today. In Ireland it was used to 'translate' the native name Maolmuire (servant of Mary).

Variations and abbreviations: Milo (Ger/Ir), Myles.

Examples: Myles Standish, 1584–1656, English colonist who sailed with the Mayflower.
Miles Kington, English writer.

MITCHELL
Origin/meaning: Hebrew 'Who is like the Lord?'

An English surname derived from the medieval pronunciation of Michael q.v. It is now coming back into use as a first name, especially in the US where family names are popular as first names.

Variations and abbreviations: see Michael.

MOHAMMED
Origin/meaning: Arabic/Swahili 'praised'.

Mohammed is a religious title and immediately indicated that a man is a Muslim. It is never a personal name, but prefixes the personal name.

Mohammed, the Prophet, died in AD 632 having created a new faith called Islam. His teachings are found in the Koran.

Variations: Mehemmet, Muhammed.

Examples: Mohammed Ali, US boxer.
Mohammed Mussadiq, 1876–1967, Persian politician and Prime Minister.

MOHAN
Origin/meaning: a Hindu name for Krishna q.v.

This was Gandhi's first name, used with the addition of the typical male suffix -das, ie Mohandas Gandhi.

MONTAGU
Origin/meaning: French 'from Mount Aigu'.

A Norman French surname. Montagu is the name of several aristocratic families including the Dukes of Manchester and Earls of Sandwich. It was adopted as a first name in the 19th century along with other, often aristocratic surnames such as Percy, Howard, Leslie etc.

Variations and abbreviations: Montague, Monte, Monty.

MORGAN
Origin/meaning: Old Welsh 'sea bright?'

A common Welsh first name and surname closely related to Mervyn q.v. Morgan was a 7th century Welsh prince who gave his name to the area of South Wales known as Glamorgan.

Variation: Morgen.

MORIARTY
Origin/meaning: Old Irish 'sea warrior'.

This is the Anglicized spelling of a native Irish name. It has sometimes been 'translated' by the saint's name, Maurice. Moriarty is Sherlock Holmes' devious opponent in the stories by Sir Arthur Conan Doyle.

MORRIS
Origin/meaning: Latin 'a man from Mauretania' (Morocco).

An early English variation of Maurice q.v. It has now become the usual surname form, although it is still also used as a personal name.

Variations and abbreviations: see Maurice.

Examples: Morris West, Australian academic and writer.
Morris Fahi, Turkish-born/English, actor and writer.

MOSES
Origin/meaning: Egyptian 'saved from the water', Hebrew 'law-giver'.

Moses was chosen by God to lead the Israelites out of slavery in Egypt to the Promised Land (see the 2nd Book of Moses-Exodus).

Mainly used as a Jewish first name and surname it was a popular Puritan first name in 17th century England and gave rise to several surnames, eg Moss, Moyce, Mossman. Moss is sometimes found as a Christian name in Wales.

Variations and abbreviations: see Maurice.
Moshe (Hebrew), Moss, Moyse, Mozes.

Examples: Sir Moses Haim Montefiore, 1784–1885, English-Jewish philanthropist.
Moses Haughton, c.1772–1848, English miniaturist.

MOYO (pron. Móyo)
Origin/meaning: Ngoni 'good health'.

This name comes from the Central African state of Malawi, formerly known as Nyasaland.

MUNGO
Origin/meaning: Gaelic 'lovable', 'most dear'.

This was an adjective used to describe St Kentigern, d.612. It came to be used as an alternative name for him and then as a Christian name, especially in the Lothian area around Glasgow where St Kentigern had taken Christianity.

Variation: Munghu. See Kentigern.

Example: Mungo Park, 1771–1806, Scottish explorer of Africa.

MURDOCH
Origin/meaning: Scots Gaelic 'man of the sea'.

A Scots first name that developed as a surname. It is similar to Murray and the Welsh Morgan and Mervyn. Now being used as a first name again.

Variation: Murtagh (Ir).

MURRAY
Origin/meaning: Scots Gaelic 'sea settlement'.

This is a Scottish place-name (Moray is a Scots county) which became a common Scottish surname. In the 19th century it was adopted as a first name, helped by the fact that it is the surname of the Dukes of Atholl and of the Earls of Moray. It quickly established itself, not just in Scotland, but in areas with a high level of Scottish immigration, particularly in Australia and Canada. It is now used without any reference to the Scottish connection.

Variation: Moray. See also Murdoch, Morgan, Mervyn.

Examples: Moray Watson, British actor.
Murray Melvin, English actor.
Nicholas Murray Butler, 1862–1947, US academic. (Address to Columbia University: 'An expert is one who knows more and more about less and less'.)

MWAI (pron. 'M wáhee)
Origin/meaning: Ngoni 'good fortune'.

A name from the Central African state of Malawi.

N

NASIM
Origin/meaning: Arabic 'discipliner'.
A Muslim name.
Variation: Nizam.

NASSOR
Origin/meaning: Swahili 'victorious'.
A name found in Tanzania in East Africa.
See also Victor.

NAT
Origin/meaning: Hebrew 'gift' or 'God has given'.
The usual short form of Nathan or Nathaniel q.v.
Variation: Natty.
Example: Nat 'King' Cole, 1919–1965, US singer and pianist.

NATHAN
Origin/meaning: Hebrew 'gift'.
This is the name of an Old Testament prophet, and is mainly used by Jewish people. It is also used as a short form of Nathaniel q.v.
Variation: Nat.

NATHANIEL
Origin/meaning: Hebrew 'God has given'.
This is the first name of the Apostle who is better known by his family name, Bartholomew. As a result Nathaniel itself was rarely used in the Middle Ages. In the 17th century Protestants, looking for names untainted by Catholic connections, re-discovered it. It is still used today although it is not very common.

Variations and abbreviations: Nat, Nataniel (Sp), Nataniele (It), Nathan, Nathanael, Nathaneal, Natty. See also Theodore and Jonathan.

Example: Nathaniel Hawthorne, 1804–1864, US writer.

NAZIR
Origin/meaning: Arabic 'victorious'.

This is a Muslim name.

Variations: Nasser, Nassor (E Africa), Nasr.

Examples: Nasr-Ed-Din, 1829–1896, Shah of Persia who visited Queen Victoria in 1873 and 1889.
Gamal Abdel Nasser, 1918–1970, Egyptian statesman, President of Egypt and of the United Arab Republic.

NEAL(e)
Origin/meaning: Old Irish 'champion'.

This is one of the many spellings of the name Neil, which is a form of Niall (Irish) and Nigel q.v. It usually appears as a surname.

Variations and abbreviations: see Nigel.

NED
Origin/meaning: a short form of names beginning with Ed- such as Edward and Edwin.

Variations: Neddie, Neddy.

Example: Ned Sherrin, English writer.

NEHEMIA (pron. Nay-em-éy-ar)
Origin/meaning: Hebrew 'Jehovah is consolation'.

Nehemiah was a Jewish servant of Artaxerxes, who lived in the 4th century BC. He obtained permission from the king to rebuild the walls of Jerusalem. The Book of Nehemiah gives an account of his work. This Biblical name was much used for two centuries by Puritans on both sides of the Atlantic but is now virtually obsolete.

Abbreviation: Neh.

NEIL (pron. Neeal)
Origin/meaning: Old Irish 'champion'.

This is a form of the Irish name Niall, which developed from the word 'niadh' and is the direct equivalent of Nigel *q.v.* Strictly speaking it is less correct than Niall because it is its genitive form, as the surname O'Neill shows. However Neil became more familiar in English-speaking countries probably because of its similarity to Neel, the medieval English form. It is also commonly used in Ireland itself, partly because the Irish use it as a short form of Cornelius, which is still a common name there and in Holland.

Variations and abbreviations: see Nigel.

Examples: Neil Armstrong, US astronaut, first man on the moon.
Neil Innes, English comedy writer.

NELSON
Origin/meaning: English 'Neil's son' from Old Irish 'champion'.

This is an English surname which developed from the Irish name Niall or Neal, the original form of Nigel. After Admiral Nelson's famous naval victories against the French, especially the Battle of Trafalgar, 1805, it came into use as a first name given to honour Nelson. The 19th century saw a great increase in the use of surnames as first names, so Nelson easily became established as a personal name. It is still in use today.

Variations and abbreviations: Nealson, Nels, Neilson, Nilson.

Examples: Nelson Riddle, US orchestra leader.
Nelson A. Rockefeller, 1906–1979, US Republican politician.

NEVILLE
Origin/meaning: French 'new city'. (Neuville is a place in Normandy.)

This is a Norman French surname which came over to England at the time of the Conquest in the form *de Nevil*. The Nevilles were an important aristocratic family in the Middle Ages. The form Nevill is the surname of the Marquess of Abergavenny. It was therefore an almost inevitable addition to the number of aristocratic surnames (Sidney, Percy, Russell, Ashley etc) which came into use in the 19th century.

Variations and abbreviations: Nevel, Nevil, Nevill.

Examples: Neville Chamberlain, 1869–1940, British Prime Minister. Neville Marriner, British musician.

NIALL (pron. Nýe-all)
Origin/meaning: Old Irish 'champion'.

A modern Irish name the equivalent of the English Nigel. Both names stem from the Old Irish 'niadh' meaning champion. The form Neil is also common in Ireland.

Variations and abbreviations: see Nigel.

NICHOLAS
Origin/meaning: Greek 'victory of the people'.

This pre-Christian Greek name was adopted as a Christian name because of the veneration for St Nicholas, a 4th century bishop of Myra in Asia Minor. Initially popular in the Eastern church (the name is still much used in Eastern Europe) his fame spread to Western Europe in the early Middle Ages. Many quite unsubstantiated legends grew up around him that associated him with miracles and good deeds affecting many parts of society. As a result he became the Patron Saint not only of Russia but of a bewildering number of groups, including sailors, pawnbrokers (his symbol is three golden balls), thieves, prostitutes and children. It is because he is Patron Saint of children that he has developed into Father Christmas or Santa Claus (Claus being a German short form of Nicholas). In many countries Santa Claus brings presents to children not on Christmas day but on December 6th, the feast of St Nicholas. Although, as a saint's name, Nicholas lost ground in Protestant countries at the time of the Reformation, in the 20th century it has recovered totally and since the Second World War has been one of the most consistently popular names in English-speaking countries.

Variations and abbreviations: Claus (Ger), Cole, Colet, Colin, Klaas (Dut), Klaus (Ger), Niccolo (It), Nick, Nickie, Nicko, Nicky, Nicol (Med Eng), Nicolas (Fr), Nikita (Russ), Niklaus (Ger), Nikolai (Russ), Nikolaus (Ger).

Examples: Nicholas Monsarrat, English novelist.
Nikolai Gogol, 1809–1852, Russian writer.
Sir Nikolaus Pevsner, 1903–1983, German-born British historian and academic.

NICK
Origin/meaning: Greek 'victory of the people'.

A short form of Nicholas q.v.

Variations and abbreviations: see Nicholas.

NICODEMUS
Origin/meaning: Greek 'victory of the people'.

This pre-Christian Greek name has the same meaning as Nicholas q.v. It was said to be the name of a secret follower of Jesus who wrote the apocryphal Gospel of Nicodemus. It was therefore adopted as a Christian name and was popular in the Middle Ages. The Puritans also favoured the name but it has become virtually obsolete over the last century.

Variations and abbreviations: Nick, Nicodemo (It), Nikodem (Ger), Nikodemus (Dut). See also Nicholas.

NICOL
Origin/meaning: Greek 'victory of the people'.

This is one of the earliest English forms of Nicholas. It was used for boys and girls. Itself a common Scottish surname it gave rise to many others, most notably Nicolson.

Variations and abbreviations: see Nicholas.

Example: Nicol Williamson, British actor.

NIGEL
Origin/meaning: Old Irish 'champion'.

This name developed from the Irish Celtic 'niadh' meaning champion. The name first went from Ireland to Scandinavia. The Normans, who were Viking in origin, adopted it and brought it to England with them in 1066, usually in the form Neel or Nele. Meanwhile other Viking invaders from Denmark and Norway had brought the name separately to the North of England and Scotland. Being a well-established medieval name it appeared in documents taking a Latin form – Nigellus. This was eventually assumed to be the true form of the name and it was given as a baptismal name in the form Nigel or Nygall, without its Latin ending. The origin of the name was forgotten and its similarity to Niger, the Latin word for black, led people to assume that this was its meaning. So Neil and Nigel came to be treated as quite separate names and continue to be to this day, although they are in fact identical in origin.

Variations and abbreviations: Neal, Neale, Neel, Nele, Neil, Neill, Neils (Scand), Nels, (Scand), Nial, Niall, Niel, Niels (Scand), Nils

(Scand).

Examples: Nigel Lawson, English politician.
Nigel Hawthorne, English actor.
Sir Nigel Playfair, 1874–1934, English actor-manager.

NINIAN

Origin/meaning: uncertain, possibly a Celtic corruption of the Latin 'vivianus' (Vivian) – 'full of life'.

This was the name of an early British missionary, St Ninian, d.432, who converted the Southern Picts of Scotland to Christianity. Its use has been almost totally confined to Scotland and the North of England where it has now become rare.

Variations and abbreviations: Ninias, Ninnidh (Ir), Nynia.

Example: Sir Ninian Stephen, Governor-General of Australia.

NKRUMAH

Origin/meaning: Akan 'ninth born'.

This is a Ghanaian name.

Example: Kwame Nkrumah, 1909–1972, Ghanaian Head of State.

NOAH

Origin/meaning: uncertain. Possibly Hebrew 'long-lived'.

This is one of the most popular Old Testament figures, the builder of the Ark and refounder of the human race (Genesis 5–10). The name was used by Puritans in the 17th century but is very unusual today. It is still used by some Gypsy families.

Example: Noah Webster, 1758–1843, US lexicographer, founder of Webster's dictionary.

NOËL

Origin/meaning: Latin/Old French 'birth day', ie 'Christmas'.

This French word for Christmas has been used as a name for children born at the Christmas season since the early Middle Ages. It was more popular in England than the native word Christmas which is also occasionally used. The form Noël was once common to both boys and girls but in the 20th century a separate feminine form, Noelle, has been formed.

Variations and abbreviations: Natale (It), Noel, Nowel (Eng), Nowell.

Example: Noël Coward, 1899–1973, English actor, playwright and composer.

NOLL
Origin/meaning: uncertain. Possibly Old Norse 'ancestor'.

The old short form of Oliver. Old Noll was the Royalists' nickname for Oliver Cromwell. In the 20th century Ollie is preferred.

NORMAN
Origin/meaning: Old English/Old German 'north man'.

This is a pre-Conquest name. It developed in England to describe the many invaders from Scandinavia, to the North of the British Isles, who repeatedly invaded the country after the departure of the Romans. The name developed at the same time on the continent in Old German, which is very similar to Old English, to describe the Viking invaders who settled in the area which came to be known as Normandy. Although it survived the Conquest the name went out of use in the late Middle Ages, but survived as a surname. It was successfully revived in the 19th century when pre-Conquest and medieval names were in vogue. It is still popular today.

Variations and abbreviations: Norm, Normand, Normann (Ger).

Examples: Norman Mailer, US writer.
Norman St John Stevas, British politician.

NORRIS
Origin/meaning: Old French 'northerner'.
This is a family name occasionally used as a first name.

Example: Norris McWhirter, co-founder of the *Guiness Book of Records*.

NORTON
Origin/meaning: Old English 'from the northern town'.
A family name occasionally used as a first name.

NURAL
Origin/meaning: Arabic 'born in daylight'.
A popular Arabic name.
Variation: Nuru (E African). See also Lucius.

O

OBA (pron. Áwba).
Origin/meaning: Yoruba 'king'.

A popular name in Nigeria. Many Nigerian names contain this word such as Obadele 'the king ie new baby arrives at the house', Obawole 'the king enters the house' and Obafemi 'the king likes me'.

OBADIAH
Origin/meaning: Hebrew: 'serving the Lord'.

This was the name of one of the Hebrew prophets written about in the Old Testament Book of Obadiah. He was a prophet at the court of Ahab, who foretold the destruction of Edom. Obadiah was used by Puritans in England and New England after the Protestant reformation. It remained in use in the US until well into the 19th century.

Its use by Anthony Trollope as the first name of the obsequious and two-faced Chaplain Obadiah Slope in his Barchester novel, *The Warden*, may well have contributed to the name's decline in popularity in England.

OBERON
Origin/meaning: Old German 'little elf-ruler'.

An alternative spelling of Auberon q.v. which was used by Shakespeare as an appropriate name for the king of the fairies in *A Midsummer Night's Dream*. Another form is Aubrey q.v.

OCTAVIUS
Origin/meaning: Latin 'eighth'.

A name given to an eighth son or child. Rarely used since the 19th century. Octavius was the brother-in-law of Julius Caesar. His daughter was the unfortunate second wife of Mark Antony. His son, Octavianus, became the Emperor Augustus.

ODO
Origin/meaning: Old German 'of the fatherland' or 'rich'.

An Old German name, popular with the Normans, who introduced it into Britain. Widespread in the Middle Ages it now survives best in the form Otto, and is a favourite German name. The girls' names Odette, Odile and Ottilie come from the same root word. St Odo of Cluny, 879–942, was the monk responsible for the 10th century monastic revival which began at the French monastery at Cluny. The Tractarians, 19th century High Church followers, revived the name in his honour.

Variations and abbreviations: Oda, Oddo, Odilo, Otho, Otto.

Example: Odo Bishop of Bayeux, 1063–1097, half-brother of William the Conqueror.

ODYSSEUS
Origin/meaning: uncertain. Possibly Etruscan 'wanderer' – sometimes given as 'hater'.

The original Greek version of Ulysses *q.v.*

OKECHUKU (pron. Okehchóoku)
Origin/meaning: Yoruba 'God's gift'.

A Nigerian name.

See also Matthew, Nathaniel, Theodore, Jonathan.

OKPARA (pron. Okpára)
Origin/meaning: Ibo 'first son'.

This name comes from Nigeria.

OLAF
Origin/meaning: Old Norse 'ancestor-inheritance/remains'.

This long-established and popular Scandinavian name is found in English-speaking countries where there are Scandinavian immigrants. Two famous historical characters ensured the name's popularity. The first was Olaf I Trygvasson, 969–1000, the Norwegian king responsible for many of the Viking raids on Britain and France until his conversion to Christianity. The second was Olaf II, 995–1030, also known as St Olaf, or Olaf the Fat, who established Christianity in Norway. The Danes who invaded Britain brought the name with them but it died out after the Norman Conquest. It probably survives as the English Oliver *q.v.* and French Olivier.

In Scandinavia it is often used as a double name, eg Karl-Olaf.

Variations and abbreviations: Ola, Olav, Olef, Olof, Olov.
Example: King Olav V of Norway.

OLIVER
Origin/meaning: uncertain. Possibly Old Norse 'ancestor-inheritance/remains,' from Anleifr. Sometimes given as 'olive tree.'

The similarity of this name to Olivarius, a late Latin word for an olive tree, coupled with the fact that it was introduced into England from France by the Normans in 1066, has supported the idea that Oliver has the same meaning as the feminine names Olive and Olivia. However the Normans were actually Viking in origin and the name is more likely to have the Old Norse meaning the Scandinavian names Olaf and Olav. Oliver was the form used in England in the Middle Ages. Like Roland its popularity was enhanced by the medieval romance tales which grew up around the life of the Emperor Charlemagne, 742–814, in a similar way to the tales of King Arthur and Camelot. Oliver was one of Charlemagne's twelve Paladins and the staunch friend of Roland. His sword was called Haute-clair and Roland's was called Durandana. The two friends fought in single combat for five days without either gaining the advantage, which is the origin of the expression, 'A Roland for an Oliver' meaning a fair exchange or tit for tat. After the death of Oliver Cromwell, 1599–1658, and the Restoration of the monarchy the name went out of fashion for about 200 years in England where it was felt to be a reminder of the civil war. In the 1970s and 80s it has become a vogue name in England and France.

Variations and abbreviations: Noll (Med Eng), Nolly, Olaf (Scand), Olav (Scand), Oliverio (Sp), Olivier (Fr), Oliviero (It), Ollie, Olly.

Examples: Oliver Tobias, English actor.
Oliver Goldsmith, 1728–1774, English novelist and playwright.
Oliver Wendell Holmes, 1809–1894, US writer.

OLU (pron. Óhlu)
Origin/meaning: Yoruba 'pre-eminent'.

This name comes from Nigeria.

Example: Olu Jacobs, British actor.

OMAR
Origin/meaning: Arab (and Swahili) 'highest'.

491

Omar, 581–564, was the second Khalif. He was the father of one of Mohammed's nine wives. His military skill extended his empire across North Africa, Persia and Syria, which is why the Muslim religion and names are found in Iran and East Africa.

Variations: Omari (Swahili), Umar.

Examples: Omar Sharif, Egyptian actor.
Omar Khayam, 1050–1123, Persian astronomer and poet.

ORLANDO
Origin/meaning: Old German 'fame-land' usually given as 'famous man of the land'.

This is the Italian form of the English Rowland and French Roland q.v. It was found in England during the Renaissance period when Italian influence was strong; Shakespeare used it in his play *As You Like It*. Virginia Woolf used it for the main character in her novel *Orlando*, 1928, and it is still used occasionally in English-speaking countries.

Variations and abbreviations: see Rowland.

Examples: Orlando Plunket-Greene, son of designer Mary Quant.
Orlando Gibbons, 1583–1625, English composer.

ORSON
Origin/meaning: Latin 'bear'.
This is the English form of the Italian name Orso. It is very rare.

Example: Orson Welles, US director and actor.

ORVILLE
Origin/meaning: Old French 'golden town.'

A rare name familiar because of the US aviation pioneer Orville Wright, 1871–1948.

OSAKWE (pron. Osárkway)
Origin/meaning: Benin 'God agrees'.

A Nigerian name. The word Os- God, appears in many Nigerian names, for example Osahar-'God hears', Osayaba – 'God forgives' and Osaze-'liked by God'. Note the similarity to the North European word for God and hence Osbert, Osmond etc.

OSBERT

Origin/meaning: Old English 'god-famous'.

One of several Old English names eg Oscar, Osborn, which contain the word Os, meaning God. It was found in Northumbria where Viking influence was strong and it has a very similar Old Norse equivalent, As. Often the names developed out of both languages simultaneously, just as many Old German names have an almost identical Old English equivalent, for the languages were very similar. Osbert was one of these old names which the Normans themselves had adopted and adapted slightly (like Roland, Bernard and many others) so it did not die out after 1066. Like Wilfred, which *had* disappeared, having no Norman version, it was revived in the 19th century as part of a general interest in Old English culture.

Examples: Osbert Lancaster, English cartoonist.
Sir Osbert Sitwell, 1892–1969, English author.

OSBORN

Origin/meaning: Old English 'god-warrior' or Old Norse 'god-bear'.

A pre-Conquest name which developed primarily as a surname in the Middle Ages. It is now found as a personal name again because family names are being increasingly used as first names.

Variations and abbreviations: Osborne, Osbourne, Ossy.

OSCAR

Origin/meaning: Old Norse 'god spear', ie 'divine spear'.

A Scandinavian name which, like Olaf, was introduced into Britain by the Viking invaders, although an Anglo-Saxon equivalent may well have existed. In Ireland it took the form Osgar which is nearer to the original Norse, Asgeirr. In Ireland the name survived, but in England it died out completely after the Norman Conquest. The poet James Macpherson, 1736–1796, published in the 1760s *Fingal* and *Temora*, two epic poems supposedly translations of the work of a 3rd century Celtic bard called Ossian. Although they were probably written by Macpherson himself and only based on fragments of an original, the poems were a runaway success throughout Europe for they were perfectly in tune with the spirit of the great Romantic revival in literature and art of the late 18th and early 19th centuries. Oscar was the name of the supposed warrior bard's son and it became a favourite name virtually overnight.

Napoleon's godson, later King of Sweden, was given the name and so it returned to its country of origin and became one of the most common Scandinavian names. Oscar Wilde, although Irish, was given the non-Irish form of the name; it was done to honour King Oscar II of Sweden whom his father, a doctor, had treated and who became Oscar's grandfather. Still popular in Europe, it became unfashionable in Britain after the sad scandal surrounding Oscar Wilde, 1854–1900, at the end of the 19th century.

Variations and abbreviations: Asger (Dan), Ansgar, Osgar (Ir), Oskar (Ger/Scand), Ossie, Ossy, Ozzie, Ozzy.

Examples: Oscar Niemeyer, Brazilian architect, designer of Brasilia.
Oscar Lewenstein, British theatrical impresario.

OSGAR
Origin/meaning: Old Norse 'god-spear', ie 'divine spear'.

The Irish form of Oscar *q.v.*

OSMOND
Origin/meaning: Old English/Old Norse 'god-protection', ie 'divine protection'.

Like Osbert, Oswald and Oscar, this name developed in several countries simultaneously. It survived the Conquest because the Normans had already adopted it. Like Osborn it developed as a surname with occasional use as a first name. Since the 19th century when surnames became acceptable as first names, it has been used again as a personal name.

Variations and abbreviations: Osmonde, Osmund, Ozzy.

Example: Osmond Bullock, English musical comedy actor.

OSRIC
Origin/meaning: Old English/Old German 'god-rule', ie 'divine rule'.

The *ric* part of this name is the same as that found in Richard, another Anglo-Saxon name which has survived more successfully. It is similar to the German word reich – kingdom, and the Latin word rex – king. Uncommon in the 20th century.

OSWALD
Origin/meaning: Old English 'god-power'.

Another Old English Northumbrian name, like Osbert *q.v.*,

which is very similar to an Old Norse name. Northumbria was frequently invaded by the Vikings. St Oswald, 605–642, was one of the great Anglo-Saxon kings of Northumbria. The name has remained in use for twelve centuries though it is not very common today.

Variations and abbreviations: Ossy, Oswell, Ozzy, Waldo.

Example: Oswald Mosley, 1896–1980, British politician.

OTTO
Origin/meaning: Old German 'of the fatherland' or 'rich'.

The version of the Old German name Odo *q.v.* which has survived most successfully into the 20th century. It was popular with the Normans who brought it to England at the time of the Conquest in all its forms. Its popularity in the Middle Ages is clear from the number of surnames eg Oates, Oddie, which come from it.

Variations and abbreviations: Odo, Oddo, Odilo, Othello, Otho.

Examples: Otto von Bismarck, 1815–1898, German statesman.
Otto Preminger, Austrian film director.
Otto Kruger, US film actor.

OWEN
Origin/meaning: uncertain. Possibly Old Scots/Irish 'young warrior' or Welsh 'lamb' or Old Welsh 'well born'.

One of the most common Welsh names both as a first name and as a surname. It is sometimes considered to be the merging of a native name with the Latin name Eugenius, and thus the equivalent of the modern name Eugene. Its popularity probably stemmed initially from the great renown of Owen Glendower (Owain Glyndwr), 1359–1416, leader of the Welsh rebellion against Henry IV. The surname Bowen is the Anglicized version of ap-Owen, son of Owen. Owen is now found in England, Owain remains the more genuine Welsh version.

Variations and abbreviations: Eugene, Ewen (Scots), Owain (Wel), Ywain (Old Wel).

Examples: Owen Hall (real name James Davus), 1854–1907, Composer of the operetta *Floradora*.
Owen Nares, 1888–1943, British-born Hollywood film actor and matinee idol.
Owen Meredith, Earl of Lytton, 1831–1891, Aristocrat and poet.

P

PADDY
Origin/meaning: Latin 'patrician'.

An Irish familiar form of Patrick *q.v.* and occasionally of the feminine form Patricia. It developed from the Irish version of the name, Pádraig.

Example: Paddy Chayefsky, US dramatic writer (Marty).

PÁDRAIG (pron. Pórreg).
Origin/meaning: Latin 'patrician'.

The native Irish form of Patrick *q.v.*

Variation: Pádraic.

Example: Pádraic Henry Pearse, 1879–1916, Irish writer and nationalist.

PASCAL
Origin/meaning: Hebrew/Latin 'of the Passover' or 'of Easter'.

A name given to boys born about the time of Easter or the feast of the Passover. Although now considered a French name it was once equally used in England. One English version, Pascoe, is still found as a surname. Paschal was the name of two Popes.

Variations and abbreviations: Paschal, Paschalis (Ger), Pascoe (Eng), Pasquale (It). See also Easter.

PAT
Origin/meaning: Latin 'patrician', ie aristocratic.

A common short form of Patrick *q.v.* Also used for the feminine form Patricia.

Example: Pat Boone, US singer.

PATRICK
Origin/meaning: Latin 'patrician' ie aristocratic.

This is a name long associated with Ireland and to a lesser extent

Scotland. From Scotland it spread to Northern England, where examples are found from the early Middle Ages, but until the last century was unusual elsewhere in England. The name was taken to the US, Canada, Australia and New Zealand in the 19th century when many Irish people emigrated. The association of the name with the Celtic areas and Ireland in particular dates back to the early 5th century. Soccat, a Scottish or Welsh Christian boy (Soccat means combatant), was captured and sold into slavery in Ireland. He escaped six years later and lived as a monk in France where he was ordained a bishop at the age of 45. He decided to return to the country of his captivity as a missionary. Before doing so he took the new name Patrick. His mission was highly successful since he converted the clan chiefs, including his former master. The rest of the people tended to follow the example of their chiefs. By the time he died c.461, aged about 90, Ireland was a Christian country. St Patrick is, of course, the Patron Saint of Ireland. For a long time the name (like Brigid and Mary) was considered too holy to use. However since the 16th century it has been the most popular masculine name in Ireland. The increased interest in native Irish culture has also seen a revival of the native spellings Pádraig or Pádraic.

Variations and abbreviations: Paddie, Paddy, Pádraic, Pádraig, Padrig (Wel), Pat, Patric, Patrice (Fr), Patrizio (It), Patrizius (Ger/Dut), Patsy.

Examples: Patrick Procktor, English painter.
Patric Dickinson, English poet.

PAUL
Origin/meaning: Latin 'small'.

Just as Timothy and Euphemia were long-established Greek personal names adopted as Christian names because they appear in the Bible, so Paul (Paullus) was an established Roman name. Its use as a Christian name is due to St Paul, who changed his name from the Jewish Saul, after his conversion to Christianity on the road to Damascus. From being one of the fiercest persecutors of Christinity he became its most energetic missionary taking the faith across the known world and earning the title Apostle of the Gentiles. He shares a feast day on June 29th with St Peter and his fame and the influence of his name have always been overshadowed by Peter. Although many English churches were dedicated to them both they tended to be known as St Peter's. The famous exception is St Paul's Cathedral. Although the name was familiar it did not come into common usage in England until after the Protestant Reformation. Puritans shunned Peter as being the name of the first Pope and Paul flourished correspondingly. In Europe Paul has always been more popular. The French equivalent of the English 'Tom, Dick and Harry' is 'Pierre, Jacques, Paul'. The pronunciation in Europe (Powle, Powlo) reflects the original Latin pronunciation which was once also used in England. Paulinus was once a separate name but is obsolete today.

Variations and abbreviations: Paavo (Finn), Pablo (Sp), Paolo (It), Paolino (It), Paulinus, Paulus, Pavel (Russ), Poul (Dan).

Examples: Paul Newman, US film actor.
Pablo Picasso, 1881–1973, Spanish painter.
Paul Verlaine, 1844–1896, French painter.

PELHAM
Origin/meaning: Old English 'Pella's homestead'.

This is an aristocratic surname, being the family name of the Duke of Newcastle and of the Earls of Chichester and Yarborough. Along with names such as Percy, Howard and Sidney it came into use in the 19th century. However, it has never become as well-established.

Example: Pelham Grenville Wodehouse, 1881–1975, English-born writer.

PENRY
Origin/meaning: Welsh 'son of Henry'.

This is a Welsh surname, a contraction of ap Henry, which is itself a contraction of mab Henry – son of Henry. The name is now also used as a first name.

Variation: Penri. See also Henry.

PERCEVAL
Origin/meaning: French 'from Percheval' a village in Normandy.

This is a Norman French surname occasionally used as a first name in England and France since the Middle Ages. The short form Percy soon became a separate surname in its own right.

Both Perceval (the surname of the Earls of Egmont) and Percy (the surname of the Dukes of Northumberland) came into use as first names in the 19th century when aristocratic surnames were fashionable. They may also have been helped by the fact that a Perceval appears in the Tales of King Arthur which were popular at the time.

Variations and abbreviations: Perce, Percival, Percy.

Example: Percival Wren, 1885–1941, English novelist, author of *Beau Geste*, 1924.

PERCY

Origin/meaning: French 'from Percheval' a village in Normandy.

This name is an early short form of the original Perceval and was brought to England by the Normans. It was primarily a surname which went through an intermediate form de Perci. As the family name of the Dukes of Northumberland it became a fashionable first name in the 19th century. It is also used as a familiar form of the first name Perceval.

Abbreviation: Perce.

Example: Percy Bysshe Shelley, 1792–1822, English Romantic poet.
Percy Thrower, English gardening expert.

PEREGRINE

Origin/meaning: Latin 'foreigner', 'traveller', 'pilgrim'.

A rare name, it has been used since the early Middle Ages to honour St Peregrinus, the Patron Saint of Modena.

Variations and abbreviations: Pellegrino (It), Peregrin (Ger), Perry.

Example: Peregrine Worsthorne, British journalist.

PERRY

Origin/meaning: 'little Peter' from Greek 'stone' or Latin 'traveller'.

This is a familiar form of either Peter *q.v.* or Peregrine *q.v.* Like many forms of Peter it is also found as a surname.

Variations and abbreviations: see Peter.

Example: Perry Como, US singer.

PETER

Origin/meaning: Greek 'stone'.

In John 1, v.42, Jesus renamed Simon saying, 'Thou art Simon, the son of Jona: thou shalt be called Cephas, which is by interpretation, a stone'. Since the gospel was written in Greek and the Greek word for stone is petros, Simon came to be known as Simon Peter and later as St Peter. As the first Bishop of Rome he was considered by Catholics as the first Pope and his name, in many forms, was therefore popular throughout Europe. In England the early form of the name, introduced by the Normans, was Piers. It is similar to the modern French Pierre. Another early form adopted from France was Perry, 'little Peter'. Peter had become the accepted form in the late Middle Ages probably because the written form, which was Latin, was Petrus. After the Reformation Peter, with its strong Catholic connotations, went out of favour in Protestant countries like England. It was extremely rare in the US until the 19th century when immigrants from Catholic countries brought it with them. During the 20th century it has been popular in all English-speaking countries, particularly Britain and Australia. The 20th century revival of the name Peter is sometimes attributed to the immense popularity of J. M. Barrie's children's book of *Peter Pan*, 1904.

Variations and abbreviations: Pär (Swed), Parry, Peadar (Ir), Pearce, Peder, Pedro (Sp), Peer (Norway), Per (Swed), Perkin (Med Eng), Perry, Pete, Pierce, Pierre (Fr), Pieter (Dut), Piero (It), Pietro (It), Pyotr (Russ), Pyrs (Wel).

Examples: Peter O'Toole, Irish actor.
Pieter Breughel, 1520–1569, Dutch painter.
Pyotr Tchaikovsky, 1840–1893, Russian composer.

PHELIM

Origin/meaning: Old Irish 'ever good'.

A popular Irish name. Sometimes 'translated' to Felix by English speakers.

Variations and abbreviations: Feiolim (Celt), Felim, Felimy.

PHILEMON

Origin/meaning: Greek 'loving mind'.

One of many pre-Christian Greek names like Timothy or Dorcas, adopted by the Puritans in the 17th century because they appear in the New Testament. One of St Paul's epistles was directed to Philemon.

PHILIP
Origin/meaning: Greek 'lover of horses'.

This is the name of one of the Apostles and was therefore much used in the Middle Ages when saints' names were popular. It has given rise to many surnames including Phillips, Phelps and Philpot. In England its inevitable loss of favour after the Protestant Reformation was hastened by the fact that it was the name of the King of Spain, England's arch-enemy, whose Armada was successfully defeated in 1588. The name has been creeping back into favour since the second half of the 19th century.

Variations and abbreviations: Felipe (Sp), Filip (Scand), Filippo (It), Lippo (It), Phil, Philipp (Ger), Philippe (Fr), Philippus (Ger/Dut), Pip.

Examples: HRH Prince Philip, husband of Elizabeth II.
Sir Philip Sidney, 1554–1586, English poet.
Fra Filippo Lippi, 1406–1469, Italian painter.

PHINEAS
Origin/meaning: uncertain. Sometimes given as Hebrew 'oracle' or Egyptian 'negro'.

This is a Biblical name adopted by 17th century Puritans, especially in New England. It has always been rare. Anthony Trollope used it for *Phineas Finn*, 1869, the story of a young politician in his Palliser series of novels.

Variation: Phinehas.

Example: Phineas Fletcher, 1582–1650, English poet.

PIERCE
Origin/meaning: Greek 'stone'.

An alternative spelling of the early form of Peter *q.v.* also Piers.

PIERS
Origin/meaning: Greek 'stone'.

The form of Peter *q.v.* introduced into Britain by the Normans in 1066. It was eventually ousted by the form Peter, which is nearer to the original Greek. However, many surnames developed from it including Pears, Pearson, Pearce and Perrin. Piers is still used today but far less often than Peter.

Variations and abbreviations: see Peter.

Examples: Piers Gaveston, d.1312, favourite of Edward II. Piers Anthony, British Sci-fi writer.

PLACIDO (pron. Plassido)
Origin/meaning: Latin 'calm'.

An adjective occasionally used as a name.

Example: Placido Domingo, Spanish opera singer.

PRINCE
Origin/meaning: Latin 'prince', 'ruler'.

This is a family name probably indicating an ancestor who worked for a prince. It is sometimes, like Earl or Duke, used as a first name.

Example: Prince Littler, 1901–1973, British theatrical impresario.

PROSPER
Origin/meaning: Latin 'successful', 'prosperous'.

Although unusual in England this name was well-established in Europe where it was given in the hope that the new child would indeed be successful and prosperous. Shakespeare used the Italian form, Prospero, for the hero of his play *The Tempest*, 1611.

Variations and abbreviations: Prospero (It), Prosperus (Ger).

Example: Prosper Mérimée, 1803–1870, French writer.

PURUSHOTAM (pron. Pooróosotam)
Origin/meaning: Sanskrit 'best of men'.

The name of a Hindu god. Found throughout India. Less common than formerly because of its length.

Q

QUENTIN

Origin/meaning: Latin 'fifth'.

Quintus was a Roman forename and also the name of a famous tribe, the Quintii, renowned for their exemplary behaviour. Two early Roman martyrs, SS Quintino and Quinto, made the name familiar and their names became altered to Quentine in France via where the name came to England. After the Middle Ages the name virtually disappeared in England but remained popular in Scotland. It was re-introduced back into England from Scotland with the publication of Sir Walter Scott's novel *Quentin Durward*, 1823.

Variations and abbreviations: Quinn, Quint, Quintilio (It), Quintin, Quinto (It), Quinton, Quntus (Ger).

Examples: Quentin Bell, writer son of Vanessa Bell, nephew of Virginia Woolf.
Quentin Crisp, English eccentric.

QUINCY

Origin/meaning: Latin/Old French 'from the fifth place', 'from the fifth son's estate'.

There are several places called Quincy in France and settlers in England at the time of the Conquest brought the name with them. It is most usual as a surname, sometimes with the aristocratic prefix *de*. Thomas De Quincy, 1785–1859, author of *Confessions of an English Opium Eater*, is an example. These aristocratic overtones may account for its use as a first name when this became fashionable in the nineteenth century.

Variations and abbreviations: Quin, Quincey, Quinn.

Example: John Quincey Adams, 1767–1848, US statesman.

QUINN

Origin/meaning: Old Irish 'counsel' or (sometimes) Latin 'fifth'.

503

A common Irish surname used as a first name. It is sometimes found as a short form of Quintin or Quincy.

Variation: Quin.

Example: Quinn Martin, US TV producer.

QUINTIN
Origin/meaning: Latin 'fifth'.

An alternative spelling of Quentin *q.v.*

Example: Quintin Hogg (Lord Hailsham), British Lord Chancellor.

R

RAFE
Origin/meaning: Old Norse/Old English 'wolf counsel'.

A variation of Ralph *q.v.* which is spelt according to the pronunciation.

RAJAN
Origin/meaning: Sanskrit 'king'.

RAJENDR
Origin/meaning: Sanskrit 'King of kings'.

This is the Gujerati version of the name. The Sikh version uses the typical Sikh addition Singh, which means 'lion'.

Variation: Rajinder Singh (Sikh).

Example: Rajendra Prasad, 1884–1963, Indian statesman.

RAJNIKANT (pron. Rjneekant)
Origin/meaning: Sanskrit 'night'.

The same as the feminine Rajni with the addition of -kant which is a polite form of address.

RAKSHA
Origin/meaning: Sanskrit 'protected'.

This is the name of a Hindu festival (usually in August) when brothers are reminded of their duty to protect their sisters.

RALPH (pron. Rafe. Modern pron. Ralph)
Origin/meaning: Old Norse/Old English 'wolf counsel'.

This (sometimes in the form Radulf) was a pre-Conquest English name. It was also popular with the Normans so it did not die out in England after the Norman Conquest. The medieval spellings, Raffe, and Rauf and later Rafe, indicate the usual pronunciation. In the US the *l* is usually sounded, just as in Anthony, Americans frequently sound the th, rather than leave the t hard. This pronunciation is becoming increasingly common in Britain.

In Scotland the *1* has always been sounded, probably because of the similarity to the name Rolph with which it is closely connected. In France the name has developed as Raoul and the English surname Rawlings indicates this was a form found in England in the Middle Ages when French influence was still strong.

Variations and abbreviations: Rafe, Ralf, Raoul (Fr).

Examples: Sir Ralph Richardson, 1903–1983, English actor.

Ralph Waldo Emerson, 1803–1882, US poet and essayist.

RANALD
Origin/meaning: Old German/Old English 'power-might'.

An uncommon spelling of Ronald, the Scottish equivalent of Reynold *q.v.* and its variation Reginald. Unlike Ronald, Ranald has remained distinctively Scottish.

RANDAL
Origin/meaning: Old English 'shield wolf'.

One of two medieval forms of this pre-Conquest name, the other being Ranulf. Randal has survived into the 20th century as well as giving rise to several surnames, including Randle, Ransom, Rankin etc. Its survival may be partly due to the ease with which it can be used as a first name from a family name.

Variations and abbreviations: Rand, Randall, Randell, Randolf, Randolph, Randy, Ranulf, Ranulph. See also Ralph, Rolph.

RANDOLPH
Origin/meaning: Old English 'shield wolf'.

The 18th century 'classical' version of the old name Ranulf, more commonly found today in the medieval form Randal *q.v.* A name used by alternate generations of the Churchill family.

Examples: Lord Randolph Churchill, 1849–1895, British conservative politician, father of Sir Winston Churchill.
Randolph Caldecott, 1846–1886, English illustrator.

RANDY
Origin/meaning: Old English 'shield wolf'.

A familiar form of Randal or Randolph *q.v.* often as an independent name in the US.

Example: Randy Newman, US songwriter and singer.

RANULF
Origin/meaning: Old English 'shield wolf'.

A medieval form of the name currently used in the form Randal *q.v.* or Randolph *q.v.*

Variation: Ranulph.

Example: Sir Ranulph Fiennes, English explorer.

RAOUL (pron. Raóol)
Origin/meaning: Old Norse 'wolf-counsel'.

The French form of the name Ralph. Both names developed from the pre-Conquest name Radulf. Raoul was one of the versions of the name introduced into England at the time of the Conquest but Ralph soon became the preferred form and Raoul is now rarely used in English-speaking countries.

RAPHAEL
Origin/meaning: Hebrew 'God has healed'.

One of the three named archangels in the Bible, together with Gabriel and Michael. Raphael was the archangel who helped Tobias in the Book of Tobit. The popularity of that story meant it was occasionally used in England in the late Middle Ages, but it has always been most popular with Jewish and Italian people.

Variations and abbreviations: Rafael, Raffaele (It), Raffaello (It), Raphael (Fr), Rafe, Ray.

Examples: Raphael (Raffaello Sanzio), 1483–1520, Italian Renaissance painter.

RAVI
Origin/meaning: Sanskrit 'sun'.

Examples: Ravi Shankar, Indian musician and composer.
Ravi Shastri, Indian cricketer.

RAVINDRA (pron. Ravindr)
Origin/meaning: Sanskrit 'sun-king of heaven'.

Variations: Rabindra, Ravinder Singh (Sikh).

Example: Rabindranath Tagore, 1861–1941, Indian poet and philosopher.

RAY
Origin/meaning: Old German 'strength', 'counsel'.

A short form of Raymond (strength-protection) *q.v.* now frequently found as an independent name. Sometimes used for girls, as a short form of Rachel, instead of the more usual Rae.

Examples: Ray Charles, US singer.
Ray Milland, Welsh film actor.

RAYMOND
Origin/meaning: Old German 'strength protection' or 'counsel protection', ie 'strong' or 'wise protector'.

A name found in Britain since it was introduced by the Normans in 1066. It is found in various forms throughout Europe and is also a surname.

Variations and abbreviations: Raimondo (It), Raimund (Ger), Raimundo (Sp), Ramón (Sp), Ray, Raymund, Reamonn (Ir), Reimund (Ger).

Examples: Raymond Barre, French politician.
Raymond Baxter, English broadcaster.

RAYNER
Origin/meaning: Old German/Old English 'counsel army' or 'strength army'.

Still frequently found as a first name (Rainer) in Germany, this name is more common as a surname in English-speaking countries.

Variations and abbreviations: Ragnar (Scand), Rainer (Ger), Rainerio (It), Rainier (Fr).

Examples: Prince Rainier of Monaco.
Rainer Maria Rilke, 1875–1926, Austrian poet.

REECE
Origin/meaning: Welsh 'impetuous'.

An Anglicized version of the popular Welsh name Rhys *q.v.*

Variations: Rees, Rice.

REGINALD
Origin/meaning: Old German/Old English 'power-might'. Sometimes given as 'powerful judgment'.

This is a late medieval version of the name Reynold *q.v.* from the form which appeared in Latin manuscripts 'Reginaldus'. The written version eventually became more familiar than the original. In Scotland the name developed into Ronald q.v. In the 19th century because of its 'aristocratic' associations Reginald became rather fashionable and more widespread. It was most popular between the World Wars.

Variations and abbreviations: Reg, Reggie, Reginaldo (It), Reginauld (Fr), Rex, Reynold.

Example: Reginald Bosanquet, 1932–1984, English television presenter.

RENÉ (pron. R'nay)
Origin/meaning: French 'reborn'.

A name with religious significance. It is common in France but only occasionally used in English-speaking countries where it is sometimes mistakenly used for the feminine form Renée.

Variations: Renatus (Ger), Renato (It).

Examples: René Descartes, 1596–1650, French philosopher.
René Cutforth, British journalist.

REUBEN
Origin/meaning: uncertain. Sometimes given as 'Behold, a son'. Possibly Hebrew 'renewer'.

This is a Biblical name. Reuben was one of the sons of Jacob and gave his name to one of the tribes of Israel. It was used by English and North American Puritans in the 17th century when Biblical names were popular. In Britain it is now regarded as an almost exclusively Jewish name.

Variations and abbreviations: Rube, Rubén (Sp), Rubin.

REX
Origin/meaning: Latin 'king'.

A name which appears in the early years of the 20th century presumably to honour the accession of a king (Edward VII) after the long reign of Queen Victoria. Sometimes used as a short form of Reginald q.v. and also Eric q.v. because it means 'king' or 'ruler'.

Examples: Rex Harrison, British actor.
Rex Whistler, 1905–1944, English artist.

REYNOLD

Origin/meaning: Old German/Old English 'power might'.

A pre-Conquest name (Regenweald) which survived the Conquest in the French form brought over by the Normans – Reynaud. From this came the English Reynold. Never a common first name it developed more successfully as the surname Reynolds. Reginald *q.v.* is a later and more familiar first name form. In Scotland the name became Ronald *q.v.* The many foreign variations (one of which is familiar as the name of the famous French car firm Renault) indicate the name's widespread popularity in Europe.

Variations and abbreviations: Ragnvald (Swed), Rainald (Ger), Reginald, Reinald (Ger), Reinaldo (Sp), Reinaldos (Sp), Reinhold (Scand), Reinold (Dut), Reinwald (Ger), Renault (Fr), Reynaud (Fr), Reynolds, Rinaldo (It), Ronald (Scot).

RICHARD

Origin/meaning: Old English 'rule hard', ie 'strong king'.

An Anglo-Saxon name, used by a Kentish king who went as a monk to Europe. The name became established in Europe where there was a similar Old German name and was introduced back into England at the Norman Conquest. One medieval variation was Ricard from which we get the short form Rick, its typical rhyming short form Dick (like Bob from Rob) and also occasionally Hick. The immense popularity of the name meant that many surnames are derived from it and its variations, such as Dickens, Richards and Hicks. A short form which has totally died out is Hud, but it survives in the surnames Hud and Hudson. The fame of Richard the Lion Heart, 1157–1199, and of the English St Richard of Chichester, contributed to the establishment of the name and for several hundred years it was generally one of the top men's names along with John, Thomas, Henry and William. The phrase 'Every Tom, Dick and Harry' indicates just how common those names were. Taken to North America by the early settlers Richard did not survive as well as the Biblical names of the period. However at the end of the 19th century it regained popularity on both sides of the Atlantic and remains well-established although in the last ten years its popularity has waned a little.

Variations and abbreviations: Diccon (Med Eng), Dick, Dickie, Dicky, Reichard (Ger), Ric, Ricard, Ricardo (Sp), Riccardo (It),

Rich, Richardt (Ger), Richart (Dut), Richie, Richy, Rick, Riocard (Ir), Ritchie.

Examples: Richard Wagner, 1813–1883, German composer.
Richard Burton, 1925–1984, Welsh actor.
Richard Attenborough, Welsh actor and film director.

RICK
Origin/meaning: either a short form of Richard 'strong king' or of names, eg Frederick, which end in -rick.

Variations: Ric, Rickie, Ricky.

Example: Rick Wakefield, British composer.

ROB
Origin/meaning: Old German 'fame-bright'.

A popular short form of Robert and Robin *q.v.*

ROBERT
Origin/meaning: Old German 'fame-bright'.

This name, originally Hrodebert, was the name of a Saxon Bishop of the 8th century. His fame made the name popular throughout the Holy Roman Empire and when that divided into two halves, (roughly corresponding to France and Germany), the name survived. Like many other names it took on a German form (see Rupert), and a French form. It was the French form, Robert, which was brought to England by the Normans. Like almost all Norman names with an Old German origin, it resembled a similar English name of Saxon origin, which meant that it was easily adopted by the English. Other examples are Richard, Albert, Alvin, Baldwin, Theodoric, Walter. Like Richard, Robert gave rise to many surnames, some of which indicate short forms where R was changed typically to H or D as well as the short form familiar today, Bob. Examples are Hobbes and Hobson, from Hob; Dobbs and Dobson from Dob; Robson and Robeson from Rob. Lob and Nob were also used as short forms in the Middle Ages and Dobbin became another name for a farm horse. A French diminutive, Robin *q.v.* became popular enough to develop as an independent name, especially in Scotland. Indeed Robert itself was much used in Scotland where three kings bore the name, including the legendary Robert de Bruce, 1274–1329, who liberated Scotland from the English. Scotland has its own short forms, Rab and Rabbie. Robert has remained consistently popular in Europe to the present day.

Variations and abbreviations: Bert, Bertie, Bob, Bobbie, Bobby, Rab, Rabbie, Riobard (Ir), Rob, Robbie, Robby, Roberto (It), Robin, Robrecht (Ger), Rupert.

Examples: Robert (Rabbie) Burns, 1759–1796, Scottish poet.
Sir Robert Menzies, 1894–1978, Australian statesman.
Robert Redford, US actor.
Robert Muldoon, New Zealand Prime Minister.

ROBIN
Origin/meaning: Old German 'fame bright'.

An originally French diminutive of Robert. The ending implies affection. In the Middle Ages Robin was an even more popular name than Robert. The fact that it is an affectionate diminutive may be the reason why it was the name given to the legendary Robin Hood, who robbed the rich and gave to the poor. Robin Goodfellow is one of the names given to the mischievous spirit usually known as Puck.

Examples: Robin Day, English broadcaster.
Robin Cousins, English figure skating champion.
Robin Knox-Johnson, round-the-world yachtsman.

ROCK
Origin/meaning: Old German 'crow'/'jay' or Old English 'rock'.

A short form of several obsolete names beginning with Roch, such as Rochbert. St Roch or Rock was a 14th century Frenchman who nursed plague victims while on a pilgrimage to Rome. In the US (it is rare in other English-speaking countries) the name Rock or Rocky is usually an English spelling of the name Rocco, the Italian form of Roch. It is generally used for boys of Italian descent. Sometimes it is a short form of the surname Rochester used as a first name.

Variations and abbreviations: Rocco (It), Roch (Fr), Rochus (Ger/Dut), Rocky.

Examples: Rock Hudson, US film actor.
Rocky Marciano, US boxer.

ROD
Origin/meaning: a diminutive of either Rodney (a place name) or Roderick (Old German 'famous ruler').

Examples: Rod Stewart, Scottish singer.

Rod Steiger, US actor.

RODERICK
Origin/meaning: Old German 'fame rule'. Usually given as 'famous ruler'.

One of the most lasting and widespread of the Old German names, Roderick is found in various forms throughout Europe. In Britain it soon became established because of its similarity to several native Celtic names; the Scottish Roderigh, the Welsh Rydderch and Rhodri and the Irish Rhuadhri. Since in Ireland and Scotland these names evolved as Rory, Rory also became known as a familiar form of Roderick. El Cid (Arab-Saeed 'Lord'), the 11th century Spanish hero of the fight to oust the Moors from Spain, was really Rodrigo (Ruy) Diaz, Count of Bivar. The name has always held romantic/heroic connotations.

Variations and abbreviations: Rod, Rodd, Roddie, Roddy, Roderich (Ger), Roderigo, Rodrigo (Sp/It/Port), Rodrigue (Fr), Rory, Rurik (Scand/Russ), Ruy (Sp).

Example: Roderick Thorp, US thriller writer.

RODNEY
Origin/meaning: Old English 'of the reed island'.

This is a surname derived from a place in Somerset. Its use as a first name began half a century before aristocratic surnames became fashionable. It was given to boys after 1782 when the daring and highly successful Admiral (later Lord) Rodney, 1719–1792, captured seven French ships together with their Admiral, de Grasse, off Dominica in the West Indies.

Variations and abbreviations: Rod, Rodd, Roddie, Roddy.

Example: Richard Rodney Bennett, English composer.
Rodney Bewes, English actor.

ROGER
Origin/meaning: Old English/Old German 'fame spear'. Usually given as 'famous spearman'.

This ancient name is found in its original form – Hrothgar – in Beowulf, the Old English epic poem. As with so many Anglo-Saxon names the Normans brought to England their own version based on the Old German, and this merged with the native version. The name has been found in its present form since the Middle Ages. Like Robert and Richard q.v. it had a short form beginning with H. which was a reminder of the

513

original pronunciation. This short form – Hodge, developed as a surname rather than a first name. Roger became an obscure country name for several centuries, but was revived in the 19th century probably as part of the general interest in medieval culture.

Variations and abbreviations: Rodge, Rodger, Rog, Rogerio (Sp), Rüdiger (Ger), Ruggiero (It), Rutger (Dut), Ruttger.

Examples: Roger Moore, English actor.
Roger Bacon, 1214–1292, English philosopher.
Ruggiero Ricci, Italian violinist.

ROLAND
Origin/meaning: Old German 'fame-land', usually given as 'famous man of the land'.

This is the French version of the name which was brought to England by the Normans in 1066. It was the most common version in the early Middle Ages when its popularity was boosted by the famous 11th century French epic poem *The Chanson de Roland*. Roland, who may or may not have existed, was said to be a nephew of the Emperor Charlemagne (742–814). He was Charlemagne's most famous Paladin, the perfect example of a courageous chivalrous Christian knight. The poem celebrates his feats and his heroic death against the Saracens as he crossed the Pyrenees. The English form Rowland later became standard until the 19th century fashion of medieval culture revived the French spelling.

Variations and abbreviations: *see* Rowland.

ROLLO
Origin/meaning: Old German 'fame-wolf'.

A Latinized version of the pre-Conquest name Radulf (similar to Ranulf/Ralph) which has survivied best in English in the form Rolph. Sometimes used as a diminutive of Rowland *q.v.*

Example: Count Rollo of Normandy, 869–932, a Viking chief who invaded France and an ancestor of William the Conqueror.

ROLPH Origin/meaning: Old German 'fame-wolf'.

A name similar in meaning and origin to Ralph and Randal *q.v.* The modern German form of this name is Rudolph, the ancient form is Radulf. It has survived better as a surname than a first name but is currently regaining some popularity.

514

Variations: Rolf, Rollo.

Example: Rolf Harris, Australian entertainer.

ROMAN
Origin/meaning: Latin 'from Rome'.

An unusual name in English-speaking countries. St Romanus was a 6th century Byzantine who wrote many hymns.

Variations and abbreviations: Romain (Fr), Romano (It), Romanus (Ger/Dut).

Example: Roman Polanski, Polish–US film director.

RONALD
Origin/meaning: Old German/Old English 'power-might'.

Like the English Reginald q.v. this Scottish name is a development of Reynold. In the 1920s and 30s Ronald was at the peak of its popularity and as a result is no longer thought of as an exclusively Scottish name.

Variations and abbreviations: Ranald, Reginald, Reynold, Ron, Ronnie.

Examples: Ronald Reagan, Filmstar and US President.
Ronald Colman, 1891–1958, British film actor.

RORY
Origin/meaning: Gaelic 'red-haired' or Old German 'famous ruler'.

The original Celtic name Ruaridh (Scots) and Rhuadhri (Irish) became Roderigh or, more familiar, Rory. This is therefore an independent name of Celtic origin. However the native Scottish name became confused with the similar sounding name Roderick q.v. which was introduced into Scotland by the Vikings. So, while Rory remains an independent name in Ireland, it is often used in Scotland as a familiar form of Roderick. A boy may be christened formally Roderick but use the Gaelic Rory for the rest of his life. The popularity of Rory in Scotland may well be due to the large number of red-headed Scots. In Ireland this native name was sometimes Anglicized as Roger.

Variations and abbreviations: Rorie, Roderick, Roger, Roy.

Examples: Rory Gallagher, Irish rock musician.
Rory Calhoun, US film actor.

ROSS
Origin/meaning: Old Scots 'of the promontory' or Old German 'fame'.

A common Scots surname which has gained popularity in the 20th century as a first name. Particularly popular in North America and Australia where there are many people of Scots descent.

Examples: Ross Macdonald, US novelist.
Ross Thomas, US thriller writer.

ROWAN
Origin/meaning: Old Norse 'rowan tree'.

A surname used as a first name, perhaps influenced by the similarity to Rowland.

Example: Rowan Atkinson, English actor.

ROWLAND
Origin/meaning: Old German 'fame-land', usually given as 'famous man of the land'.

This spelling was the most usual in England from the late Middle Ages until the 18th century. In the 19th century the fashion for medieval culture led to a preference for the version brought to England by the Normans – Roland q.v. Roland was the legendary hero of a French epic poem. Rowland is the subject of an early English legend, a supposed son of the legendary 5th century British King Arthur. An early ballad about him, *Childe Rowland*, was very popular. He had an elder sister called Helen and with the aid of Merlin rescued her from Elf-land where the fairies had taken her.

Variations and abbreviations: Orlando (It), Roland (Fr/Ger), Rolando (It/Port/Sp), Roldan (Sp), Rolland, Rollo, Rolly, Rowley, Rowly, Ruland (Ger).

Example: Sir Rowland Hill, 1795–1879, English originator of the penny post.

ROWLEY
Origin/meaning: either Old German 'famous man of the land' (a familiar form of Rowland), or Old English 'dweller at the rough clearing' (a surname from a place name).

ROY
Origin/meaning: Celtic 'red' 'red-haired'.

Sometimes thought to be the equivalent of the Spanish Ruy – ruler, through the French word roi – king. It is also found as a short form of the US name Leroy. Roy is in fact a name similar to Rory *q.v.* a Scots name meaning a red-haired as opposed to a dark-haired man, (who would be Dougal or its Irish equivalent, Doyle). Rob Roy, the legendary Scottish Highland adventurer, was red-headed. His real name was Robert MacGregor. An equivalent name is Rufus, a Latin word meaning red-haired. Roy has become so popular in English-speaking countries it is no longer considered a Scottish name or given exclusively to red-headed children.

Variations and abbreviations: Rory (Scot/Ir), Ruffino (It), Rufus.

Example: Roy Strong, Art historian.
Roy Rogers, US singing cowboy.
Roy Jenkins, British politician, founder-member SDP.

RUDOLPH
Origin/meaning: Old German 'fame-wolf'.

A modern German form of a pre-Conquest name, more familiar in English-speaking countries as Rolph.

Variations and abbreviations: Rodolf, Rodolphe (Fr), Rolph, Rudolf, Rodolf, Rodolfo (It), Rodolphe (Fr), Rudolf, Rudy. See also Ralph and Randal.

Examples: Rudolf Valentino (Rodolfo Guglielmi), 1895–1926, Italian-American film idol.
Rudolph Diesel, 1858–1913, German engineer, inventor of the diesel engine.

RUFUS
Origin/meaning: Latin 'red-haired'.

This originated as a nickname and was used by the Romans. An early example is William the Conqueror's son who was known as William Rufus, because of his red hair. It has never been a common name in England or in the Celtic areas, where the native names Rory and Roy have the same meaning. It was not uncommon in 18th and 19th century America. Sometimes used by Jewish people to 'Anglicize' Reuben.

Variations and abbreviations: Rory, Roy.

Example: Rufus Daniel Isaacs, 1st Marquess of Reading 1860–1935. English lawyer and statesman.

RUPERT
Origin/meaning: Old German 'fame-bright'.

This comes from Rupprecht, the German version of the Saxon name Hrodebert. The French version Robert q.v. was introduced into England by the Normans in 1066 and has been consistently used since the Middle Ages. Rupert did not reach England until the 17th century when it was introduced by Prince Rupprecht, 1619–1682, a son of the Elector Palatine. A nephew of Charles I he fought valiantly on his behalf in the English Civil War and earned the nickname 'The Mad Cavalier'. His real name proved a problem for the English, many of whom called him Prince Robert. However, an English version of Rupprecht eventually evolved as Rupert. It has never become properly established in North America or Australia.

Variations and abbreviations: Ruppert, Rupprecht, Ruprecht.

Example: Rupert Brooke, 1887–1915, English poet.

RUSS
Origin/meaning: French 'little red head'.

Short form of Russel q.v. sometimes used as an independent name.

Example: Russ Abbot, English comedian.

RUSSELL
Origin/meaning: French 'little red head'.

An aristocratic surname (it is the family name of the Duke of Bedford) it came into use as a first name in the 19th century along with others such as Sidney, Percy and Selwyn. Very popular in Australia, Canada and Scotland in the 1940s and 50s, now becoming more frequent in England.

Variation and abbreviations: Russ, Rusty.

Example: Russell Harty, British broadcaster and writer.

RUY
Origin/meaning: Old German 'ruler'.

A Spanish short form of Roderick q.v. found in parts of the US, sometimes thought to be the equivalent of Roy q.v.

Example: Ruy Diaz, known as El Cid, 11th century Spanish freedom fighter.

S

SABIN
Origin/meaning: Latin 'Sabine man'. A member of the ancient tribe whose lands bordered on Rome.

This virtually obsolete English name is the equivalent of the feminine Sabina. It is still used in Europe.

Variations: Sabino (It), Sabinus (Ger), Savin (Fr), Savinien (Fr), Savino (It).

Example: Savinien Cyrano de Bergerac, 1619–1655, French writer.

SACHA
Origin/meaning: Ancient Greek 'defender of men'.

A short form of Alexander, or Alexandra *q.v.* frequently found recently as an independent first name for both boys and girls.

Variations and abbreviations: Sascha, Sasha.

Examples: Sacha Distel, French singer.
Sacha Guitry, 1885–1957, French actor and playwright.

SACHEVERELL (pron. Sashéverall)
Origin/meaning: Old French 'from Saute de Chevreuil'.

This surname has been used from time to time in England as a first name, since the 18th century. It was probably given to honour Dr Henry Sacheverell, 1674–1724, whose right-wing preaching made him immensely popular for a while. The Sitwell family have used the name since the 18th century to honour William Sacheverell, 1638–1691, a Liberal politician, the 'First Whig'.

Example: Sacheverell Sitwell, English poet and art critic.

SADIQ
Origin/meaning: Arabic 'faithful'.

519

A popular Muslim name.

Variation: Sadiki (E African).

SAID (pron. Séye-eed)
Origin/meaning: Arabic 'happy' or 'fortunate'.

A traditional Muslim name.

Variations: Saeed, Sayed.

SALIM
Origin/meaning: Arabic 'peace'.

A popular Muslim name. The feminine version is Salama. 'Peace' is a traditional Muslim greeting.

Variation: Selim.

SAM
Origin/meaning: Hebrew 'name of God'.

A familiar form of Samuel *q.v.* and occasionally of the feminine Samantha *q.v.*

Variations: Sammie, Sammy.

Example: Sammy Davis, Jnr, US singer and entertainer.
Sam Peckinpah, US film director.

SAMSON
Origin/meaning: Hebrew 'child of Sham' (the sun god).

A Biblical hero Samson, with his immense strength, was the scourge of the Philistines. Delilah seduced him into revealing that his strength came from his hair, and then cut it off while he slept. A 6th century Welsh missionary saint called Samson was popular in other Celtic regions including Brittany and Normandy. (One of the Scilly Isles is named after him.) The name was introduced into England at the Norman Conquest, 1066, in this roundabout fashion. It is an unusual name today.

Variations and abbreviations: Sam, Sammy, Sampson, Sansom, Sanson (Sp), Sansone (It), Simson.

Example: Henry Sampson Woodfall, 1739–1805, English printer and journalist.

SAMUEL

Origin/meaning: Hebrew 'name of God'. Possibly 'Sham is God' – see Samson. Occasionally 'summer traveller', ie 'Viking'.

This is a Biblical name. Samuel was the great prophet whose life and work is covered by the ninth and tenth books of the Old Testament. Rare before the 16th century Protestant Reformation, it is one of the few popular Puritan names which have not returned to obscurity. Another is Timothy. When Samuel was used in Ireland and Scotland it may have been to translate the similar Gaelic name for a Viking. It is one of many traditional names currently enjoying a revival after the 1960s period of rather fanciful names.

Variations and abbreviations: Sam, Sammy, Samuele (It).

Examples: Samuel Beckett, Irish playwright (*Waiting for Godor*). Samuel Pepys, 1633–1703, English diarist.

SANDY

Origin/meaning: Greek 'defender of men' or 'red-haired'.

This is a familiar form of Alexander *q.v.* or a nickname, usually given to someone with red hair.

Example: Sandy Gall, British television newscaster.
Sandy Lyle, British golfer.

SAUL

Origin/meaning: Hebrew 'asked for'.

This is a Biblical name with two important namesakes; the first King of Israel, whom the tribes of Israel asked for (I Samuel 8), and St Paul, whose original name was Saul. Used in the 17th century when Biblical names were popular among Puritans, it is now found mainly among Jewish people.

Variations and abbreviations: Erasmus, Sol, Sollie, Solly, Zollie, Zolly.

Example: Saul Bellow, US novelist.

SAXON

Origin/meaning: Old English 'of the short sword'.

This word was used by the Romans to describe the Germanic people (of Saxony) who later invaded Britain after the decline of the Roman Empire. It is now primarily a surname which is occasionally used as a first name.

Abbreviations: Sax, Saxe.

Example: Sax Rohmer, pseudonym of Arthur Ward, 1886–1959, English author (*Dr Fu Manchu*).

SAYER
Origin/meaning: Old German/Old English 'people's victory'.

A medieval first name now found mainly as a surname. It is still found occasionally as a first name when given as a family name, particularly in the US.

Variation: Sear.

SCOTT
Origin/meaning: Old English 'Scottish'.

A surname used as a first name, initially in the US but currently something of a vogue name in Britain and Australia.

Variations and abbreviations: Scot, Scotty.

Examples: Scott Walker, US singer.
Scott Joplin, 1868–1917, US ragtime pianist.

SEAMUS (pron. Shamus)
Origin/meaning: uncertain, possibly Hebrew 'supplanter'.

The Irish version of James or Jacob *q.v.*

Variations: Seumus (Scots), Shamus.

SEAN (pron. Shawn)
Origin/meaning: Hebrew 'Jehovah has favoured'.

An Irish form of John *q.v.* through the French form Jean. It is increasingly used by non-Irish people and misspelt Shawn. An even older Gaelic form of John is Eóin *q.v.*

Variations and abbreviations: Shaun, Shawn. See also John.

Example: Sean Connery, Scottish actor (James Bond).

SEBASTIAN
Origin/meaning: Greek 'venerable' and Latin 'from Sebastia'.

Since the town Sebastia took its name from the Greek word (Sevastos) both meanings apply to this name. Sebastian was a popular European name because of the veneration for St Sebastian. This saint was particularly well known because the manner of his death (he was shot with arrows and then cudgelled to death) made a striking subject for many paintings. In England the name has only recently become widespread, although earlier it came to the West Country from Northern France. There it was found as often in the shortened French form Bastien. Shakespeare used the name for Viola's twin in his play *Twelfth Night*.

Variations and abbreviations: Bastian, Bastien, Seb, Sebastiano (It), Sébastien (Fr), Sebastianus (Ger).

Examples: Sebastian Coe, British athlete.
Sébastien Érard, 1752–1831, French harp-maker.

SECUNDUS
Origin/meaning: Latin 'second'.

A name sometimes given to a second son.

Variation: Secondo (It).

SEFTON
Origin/meaning: Old Norse/Old English 'dwelling in the rushes'.

A surname which derived from a place name. It is occasionally used as a first name.

SEIORSE (pron. Schorsch)
Origin/meaning: Greek 'farmer'.

This is the Irish Gaelic form of George *q.v.*

SELWYN
Origin/meaning: Old English 'friend of the house'.

An Old English name which developed as a surname rather than a first name. In the 19th century when surnames became fashionable as first names, it came back into use as a first name, perhaps influenced by the name of Bishop Selwyn (of New Zealand and later Lichfield) who found Selwyn College, Cambridge. It is most commonly found in Wales.

Variation: Selwin.

Example: Selwyn Lloyd, British politician.

SEPTIMUS
Origin/meaning: Latin 'seventh'.

A name given to a seventh son or seventh child, particularly in the 19th century. Sometimes given without regard to numerical order.

Example: Septimus Harding, the Warden in Anthony Trollope's Barchester novels.

SERGIUS
Origin/meaning: uncertain. Possibly Etruscan 'fisherman'.

A popular name in Russia and other areas of the Orthodox Church because of two saints, one a Roman martyr, d.303, whose cult was very strong and the second St Sergius of Radonegh, 1314–1392, a Russian abbot and mystic. Rare in English-speaking countries.

Variations and abbreviations: Serge, Sergé (Fr), Sergei (Russ), Sergio (It).

Examples: Sergei Prokofiev, 1891–1955, Russian composer. Sergei Eisenstein, 1898–1948, Russian film director.

SETH
Origin/meaning: Hebrew 'substitute'.

This was the appropriate name given to the son born to Adam and Eve after the murder of their second son Abel, by his brother Cain (Genesis 4). As a Biblical name and perhaps because of its meaning it was popular in the 17th century, both in England and New England. It has now become rare in Britain, although it is still current in the US.

Example: Seth Thomas, 1774–1859, American clock maker.

SEXTUS
Origin/meaning: Latin 'sixth'.

A name given to a sixth son or child. Rare today.

Variation: Sixtus.

SHAH JEHAN
Origin/meaning: Sanskrit 'ruler of the world'.

This Muslim name is given to honour Shah Jehan, 1592–1666, the 5th Mogul Emperor. His father was Jehangir q.v. and his son was Aurangzeb q.v. Shah Jehan, unlike his father and son, is remembered as a just and able ruler. He waged several wars to increase the territory of the empire. The Taj Mahal, the most famous building in India, was built by him as a mausoleum for his adored wife Mumtaz Mahal.

Variation: Shah Jahan.

SHAMUS
Origin/meaning: uncertain, possibly Hebrew 'supplanter'.

An English phonetic spelling of Seamus, which is the Irish equivalent of Jacob or James q.v.

SHANE
Origin/meaning: Hebrew 'Jehovah has favoured'.

An Anglicized spelling of Sean q.v. the Irish version of John.

Variation: Shan.

SHANKAR (pron. Sankar)
Origin/meaning: Hindu. Another name for Shiv q.v.

Shankar was a famous Hindu Saint who helped defend India against Moslem invaders.

Example: Shankar, one of the singers of Shankar Jaykishan.

SHASHI
Origin/meaning: Sanskrit 'moon'.

This can be turned into a girl's name with the addition of the suffix's -bai or -ben q.v.

See also Chandra and Indu (feminine).

Example: Shashi Kapoor, Indian film actor and director.

SHAUN
Origin/meaning: Hebrew 'Jehovah has favoured'.

An English phonetic spelling of Sean q.v.

Variation: Shawn.

SHEHR-KHAN (Seer-Khan)
Origin/meaning: Sanskrit 'Emperor lion'.

Khan (Emperor) is another of the male Moslem 'group' names which can indicate social status.

Variation: Shere. See also Babar, Leonard, Llewellyn, Simba, Singh, Tau.

SHIV (pron. Seev)
Origin/meaning: Hindu 'destruction'.

Shiv is a Hindu god known in English-speaking countries as Lord Shiva. In modern Hinduism devotion to Shiv or Vishnu are the two major subdivisions. Shiv is the Lord of all creatures who supports the world by his constant meditation. Paradoxically he is also the god of death.

Example: Shiva Naipaul, Trinidadian novelist.

SHOLTO
Origin/meaning: Old Scots 'sower'.

A name used by the Scottish Douglas family since the 18th century to honour their alleged ancestor Sioltaich Dhu Glas. Occasionally used by other Scots.

SHURESH (pron. Suress)
Origin/meaning: Hindu 'supreme god'.

This is an alternative name for Indra (pron. Indr). In early Hindu mythology he was the warrior king of the gods.

Variations: Surinder-Singh (Sikh), Surendra (Gujerati).

SIDNEY
Origin/meaning: Latin/Greek 'follower of Dionysos'.

This aristocratic surname is a contraction of St Denis, a French place name. It is a similar contraction to Sinclair for St Clair and Semple for St Paul. In the 19th century along with names like Howard, Herbert, Cecil etc it was part of a vogue for aristocratic surnames. As a first name it had the additional boosts to its popularity of being the surname of the much admired Elizabethan poet Sir Philip Sidney, 1554–1586, and the influential republican politician Algernon Sidney, 1622–1683, who was highly regarded by 19th century Liberals. The city of Sydney, Australia, was named after the Secretary of State at the time of its foundation, Thomas Townshend 1st Viscount Sydney, 1733–1800. Familiarity

526

with the city's name has undoubtedly accounted for the popularity of the alternative spelling of the name. Sidney is sometimes used as a feminine name.

Variations and abbreviations: Sid, Sydn, Sydney.

Examples: Sidney Poitier, US film actor.
Sydney Smith, New Zealand poet and critic.

SIEGFRIED
Origin/meaning: Old German 'victory peace'.

A popular German name used infrequently in Britain since the end of the 19th century. This was the direct result of the influence of Richard Wagner's opera cycle *The Ring*, in which the hero's name is Siegfried.

Example: Siegfried Sassoon, 1886-1967, British war poet and writer.

SILAS
Origin/meaning: Latin. From Silvanus, the Roman god of uncultivated land or woodland.

Silas is the more accepted form of the name Silvanus in English-speaking countries. It is close in origin to the name Silvester. Both Silvanus and Silas are names found in the Bible (2 Corinthians 1 v.19, and Acts 15-18). Because of this they (particularly Silas) were widely used from the 17th century after the Protestant Reformation caused a reaction against Catholic saints' names. However, Silas, like Timothy, is really a pagan name, which has only become a Christian name through association. After the 18th century Silas began to decline in popularity. This decline was accelerated in the US by the association of the name with drunkenness. It is now rare.

Variations and abbreviations: Si, Silvain (Fr), Silvan, Silvano (It), Silvanus (Ger/Dut), Silverio (It/Sp), Silvio (It/Sp), Sylvain (Fr), Sylvanus.

Example: Silas Marner, hero of George Eliot's novel of the same name, 1861.

SILVANUS
Origin/meaning: Latin. The name of the Roman god of uncultivated land or woodland.

See Silas, Silvester.

SILVESTER

Origin/meaning: Latin 'of the woodland'.

A name similar to Silas q.v. This was a reasonably widespread name in the Middle Ages, probably because there were three Popes who used the name. It survived the Reformation but has never been popular since in English-speaking countries, except in Catholic Ireland. The feminine form is usually taken to be Silvia, but there is an Italian feminine Sylvestra.

Variations and abbreviations: Silvanus, Silverius, Silvestro (It), Silvius, Sylvester, Sylvestre (Fr).

Example: Sylvester Stallone, US film actor and director.

SIMBA

Origin/meaning: Swahili 'lion'.

A name familiar to the West because it was often given to lions in captivity and in literature.

See also Leo, Tau.

SIMEON

Origin/meaning: uncertain. Usually given as Hebrew 'hearkening' but may be a non-Hebrew name adapted by the Israelites.

This is the usual Old Testament form of the Hebrew name Shim'on given as Simon in the New Testament. Although really the same name they are now commonly treated as two separate names. Simeon, being the name of one of the tribes of Israel, was at its most popular in the period of Biblical names after the Reformation. It is now rare.

SIMON

Origin/meaning: uncertain. Usually given as Hebrew 'hearkening' Being the Greek influenced version of the name Shim'on or Simeon it may also incorporate the Greek word meaning 'snub-nosed'.

This New Testament version of the name Simeon is the one most favoured in English-speaking countries. In the Middle Ages it rivalled Thomas, John and Peter as the most popular of the names taken from the New Testament. Indeed Simon owed part of its popularity to the fact that it was the original name of Peter, the head of the Apostles and the first Bishop of Rome. Like all the most popular Christian names it gave rise to a large number of surnames, such as Simons, Simpkins, Simpson and Simmonds. In the 1960s and 70s it has enjoyed a vogue in Britain and Australia.

Variations and abbreviations: Semjon (Russ), Si, Sim, Simeon, Siméon (Fr), Simmie, Simone (It), Simpkin, Symon, Symond (Med Eng), Ximines (Sp).

Examples: Simon Bolívar, 1783–1830, South American liberator.
Simon Cadell, British actor.
Simon de Montfort, Earl of Leicester, 1208–1265, English soldier, who helped create Parliament.

SINCLAIR
Origin/meaning: French. A contraction of St Clair, a town in Normandy.

This is one of the aristocratic surnames, like Howard, Percy, Sidney, etc which were so popular as first names in the 19th century. It is the family name of the Earls of Caithness.

Example: Sinclair Lewis, 1885–1951, US novelist.

SINGH
Origin/meaning: Sanskrit 'lion'.

This is a Sikh name from the Punjab region. It is not used on its own but is added to other male names (which may also be common in other areas of India) as a form of politeness, eg Rajinder Singh.

See also Leo, Shehe and Simba.

SIÔN (pron. Sheón)
Origin/meaning: Hebrew 'Jehovah has favoured'.

This is the native Welsh form of John q.v. Anglicized Welsh forms of John include Evan and Owen.

Variation: Sionyn (dim). See also John.

SIÔR (pron. Shaw)
Origin/meaning: Greek 'farmer'.

This is the Welsh form of George q.v.
Variation: Shaw.

SLOAN
Origin/meaning: Old Irish 'warrior'.

A surname used as a first name.

Variation: Sloane.

Example: Sloan Wilson, US novelist.

SOL
Origin/meaning: Hebrew 'asked for' or 'little man of peace'.

A short form of either Saul q.v. or Solomon q.v.

Variations: Sollie, Solly, Zollie, Zolly.

Example: Solly Zuckerman, British-South African scientist.

SOLOMON
Origin/meaning: Hebrew 'little man of peace'.

A Biblical name referring to David's son, King Solomon, who was famous for his wisdom. This was a common medieval name especially in the form Saloman but it fell out of favour. It enjoyed a revival among Puritans in England and North America during the 17th century period of Biblical names. Nowadays it is almost totally confined to Jewish people who also use it as a surname.

Variations and abbreviations: Salomo, Salomon (Fr/Ger), Salomón (Sp), Salomone (It), Selim (Arab), Sol, Solly, Soloman, Sulaiman (Arab). See also Salome.

SPENCER
Origin/meaning: Old French 'steward' or 'butler'.

This is the English equivalent of the Scots surname Stuart. The steward was the 'dispenser' of household supplies. Used as a first name in families connected with the Spencer family and the Spencer-Churchill family (the Dukes of Marlborough) it became more widespread in the 19th century when aristocratic surnames were fashionable as first names.

Variation: Spenser.

Examples: Spencer Perceval, 1762-1812, British Prime Minister (assassinated).
Spencer Tracy, 1900-1967, US film actor.

STANLEY
Origin/meaning: Old English 'stony meadow'.

An aristocratic surname, the family name of the Earls of Derby, it has been used as a first name since the 19th century. Its popularity may have been helped along by the renown of the famous explorer Henry Stanley, 1841-1904. It is sometimes used by immigrants to English-speaking countries to 'Anglicize' the Polish name Stanislas.

Variations and abbreviations: Stan, Stanly.

Examples: Stanley Baldwin, 1867-1947, British Prime Minister. Stanley Matthews, British footballer.

STEPHEN
Origin/meaning: Greek 'wreathed' or 'crowned'.

This name comes from the wreath or crown of laurel leaves given to a victorious athlete in ancient Greece. It was a common pre-Christian name which, like Timothy, Silas, Dorcas and numerous other pre-Christian Greek names, was adopted as a Christian name because of the fame of an early Christian. St Stephen was the first known Christian martyr who died c.35. His story is told in Ch. vi and vii of the Acts of the Apostles. The name was extremely popular in Eastern Europe in the forms Stefan or István, and five kings of Hungary, including one Saint, bore the name. It was introduced into England at the Norman conquest and was the name of one Norman king of England, Stephen of Blois, 1097-1154.

Variations and abbreviations: Etienne (Fr), Esteban (Sp), Estevan, István (Hung), Stefan (Ger/Pol), Stefano (It), Steffan (Wel), Stephan, Stéphane (Fr), Stephanus, Steve, Steven, Stevie, Stevy, Stevyn (Med Eng), Ystffan (Wel).

Examples: Stevie Wonder, US singer.
Stephen Sondheim, US composer.
Stephen Spender, English poet.

STEVEN
Origin/meaning: Greek 'wreathed' or 'crowned'.

An alternative spelling of Stephen q.v.

STEWART
Origin/meaning: Old English 'animal keeper' or 'steward'.

An alternative spelling of Stuart q.v.

Example: Stewart Granger, British film actor.

STUART
Origin/meaning: Old English 'animal keeper' or 'steward'.

This Scottish surname is particularly famous as the name of the Scottish royal family. It was 1371 when one of the hereditary stewards of Scotland came to the throne as Robert II. Although the last Stuart monarch was Queen Anne, d.1714, the present Queen Elizabeth II has Stuart ancestors. In the 19th century Scottish surnames, like aristocratic names, became generally popular, and today Stuart is not exclusively a Scottish name. Scottish clan names are particularly popular in Australia and Canada.

Variations and abbreviations: Steuart, Stew, Steward, Stewart, Stu. See also Bruce, Cameron, Douglas, Graham.

Example: John Stuart Mill, 1806–1873, English philosopher.

SUDHAKAR (pron. Soothoh-kar)
Origin/meaning: Hindi 'treasure of nectar'.

The masculine equivalent of Sudha q.v. Found fairly generally throughout India.

SULAIMAN
Origin/meaning: Arabic 'peaceful'.

This is a Muslim name closely related to Salim, another popular Muslim name. It is the same name as Solomon q.v.

Variation: Suleimano.

Example: Sulaiman the Magnificent, 1494–1566, Sultan of the Turkish Ottoman Empire.

SULTAN
Origin/meaning: Arabic 'ruler' or 'emperor'.

This is a Muslim title of respect similar to Khan. It does not always mean that a person is a government ruler in the Western sense.

T

TAD

Origin/meaning: uncertain, possibly Hebrew 'praise'.

A short form of Thaddeus *q.v.* found mainly in the US as an independent name. Popular among Irish and Polish communities.

TALBOT

Origin/meaning: Old French 'cut faggot' or 'wood-cutter'.

A medieval name which developed mainly as a surname. It is the family name of Baron Talbot of Malahide, and the Talbot family goes back to the time of the Conqueror. Probably because of its aristocratic connections, this surname was re-introduced as a first name in the 19th century.

Talbot was also the name of a ferocious hunting dog.

Variation: Talbert.

TAM

Origin/meaning: Aramaic 'twin'.

Scottish form of Thomas, as in Robert Burns' poem *Tam O'Shanter*. It is sometimes given as an independent name.

Example: Tam Dalyell, British MP.

TAMAR

Origin/meaning: Hebrew 'palm tree'.

A masculine version of the more familiar feminine name Tamara *q.v.*

TANCRED

Origin/meaning: Old German 'grateful counsel'.

This is the usual English form of the Old German Thankred. As well as bringing the name over to England in 1066, the Normans introduced it into another of their kingdoms in Southern Italy. One particularly famous Norman who held the name came from this kingdom of the Two Sicilies. He was the Tancred,

1078–1112, who led the First Crusade against the Saracens in the Holy Land. As a result the name always held crusading overtones. In 1847 Benjamin Disraeli published a novel on the theme of Zionism called *Tancred, The New Crusade*.

Variations: Tancrède (Fr), Tancredi (It), Tankred (Ger).

TARIQ
Origin/meaning: uncertain. Possibly Arabic 'conqueror'.

A Muslim name. Tariq was a Moslem general who led the Moorish invasion of Southern Spain.

Variation: Tarik.

Example: Tariq Ali, Pakistani journalist and left-wing activist.

TATE
Origin/meaning: Old German/Old English 'glad' or 'dear'.

An early name which developed principally as a surname. It is still viable as a first name and has also been used as a family surname given as a first name.

TAU
Origin/meaning: Tswana 'lion'.

A name from Botswana.

See also Leo, Shehr, Simba, Singh.

TEAGUE (pron. Theeg)
Origin/meaning: Old Irish 'poet'.

Like Thaddeus *q.v.* in Ireland this name developed as an easier way of saying the Old Gaelic Tadhgh (Theeg). It is also found as a surname. Once considered typically Irish rather as Paddy is today.

Variations and abbreviations: Teige, Thaddeus, Thaddy, Timothy.

TEDDY
Origin/meaning: either Old English 'rich ward' or Greek 'gift of God'.

A familiar form of Edward *q.v.* or Theodore *q.v.*

TERENCE
Origin/meaning: from Terentius, the name of an ancient Roman tribe. Meaning obscure. Also Old Irish 'tower of strength'.

A Roman name, which like several others, eg Cornelius, was used by the Irish to translate a native name which has a separate meaning of its own. In this case the native name is Turlough. It has only been introduced into English-speaking countries from Ireland in the last century. The short form Terry used to be an independent name, an English form of Theodoric.

Variations and abbreviations: Terencio (Sp), Terenziano (It), Terenzio (It), Terrence, Terry.

Examples: Terry Thomas, English film actor.
Sir Terence Rattigan, 1911–1977, English playwright.

TEWDWR (pron. Tudor)
Origin/meaning: Greek 'gift of god.'

The Welsh version of Theodore *q.v.* usually given the English spelling Tudor *q.v.*

THADDEUS
Origin/meaning: uncertain, possibly Hebrew 'praise'.

There are many instances of the name Thaddeus and its short form Thady in Ireland where it was probably used to translate the Old Irish name Tadgh (pron. Theeg) 'a poet'. In the Bible, (Matthew ch.10 v.3), it is given as the surname of one of the Apostles, Lebbaeus. As a Biblical name it was used in the 17th and 18th centuries in England and New England but by the 19th century it was obsolescent. It has remained more popular in Eastern Europe.

Variations and abbreviations: Fadej (Russ), Tad, Tadd, Taddeo (It), Tadeo (Sp), Tadeusz (Pol), Thad, Thaddoeus, Thaddäus (Ger), Thaddés (Fr), Thady.

Example: Tadeusz Kosciusko, 1746–1817, Polish patriot.

THEOBALD
Origin/meaning: Old German/Old English 'bold folk'.

The medieval version of this pre-Conquest name was pronounced Tibald/t. An example of this is Tybalt, one of the characters in Shakespeare's *Romeo and Juliet*. However the spelling gradually evolved to Theobaldus in Latin documents perhaps because it was assumed, like Theodore, to have some connection with the Greek word Theo-god. Like most popular medieval names it gave rise to several surnames, all of which emphasize the old

pronunciation, eg Tibbles, Tibbet, Tibbit, etc. The common cats'
name, Tibby or Tibbles, refers back to a cat named Tybalt in the
medieval folk-tale cycle, *Reynard the Fox*.

Variations and abbreviations: Dietbold (Ger), Tebaldo (It),
Teobaldo (It/Sp), Thebault (Fr), Theo, Thibaud (Fr), Thibaut
(Fr), Tibald, Tibold (Ger), Tiebout (Dut), Tybalt.

THEODORE
Origin/meaning: Greek 'gift of God'.

This is a popular name in Eastern Europe where St Theodore, an
early martyr, is greatly venerated, along with St Demetrius and
St George. It has never been common in English-speaking
countries although it had some popularity in the 19th century
when it was re-introduced by the High Church movement along
with names of other saints popular in the Eastern Church, such
as Basil and Cyril. Theodore Roosevelt, 1858–1919, helped to
popularize the name in the US where the typical short form is
Teddy. It was from Roosevelt that the Teddy bear got its name.

Variations and abbreviations: Fedor (Russ), Fyodor (Russ), Ted,
Teddy, Tewdr (Wel), Teodoro (It), Theo, Théodore (Fr), Tudor
(Wel). See also Jonathan, Matthew, Nathaniel, Donatus.

Examples: Fyodor Dostoevsky, 1821–1881, Russian novelist.
Theodore Dreiser, 1871–1945, US novelist.

THEODORIC
Origin/meaning: Old German 'ruler of the people.'

The Old German form of the modern German name Dietrich
and the Dutch Diederick from which the English Derek *q.v.* is
derived. In the Middle Ages the English form was Terry from the
French version Thiérry. Theodoric is rare in English-speaking
countries today and Terry is used as a short form of Terence.

THEOPHILUS
Origin/meaning: Greek 'loved by God' or 'lover of God'.

This name, rare today, was one of the most popular 17th
century Biblical names. It is the name of the man to whom the
Gospel according to St Luke and the Acts of the Apostles are
written. It may in fact not have been one person at all but a name
used, because of its meaning, to address the Bible to all
'lovers of God'.

536

Variations and abbreviations: Theo, Théophile (Fr).

Examples: Théophile Gautier, 1811–1872, French poet and novelist.
Theophile Marzials, 1850–1920, English songwriter.

THOM
Origin/meaning: Aramaic 'twin'.

A form of Thomas *q.v.*

Example: Thom Gunn, British poet.

THOMAS
Origin/meaning: Aramaic 'twin'.

This is one of the most popular names in Europe and English-speaking countries. It was the name of one of the Apostles. His real name was Judah and Thomas was a nickname to distinguish him from St Jude and from Judas. His twin was said to be a woman called Lysia. Like Benedict Thomas was a priest's name until after the Norman Conquest when it quickly gained general popularity. This was considerably boosted by the reverence for St Thomas à Becket. An Archbishop of Canterbury, he was killed in 1170 at the instigation of Henry II who bitterly resented his assertion that the power of the church overrode the power of the King. Canterbury quickly became one of the most famous shrines in Europe and Thomas along with John and William, one of the most common English names. There are several feminine variations, including Thomasina and Tamsin *q.v.* The familiar and short forms Tommy and Tom are found in many old expressions and rhymes, eg 'Tom, Dick and Harry' and 'Tom, Tom, the Piper's Son', and Tommy means private in the British army etc. All these are indications of the popularity and familiarity of the name. So too is the number of associated surnames eg Tompkins, Thomson, Thomsett, Tomlin.

Variations and abbreviations: Tam, Tamas, Tammie, Tammy, Thom, Tom, Tómás (Sp), Tomas (Ir), Tomaso (It), Tompkin, Tommie, Tommy.

Examples: Thomas (Fats) Waller, 1904–1943, US jazz composer.
Thomas Jefferson, 1743–1826, 3rd US President.

THOR
Origin/meaning: Old Norse 'strength'. Thor was the Norse god

of thunder and war.

This name is not usually found independently in English-speaking countries, but is usually a short form of Thorold. The English name for the god Thor was Thunor.

Variations: Thore (Dan), Tore (Swed). See also Thora.

Example: Thor (pron. Toor) Heyerdal, Norwegian anthropologist.

THOROLD
Origin/meaning: Old Norse/Old English 'strength of Thor'.

This was a popular name both before the Norman Conquest and afterwards, when the Norman French version Torald was more usual. It led to many surnames including Tyrrel and Turrell.

Variations and abbreviations: Thor, Thorald, Thorvald, Thorwald, Torald, Torvald (Swed), Turlough (Ir), Turold.

THURSTAN
Origin/meaning: Old Norse/Old English 'Thor's stone'.

A surname from East Anglia (there was most Viking influence on the East coast of Britain) which is also used as a first name. Sometimes said to be the origin of the name Tristram q.v.

Variations: Thurston, Tristram.

Example: Thurston Dart, British musician and writer.

TIMOTHY
Origin/meaning: Greek 'honour to God'.

This is a Greek name pre-dating Christianity. It was the name of St Paul's companion in the Acts of the Apostles. Two of Paul's letters are addressed to Timothy. Although it is now a very familiar name it did not come into use until the period of Biblical names after the Protestant Reformation, when it became popular with English and American Puritans. Unlike other Puritan names, such as Obadiah or Theophilus, it has stood the test of time and has been fairly popular in English-speaking countries in the post-war period. The name is a popular one in Ireland where, like Thaddeus and Teague, it has been used to 'translate' the native Tadhg.

Variations and abbreviations: Tim, Timmie, Timmy, Timoteo (It/ Sp), Timothée (Fr), Timotheus (Ger/Dut).

Examples: Timothy Bottoms, US actor.
Timothy Raison, British politician.

TITUS
Origin/meaning: uncertain, possibly Greek 'honoured'.

A Latin name, derived from the Greek, and rare today. One of
the followers of St Paul, to whom he wrote one of his Epistles,
was called Titus. As a Biblical name it was popular in the 17th
century. An example is Titus Oates, 1649–1705, who took part
vigorously in the persecution of Catholics and was convicted of
perjury.

Variation: Tito (It).

Example: Titto Gobbi, Italian opera singer.

TOBIAS
Origin/meaning: Hebrew 'God is good'.

The Greek form, used in the Bible, of the Hebrew name Tobiah.
The more familiar English form is Toby *q.v.* although in the
period of Biblical names Tobias was also used. Tobias was the
son of Tobit in the Book of Tobit (Apocrypha).

Example: Tobias Smollett, 1721–1771, Scottish novelist.

TOBIT
Origin/meaning: Hebrew 'son of Tobias'.

Despite its slightly different meaning this name is now usually
considered a variant of Toby *q.v.*

TOBY
Origin/meaning: Hebrew 'God is good'.

The English form of Tobiah, generally more popular than the
Greek form, Tobias *q.v.* Although there are no known examples
of this as a Christian name in the Middle Ages, the existence of
several surnames which clearly derive from it (Tobin, Tobit, etc)
indicate it must have been fairly widespread particularly since
the Book of Tobit (omitted from the Authorized Version of the
Bible) was a popular Biblical story in the Middle Ages. It tells the
story of the pious Tobit (which means 'son of Tobiah' in Hebrew)
and his own son Tobias. Other indications of the popularity of
the name are its use for Mr Punch's dog (in the Bible Tobias
owned a dog) and for the Toby jug.

Variations and abbreviations: Tobia (It), Tobiah, Tobias (Ger), Tobie (Fr), Tobin, Tobit, Toby.
Example: Sir Toby Belch in Shakespeare's *Twelfth Night*.

TOM
Origin/meaning: Aramaic 'twin'.

A common short form of Thomas, often used as an independent name.

Examples: Tom Watson, US golf champion.
Tom Lehrer, US songwriter.

TONY
Origin/meaning: Latin Antonius – the name of one of the great Roman families.

The most popular short form of Antony *q.v.* sometimes given as an independent name.

Example: Tony Curtis, US film actor and director.

TORQUIL
Origin/meaning: obscure, possibly Old Norse 'Thor's cauldron'.

This is the Gaelic version of an Old Norse name introduced into Scotland and the North of England by the Vikings from the 8th–11th centuries. It is still found occasionally today, particularly in Scotland, and is the source of several surnames, eg Thirkettle.

Variations: Thorkill, Thorketill, Torcull.

TREFOR
Origin/meaning: Old Welsh 'large settlement'.

The Welsh original of Trevor *q.v.*

TREVOR
Origin/meaning: Old Welsh 'large settlement'.

This is a Welsh place name which is found as a given name or surname as far back as the 10th century. The Welsh form is Trefor and Trevor is the now more familiar English version. The Welsh origin of the name now seems largely forgotten. During the 20th century Trevor has become well-established in English-speaking countries having been almost non-existent before.

Abbreviation: Trev.

Examples: Trevor Francis, British football player.
Trevor Howard, British film actor.

TRISTAN
Origin/meaning: uncertain. Either Old Welsh 'herald', Latin/French 'sad' or Old Norse 'Thor's stone'.

The French form of Tristram *q.v.*

Variation: Tristano (It).

Example: Tristan Corbiére, 1845–1875, French writer.

TRISTRAM
Origin/meaning: uncertain. Either Old Welsh 'herald', Latin 'sad' or Old Norse 'Thor's stone'.

There may be an element of all these definitions in Tristram for the name seems to have developed independently in several countries. Certainly the Latin/French words for sad, tristis/triste, have set the tone for or reflected the sad tale of Tristram and Iseult (Tristan and Isolde). This Arthurian romance which may date back as far as the 6th century was popular in the Middle Ages (see Isolda), and the name was not uncommon. It is now rare.

Variations: Thurstan, Tristan (Fr), Tristano (It), Tristran, Trystram.

Examples: Tristram Shandy, hero of the novel of the same name by Laurence Sterne, 1713–1768.
Tristram Hillier, RA, 1906–1983, British artist.

TROY
Origin/meaning: Old Irish 'foot soldier' or a place name after Troy in Greece or Troyes in France.

Greek and North African town names were often given to settlements in North America after the civil war as if to emphasize the similarity between Greek democracy and the struggle to overthrow colonial tyranny. For the same reason these city names were sometimes used as personal names. This would account for a small percentage of times the name occurs. Troy is also a fairly common British surname either indicating a family descended from a foot soldier or coming from the French town Troyes which also gave its name to Troy weight. The name is therefore usually a family name given as an independent name.

It has been used mainly in the US and mainly in the 20th century.

Example: Troy Donahue, US actor.

Troy Kennedy Martin, British screenwriter.

TRUMAN
Origin/meaning: Old English 'faithful man'.

This is a surname used as a first name which may sometimes honour Harry S. Truman, 33rd US President.

Example: Truman Capote, US novelist, author of *Breakfast at Tiffany's*.

TURLOUGH (pron. Turlow)
Origin/meaning: Old Irish 'like Thor' or 'full of strength'.

This was once a very common Irish name. It was often 'translated' into the more familiar Terence or Terry *q.v.*

See also Thor, Thorald, Thurstan.

Variations: Toirdealbhach (Old Irish), Turlozgh.

TY
Origin/meaning: a short form of names beginning with Ty. Most are surnames used as first names, eg Tyler, Tynan.

Example: Ty Hardin, US actor.

TYLER
Origin/meaning: English 'tiler', 'tiler-maker'.

An English surname fairly frequently found as a first name.

TYRONE Origin/meaning: Old Irish 'land of Owen'.

This is an Irish place name (County Tyrone), and an aristocratic surname – the Earl of Tyrone is the elder son of the Marquess of Waterford.

Examples: Tyrone Power, 1913–1958, US film actor.

Tyrone Guthrie, 1900–1971, English theatrical producer.

U

ULICK
Origin/meaning: Old Irish 'mind reward'.

A native Irish name sometimes 'translated' as Ulysses *q.v.*

Variation: Uillioc.

Example: Ulick O'Connor, Irish biographer and playwright.

ULRICH
Origin/meaning: Old German/Old English 'wolf ruler'. Originally Wulfrich.

The wolf was a symbol of nobility and strength. It is a rare name now in Britain although for hundreds of years after the Norman Conquest it was popular, usually with the spelling Ulric. In Germany and Switzerland, it is still popular, together with the feminine version Ulrike *q.v.*

Variations and abbreviations: Udo, Ulderico (It), Ulric, Ulrico (It), Ulrik (Scand).

Example: Ulrich Zwingli, 1484–1531, Swiss religious reformer.

ULYSSES
Origin/meaning: uncertain, possibly Etruscan 'wanderer'. Sometimes given as 'hater'. In Ireland 'mind reward'.

This is the Latin form of Odysseus, the name of a Greek hero of the Trojan wars whose journeyings are described in Homer's epic poem *The Odyssey*. It was used occasionally after the Renaissance had stimulated an interest in classical names. It is rare in English-speaking countries but is found in Ireland where it was used to translate the native names Ulrick *q.v.* and Uileos. The Irish writer James Joyce used it as the title of one of his novels published in 1922. In the US it has been used to honour Ulysses S. Grant.

Variations and abbreviations: Uileos, Uillioc (Ir), Ulick (Ir), Ulises (Sp), Ulisse (It).

Example: Ulysses Simpson Grant, 1822–1885, US Unionist

General and 18th President.

UMAR
Origin/meaning: Arabic 'highest'.
An alternative form of Omar *q.v.*

UMESH (pron. Ooméss)
Origin/meaning: Sanskrit 'husband of Uma'.
This is another name for Shiv *q.v.* (Lord Shiva) as Uma was a re-incarnation of Parvati *q.v.* Shiva's wife.

UNI
Origin/meaning: Yao 'life'.
A name from Malawi in Central Africa.
See also Zoë (f).

URBAN
Origin/meaning: Latin 'of the town'.
A popular name in the medieval church – there were eight Popes who used the name, three of whom were Saints. It is now rare.
Variations and abbreviations: Urbain (Fr), Urbano (It/Sp).

URI
Origin/meaning: Biblical. Meaning unknown.
This name is found in 1 Chronicles 2:20.
Example: Uri Geller, Israeli 'spoon-bender'.

URIAH
Origin/meaning: Hebrew 'light of Jehovah'.
This is a Biblical name (II Samuel ch.11) used occasionally by Puritans after the 16th century Protestant Reformation. Uriah was the Hebrew name used to translate a Hittite name very similar to it. King David sent Uriah the Hittite into the front line of battle to be killed in order that he might marry Uriah's wife Bathsheba *q.v.* himself.

Examples: Uriah Heep, the oily villain of Dickens's *David Copperfield*, 1850, helped to ensure the name's unpopularity.

V

VALENTINE
Origin/meaning: Latin 'strong', 'healthy'.

Well known because of St Valentine the Roman martyr, whose feast day (February 14th) coincided with a pagan festival in which young people chose partners. This tradition was retained by the new Christian religion. In the 19th century the feast day gained a new lease of life with the introduction of the custom of sending Valentine cards.

Also found as a surname and a feminine name.

Abbreviations: Val, Valentijn (Dut), Valentin (Fr/Ger/Scand/Sp), Valentino (It).

Example: Valentine Dyall, English actor.

VALERIAN
Origin/meaning: Latin 'strong' or 'influential'. From the patrician Roman name Valerius.

An uncommon name but one which has been in continuous use in England since the Middle Ages.

Variations and abbreviations: Valeriano (It), Valererio (It), Valerius, Valéry (Fr).

Examples: Valéry Giscard d'Estaing, former French President. Arthur Valerian Wellesley, 8th Duke of Wellington, 1769–1852, British general and victor at Waterloo.

VAN
Origin/meaning: Dutch 'of', 'from' which implies 'noble descent'.

Dutch names beginning with Van usually signified aristocratic roots and influence over a certain area, in the same way as the German von or the French de. This gives the name its alternative meaning. It is popular as an independent name in countries like the US and Australia, which have large populations of Dutch descent. Uncommon in Britain.

Examples: Van Morrison, Irish singer.

Van Johnson, US actor.

VANCE
Origin/meaning: Middle English 'thresher'.

A US first name, probably from a surname. Rare in Britain.

VAUGHAN
Origin/meaning: Old Welsh 'little'.

This is a Celtic name which is usually a surname. It probably became popular in the 19th century because it is the family name of the Earls of Lisburne and aristocratic surnames were fashionable at the time.

Variation: Vaughn.

Example: Ralph Vaughan Williams, 1872–1958, British composer.

VERE
Origin/meaning: 'from Ver' (an area of Normandy).

A surname introduced at the Conquest. Its aristocratic connections made it an ideal candidate for adoption as a first name during the 19th century when this became common practice.

Example: Vere Harmsworth, Viscount Rothermere, newspaper proprietor.

VERNON
Origin/meaning: Latin 'springlike' or Old French 'little alder grove'.

Either a masculine form of the Latin word Verna or a typical 19th century adoption of an aristocratic surname. Richard de Vernon came to England with the Conqueror and it is the family name of Barons Lyvedon and Vernon.

Variations and abbreviations: Vern, Verne, Verney.

Example: Vernon Dobcheff, Anglo-Bulgarian actor.

VICTOR
Origin/meaning: Latin 'victor', 'conqueror'.

Although a name introduced into Medieval England this name only became popular in the 19th century as the masculine form of Victoria.

Variations and abbreviations: Vic, Vick, Viktor (Ger), Vitorio (Sp), Vittorio (It). See also Vincent.

Examples: Victor Hugo, 1802–1885, French writer.
Victor Mature, US film actor.

VIDAL
Origin/meaning: Latin 'vital' or 'belonging to life'.

A Spanish form of the rare English name Vitalis q.v. A more current English equivalent is Vivian q.v.

Example: Vidal Sassoon, British hairdresser.

VIJAY
Origin/meaning: Sanskrit 'victory'.

Variation: Viajay.

Example: Vijay Amitraj, Indian tennis player.

VIKRAM/A (the final a is not pronounced)
Origin/meaning: Sanskrit 'record-breaker'.

Vikram, whose full title was Vikramaditya (Vikram of the eternal) was a legendary Indian Raja (king) possibly based on the real King Chandragupta II, 375–415. However in India many people count the modern era from 400 years earlier (58 BC) and call this the Vikram era. Chandragupta himself probably used the name Vikramaditya to bolster his own prestige. From the gods Vikram received the power of flight and the ability to communicate with animals and birds. His many exotic adventures are an Indian equivalent of the tales of the Arabian nights.

VINAY
Origin/meaning: Hindi 'courtesy'.

VINCENT
Origin/meaning: Latin 'conquering'.

This name was used in Medieval England to honour St Vincentius of Saragossa who was martyred by the Emperor Diolectian at the beginning of the 4th century. In later centuries the reputation of St Vincent de Paul, 1576–1660, made Vincent a popular name with Catholics in many European countries.

Variations and abbreviations: Vicente (Sp), Vin, Vince, Vincente,

Vincenzo (It), Vinny, Vinzent, Vinzenz (Ger). See also Victor.

Examples: Vincent Price, Hollywood actor, specializing in horror movies.
Vincent van Gogh, 1853–1890, Dutch painter.

VIRGIL
Origin/meaning: Latin 'staff bearer'.

Publius Vergilius Maro (Virgil), 70–19 BC was one of the best known Roman poets. The name Virgil survives because of him and St Virgil of Salzburg, d.784. Never popular in England it is found in Europe and the US.

Variations and abbreviations: Verge, Vergil, Vergilius, Virgile (Fr), Virgilio (It), Virgilius. See also Aeneus.

Examples: Virgil Thomson, US composer.
Virgil Grissom, US astronaut.

VISHNU
Origin/meaning: Hindu. The name of one of the greatest of the Hindu gods.

According to the Hindu religion Vishnu is probably the greatest of all the gods, although he himself acknowledged the supremacy of Shiva q.v. Hindus see the history of the world in terms of cycles. At crucial points in the cycle Vishnu is incarnated and comes to earth to help. Each cycle has its own incarnation and the three best known are Rama q.v. Krishna q.v. and Buddha.

VITALIS
Origin/meaning: Latin 'vital' or 'of life'.

A name introduced into England after the Norman Conquest, it became both a first name and surname. Rare now in English-speaking countries, it is still found in various forms in Europe, including this form in Germany.

Variations and abbreviations: Vial (Fr), Vidal (Sp), Vitale (It).

VITUS
Origin/meaning: Latin 'alive'.

Rare in England but more common in Europe, particularly in Italy. St Vitus is the saint whose intercession is called for by those with nervous diseases. One illness (St Vitus dance) is named after him. The Old French form Wido became confused with Guido and thus with the name Guy *q.v.*

Variations and abbreviations: Veit (Ger), Vitas, Vito (It). See also Guy, Vitalis, Vivian.

Example: Vitas Gerulaitis, US tennis player.

VIVIAN
Origin/meaning: Latin 'full of life'.

A rare masculine name which, as Vivianus, dates back to the early Middle Ages. There is a feminine version, Vivien *q.v.* and the masculine spelling is sometimes used for girls. Another name Vitalis, now more or less obsolete in English-speaking countries, has the same meaning.

Variations and abbreviations: Viv, Vivien (Fr), Viviano (It), Vyvyan.

Examples: Vyvyan Holland, 1886–1962, English writer, son of Oscar Wilde.
Sir Vivian Fuchs, English explorer.

VLADIMIR
Origin/meaning: Slavic 'famous prince'.

Prince and Saint, Vladimir, 955–1015, is credited with the definite conversion of European Russia to Christianity. The name has been consistently popular since then among people of Slavic origin.

Examples: Vladimir Ashkenazy, Israeli pianist.
Vladimir Petrovic, Yugoslav/British footballer.

W

WALDO
Origin/meaning: Old German 'rule'.

An independent first name and a surname which probably derived from other German names such as Waldemar, Waldebert, or even from Oswald. The Astor family name Waldorf probably comes from an Old English name with a similar meaning.

Example: Ralph Waldo Emerson, 1803–1882, American essayist and philosopher.
Waldo Frank, 1889–1967, US novelist and journalist.

WALID
Origin/meaning: Arabic 'new born'.

This is a Muslim name.

Variation: Waleed.

WALLACE
Origin/meaning: Old Scots 'from Wales' or 'Welsh'.

A famous Scottish surname initially used as a first name in the 19th century when aristocratic surnames were fashionable. The alternative spelling, Wallis *q.v.* is sometimes used for girls.

Variations and abbreviations: Wal, Wally.

WALLY
Origin/meaning: Old Scots 'from Wales' or 'Welsh'.

A familiar form of Walter, Waldo, Wallace now found as an independent name.

Example: Wally Herbert, English explorer.

WALT
Origin/meaning: Old German 'rule-people'.

A short form of Walter (and perhaps of Walton) now commonly found as an independent name in the US.

Example: Walt Whitman, 1819-1891, US poet.
Walt Disney, 1901-1966, US, creator of Mickey Mouse and Disneyland.

WALTER

Origin/meaning: Old German/Old English 'rule-people'.

The Norman version of this name was very popular. Introduced at the time of the Conquest it quickly absorbed the Old English version which was much closer to the Teutonic original. One of the most popular short forms Wat, indicates that in the Middle Ages the pronunciation was Water.

Like all popular names it gave rise to many surnames, for example Waters, Watts, Walters, Watkins etc.

Variations and abbreviations: Gauthier (Fr), Gautier, Gualterio (Sp), Gualtiero (It), Gwaleter (Wel), Wally, Walt, Walther (Ger), Wat.

Examples: Sir Walter Raleigh, 1554-1618, English explorer and poet.
Sir Walter Scott, 1771-1832, Scottish novelist and historian.
Wat Tyler, d.1381, leader of a peasants' rebellion against Richard II.

WARNER

Origin/meaning: probably Old German 'of the Verini tribe'. Sometimes given as 'protecting warrior'.

A family name used as a first name, it may have developed as a surname from the Norman Christian name Garnier. It is the same name as Warren q.v.

Variations and abbreviations: Werner (Ger), Wernher (Ger).

Example: Warner Baxter, US film actor.

WARREN

Origin/meaning: probably Old German 'of the Verini tribe'. Sometimes listed as 'defender'.

Almost identical in meaning and development to Warner q.v. Warren developed almost exclusively into a surname in the Middle Ages. Its use as a first name has been revived in the last 100 years, particularly in America. In Britain it usually indicates a family connection.

Variations and abbreviations: Garnet, Warin, Waring.

Examples: Warren Harding, 1865–1923, US President.
Warren Beatty, US film actor.
Warren Hastings, 1732–1818, First English Governor General of India.

WASHINGTON
Origin/meaning: Old English 'home of the Wassa folk'.

There are several English places with this name. Washington in County Durham gave its name to the family of George Washington, first President of the US. As a result this surname has periodically been popular as a first name in the US, although rare elsewhere.

Example: Washington Irving, 1763–1859, US writer, author of *Rip Van Winkle*.

WAYNE
Origin/meaning: Old English 'wagon'.

A surname, sometimes a short form of Wainwright (wagon-mender). Frequently found as a first name in the US because of film actor John Wayne and the hero of the Revolution General Anthony Wayne. Popular in Britain in the 1950s and 60s.

Examples: Wayne Eagling, British ballet dancer.
Wayne Sleep, British ballet dancer.

WILBUR
Origin/meaning: either Old German 'resolute defence' or Dutch 'wild farmer'.

This name, so popular in the US but rare in other English-speaking countries, may have either or both of the above meanings. In both cases it derives from a surname, the English Wilber/Wildbore or Dutch Wildeboer. Occasionally it is mistakenly listed as a form of Gilbert, because of its similarity to the German Wilbert (bright/strong will) which has a French form Guilbert.

Variations and abbreviations: Will, Wilber.

Example: Wilbur Wright, 1867–1912, American pioneer aviator.
Wilbur Smith, South African novelist.

WILFRED
Origin/meaning: Old English 'will peace', ie 'determined for peace'.

This Old English name usually found before 1066 as Wilfrith, did not survive the competition of the new names which arrived with the Conquest. In the 19th century it was revived with similar names, like Cuthbert and Ethelbert, by followers of the Oxford Movement for religious reform who wished to honour the early church missionary St Wilfrith, 634-709.

Variations and abbreviations: Fred, Wilf, Wilfrid, Will.

Examples: Wilfrid Hyde-White, British actor.
Sir Wilfred Laurier, 1841-1919, Canadian statesman.

WILL
Origin/meaning: a short form of William q.v. and sometimes of other names beginning Wil eg Wilbur, Wilfred q.v.

This is commonly found as an independent name, especially in the US.

Example: Will Hay, 1888-1949, British actor/comedian.

Will Fyffe, 1885-1947, Scottish comedian.

WILLIAM
Origin/meaning: Old German 'will helmet', ie 'helmet of resolution'.

One of the most consistently popular names in England (and later in the US, Canada and Australia) since it was introduced in the old forms Willelm and Guillamo by William the Conqueror in 1066. It has numerous variations and short forms and they are the source of many surnames such as Williams, Wilson, Willis, Wilkinson etc. Will used to be the most common short form but in the last few hundred years Bill and Billy have become more popular. Like many tried and tested traditional names it is currently enjoying a revival.

Variations and abbreviations: Bill, Billie, Billy, Guglielmo (It), Guillaume (Fr), Guillermo (Sp), Gwylim (Wel), Liam (Ir), Vilhelm (Scand/Slav), Wilhelm (Ger), Will, Willem (Dut), Willie, Willis, Willy.

Examples: William Shakespeare, 1564-1616, English playwright.
William Butler Yeats, 1865-1939, Irish poet.

William Mackenzie King, 1874–1950, Canadian statesman.
William Tecumseh Sherman, 1820–1891, C-in-C of the US army.
William Caxton, 1422–1491, first English printer.
HRH Prince William of Wales, b.1982.

WILMOT
Origin/meaning: Old German 'helmet of resolution'.

A medieval first name from the same root as William *q.v.* It may also be used as a girl's name.

WILSON
Origin/meaning: Old German 'helmet of resolution', Medieval English 'son of William'.

An early variation of William *q.v.* used as a surname and now frequently transferred back as a first name, especially in the US.

Example: Wilson Pickett, US singer.

WINDSOR (pron. Winzer)
Origin/meaning: English place name, 'boundary river bank'.

A surname (since 1917 that of the British Royal family) sometimes used as a first name.

Example: Windsor Davis, Welsh actor.

WINSTON
Origin/meaning: Old English 'friend's farm' (the name of a small village in Gloucestershire).

The family name of the grandmother of John Churchill, 1st Duke of Marlborough. He held it as a second name and it is still a regularly used name in the Churchill family. Sir Winston Churchill was a grandson of the 7th Duke of Marlborough. His fame as leader of Britain during the Second World War made the name popular although surprisingly less so in Britain than elsewhere.

Variations and abbreviations: Win, Winnie, Winny.

Examples: Sir Winston Churchill, 1874–1965.
Winston Churchill 1871–1947, US historical novelist.
Winston Graham, English novelist, author of the *Poldark* novels.

WOLF
Origin/meaning: Old German 'approach of the wolf'.

An uncommon English name similar to the German name Wolfgang. Also found as a surname and consequently adopted as a first name. In German-speaking countries it is often the short form of the large number of names beginning Wolf, eg Wolfger, Wolfram, Wolfgand.

Variations: Wolfe, Wolff, Wolfie, Wolfy, Wulf (Old Eng).

Example: Wolfe Tone, 1763–1798, Irish rebel leader.

WOLFGANG
Origin/meaning: Old German 'approach of the wolf'.

A South German/Austrian name world famous because of the Austrian composer Wolfgang Amadeus Mozart, 1756–1791.

Variations and abbreviations: Volfango (It), Wolf, Wolfe, Wolfie, Wolfy, Wulf.

Example: Johann Wolfgang von Goethe, 1749–1832, German poet and philosopher.
St Wolfgang, 925-994, Bishop of Swabia.

WOODROW
Origin/meaning: 'from the lane in the woods'.

An English surname used as a first name.

Abbreviation: Woody.

Example: Woodrow Wyatt, English MP and writer.
Thomas Woodrow Wilson, 1856–1924, 28th US President.

WYNNE
Origin/meaning: Welsh 'white/fair'.

A form of Gwyn q.v. It is found as part of many Welsh names as well as a name in its own right. It has also become a Welsh surname and is often used as part of a double name such as Wynne-Jones.

X

XAN
Origin/meaning: Ancient Greek 'defender of men'.
A short form of Alexander *q.v.*

XANTHUS
Origin/meaning: Greek 'golden yellow' or 'golden-haired'.
A rare masculine form of Xanthe.
Variation: Xan.

XAVIER (pron. Sp Havierr, Eng Zayvier).
Origin/meaning: Arabic 'bright' or 'splendid'.
The surname of the Spanish missionary St Francis Xavier, 1506–1552. It is a popular name among Catholics, particularly of course in Spanish-speaking countries.
Variations: Javier, Xaver (Ger).

XIMENES (pron. Sp Hímanath, Eng Ziminez)
Origin/meaning: Hebrew 'hearkening'.
A Spanish form of Simon *q.v.*

Y

YAQUB
Origin/meaning: Arabic 'supplanter'.
This is the same name as the Hebrew Jacob and English James.

YEHUDI
Origin/meaning: Hebrew 'praise of the Lord'.
A Jewish form of Jude *q.v.* as is Judah.
Variations and abbreviations: see Jude.
Example: Yehudi Menuhin, US-born violinist.

YESTIN
Origin/meaning: Latin 'just'.
The Welsh version of Justin.
Variation: Iestin.

YOGESH (pron. Yogess)
Origin/meaning: Sanskrit/Gujerati 'expert at yoga'.

YUSUF
Origin/meaning: Arabic 'he shall add (to his power)'.
This is the Muslim form of the Hebrew name Joseph *q.v.*
Variations and abbreviations: see Joseph.
Example: Salah-al Din Yusuf ibn Ayyub, 1137–1193, (Saladin) Sultan of Egypt. In 1187 he captured Jerusalem and provoked the third Crusade.

YVES
Origin/meaning: Old German Iv 'yew'.
The French version of the English Ivo *q.v.* or Ives, common in Medieval France, particularly in Brittany and still popular today.
Variation: Yvon.
Examples: Yves Montand, French actor.
Yves St Laurent, French courturier.

Z

ZACCHAEUS

Origin/meaning: Hebrew 'the Lord has remembered'.

The Latinized version of the short form of Zachariah (see Zachary). Zacchaeus (Luke 19) was a small man, a publican, who climbed a sycamore tree to get a good view of Jesus. This is one of the Biblical names popular with 17th century Puritans in England and New England.

ZACHARY

Origin/meaning: Hebrew 'the Lord has remembered'.

This is the English version of the Biblical name Zachariah or Zacharias. It is the name of a king of Judah and a prophet. One of the last Books of the Old Testament is named after him. Taken up by 17th century Puritans it has become almost obsolete in England in the present century but is still found in the US, particularly in one of its short forms.

Variations and abbreviations: Zacarias (Sp), Zaccaria (It), Zacharias, Zachariah, Zacharian, Zacharie (Fr), Zack, Zacky, Zak, Zechariah, Zeke.

Example: Zachary Taylor, 1784–1850, 12th US President.
St Zachary, d.752, an early Pope.
Zachary Scott, US film actor.

ZADOK

Origin/meaning: Hebrew 'righteous' or 'just'.

A Biblical name, the best known holder being Zadok the Priest (Kings I) whose Anthem is sung at the Coronation of English monarchs. Rare after the 17th century.

Variation: Zadoc.

ZAID

Origin/meaning: Arabic 'increase'.

A common Muslim name.

Variations: Zaeed, Zayed, Ziyad.

ZANE
Origin/meaning: uncertain. Sometimes given as a form of John – Hebrew 'Jehovah has favoured'.

Example: Zane Grey, 1875–1939, US novelist whose Western novels formed the basis of many Hollywood films.

ZARED
Origin/meaning: Hebrew 'ambush'.

ZAVIER (pron. Záyvyer)
Origin/meaning: Arabic 'bright'.

One of the Anglicized versions of Xavier q.v.

Variation: Zaver.

ZEBEDEE
Origin/meaning: Hebrew 'gift of the Lord'.

Zebedee was the father of the Apostles James and John (Mark ch I:19)

Variations and abbreviations: Zeb, Zebadiah, Zebediah.

ZEBULUN
Origin/meaning: uncertain. May be Hebrew 'dwelling place'.

Biblical. The name of the founder of the tribe of Israel (Gen. ch.30 v.20). It was popular among 17th century Puritans in England and New England but is now rare.

Variations and abbreviations: Lonny, Zeb, Zebulin, Zebulon.

ZEDEKIAH
Origin/meaning: Hebrew 'God is just'.

One of the Biblical names popular among 17th century Puritans. The last king of Judah, Zedekiah, was captured and taken to Babylon after rebelling against Nebuchadnezzar (2 Kings ch.24-25).

ZEKE
Origin/meaning: Hebrew 'the Lord has remembered' or Hebrew 'God is strong'.

A short form of Zachary or Ezekial, found as an independent name in the US.

ZENON
Origin/meaning: Greek 'gift of Zeus'.

In Greek mythology Zeus was the father of the gods. The name is found in St Paul's Epistle to Titus as Zenas.

The Greek philosopher Zeno, 490–430 BC, was founder of the Stoics.

Variations and abbreviations: Zenas, Zeno, Zénon (Fr), Zénos.

ZOLLY
Origin/meaning: Hebrew 'asked for' or Hebrew 'peace'.

A short form of Saul or Solomon q.v. mainly used by Jewish people.

Variation: Zollie.

THE END